THE ENLIGHTENMENT

THE ENLIGHTENMENT

A Comparative Social History 1721–1794

THOMAS MUNCK

Senior Lecturer in History, University of Glasgow

A member of the Hodder Headline Group
LONDON
Co-published in the United States of America by
Oxford University Press Inc., New York

First published in Great Britain in 2000 by
Arnold, a member of the Hodder Headline Group,
338 Euston Road, London NW1 3BH

http://www.arnoldpublishers.com

Co-published in the United States of America by
Oxford University Press Inc.,
198 Madison Avenue, New York, NY10016

British Library Cataloguing in Publication Data
A catalogue record for this book is available from the British Library

Library of Congress Cataloging-in-Publication Data
A catalog record for this book is available from the Library of Congress

ISBN 0 340 66326 X (hb)
ISBN 0 340 66325 1 (pb)

1 2 3 4 5 6 7 8 9 10

Production Editor: Rada Radojicic
Production Controller: Sarah Kett
Cover Design: Thomas Munck

Typeset in 10/12pt Sabon by York House Typographic Ltd, London
Printed and bound in Great Britain by MPG Books Ltd, Bodmin, Cornwall

What do you think about this book? Or any other Arnold title?
Please send your comments to feedback.arnold@hodder.co.uk

Contents

Preface   vii

1 The enlightenment   1

   Enlightenment in national context   3
   Enlightenment and counter-enlightenment   7
   Nature, man and science   11
   The 'public sphere' and its limits   14
   Enlightenment and political power   18

2 Tradition and communication in daily life   21

   Popular and elite culture   22
   Rural interaction and peasant action   26
   Religious observance and beliefs   29
   Processions, festivals and the use of open space   37
   Street life, public entertainment and the theatre   40

3 Broadening the horizon: ways and means   46

   Literacy   46
   Education   52
   Prints, pictures and the eye of the beholder   60
   Venues of contact, conversation and debate   65
   Political radicalism in the 1790s   72

4 Books and readers   76

   Book production and distribution   77
   Copyright and profits   80
   Censorship before the reforms   84
   Changing demand for books   89

Libraries and book clubs   98
The impact of the book: two case studies   99
Pamphlets and politics   103

5 The press   106

The *Tatler* and the *Spectator*   109
The growth of press output and readership   111
The French-language press before the Revolution   117
The press, enlightenment and change   122
Revolutionary media   128

6 Reason and the dissolution of certainties   132

State legislation on toleration   133
The churches under scrutiny   139
Censorship reform and state hesitations   142
The judiciary and the law   146
Crime and punishment   150
Treatment of the sick   156

7 Property, the underprivileged and reform   163

Taxation   164
Political economy, cameralism and the physiocrats   168
Rural reform   172
Poverty   181
Slavery and enlightenment   186

8 State, nation and individual in the late eighteenth century   193

Social structure, 'the people' and public consensus   194
Nation, homeland and patriotic identity   199
Political rights and representation in revolutionary France   203
Representing the other half: women and public life   211
The revolution of popular politics   214

9 Conclusion   220

Select bibliography   224
Index   240

Preface

This book is about communication and debate in the eighteenth century – about the diffusion of information and the spread of more open discussion. Many of the great minds of the enlightenment make an appearance, but, remarkable though their achievements are, they are not the real focus of interest. Instead, I have attempted to explore what the enlightenment may have meant not just for European high society, but also for those broader and only partially educated social groups of whom Voltaire was at times so famously dismissive. The book is written in the belief that changes in attitudes and beliefs during the eighteenth century can be studied at least as fruitfully from the vantage point of more ordinary people – those who read newspapers, frequented coffee-houses or societies, shared in popular entertainments, became interested in current social issues, or simply walked round town with an open mind.

It is a commonplace that each generation refashions its own past history, and the enlightenment has had its very full share. In recent years much work has been devoted to the enlightenment 'in national context' – emphasising characteristics which distinguish the cultural, linguistic and intellectual life of one country or region from that of its neighbours. Profitable as this debate has been, it seems to me less than the whole story. One key feature of the eighteenth century, judging in particular from books and periodicals, was a growing interest in the life of nations and cultures other than the reader's own – not only within Europe but also in the Americas and the Far East. Montesquieu's *Persian Letters* (1721) is a perfect illustration of the impact such open-minded comparison can make at all levels of understanding. His book was the source of two ideas which have fundamentally coloured the interpretation of the enlightenment offered here. One is that, even though we recognise all the variant 'national' forms of enlightenment in Europe, we need to remember that to many contemporaries the fundamentals of reason and enlightening were valid throughout Europe and North America irrespective of national boundaries. The second is that, for all the deep social divisions in European society, the enlightenment was not merely an elite intellectual pastime, but a real process of emancipation from inherited values and beliefs, with as much potential impact on ordinary Europeans as travelling had on Montesquieu's fictional Persian gentleman, Rica. Such emancipation was most obvious in the larger and more buoyant urban centres of north-western Europe, and there is good reason to believe that rural and provincial society was slow and sometimes reluctant to follow suit. Even so, anyone who compares what was read and what was debated in the early 1790s – and by whom – with the equivalent three generations earlier will surely recognise that the change was enormous and socially pervasive.

Specific chronological and geographic limits have been adopted here, in order to give a clearer focus. First of all, the term 'enlightenment' is used to denote the generally accepted historical period – the eighteenth century. Precise delimiters can be endlessly debated, with little profit. It makes practical sense to start around 1721 (the publication of Montesquieu's *Persian Letters*, at a time when the troubled last years of Louis XIV could be studied more dispassionately); and ending not with the start of the French Revolution but rather with its change of direction by 1794 – also the year of death of two of the last great *philosophes*, Condorcet and Lavoisier. Such dates are evidently just for convenience: as with all historical periodisation, there is no decisive start or finish, and chronological markers should not be allowed to disguise either the extent to which the roots of the enlightenment are to be found in the age of Newton, Locke and Bayle, or the extent to which many of the issues of the enlightenment, like the interminable *Encyclopédie méthodique* (1782–1832), refused to be buried.

Rather more difficult is the question of geographic limitation. Many historians would argue that most of Europe and much of North America belong; and that the process of self-discovery involves European reactions to other world cultures. Equally, work in progress suggests that southern and eastern Europe will eventually provide interesting ground for comparison. But for the moment, and in order to achieve a clearer focus on detail, the emphasis is more selective. This book largely concentrates on the enlightenment epicentre: on France, without which no study of the enlightenment would make sense; on England and Scotland, which led the way in terms of liberalisation and in some aspects of social comment; and on other relevant parts of Protestant Europe (especially the northern parts of the German-speaking lands). The focus is on the urban environment, and in particular on the eighteenth-century 'golden triangle' of Paris, London and Hamburg.

This epicentre is marked out in the later eighteenth century by one crucial characteristic. As we shall see, a number of complex and interrelated factors helped to ensure that basic literacy was very widespread across all social classes in Britain, north-eastern France, northern Germany, the Netherlands, and Scandinavia – not just amongst men but also increasingly women. Both old and newer means of communication evolved crucially in those parts where the enlightenment had the widest social impact. Ability to read was not indispensable for contact with innovative ideas and debate, but it undoubtedly helped. Print provided a vital and autonomous medium of diffusion – arguably becoming a mass medium in an age with no other reliable form of mass communication. But since we are dealing with the social context in which debate grew and ideas spread, it is of importance to include those high literacy areas (like the Netherlands and Scandinavia) which made few radically innovative contributions of their own, but did allow increasingly unrestricted diffusion. In short, we are dealing not just with the area of *enlightenment*, but also with an area where some of the conditions were right for more widespread *enlightening*.

Concentrating on north-western and northern Europe as an area suitable for comparative historical analysis nevertheless entails some problems. Important parts of Europe have been given less prominence here than they might deserve – above all the Italian peninsula, which presents a particular problem for those without access to Italian, given that the crucial parts of Franco Venturi's summative assessment have yet to be translated (see p. 2). But the unique political–ecclesiastical environment of the Italian peninsula created conditions which have still not been fully untangled in terms of the types of research on which this book relies; and in any case literacy rates (if not as poor as in the Iberian peninsula and in eastern Europe) were much lower than in the north-west. Even within the north-west, however, thematic selectivity has been prioritised over geographic coverage. Copenhagen was not Edinburgh, Hamburg was not London – and no place on earth might appear even superficially similar to Paris. Enlightenment studies have in recent years tended to emphasise, often fruitfully, the confines of a national or regional framework. But an exclusive concentration on, say, the French or the Scottish enlightenment may make us overlook some important common features. The eighteenth century was a period of growing awareness of national identity, certainly, but it was also a period of refreshing cosmopolitanism and open-mindedness, of linguistic versatility, and of a flourishing cross-national 'republic of letters' (network of scholars). So in attempting a comparative study of the core area of the enlightenment, this book does not aim to understate regional diversity or to belittle genuine differences, but rather to bring them out in order better to understand each of the societies and communities concerned.

The last three chapters of this book move from the process of communication to the actual impact of 'enlightening' in a number of specific areas – paying close attention, as any social history of the period now surely must, to the changing interface between the individual subject or citizen on the one hand, and the complex structures of government and collective authority on the other. A generation ago, constructs like 'enlightened despotism' or 'enlightened absolutism' were used for the eighteenth century without much controversy. But historians have long since recognised that governments did not always take the lead in imposing supposedly benevolent enlightened reform on their territories – indeed not infrequently they were compelled to *follow* in order to maintain political credibility in a rapidly changing environment. Recent research has immeasurably improved our understanding of the context of what we might call enlightened reform, particularly in the Habsburg lands, Russia, and many of the German states. Some of these reform schemes also naturally lend themselves to comparative study. Those attempted by Joseph II after 1780, for example, provide some interesting parallels with contemporary Danish initiatives; whilst the remarkable constitutional experiments of Joseph's brother Leopold in Tuscany went well beyond what most other European rulers were prepared to contemplate. Generally speaking, however, wider public debate in southern and eastern Europe lagged well behind that of the north-west. Part of the explanation for this is no doubt to be found in the restraints of tradition, in state-backed religious conservatism, in the far lower overall literacy rates, and in the persistence in some states of censorship controls of a kind that were being abandoned or were becoming unenforceable in the north-west. The diffusion of enlightened debate in central and southern Europe was also dampened by the absence of that explosive economic growth which loosened social barriers, facilitated consumer spending, raised expectations and spawned genuine liberalisation in north-western Europe in the century before the French Revolution.

Because of the rapidly increasing complexity of social and political relationships in much of Europe in the course of the eighteenth century, the notion of enlightened reform driven solely, or even primarily, by a supposedly enlightened central government hardly seems tenable any longer as a norm. Indeed it is probable that, if we retain the term 'enlightened absolutism' at all, we shall increasingly come to associate it solely with those parts of Europe that lagged behind in terms of social and economic change – where rulers appeared to have the kind of authority which might tempt them to try, like Joseph II, to impose reform without much of the preparatory groundwork, and where 'accountability' in practice was sacrificed for the sake of power politics and military consolidation. If that is the case, we may well be heading towards a clearer understanding both of the nature of government in this period, and the significance for the north-west of the process of 'enlightening' across society as a whole.

* * *

The purpose of this book, therefore, is to attempt to look at the eighteenth-century enlightenment from a perspective which is much more socially inclusive than has hitherto been the norm. Trying to throw light on how, and how far, the diffusion of ideas actually took place is bound to involve exploration of some unusual historical territory. This could not even have been contemplated without the work of scholars across a number of different disciplines: the footnotes and bibliography are a token acknowledgement of these wide-ranging debts, and may also help to remind readers of the range and quality of much recent work. For reasons of space, references to more specialised material in the notes are not necessarily repeated in the selective bibliography at the end – in other words, notes and bibliography are to some extent complementary, and readers seeking references to work on specific topics will want to use the index to locate relevant sections. Throughout this book, all translations from French, German and the Scandinavian languages, except where otherwise indicated, are my own. Eighteenth-century book and periodical titles mentioned in the text are also often rendered in English, but such a rendering cannot be taken as an indication that the work itself was actually translated at the time (or has been since). As will become apparent (p. 4), contemporary translation practices are themselves of great significance.

Whilst this book owes a great deal to recent scholarly debate, its actual realisation depended on much else. First and foremost, Glasgow University allowed me an initial generous leave of one year to start the project, followed by another shorter period of leave at the end to ensure its completion. The significance of such periods of leave, allowing intensive exploration of new research territory, cannot be overstated. But the project also relied on the resources of several libraries, and on the patience of their staff in the face of sometimes elusive requests. In particular, it is a pleasure to single out Glasgow University Library – and not least its Special Collections, which have provided a wealth of material for this book. Having substantial source material, as well as complete runs of serials such as the *Studies on Voltaire and the Eighteenth Century (StVEC)* a few hundred yards from one's desk is not a trifle.

On a more personal level, successive Heads of Department have been not only constant in their support and friendship, but also trusting in their belief that the undertaking was realisable: Professors Hew Strachan, Alan Smith, David Bates and Evan Mawdsley. Closer to this particular field, Hamish Scott of the University of St Andrews provided me with some invaluable suggestions at the start of the project, whilst Simon Newman, Chris Black, Tricia Allerston and many other colleagues at Glasgow University and elsewhere have been generous with advice, suggestions and pointers of all kinds. Two colleagues need special mention – Simon Dixon and Colin Kidd. Their own work in cognate fields has been a wonderful source of inspiration to me. But they have also, in taking on the burden of reading drafts of this book, added immeasurably and directly to its clarity of purpose. Whilst it goes without saying that they are in no way responsible for any remaining weaknesses, their lucid questioning and friendly encouragement went far beyond what I could reasonably expect.

It was thanks to an almost chance conversation with Christopher Wheeler of Arnold that I originally formulated this project in detail; he has been both wonderfully encouraging and patient in waiting for the result. But I also owe a real debt to many students who in recent years have taken my Honours courses, contributed to graduate seminars, and tackled some impossibly big questions: their responses and ideas encouraged me to attempt a fuller answer – certainly not a definitive one, but one which may perhaps go some way towards clarifying what the enlightenment may have meant to those who in the eighteenth century were not themselves full-time scholars.

Thomas Munck
University of Glasgow
June 1999

1

The enlightenment

A generation ago, there would have been no particular need for a book on the enlightenment to start with more than a cursory definition of its subject. A number of durable works on the core ideas of the enlightenment had created something of a consensus which, despite differences of approach, seemed unproblematic.[1] French eighteenth-century writers were seen as both the formative and the dominant influence. Their inspiration had come primarily from Locke, Newton and Pierre Bayle, and their group identity was summarised in the term *philosophe* – a French word used by contemporaries to denote the liberal thinkers, intellectuals and writers of mid-eighteenth-century Paris. The key figure always was – and indeed still is – Montesquieu (1689–1755), whose delightful *Persian Letters* of 1721 set much of the agenda, and whose substantial treatise on the *Spirit of the Laws* (1748) remained one of the most frequently cited texts right through the period of the American and French revolutions. Rather less weighty in terms of systematic ideas, though much appreciated by contemporaries for his literary style, wit and satire, was Voltaire (1694–1778), whose network of famous correspondents around Europe was enormous even by the standards of that epistolary age. The trinity of the enlightenment was completed by Rousseau (1712–78), the most eccentric of the three – a perpetual rebel, a self-proclaimed spokesman for truth and sincerity in an age prone to empty

1 A good example is Peter Gay, *The Enlightenment: An Interpretation*, 2 vols. (New York, 1966–69); but see also notably the works of Hazard, Cassirer, Crocker, Cobban, Berlin, Gay, Hampson and Wade listed in the bibliography at the end of this book. Some of the differences of approach amongst these writers were surveyed by one of them, L.G. Crocker, 'Interpreting the enlightenment: a political approach', *Journal of the History of Ideas* 46 (1985), 211–30. This chapter, however, will not attempt a historiographical survey: for that, a good starting point is found in D. Outram, *The Enlightenment* (Cambridge, 1995), 3–13 and in R. Porter, *The Enlightenment* (Basingstoke, 1990), both of which also have annotated bibliographies. On the definition of *philosophe*, see Dumarsais' article from the *Encyclopédie*, translated in I. Kramnick, *The Portable Enlightenment Reader* (Harmondsworth, 1995), 21–2.

flattery, an educational reformer (in *Émile* of 1762), an early Romantic (in *La Nouvelle Héloïse* of 1761), a communitarian (in theory if not by personal preference), and a political innovator (in *The Social Contract* of 1762). Vast amounts of scholarship have accumulated on these three, but more recent work has underlined the pivotal importance of some additional figures: first and foremost Diderot (1713–84), editor of the *Encyclopédie* (1751–65/72) and author of some powerful works not all of which he risked publishing in his lifetime; scientists such as Maupertius (1698–1759), Buffon (1707–88) and Lavoisier (1743–94); the playwright, ambassador, publisher and entrepreneur Beaumarchais (1732–99); the mathematician Condorcet (1743–94); the economist Quesnay (1694–1774), founder of the physiocrat group; and an array of other influential writers covering most fields of learning from oriental languages to materialism.

Innovative work on other parts of Europe, however, has made it clear that not all of the enlightenment was quintessentially French. Over a long and distinguished career the historian Franco Venturi did more than most to clarify the context and substance of the enlightenment from a distinctive Italian angle, encouraging renewed interest not just in Vico (1668–1744), Galiani (1728–87) and Beccaria (1738–94), but also in the many government advisors and reformers that made enlightened reform a reality in the states of Italy and elsewhere in Europe.[2] Obvious parallels have been drawn with the enlightenment in the German-speaking world, whose leading thinkers Kant (1724–1804), Moses Mendelsohn (1729–86) and Herder (1744–1803) departed in fundamental ways from French Cartesian logic and detached rationality. On the literary front Lessing (1729–81) emphatically rebelled against French cultural norms, whilst the visionary writers Goethe (1749–1832) and Schiller (1759–1805) explored the irrational inner being, launching, with Herder, the German literary and musical protest movement of self-realisation known as *Sturm und Drang* ('storm and stress'). Although the German enlightenment remained deeply indebted to the French, it was also significantly influenced by some of the leading Scots philosophers, notably Thomas Reid (1710–96), David Hume (1711–76), Adam Smith (1723–90) and Adam Ferguson (1723–1816) – who as a result are at last being located more convincingly in their European historical context. Recognising such a diversity within the European enlightenment has in turn encouraged historians to look for an English enlightenment – or, perhaps more convincingly, to redefine the English-language enlightenment which also embraced Dublin and the North American colonies.

As a result, a single and concise definition of the enlightenment may seem elusive. But this chapter will, in surveying some areas of debate in recent

---

2 F. Venturi, *Settecento riformatore*, 5 vols. (Turin, 1969–91), vols. 3–4 of which have been translated by R. Burr Litchfield under the title *The End of the Old Regime in Europe* (Princeton, 1989–91); see also J. Robertson, 'Franco Venturi's Enlightenment', review article in *Past and Present* 137 (1992), 183–206.

years, suggest that a lack of simple definition is in reality a positive gain: neither the individuals who contributed directly to the enlightenment, nor the wider repercussions of new ways of thinking, can or should be over-rigidly compartmentalised. Instead, we might look on the enlightenment as many different (and not necessarily always fully compatible) strands, some of which can be said to make up a real core, surrounded by other looser threads whose significance is open to interpretation.

Enlightenment in national context

It would be easy to add many more names to the array of great thinkers listed above, and to extend the range into Russia, the Habsburg lands, Scandinavia and the Iberian peninsula. In 1981, such an approach was given a specific slant with the publication of a volume of essays which sought to define the enlightenment from a national point of view,[3] or at least from within the framework of the different cultural and political contexts of various parts of Europe. In so far as most of educated Europe, including the intellectual leaders already mentioned, genuinely aspired to be cosmopolitan in their outlook, enthusiastic travellers and linguists, devotees of cultural and anthropological comparisons covering the known world, and at least in theory deeply sceptical of parochialism and insularity, the 'nationalist' approach to the enlightenment is bound to have its limitations. Nonetheless, it has been established beyond reasonable doubt that the enlightenment was European-wide, and that its main strands at least after mid-century were not all French-inspired.

There were pressures in opposing directions. On the one hand, the linguistic skills and enthusiasm for travel common amongst the elite strengthened mutual appreciation, and nourished the international 'republic of letters' – that informal network of contacts and correspondence which was so essential to the world of learning of the early modern period. Equally, with Latin declining as the international language of scholarship, translations of the

---

3 R. Porter and M. Teich, eds., *The Enlightenment in National Context* (Cambridge, 1981). The high quality of many of the chapters in this volume gave impetus to a re-assessment of the enlightenment which was in fact already under way. On the Italian dimension, see the work of Venturi cited in the previous footnote. For an overview of the key characteristics of the German enlightenment, see notably T.C.W. Blanning, *Reform and Revolution in Mainz 1743–1804* (Cambridge, 1974), 1–38; J.B. Knudsen, *Justus Möser and the German Enlightenment* (Cambridge, 1986), 3–30; F. Kopitsch, ed., *Aufklärung, Absolutismus und Bürgertum in Deutschland* (Munich, 1976). On the Scottish enlightenment in a comparative context see J. Robertson, 'The Scottish Enlightenment', *Rivista Storica Italiana* 108 (1996), 792–829, and his innovative discussion of 'The Enlightenment above national context: political economy in eighteenth-century Scotland and Naples', *Historical Journal* 40 (1997), 667–97; on Scottish and British identities, see C. Kidd, *Subverting Scotland's Past: Scottish Whig Historians and the Creation of an Anglo-British Identity, 1689–1830* (Cambridge, 1993), and his 'North Britishness and the nature of eighteenth-century British patriotisms', *Historical Journal* 39 (1996), 361–82.

major works of the period became more common. Translation and cross-cultural communication during the eighteenth century, however, needs a great deal more research: recent work indicates that translators at the time did not always try to be demonstrably 'accurate', and might act more as mediators by adapting an original work to the mind-set of the intended readership.[4] Similarly, reviews of, commentaries on and selective quotation from works as complex as Montesquieu's rather digressive *Spirit of the Laws* were bound to produce further distortions. This underscores a trend which increasingly cut across the grain of cosmopolitanism: a growing interest in national identity and in the distinctive historical and institutional features that marked different societies apart. As we shall see, both the book trade and the newspaper industry expanded enormously during the eighteenth century, and each had the capacity to profit as much from European cosmopolitanism as from particularism. But the increasing diffusion of new ideas and new ways of thinking downwards through society, about which this book is chiefly concerned, was bound to reduce the relative significance of the esoteric and idealised 'republic of letters', whilst strengthening more pragmatic and sometimes local interests. In the last decades of the century, patriotism, always part of enlightened debate, began to mutate into stronger national consciousness (p. 199). Whether it fostered new forms of xenophobia, or merely helped embellish older prejudices, is a question which has not yet been satisfactorily resolved.

Approaches to the actual structure and development of knowledge itself also differed within Europe. As long as one individual could still hope to embrace a good part of the entire corpus of learning of western Christendom, system-building had remained a common and understandable scholarly preoccupation. In the German world Leibniz (1646–1716), one of the last great universalists and a rival of Newton, together with his less original pupil Christian Wolff (1679–1754), attempted to systematise what was known at the time as the science of morals (metaphysics and moral philosophy). Wolff had a lasting impact on enlightened thinkers outside France, his teaching and his extensive writings eventually providing a foundation for the cameralist approach to state reform (p. 168). A very different attitude was adopted by

---

4 A study of translation patterns across Europe is complicated by the widespread use of French as the standard language amongst the educated everywhere. For other European languages, however, we are only beginning to see the scale of the problem: the most striking work to date is that of F. Oz-Salzberger, *Translating the Enlightenment: Scottish Civic Discourse in Eighteenth-Century Germany* (Oxford, 1995). See also B. Fabian, 'English books and their eighteenth-century German readers', in *The Widening Circle: Essays on the Circulation of Literature in Eighteenth-Century Europe*, ed. P. Korshin (Philadelphia, 1976), 117–96; and M. Kuehn, *Scottish Common Sense in Germany, 1768–1800: A Contribution to the History of Critical Philosophy* (Kingston/Montreal, 1987). For a different part of Europe, see M. Kennedy, 'Readership in French: the Irish experience', as well as M. Kennedy and G. Sheridan, 'The trade in French books in eighteenth-century Ireland', both in *Ireland and the French Enlightenment, 1700–1800*, ed. G. Gargett and G. Sheridan (Basingstoke, 1999), 3–20 and 173–96 respectively, which offer evidence of quite widespread knowledge of French in Ireland.

the French *philosophes*, especially after the abbé de Condillac (1714–80) in his *Treatise on Systems* of 1749 dismissed abstract metaphysical system-building as verbal sophistry. Yet Diderot's co-editor in the early years of the *Encyclopédie*, the mathematician d'Alembert (1717–83), was not opposed to all systematisation, and added to his Preliminary Discourse in volume 1 (1751) a map of knowledge trying to schematise all the main disciplines. System-building also found some resonance in Scotland, notably with Adam Smith who, though never completing the enterprise, thought of his *Theory of Moral Sentiments* (1759) and *The Wealth of Nations* (1776) as parts of a more comprehensive and coherent intellectual structure, into which his unpublished lectures on jurisprudence and other work might one day have fitted. Others in Europe were attracted by more realisable subsets of knowledge – for example Jean-Philippe Rameau, whose *Traité de l'harmonie réduite à ses principes naturels* (*Treatise on Harmony Reduced to its Natural Principles*, 1722) was the first of many works he published to explain his theoretical system of music. Increasingly, however, the consensus amongst eighteenth-century intellectuals was to move away from the kind of ideal entertained by Descartes a century earlier, of a total body of knowledge built on a single set of intellectual principles.[5]

A near-universal admiration for the civilisation of classical Greece and Rome provided inspiration for writers like Alexander Pope (1688–1744) and the historian Gibbon (1737–94), but did little to foster a European-wide unity of purpose. The so-called quarrel of the Ancients and the Moderns, over whether intellectual development could ever aspire to go beyond the classical inheritance, lost much of its impetus after 1700 as the intellectual agenda changed. Both French and British politicians continued to admire the oratorical skills and majestic grandeur of the great writers of antiquity, consciously imitating and adapting some of their characteristics, but (as we shall see in the last three chapters of this book) the purpose to which they applied such skills differed significantly. Overall, the predominant trend in the enlightenment was towards recognition of fruitful diversity, a combination of some degree of open-mindedness with inquisitiveness, and a constructively critical re-assessment of the history and inheritance of the past. Reason itself was a prominent tool to be applied to any part of the inherited system of beliefs and ideas, and to fresh empirical observation. But even here the consensus was open to challenge: Rousseau influenced a whole generation potentially to reject the cold detachment of logic and reason, while Kant elevated innate ideas to a dominant role in his concept of truth. A sometimes quite bitter conflict persisted between those who gave prominence to metaphysical innate ideas, as against those who preferred the sensationism

5 R. Darnton, 'Philosophers trim the tree of knowledge: the epistemological strategy of the Encyclopédie', in his *The Great Cat Massacre and other Episodes in French Cultural History* (Harmondsworth, 1985), 185–207. That the musical dimension was far more than a fringe issue in French enlightened thinking is demonstrated by T. Christensen, *Rameau and Musical Thought in the Enlightenment* (Cambridge, 1993).

(pure empiricism, knowledge gained from the senses alone) derived from Locke and Newton, and central to most of the French enlightenment. Seeing this in terms of 'national' tendencies (or even common trends within a single group like the *philosophes*) clearly has only very limited validity. That said, it is commonly accepted as a rough generalisation that the metaphysical approach was more common in the German lands, where religion, corporate tradition and paternalist authority were all well engrained and remained largely unchallenged; whilst amongst the *philosophes* in Paris, if not in France generally, all inherited values seemed increasingly vulnerable to empirical re-evaluation. In practice, such a contrast may have had something to do with the fact that the most influential contributors to the French enlightenment were outsiders, living as freelance writers, perhaps with the help of private patronage; whilst in the German lands, as in Scotland, most were in secure professional jobs (often in government or the legal service, in education, or even in the church). But there were also fundamental differences of style and temperament: whilst flamboyant French cultural influences understandably remained strong throughout eighteenth-century Europe, their tendency to rhetoric, gesture and superficiality did not attract universal admiration. In the Catholic states of southern Germany, for example, French influences were minimal: the Catholic *Aufklärung* derived far more from state-sponsored reform and from the moderate practical ideas picked up by the professional elite in their studies at the more liberal north German (but Protestant) universities. By contrast, British influences on the continent, already significant in the second quarter of the century because of the work of Newton and Locke, revived after the conclusion of peace in 1763 into something akin to Anglomania. All over Europe (not least in France itself) the relaxed prosperity and apparent informality of the British way of life were greatly admired and even imitated, though in later years this was offset especially in France by criticism of the unedifying factionalism of British politics.[6]

Recognising the different regionally and culturally determined strands in the enlightenment has made the task of locating a coherent core increasingly difficult. As John Robertson has argued, the 'national' perspective may be introducing distortions of its own: 'as what counts as enlightened in each national context has been extended, so scholars' awareness of the interconnectedness of Enlightenment intellectual activity – of the international passage of ideas, books and thinkers – has become attenuated'.[7] Confirming the Parisian *philosophes* as the cutting edge of much radical re-evaluation in mid-eighteenth-century Europe, and identifying the particular religious,

6 J. Grieder, *Anglomania in France, 1740–1789: Fact, Fiction and Political Discourse* (Geneva, 1985); M. Maurer, *Aufklärung und Anglophilie in Deutschland* (Göttingen, 1987); S. Maza, 'Luxury, morality and social change: why there was no middle-class consciousness in prerevolutionary France', *Journal of Modern History* 69 (1997), 199–229, esp. 220f.
7 J. Robertson, 'The Enlightenment above national context: political economy in eighteenth-century Scotland and Naples', *Historical Journal* 40 (1997), 671.

political and social circumstances that led to specific forms of debate in individual areas, should not prevent us from seeing the considerable common ground in terms of basic attitudes over much of the rest of at least urban Europe. For the purposes of this book we shall drop the capital letter and often the definite article preceding 'enlightenment'; however, this is intended not to indicate a further diminution in the overall meaning of its subject, but rather to emphasise that for most participants enlightenment was much more than the attainment of a specific set of ideas. As Kant made clear in his often-quoted popular piece of 1784, 'Was ist Aufklärung?' ('What is enlightenment?'),[8] it was the process of discovery, the active and critical engagement of the individual, that mattered, not necessarily the end result. Such an approach may at times make for a very broad and inclusive definition of enlightened ideas, complete with internal contradictions and inconsistencies of detail. But it may also help us to recognise the framework of geographic comparison and international cross-fertilisation which was itself one of the most important contemporary sources of inspiration.

Enlightenment and counter-enlightenment

Defining enlightenment as an attitude of mind, rather than a coherent system of beliefs, may seem evasive and undiscriminating. As a working hypothesis, however, it has some merits; and given that many contemporaries (including Kant and his fellow-contributors to the discussion in Berlin in the early 1780s) could reach no agreement regarding the bounds of *Aufklärung*, we may be entitled to some latitude as well. But what of the 'opposition' feared by many *philosophes*? Was it a smokescreen to conceal their own often bitter feuds, a real anti-enlightenment distinct from the rest, or just a more conservative way of tackling the same questions constructively? In other words, was there a real debate between opposing points of view which, at their extreme, included facile, trendy or irresponsible intellectuals on one side, and incorrigibly reactionary traditionalists on the other? Many individuals who regarded themselves as enlightened were clearly in practice less than ideally tolerant of others with divergent opinions – the *philosophes* themselves, for example, were known to press for a denial of freedom of expression to conservative religious writers whom they believed had succumbed to superstition and ignorance. Such partisan claims to a monopoly on truth hardly seem compatible with a spirit of open-mindedness, and might make one wonder whether those of a more conservative bent who were

8 Many translated versions exist of this short piece, amongst them that provided by I. Kramnick in *The Portable Enlightenment Reader* (Harmondsworth, 1995), 1–7. Not all of the text is as straightforward as it seems at first sight: further discussion of the context in which it was written is found below, p. 69; see also H.B. Nisbet, '"Was ist Aufklärung?": the concept of Enlightenment in eighteenth-century Germany', *Journal of European Studies* 12 (1982), 77–95.

nonetheless engaged in serious discussion might also have a claim to being part of the process of enlightening.

Amongst the key issues that have helped us redefine the boundaries of enlightenment is the complex nature of religious belief itself. It was once taken for granted that one of the distinguishing characteristics of the enlightenment was religious scepticism. The atheism of d'Holbach (1723–89), the devastating doubt of Hume, the materialism of La Mettrie (1709–51), the caustic anti-clericalism of Voltaire, and the ironic cross-cultural comparisons of the *Encyclopédie* (p. 134) might all be taken as indications that religious revelation was being re-classified as a form of superstition. There is no denying that that was what Diderot had in mind, and that his view was shared by some of the French elite. But personal beliefs are elusive, and where we have some evidence – for example in Rousseau's extraordinary *Confessions* (1782) – enormous problems immediately become apparent. There is now general agreement that outright anti-clericalism is of little value as a criterion of enlightenment in most of Catholic Europe outside the salons of Paris, and for historical reasons even less so in the Lutheran world – where someone like Herder could at one and the same time, without obvious self-contradiction, serve as a clergyman, philosopher, historian, and leading figure in the literary *Sturm und Drang* movement which heralded Romanticism.

Religion and enlightenment were manifestly not mutually exclusive, nor were the established churches necessarily anti-enlightened. The Sorbonne, Oxford and Cambridge were centres (and at times censorious judges) of religious orthodoxy, but many of the higher clergy who trained in these institutions were anything but narrow-minded reactionaries constrained by their background.[9] In France, recurrent criticism of the church came about not so much because it was unresponsive, but rather because of its strong institutional links with the crown (against, for example, the *parlements* and the other corporate law courts of France), its privileged position within the traditional social hierarchy, and its perceived reactionary control of the censorship system which so obviously threatened and frustrated iconoclast authors in France (p. 86). In England, by contrast, the spread of dissent in the seventeenth century, together with the revivalist movements of the eighteenth, ensured there was no single church and hence no single intellectual strait-jacket against which to rebel. That is one of the reasons why the identity of the English enlightenment has proven elusive. Whether, for example, the lexicographer and writer Samuel Johnson (1709–84) can be regarded as an example of counter-enlightenment (because of his hostility to

9 For example, A. Kors, *D'Holbach's Coterie* (Princeton, 1976), documents fully the evidence for atheism amongst this famously radical circle of *philosophes*, which included a former cleric, the abbé Raynal (1713–96), and a Sorbonne-trained theologian, Morellet (1727–1819). Even more notorious in the last years of the old order were men like Loménie de Brienne, archbishop of Toulouse and Sens though reputedly an atheist; or Talleyrand, bishop of Autun, famous for his colourful private life and his insatiable political ambition.

the French *philosophes*, and his generally conservative instincts) is an open question.[10]

Scotland occupies an interesting intermediate position: like Scandinavia, it was only just freeing itself from a severe and unforgiving religious past, but the heat of theological feuding seems to have dissipated remarkably quickly, despite recurrent internal splinterings and the resilience of Calvinist fundamentalism. Many of the Lowland clergy were great readers, enthusiastic contributors to historical studies, willing participants in social analysis – but often noticeably reticent in matters of theological debate. Particularly striking is the informal circle known as the Moderates, whose leader, the clergyman and scholar William Robertson (1721–93), might almost have seemed in agreement with moderate French *philosophe* opinion in recognising that there was logically no way of resolving or reconciling differences of religious interpretation, and hence little point in allowing theological disputes to escalate into interminable confrontation. The Moderates gained a predominant influence on the development of the Church of Scotland (of which Robertson was Moderator in 1763), but arguably had less impact on popular attitudes generally: Robertson himself became a key target of the Edinburgh rioters protesting against proposals for Catholic relief during 1778–79.[11]

Even in the case of France itself, a clear demarcation line between enlightenment and counter-enlightenment is proving problematic. Those critical of the *philosophes*, or willing to defend religion and the institutional church, were not necessarily hostile to rational debate as such. They might be influenced by the kind of Jansenism that evolved from the 1740s, nourished by the probing religious analysis of such journals as the *Nouvelles ecclésiastiques* (1728–98). As we shall see (p. 138), Jansenist members of the *parlements* came to embody a traditionalist opposition to the monarchy largely independent of the *philosophes*, but arguably at least as influential in political terms. There were other groups of intellectuals who made a priority of criticising the *philosophes*, prominent among them the circle surrounding Fréron's journal *Année littéraire* (*Literary Yearbook*, launched 1754). By means primarily of extended reviews, this journal maintained a sharp and sustained focus on the inconsistencies, superficialities and intellectual shortcuts evident in much French enlightened writing. Until his death in 1776 Fréron remained personally at the forefront of this attack, but he also commissioned work from less well-known contemporaries, including Gilbert and Sabatier, and maintained close contact with the journalists Royou

---

10 See for example R. Shackleton, 'Johnson and the Enlightenment', in his *Essays on Montesquieu and on the Enlightenment* (Oxford, 1988), 243–56; but notice also the evidence for his consistent conventionality and traditionalism in N. Hudson, *Samuel Johnson and Eighteenth-Century Thought* (Oxford, 1988).

11 R.B. Sher, *Church and University in the Scottish Enlightenment: The Moderate Literati of Edinburgh* (Edinburgh, 1985), 277–97, which also includes a very full and helpful bibliography.

(1741–92) and Geoffroy (1743–1814), both of whom became prominent conservative newspaper editors in the Revolution. Fréron also had links with the notorious and fiercely independent lawyer Linguet (1736–94), who cannot be fitted into any neat category in the complex alliances of the later enlightenment.[12]

Significantly, Rousseau was to a large extent spared by Fréron's team, and it is not difficult to see why. Rousseau defies all categorisation, and (as if almost to prove it) managed to quarrel irretrievably with most of the *philosophes* who had once been his friends, as well as with David Hume and many others. He was never part of a counter-enlightenment, however defined, but his demonstrative retreat from Paris into the countryside in 1756 was meant to tell the world that he believed that no truth or virtue could be found there. He became a lifelong refugee, instinctively distrustful of everyone, seemingly convinced (especially once Voltaire started his viciously personal attacks on him) that there was a conspiracy against his work. His belief in the innate goodness of natural man, his cultivated naïvety, his return to a kind of purified religious faith, and his willingness sometimes to prioritise sensibility and nostalgic sentimentality over reason, marked him out as the creator of an alternative enlightenment – highly influential in its own right, but other-worldly and Utopian to the point that compromise with mainstream enlightenment became intellectually as well as temperamentally impossible.[13]

To complicate matters, there were scholars outside France who rejected both Rousseau and the *philosophes*. One of them, Elie Luzac (1721–96), was part of a family of Huguenots who had fled from France to the United Provinces. Luzac worked all his life in Leiden, as a major publisher, prolific author and participant in the republic of letters. Amongst his close friends was Samuel Formey, also a Huguenot exile, secretary of the Berlin Academy of Sciences and member of the lively if secretive Mittwochsgesellschaft (1783–98) which included many leading German intellectuals (see p. 69). Luzac had caused a storm already in 1747 by publishing La Mettrie's materialist *L'homme machine* (*Man a Machine*), and became an outspoken critic of restrictions on freedom of the press. But, as representative of what has been called a 'rational, tolerant and liberal Protestant enlightenment', he found the *Encyclopédie* too superficial to foster rational analysis, and Rousseau too close to the kind of primitivism that might destroy civilisation as he knew it (a primitivism which he later saw embodied in the Dutch Patriot movement of the 1780s). Temperamentally, he was much closer to

---

12 D.M. McMahon, 'The counter-enlightenment and the low-life of literature in pre-revolutionary France', *Past and Present* 159 (1998), 77–112; D.G. Levy, *The Ideas and Careers of Simon-Nicolas-Henri Linguet: A Study in Eighteenth-Century French Politics* (Urbana, 1980).

13 M. Hulliung, *The Autocritique of Enlightenment: Rousseau and the Philosophes* (Cambridge, Mass., 1994). For an interpretation of his impact, see also C. Blum, *Rousseau and the Republic of Virtue: The Language of Politics in the French Revolution* (Ithaca, 1986).

Wolff, whose writings he made accessible to a French audience, and to Adam Smith, whose *Theory of Moral Sentiments* of 1759 he commented on in great detail.[14]

It would seem difficult to deny, on the basis of this kind of evidence, that creating a clear antithesis between enlightenment and counter-enlightenment, over religious issues or anything else, is frequently unhelpful. Rousseau's rebellion, and the difficulties he had trying to ensure that his works were understood the way he would want them to be, is perhaps the most obvious warning against over-simplification. Many other individual contributors to the great debates of the period can also be firmly categorised under either rubric only if we are prepared to ignore apparent 'contradictions' within their writings. It is doubly unhelpful when we remind ourselves that personal attitudes were liable to change within a lifetime, either with – or, as in Luzac's reaction to the Dutch Patriot revolt, against – contemporary trends. Much work has been done in recent years, notably by Robert Darnton (below, p. 96), to show just how volatile, perhaps even fashion-driven, the French enlightenment was in its later stages. By then much of central and eastern Europe was catching up with the more moderate strands of French thought, absorbing those of its key ideas that did not clash obviously with their own core values. Whether the more extreme forbidden and under-ground literature that seemed to sell in France after 1763 reached the rest of the European market in any significant quantity is not yet clear, but the control mechanisms in force in the Habsburg lands and in Scandinavia, combined with the barriers of language and culture for the less well educated, would suggest that its impact was bound to be limited. The diffusion of certain types of ideas, then, was contingent on a variety of factors, some to do with cultural and regional characteristics, some to do with perceived alignments and 'parties' within the enlightenment and amongst its critics, but probably many more dependent on the particular social circumstance and personal attitude of originators and potential recipients alike.

Nature, man and science

Phrases to do with 'nature' and 'natural' are sprinkled liberally throughout eighteenth-century discourse – with little attempt at precision. Sometimes, as in 'natural religion', it implies something generic, instinctive, not contingent on cultural constructs. Similarly, the idea of a 'law of nature' (a general law stemming from the unspecified innate characteristics of nature as discerned by man) could be developed as a corrective to existing law, just as 'natural rights' became a concept around which to build a fairer society; even the 'state of nature', a kind of primitivism that Hobbes had once deemed brutish

14 W.R.E. Velema, *Enlightenment and Conservatism in the Dutch Republic: The Political Thought of Elie Luzac* (Assen/Maastricht, 1993), 3–32 and *passim*.

and short, eventually came to be seen by Rousseauists as a virtuous condition. Nature played a large if fairly diffuse part in the popularised versions of key intellectual and scientific issues which so enthralled contemporary opinion. Debate on a whole range of subjects, from psychology and sense perception to gender or race, came to be conducted on the basis not merely of inherited philosophical abstracts (or old prejudices), but increasingly also of a great deal of new and innovative work affecting all of the sciences.[15] However, the status of knowledge about the physical world was itself the object of discussion. On the one hand, the use of the terms 'natural history' and 'natural philosophy' to describe what we would now call the biological and physical sciences was not merely a matter of different nomenclature, but rather a reflection of the essential unity of all traditional forms of learning (philosophy), with theology as a central guiding framework. There was no assumption that the divinely ordained universe would necessarily be distinct from the natural world governed by universal laws of nature. Thus the systematic work of Linnaeus (1707–78) in designing a comprehensive framework for the classification of all living things (significant especially for plant taxonomy) could also be regarded as a step forward in revealing the totality of God's creation. For some, however, knowledge about the physical world was regarded as the least reliable 'philosophy': the all-embracing doubt that Descartes had tried to eliminate deductively in the early seventeenth century continued to pose a major challenge to all forms of knowledge, and, as Hume made clear, in particular to those dependent on sense perceptions. Locke had suggested a partial solution to this difficulty by adopting a subtle combination of empiricism and intuition, which in the eyes of some (like the Irish philosopher George Berkeley, 1685–1753) might remove threats to religious belief itself. By contrast, Condillac in his *Traité des sensations* (*Treatise on Sensations*, 1754) used Locke to build his rather shallow theory of sensationism, in which sense perception became the sole basis for knowledge about the 'real' natural world.

Natural philosophy remained throughout the eighteenth century primarily in the hands of non-specialists, notably the gentlemen amateurs who were its most prominent practitioners, and the *philosophes* who popularised some of its more exotic findings. Except for medicine, there was little explicit training in basic scientific methodology anywhere in Europe until the reforms in the Scottish and north German universities gathered momentum in the second quarter of the century.[16] In chemistry a final break with traditional alchemy really only came with the work of Joseph Black (1728–99) at Glasgow and

15 L. Schiebinger, 'The anatomy of difference: race and sex in eighteenth-century science', *Eighteenth-Century Studies* 23 (1989–90), 387–405, illustrates experimental and theoretical work on these two particular fronts. A helpful set of essays exploring a much wider range of eighteenth-century work is provided by C. Fox, R. Porter and R. Wokler, eds., *Inventing Human Science: Eighteenth-Century Domains* (Berkeley, 1995).

16 See for example R.L. Emerson, 'Scottish universities in the eighteenth century', *StVEC* 167 (1977), 453–74; and his 'Science and the origins and concerns of the Scottish enlightenment', *History of Science* 26 (1988), 333–66.

Edinburgh universities from the 1750s onwards, and in Paris with the quantitative research of Lavoisier on combustion, oxygen and the properties of elements and compounds. Much popular interest in the physical and natural sciences continued to be met by theoretical treatises with little empirical basis, by meetings of the many provincial academies and scientific societies that came into existence all over Europe from the later seventeenth century onwards, and, increasingly for the applied sciences, by means of the public lecture-demonstrations that enterprising enthusiasts undertook round the fashionable consumer markets and fairs of the more prosperous parts of Europe. Inevitably, popular science tended to focus on the weird, the entertaining and the spectacular, rather than on the more complex theoretical issues of the cognitive process itself or of the mechanics of the physical world. Contemporary attention was caught by volcanic activity, the exotic flora and fauna of distant worlds, innovative iron bridge-building techniques, sexual reproduction and heredity, Benjamin Franklin's kite-flying experiments during thunder storms, Montgolfier's balloon-flying, Mesmer's so-called 'animal magnetism', and other novelties. However, there was also a growing interest in quantification and scientific measurement of natural phenomena and time, some of which had immediate beneficial results in terms of maritime navigation, cartography, standardisation of weights and measures (including the metric system), and even aspects of political economy and public administration.[17]

In the long run, such interests may have furthered a gradual separation of natural philosophy from theology, and of the applied sciences from religion. Ever since the scientific revolution of the late sixteenth and early seventeenth centuries, the potential for clashes between stated church dogmas and the empirical evidence of observation had been obvious. To some, like the radical free thinker and experimental scientist Joseph Priestley (1733–1804), there was no real conflict of interest, and he continued to serve as a dissenting preacher whilst furthering his experimental scientific work. Yet conventional religious beliefs were liable to be challenged, notably by the work of scientists who adopted an evolutionary view of the natural world at odds with the church's chronological interpretation of the Book of Genesis. Buffon's hugely successful *Natural History*, of which the first three (of many) volumes appeared in 1749, documented evidence of evolutionary processes stretching over a much longer period.[18] In Edinburgh, James Hutton (1726–97) published the first part of his *Theory of the Earth* in 1785, laying the foundations for the modern interpretation of the long-term geological evolution of the planet, again at variance with the formal teachings of the church.

Less controversial, but ultimately closer to the central interests of the enlightenment all over Europe, was the study of social man – systematic

17 T. Frängsmyr, J.L. Heilbron and R.E. Rider, eds., *The Quantifying Spirit in the Eighteenth Century* (Berkeley, 1990).
18 J. Roger, *Buffon: A Life in Natural History* (Ithaca, 1997) provides an excellent analysis of the priorities and nature of Buffon's research.

analysis of the detailed workings of human society itself. Also referred to as the 'science of man' or 'moral philosophy', it sought to extend the moral reflections on human nature favoured by earlier generations into a systematic scientific discipline. Provided we allow for changes in nomenclature and in academic content over time, we might describe the 'science of man' as consisting of what we would now call psychology, religion and ethics, parts of jurisprudence, sociology, political science, political economy, history and economics, together with the theoretical and philosophical basis for each of these areas. But in essence the 'science of man' dealt with civil society, the moral principles of civic rights and obligations, and the mechanics whereby progress towards stability and prosperity might be achieved. For many of the key contributors to the enlightenment, and especially the French *philosophes*, cross-cultural comparisons provided the ideal material with which to illustrate (obliquely where necessary) the problems and factors shaping modern society, including the role of environment and individualism. The historical dimension was strong especially amongst the Scots, though for them and the Germans religious and moral concerns proper also figured prominently. And probably everyone – even Rousseau – agreed that the arts (especially music and literature) could make a vital contribution in improving moral instincts and raising the self-consciousness of mankind. Amongst the striking contributions to the 'science of man' we might therefore include Swift's *Gulliver's Travels* of 1726, Mercier's *The Year 2440* of 1771, Fuseli's engraving *The Nightmare* ten years later, Mozart's opera *The Magic Flute* first performed in 1791, and much else besides – as well as innumerable lesser works of fiction some of which are now all but forgotten. As we shall see in the last three chapters of this book, the scope for detailed analysis of human society, experimentation, and even practical reform was virtually boundless.

The 'public sphere' and its limits

The history of ideas is central to any understanding of the enlightenment; but so is the need to evaluate the context in which the major writers worked, the environment which turned some into household names whilst ignoring others, and the mechanisms which influenced the reception of new ideas amongst a growing number of contemporaries who did not necessarily have the intellectual stamina to read major publications. Discussion of these issues now often takes its starting point in two influential works of philosophical sociology written 40 years ago – Habermas's exposition of what he called the *bürgerliche Öffentlichkeit* (translatable as the 'public sphere' or public opinion), and Koselleck's exploration of related ideas specifically in the context of the enlightenment.[19] Their relevance here lies in the impetus they have given to innovative research on the growth of public discussion and the formation of public opinion. In the eighteenth century public opinion was fostered primarily through the medium of print, through debating societies and political clubs, through academies and libraries, and through other forms of what Habermas described as 'bourgeois' sociability – in other words through structures which were essentially independent of the absolute state, and could therefore provide a platform for criticism. We can discount the use of the term 'bourgeois', which few historians regard as helpful for this period. In Chapter 8 we shall return at greater length to the nature of opinion, and to the problems of separating 'public' from 'private' in the eighteenth century (p. 199); here it is more important to outline what the 'public sphere' might now be understood to mean.

Common sense suggests that there always has been some kind of collective opinion, as well as an array of different forms of public 'interface' between the state and the people it governs. The Reformation and Counter-Reformation period undoubtedly strengthened the role both of private religious belief and of the individual conscience in making judgements about society and its government. In the case of civil war and interregnum England (1639–60) such judgements became sufficiently powerful to threaten not only the political structure of the state itself, but also some of the most fundamental relationships within society, for example regarding the distribution of property. The eighteenth century may not have added greatly to the fundamental principles and intellectual constructs around which criticism and debate were formulated. But, as Chapters 2–5 will seek to demonstrate, it did bring very significant changes regarding the settings where debate might develop, the mechanisms by which it might be furthered (not least through print), and the kinds of people – especially in urban society – who might be reached.

Originally, in the Habermas–Koselleck discussion, much was made of an essentially binary divide between on the one hand the private realm (consisting of civil society, the family and the individual), and on the other a consolidated public authority (central government, usually in the form of absolute monarchy). In between these two was an area of intersection covering a 'public sphere' in politics, urban sociability and the press. Today, such a schematic view seems over-simplified, and most historians would opt for a rather more nuanced analytical framework. The state itself was a

19 R. Koselleck, *Critique and Crisis: Enlightenment and the Pathogenesis of Modern Society* (German original 1959; English translation Oxford, 1988); J. Habermas, *The Structural Transformation of the Public Sphere: An Inquiry into a Category of Bourgeois Society* (German original 1962; translation Oxford, 1989). The very wide agenda of each of these books will not be considered here, but for a helpful introduction to the impact of these works on historical studies, see A.J. la Vopa, 'Conceiving a public: ideas and society in eighteenth-century Europe', *Journal of Modern History* 64 (1992), 79–116; and D. Goodman, 'Public sphere and private life: toward a synthesis of current historiographical approaches to the Old Regime', *History and Theory* 31 (1992), 1–20.

composite of what nowadays we would call public and private: the king a public symbol but also a private magnate, his exercise of power and patronage designed precisely to blur such a distinction; surrounded by a court or royal entourage consisting of the long-established aristocracy, more recent service nobles, professional bureaucrats, venal office-holders, essentially 'private' financiers with a stake in the fiscal and entrepreneurial machinery of the state, and many others. Each of these groups might have their own network of contacts, and their own way of defining and expressing their personal interests. The same could be said of the many official groupings outside the immediate environment of the court: in Britain the network of connections that made up Commons and Lords in Parliament, in France the powerful and well-read *robe* nobility who staffed the Parisian and provincial *parlements* and special courts. All over Europe there were carefully defined and exclusive corporations of lawyers, regional and local administrators (some dependent on the state, others less so), perhaps provincial Estates or other regional assemblies, and strong municipal oligarchies; as well as a rich profusion of professional organisations, guild officialdom, parish councils, church wardens and elders, boards of overseers for hospitals and poor relief structures, religious orders and confraternities, journeymen's associations, and much else. Each could serve as a forum of communication and perhaps of debate, as a pressure group, or just as a social network. If we add more 'private' organisations such as clubs, reading societies and libraries, Masonic lodges,[20] voluntary societies, journal subscribers, not to mention the ubiquitous 'republic of letters' and other informal correspondence networks, several conclusions readily spring to mind. First, any divide between 'public' and 'private' is virtually meaningless in the eighteenth century, as contemporaries did not think or operate with such a distinction in mind. Second, what might be called 'political authority' was exercised by a wide array of different and sometimes rival interests – at local level typically ranging from the private landowner acting as provincial governor, tax collector or recruitment agent, to the venal office-holder in a largely honorary post choosing to collect fees for the 'public' services that were actually carried out for him by a deputy. And we need to remember that any one individual could be a member of several overlapping interest groups, each with their own form of 'sociability', each with their distinct attitudes to current affairs, philosophical debates, social policy and local power struggles. Of course it was all held together by invisible norms of deference, and by knowledge and experience

20 The significance of Freemasonry as a network (or even as a set of beliefs distinct from the enlightenment as a whole) has been debated extensively but inconclusively. See notably M.C. Jacob, *The Radical Enlightenment: Pantheists, Freemasons and Republicans* (London, 1981) and the critical review of it by G. Gibbs in the *British Journal for the History of Science* 17 (1984), 67–81; M.C. Jacob, *Living the Enlightenment: Freemasonry and Politics in Eighteenth-Century Europe* (Oxford, 1992); H. Reinalter, ed., *Aufklärung und Geheimgesellschaften: zur politischen Funktion und Sozialstruktur der Freimaurerlogen im 18. Jahrhundert* (Munich, 1989); G. Gayot, *La franc-maçonnerie française: textes et pratiques, xviiie–xixe siècles* (Paris, 1980).

of how to work the system; but those links are not always easy for the historian to identify, and reducing a complex network into neat rubrics is almost bound to entail the risk of serious distortion. We have to take eighteenth-century society as it was, without more simplification than necessary. The next few chapters will suggest that the cultural and communication systems – especially in urban society – were, as we would expect, of comparable complexity.

What has been said so far applies primarily to adult men. Women did have access to some networks, notably those based on the parish and its related poor relief and medical systems, and of course those based on the extended family; but they had only partial access to guild structures and occupational networks, and (except during riots) hardly any to structures that could be construed as political. Their most readily accessible way of self-expression was through writing: either as contributors to the huge market for novels and other forms of fictional writing (in which women were also major consumers), or, less commonly, as modest (or pseudonymous) authors of non-fiction. Women were valued for their sensitivity and sensibility, their subtle compassion and their understanding of the pathetic and emotional elements in literature and the arts. They were deemed inferior in the qualities which according to eighteenth-century gender stereotypes were supposed to be 'masculine', such as clarity of logic or participation in critical political debate. As spouses they might serve as power-brokers, but (as for example Madame Roland discovered) it was difficult to do so without incurring the risk of being criticised as an unnatural meddler or licentious schemer. Contemporary males often used Rousseau as justification for enhancing what they saw as 'natural' distinctions of gender, and for criticising women who exceeded their pre-determined (essentially domestic) sphere. Women of high social standing could host salons and intellectual dinner parties, and to a considerable extent control the agenda on such occasions; but they were not often major or original contributors to discussion, and were certainly meant to take a passive role (if any role at all) in the 'republic of letters'. As we shall see in Chapter 8, the cause of emancipation of women did not make much progress during the French Revolution.[21] Overall, the 'public sphere' expanded greatly during the eighteenth century, but much more so for men than for women.

21 D. Goodman, *The Republic of Letters: A Cultural History of the French Enlightenment* (Ithaca, 1994), 73–135 and *passim*; L. Steinbrügge, *The Moral Sex: Woman's Nature in the French Enlightenment* (Oxford, 1995); J. Landes, *Women and the Public Sphere in the Age of the French Revolution* (Ithaca, 1988), 39–89 and *passim*; S.E. Melzer and L.W. Rabine, eds., *Rebel Daughters: Women and the French Revolution* (New York, 1992); O. Hufton, *The Prospect before Her: a History of Women in Western Europe*, vol. 1 (London, 1995) 436–57; S. Mazah, 'Women, the bourgeoisie and the public sphere', *French Historical Studies* 17 (1991), 935–50; W. Stafford, 'Narratives of women: English feminists of the 1790s', *History* 82 (1997), 24–43. It might be noted, however, that the role of women in publishing, though sometimes difficult to trace reliably, may have been quite significant: see for example K. Wilson, *The Sense of the People: Politics, Culture and Imperialism in England, 1715–1785* (Cambridge, 1995), 48–54.

Enlightenment and political power

During the later eighteenth century the nature of politics itself changed. For many years historians have used the term 'enlightened absolutism' (or less helpfully 'enlightened despotism') to describe what they see as a form of personal rule tempered by awareness of public consensus around a programme of enlightened reform.[22] We shall examine some aspects of this reform programme, and the role of 'public opinion' in its formulation and implementation, later in this book; at this stage we should note the varying relationship across Europe between leading thinkers and those who exercised actual political influence. For example, the leading lights of the Scottish enlightenment had access to none of the levers of political power which their German counterparts could sometimes operate, and only the most indirect political influence. Yet this does not seem to have caused them undue concern: were they satisfied with the peculiarly British form of consensus politics in which they now had some share, albeit an ill-defined one, or did they tacitly recognise that political influence in later eighteenth-century absolutist Europe was in fact mostly illusory anyway?

The French *philosophes* have often been regarded as 'outsiders', both socially and politically – that is, their main impact was through criticism and through their influence on public opinion, rather than directly on government. This may be true of some of them, but the generalisation does not always stand up to closer scrutiny. The physiocrats, in particular, came to exercise considerable direct influence, not just whilst one of their foremost contributors, Turgot, held the highest financial office of the state (as Controller General, 1774–76), but also over the following years (even after 1789) when physiocratic fiscal policies were partially absorbed into central government thinking. Interestingly, physiocratic ideas also had a significant impact on the policies of Frederick II of Brandenburg-Prussia (an avid reader of everything French), and on the great ministers of the Habsburg state, especially Kaunitz. Indeed Kaunitz, like Sonnenfels, van Swieten and some of the other major advisors serving Maria Theresa, was a prime example of the potentially close relationship between politics and enlightenment: an extremely well-read, independent-minded, and extraordinarily energetic man, he was at the same time sufficiently well in tune with the realities of political life to serve both the old-fashioned Maria Theresa and her impatiently iconoclastic son Joseph II. This kind of cooperation, however, may

22 H.M. Scott, ed., *Enlightened Absolutism: Reform and Reformers in Later Eighteenth-Century Europe* (Basingstoke, 1990) provides a good starting point for comparison of the main examples across Europe. See also D. McKay and H.M. Scott, *The Rise of the Great Powers, 1648–1815* (London, 1983); A. Lentin, *Enlightened Absolutism: A Documentary Sourcebook* (Newcastle-upon-Tyne, 1985); F. Venturi, *The End of the Old Régime in Europe, 1768–1776* (Princeton, 1989) and his *The End of the Old Régime in Europe, 1776–1789*, 2 vols. (Princeton 1991); and the very large literature on individual states during this period.

have come at a price: fairly strict controls on public debate were maintained, and it is striking, for example, that details of the American constitutional discussions in the 1770s and 1780s were not as readily available in the German lands as in Britain or France.[23]

By 1793, the term 'statesman' had become a term of abuse attached to Girondins and others perceived to modify their principles to suit their ambitions; but for the period before 1789 we are entitled to use the term more freely to describe some of those who saw no unbridgeable conflict between philosophical interests and political power. The American intellectual politicians Benjamin Franklin (1706–90) and Thomas Jefferson (1743–1826) may have had the easiest task, in that they were assisting in the construction of a new political system; in Europe, long historical memories and traditions complicated matters. Contrary to what we might expect, however, strong or autocratic government was not necessarily the most effective way of promoting 'enlightened' reform: there were many more outstanding and influential minds in the service of the Habsburg government, for example, than there were in the close entourage of Frederick II of Prussia. Similarly, the Danish government after 1784, in the hands of a very young and inexperienced crown prince, had far more distinguished and genuinely effective advisors than the temperamental and autocratic Gustavus III of Sweden – even though the formal framework of government of each (Denmark–Norway being very absolutist, Sweden nominally a parliamentary monarchy) might have suggested that the opposite should have been the case. France itself, as we shall see, had a string of able and significant ministers from the end of Louis XV's reign onwards: the crown was sufficiently weak to be forced to tolerate considerable discussion and consultation, but unfortunately it also proved too weak to provide effective leadership. In short, continental European experiences in the later eighteenth century suggest that the relationship between enlightenment and political power was rather more complicated than the traditional image of an 'enlightened monarch' may convey. As one recent historian has indicated, autocratic reform could prove superficial and ineffective, whereas

> a climate of opinion can be subtler and more pervasive, and it shows that power is permeable. A climate of opinion is the result of having ideas lying round where people – including the powerful – are bound to

23 On the tendency to political conservatism in the German press, and its support for strong government against popular radicalism, see J.D. Popkin, 'The German press and the Dutch Patriot movement, 1781–87', *Lessing Yearbook* 22 (1990), 97–111. See also H. Dippel, *Germany and the American Revolution 1770–1800* (Chapel Hill, 1977). *The Catalogue of English Books Printed before 1801 Held by the University Library at Göttingen* (Hildesheim, 1987) indicates just one up-market edition in German of, for example, Tom Paine's *Common Sense* issued in 1777 (the year after the American original), and one translation of Part I of his *Rights of Man* in Leipzig immediately in 1791. By contrast, debate on the details of American political innovations was lively in Britain, and remarkably extensive also in pre-revolutionary France thanks in part to the colourful ambassadorial role of Benjamin Franklin.

find them; ideas which seem at first to have no risks attached, which seem harmless, interesting, entertaining even, in the way bourgeois social circles according to Kant's account found them entertaining.[24]

Effective government in the later eighteenth century seemed to depend not so much on its formal machinery and political traditions, as on its amenability to share the 'public sphere' – not in an adversarial role, but in something that could be construed as a partnership.

*   *   *

Any definition of the enlightenment, and its social and political context, must now to some extent be dependent on the eye of the beholder. Since this book is a social history, and not primarily a history of intellectual ideas, it takes a broad and inclusive approach. The emphasis throughout will be on means of communication, actual or potential exposure to different ways of thinking about a broad range of problems, challenges to accepted norms and inherited beliefs, and potential reinforcement of the resulting questioning both by means of public discussion and by means of experimentation with actual reform initiatives. The intention is not to measure the enlightenment by tangible results (important though some of these may be), but rather to see it as a process of emancipation. Like all such processes it created contradictions and revealed inconsistencies that can easily be held up as faults. One might be tempted to see many of the *philosophes*, with all their armchair radicalism, as little more than players in the intellectual games of the glittering salons of a profoundly inegalitarian and at times authoritarian society – or as shrewd manipulators in a growing consumer market. That, however, would in my view be a profound misreading, and we should not allow twentieth-century cynicism to discredit the sincerity of another age. An open-minded reading of the books, pamphlets, newspapers and government reports of especially the second half of the eighteenth century will reveal enthusiasts, dreamers and committed reformers – alongside pedants, cynics and hedonists. The real achievement of the age, perhaps, is to have humoured and tolerated most of them for most of the time – to have allowed a Diderot to explore the full boundaries of acceptability within the public domain, whilst convincing him wisely to reserve the most provocative ideas for private conversation and correspondence. Above all, the enlightenment was more than the sum of its individual (if considerable) parts: it was a period where public opinion, though very different from our own, acquired significant new momentum.

24 T.J. Reed, 'Talking to tyrants: dialogues with power in eighteenth-century Germany', *Historical Journal* 33 (1990), 63–79, quoted from 70f. For a wider discussion, see also C.G. Stricklen, 'The philosophe's political mission: the creation of an idea, 1750–1789', *StVEC* 186 (1971), 137–228; and J.v.H. Melton, 'From enlightenment to revolution: Hertzberg, Schlözer and the problem of despotism in the late Aufklärung', *Central European History* 12 (1979), 102–23.

2

Tradition and communication in daily life

The major achievements of eighteenth-century creative and innovative thinkers may seem relatively familiar in the abstract, as ideas and intellectual processes. However, when we turn to the social context in which these changes occurred, we enter less well-charted territory. How directly were specific works of the enlightenment influenced by the environment in which they were created, and what kinds of impression did such works make outside the community of *philosophes*, writers and scholars who read and discussed each others' works? In what respects, if at all, did the conceptual world of ordinary Parisians or Londoners change in the course of the eighteenth century? What about those who were more distant from city life, or who were not habitual readers? How effective were different forms of communication, and what purposes could they serve?

If we were to ask equivalent questions even about modern society we would have some difficulty finding conclusive evidence. For the eighteenth century, the problems are bound to be much greater. Letters, diaries, fictional literature and other descriptive material can help provide some impression of what went on in the salons, academies and coffee-shops of the better-off. Even what contemporaries sometimes called the 'middling sort' (consisting of professionals, lesser officeholders, merchants, manufacturers and others living comfortably above the bread-line) have left enough clues to keep social historians busy. But skilled and semi-skilled workers, domestic service staff, apprentices and wage-earners – let alone unskilled labourers, most of the rural population of Europe, their households, and above all the women – are much more difficult to approach. Even amongst the increasing number of adults who had somehow learnt to read adequately, writing remained a relatively rare skill, used primarily in formal or exceptional circumstances. In other words, we face some quite fundamental problems of evidence in trying to study the diffusion of the enlightenment outside the charmed circles of the well-to-do. Some of this evidence will be examined in detail in later chapters.

Here we shall start by outlining those forms of communication that remained essentially traditional in nature, and did not rely primarily on the printed word.

Popular and elite culture

Despite intensive research in recent years, there is very little agreement about what early modern European popular culture really was. At first sight, there are no great difficulties with the dictionary definition. In the words of one historian,[1] we might define culture generally as a 'system of shared meanings, attitudes and values, and the symbolic forms . . . in which they are expressed or embodied'. What we are referring to is a comprehensive culture intelligible to all members of a society, a common culture embracing the whole gamut of assumptions, ideas, beliefs, linguistic norms, forms of expression and accepted imagery which underpin all forms of communication in a society. Problems arise, however, as soon as we start using the phrase 'popular culture' (unofficial, organic, meaningful to ordinary people) in contrast to 'elite culture' (perhaps officially sponsored, sometimes implying status and exclusivity, and always contingent on wealth, education and 'good taste'). At first sight such a differentiation seems logical enough. By the eighteenth century, after all, elite culture is fairly readily identifiable and relatively homogeneous over much of western and central Europe. Given enormous differences of wealth, material culture and education, the elite are bound to have had values significantly different from those of the great majority of society. There is certainly no lack of evidence that the eighteenth-century elite, from workhouse governors and economic theorists to Marie Antoinette acting out rustic fantasies, were not only heavily patronising towards the poor, but determined to set themselves apart from ordinary people: rich against poor, literate against illiterate, polite against rough, respectable against rowdy or vulgar. Yet just as the actual fabric of eighteenth-century society itself has on closer examination proved far more complex than historians first assumed, so plausible demarcation lines between different cultural layers, and the characteristics of each, have proved elusive.

It used to be argued that popular culture, a system of values traditionally shared by all, began (perhaps in the Reformation and Counter-Reformation period) to become differentiated from that elite culture which it had hitherto in part incorporated; and that the polarisation between the two by 1800 had led not only to some degree of mutual incomprehension, but also to social alienation and renewed efforts of reform or repression by the elite. The

---

1 This is the definition developed by Peter Burke in his innovative studies over the last two decades, cited and commented upon by Tim Harris in the introductory essay, 'Problematising popular culture', in *Popular Culture in England, c. 1500–1850*, ed. T. Harris (London, 1995), 1–11.

chronology of such a repression of popular culture has proved problematic: after all, attempts especially by religious leaders to change popular (often pagan) practices had started well before the Reformation, and the history of witchcraft and other forms of superstition indicate how slow and ineffective 'elite' reform often was. Similarly, it has been recognised that interaction between elite and popular culture took different forms, depending on the context of religious divisions, educational change, administrative developments and the emergence of professional bureaucracies.

Recent work, however, has questioned the polarisation thesis more fundamentally. The sheer diversity of customs and traditions across different regions (urban against rural, dairy as against arable country) and across different social groups (for example journeymen against vagrants) suggests that we are faced with highly complex overlapping subcultures, co-existing but not always fully and mutually comprehensible. There were also clear contrasts even within single social levels (between for example the customs of individual trade guilds, or more significantly between the culture of working women and that of their husbands). On the other hand, there was a great deal of mutual interaction across social divides, graphically illustrated in the tall buildings of Paris, where the wealthiest lived on the main floors above shop and street level, and the poorest on the eighth to ninth floor or attic of the same house. Mutual economic dependence and constant social contact made cultural interaction inevitable. No doubt there would be plenty of friction, and perhaps some mutual assimilation; but once we recognise the richness of intermediate layers between rich and poor, then notions of straight polarisation seem increasingly simplistic.[2]

If we accept this sociological complexity of especially urban culture, it follows that the already serious problem of reliable evidence becomes more intricate. The vestiges of oral culture (ballads, songs, legends and folk tales) only survive because someone wrote them down, more often for commercial gain than as an authentic contribution to the genre. Writing skills were still too rare in the eighteenth century to have left much genuine popular output.

2　The issues discussed here are covered far more fully in the classic work on the subject, namely P. Burke, *Popular Culture in Early Modern Europe* (London, 1978), 270–81 and *passim*. Amongst those arguing that popular culture was destroyed by the elite, especially through moral–religious repression and education, an uncompromising presentation is found in R. Muchembled, *Popular Culture and Elite Culture in France 1400–1750* (Baton Rouge, 1985; translated from the French original of 1978). For recent and more balanced surveys, see *Popular Culture in England, c. 1500–1850*, ed. T. Harris (London, 1995), esp. 1–27; R.A. Houston, *Scottish Literacy and the Scottish Identity* (Cambridge, 1985), 193–210 and 214–26; as well as the short but helpful surveys by R. Chartier, 'Culture as appropriation: popular cultural uses in early modern France', in *Understanding Popular Culture: Europe from the Middle Ages to the Nineteenth Century*, ed. S.L. Kaplan (Berlin, 1984), 229–53; by B. Scribner, 'Is a history of popular culture possible?', *History of European Ideas* 10 (1989), 175–91; and more recently, by B. Reay, *Popular Cultures in England 1550–1750* (London, 1998), 198–223. For interesting case study material, see notably J.-L. Ménétra, *Journal de ma vie: compagnon vitrier au 18e siècle*, ed. D. Roche (Paris, 1982); and A. Jarrick, 'Världen enligt Hjerpe eller några folkliga skriftprov från upplysningstiden', *Historisk Tidskrift* (Stockholm) 111 (1991), 503–39.

Of necessity, therefore, we often have to turn to the indirect evidence found in sources compiled mostly from the point of view of outsiders. Church and judicial records, for example, are full of case histories from which a rich and colourful impression of community life can be reconstructed, but the formal versions that have survived are necessarily those of clerks and officials, with the real views of participants represented only patchily in personal depositions and supportive material. Fuller contemporary descriptions of urban culture, festivities and processions, as well as prints and other visual material, must also be treated with caution since they were usually composed by, and often for, outsiders.

One possible access route for historians of popular culture might be found in the mass-produced chapbooks and cheap pamphlets so common in this period. In France, the *bibliothèque bleue* (so called because of the cheap coloured paper covers) had emerged in the seventeenth century as a clearly identifiable genre. By the eighteenth century over a hundred printer–publishers in the major provincial towns of France were involved in the trade, mostly in the more literate northern and eastern parts of France. Distributed by itinerant pedlars as well as by regular bookshops, these small blue books undoubtedly sold well – perhaps over a million copies annually in mid-eighteenth-century France alone. In England a very similar development occurred, with some publishers specialising in the huge print-runs of cheap material which the popular market could now sustain.

The *bibliothèque bleue* and the chapbook were in part derivative – consisting of simple timeless tales and devotional works that were expected to be in fairly continuous demand, alongside simplified and shortened versions of books originally intended for a higher market, such as Rabelais' *Gargantua* and *Pantagruel* (first published 1532–34), Bunyan's *Pilgrim's Progress* (1678–84), or Defoe's more recent *Moll Flanders* (1722). Prices were deliberately held low through large print-runs: often in the range of 2–4 pence in England, and often less than 1 sol in France. Illustrations might well be included, typically crude woodcuts of only tenuous relevance to the text itself. But even here market forces made an impression in the course of the eighteenth century, with texts made more attractive through suggestive title pages, better woodcuts, paragraph divisions and other aids to easier reading. The chapbook was not a static genre, impervious to change; but it tended to lag behind the kind of substantial shift in reading interests that we shall observe in a later chapter in connection with more up-market book production.[3]

Although authors are rarely named, much of the output was evidently

3 The most thorough recent study of the French market is L. Andries, *La bibliothèque bleu au dix-huitième siècle: une tradition éditoriale*, St VEC 270 (1989), 9–24 and *passim*. See also R. Chartier, *The Cultural Uses of Print in Early Modern France* (Princeton, 1987), 240–64; P. Rogers, *Literature and Popular Culture in Eighteenth-Century England* (Brighton, 1985), 162–96; and N.Ó. Ciosáin, *Print and Popular Culture in Ireland, 1750–1850* (Basingstoke, 1997).

written by people who might, like the writer Restif de la Bretonne
(1734–1806), originally have come from peasant stock but were hardly any
longer of low social position: in other words, the chapbook market was
written for the people, but not by the people. Many of the texts relied on
stock moral and pious themes, often simply reprinting old material. Sometimes they were enlivened by the burlesque, the picaresque and the grotesque,
occasionally they had a belated hint of the new intellectual ideas of the times
(for example in travel accounts), but more often they were couched in
traditional religious, devotional, fictional or mythological–historical terms.
Even the popular accounts of the last hours of convicted criminals mostly
reinforced contemporary assumptions of morality and obedience: any
awareness of social injustice, for example, is difficult to find, and occasional
political satire is never sustained. Only a small proportion of the booklets
were meant for practical orientation, notably the guides to popular medicine
or to improved literacy.

If the blue books in France were to be regarded as a reliable reflection of
popular interests, we might well conclude that provincial and rural readers
were much less discerning than those of Paris, and that popular social and
political awareness was slow to develop before the Revolution. On comparable evidence, the overall impression in England or other parts of Europe
would probably be much the same. But there are clearly problems in trying to
use this kind of material as a guide to popular culture, let alone as an
indicator of the diffusion or reception of new characteristics. As noted, it
seems unlikely that the authors were themselves normally writing from
personal experience, or even aiming to appear as if they were. More tellingly,
perhaps, we cannot even be sure who the buyers and readers really were: did
they extend right across society (including the elite, in whose libraries some
are found), or was the market primarily amongst the lesser urban and
wealthier rural consumers who might have the time and leisure to read, or
even amongst those who read only occasionally and falteringly?

If chapbook material is not quite what it seems at first sight, what about
more substantial contemporary works which explicitly described aspects of
cultural tradition and change? Amongst such works one might note Antoine
Court de Gébelin's *The Origins of Language and Writing* (1775), Legrand
d'Aussy's *History of the Daily Life of the French* (1782), and many others.
That scholars started exploring these areas, not (as administrators and
religious reformers had done in the past) out of professional need, but out of
intellectual curiosity, is interesting in its own right. But given eighteenth-
century research methods we again need to be cautious. Arguably, their work
cannot be considered any more reliable, as evidence of reality, than for
example Diderot's *Supplement to the Voyage of Bougainville* (1772) – which
comments on someone else's description of Tahitian civilisation.

It might therefore seem that we shall never know much about the level of
awareness of news and current affairs in the street and the coffee-shop, or
about what was said between neighbours or at family meal-times – beyond

the exaggerated and possibly quite atypical reflections that we see in news-papers, in Louis-Sébastien Mercier's *Tableau de Paris*, in Gillray's cartoons, or in the secret reports of the Paris police and their spies. Such a conclusion, however, may be premature. The approximate contours of common value-systems, and their change over time, can be discerned if we are prepared to accept indirect, refracted and at times fuzzy evidence across a wide spectrum. Some of this evidence will be examined in the following sections.

Rural interaction and peasant action

As we shall observe in various contexts in the next few chapters, rural society is not the obvious place to start looking for signs of social and cultural innovation. The source material itself is very inadequate. Most of what survives was written by others, and peasants in this period who kept diaries or recorded events in their lives are by definition exceptional. The most common written evidence consists of manorial accounts, legal records and peasant petitions, none of which provide a picture which can be regarded as remotely representative. Even the rich evidence of the *cahiers de doléances* (booklets of grievances prepared for the Estates General in France in 1789) is difficult to use. Such problems, however, are not sufficient grounds for discarding rural society as irrelevant to our concerns. There was a great deal of interaction between rural and urban worlds, and we cannot understand the latter properly without appreciating the more primitive environment from which many urban migrants originated.

Rural recreations and entertainments were tradition-based, and on the whole less driven by entrepreneurial innovation and profit than in the urban environment. Market days and seasonal hiring fairs might still include pedlars selling flysheets, jugglers and charlatans, shows, and more organised entertainments such as bear-baiting, bull-running or cock-fighting. But smaller communities would necessarily have to rely mostly on their own resources, including team sports and dances – with the landowning elite perhaps patronising the event and supplying refreshments, but otherwise deliberately keeping their distance in accordance with their view of social distinctions. Festivals and fairs served several purposes: they helped bond the community, and allowed younger people some degree of social and sexual licence. But they also provided a safety valve for social tensions, through the controlled and temporary carnivalesque inversion of social norms, the mock-ing mimicry of figures of authority, or the shaming 'charivari' against individuals deemed to have broken specific norms of behaviour. They were part of a range of traditionally accepted forms of expression and criticism, which, during the more serious periods of economic disasters such as 1770–75, might well erupt into riots. Whatever form it took, however, collective action tended to react against innovation and against perceived changes from accepted norms. Not without reason, rural society in most of eighteenth-century Europe was typically regarded as conservative and tradition-bound – even where (as in parts of England and the area from northern France to Holstein) newer forms of husbandry, enclosures of commons or encroachment on traditional forms of animal husbandry had already brought noticeable economic change.

This image of continuity, social conservatism and relative impermeability to outside ideas in rural Europe may hold good for most of Europe, most of the time. Yet it has not remained unchallenged with regard to the last decades of our period, and recent research has unearthed evidence of significant changes of perception even in some of the most tradition-bound regions. In Brandenburg and Silesia after 1763, for example, there appears to have been such a noticeable rise in peasant litigation against landowners that the crown tried to stem the tide by explicit prohibitions. Not only did this fail to have any noticeable calming effects, but in some areas peasants even defied well-engrained seigneurial authority, challenging punitive reprisals and the customary restrictions of serfdom by systematically undermining labour requirements and refusing to respect judgements in law.[4]

In Denmark, where seigneurial demands for labour services were also particularly oppressive, there was a significant increase in peasant complaints during the period 1788–90. There was also an unprecedented rash of labour-service strikes, increasing from nil in 1787 to 5 in 1788, 20 in 1789 and 26 in 1790 – many of them minor confrontations, but significantly scattered over most of the country and causing great alarm amongst landowners. Over the previous decades, gradual technical reform of agriculture (including voluntary enclosure and the introduction of new crops) had already gained wide acceptance amongst the peasantry. But rural literacy was not high, and there is little evidence before 1788 of the Danish peasantry being capable of sustained or coordinated agitation. The economic environment fluctuated widely, as in previous years, but cannot alone account for changing attitudes. What triggered the more frequent confrontations of 1789–90, it seems, were the expectations raised by apparent changes in government policy itself – expectations that must have been transmitted largely by word of mouth, through rumours and through the reports of those few who had the necessary contacts in Copenhagen. From 1787, a measured legislative transformation of rural social and economic relations had indeed been launched by the government, spearheaded by the initiatives of the Rural Reform Commission of 1786, but the process had been intended to be strictly controlled and gradual. Landowners and the Copenhagen intelligentsia had taken sides early on; but peasant reactions indicate that they were not mere

---

4 W.W. Hagen, 'The Junkers' faithless servants: peasant insubordination and the breakdown of serfdom in Brandenburg-Prussia, 1763–1811', in *The German Peasantry*, ed. R.J. Evans and W.R. Lee (London, 1986), 71–101; E. Melton, 'The decline of Prussian *Gutsherrschaft* and the rise of the Junker as rural patron, 1750–1806', *German History* 12 (1994), 334–50.

spectators, and that they, too, were becoming increasingly aware of just how much was at stake.[5]

France had a centuries-old tradition of large-scale and often violent peasant revolts, which, although subsiding in the late seventeenth century, had shown signs of revival in the turbulent years of 1770–75. Grievances were often primarily economic, but had in the past also included very wide-ranging fiscal, social and political demands. The eruptions in many parts of France in late July and August 1789, the so-called Great Fear, thus stand out more for their intensity and political repercussions than for their intrinsic novelty. Significantly, however, there are signs during the previous year that the uncertainty at the centre of French politics was beginning to be felt everywhere – even in some rural communities. Parish priests, lawyers, travellers and other cultural intermediaries, whose statements do not necessarily have the benefit of hindsight, indicate that peasant demands in 1788 already included not only calls for seigneurial restraint, tax relief and stricter control of royal officials, but also criticism of crown finances generally, and, more ominously, support for local *parlements* and magistrates against central authority. Well before the compilation of the *cahiers de doléances* early in 1789, 'some peasants in some parts of France … knew about and responded to political developments and were able to relate particular problems of village life to broader national currents. They had a certain political consciousness', even if they had little or no access to print culture and had to rely on intermediaries for news.[6]

However, rural unrest was nothing new, and we must resist the temptation to read more into such modest evidence than it warrants. The peasantry – without much education, without habitual access to print, without a vote (except for some in France from 1789), without much scope for anything more than sporadic collective action, and indeed most often without any

---

5 C. Bjørn, 'The peasantry and agrarian reform in Denmark', *Scandinavian Economic History Review* 25 (1977), 117–37; and his *Bonde, Herremand, Konge: Bonden i 1700-tallets Danmark* (Copenhagen, 1981). For a brief survey of the political background, see T. Munck, 'The Danish reformers', in *Enlightened Absolutism: Reform and Reformers in Later Eighteenth-Century Europe*, ed. H.M. Scott (London, 1990), 245–63.

6 V.R. Gruder, 'Can we hear the voices of peasants? France, 1788', *History of European Ideas*, 17 (1993), 167–90, esp. 182; see also H.L. Root, 'Challenging the seigneurie: community and contention on the eve of the French Revolution', *Journal of Modern History* 57 (1985), 652–81. There is an extensive literature on the *cahiers*: see notably R. Chartier, *The Cultural Uses of Print in Early Modern France* (Princeton, 1987), 110–44; J. Markoff, 'Peasant grievances and peasant insurrection: France in 1789', *Journal of Modern History* 62 (1990), 445–76, which he has followed up in his study of *The Abolition of Feudalism: Peasants, Landlords and Legislators in the French Revolution* (Philadelphia, 1996); as well as the observations of P.M. Jones, *The Peasantry in the French Revolution* (Cambridge, 1988), 58–67. Both the pre-1789 reports and the *cahiers* suffer from the weakness of being indirect transmissions, written (hence no doubt filtered) by others, and probably as representative of their authors' views as of the peasant grievances they purport to transmit; yet they cannot be dismissed as having no foundation. On the evidence of rural reading in the responses to abbé Grégoire's survey of 1790, see R. Chartier, 'Figures of the "other": peasant reading in the age of enlightenment', in his *Cultural History: Between Practices and Representations* (Cambridge, 1988), 151–71.

social coherence at all – did not have much scope for acquiring a permanent political presence. With the exception of the Austrian lands in the early 1770s, and France in both 1775 and 1789, eighteenth-century rural unrest in western Europe was nearly always small-scale and sporadic, minor confrontational incidents rather than significant riots. Peasant unrest remained pragmatic and traditionalist in aims; many issues of 'national' politics would have seemed abstract, if not altogether irrelevant, to the vast majority of villagers. Nevertheless, the three cases just cited are sufficient to warn us against the assumption that rural society was mostly malleable and passive. Certainly, transmission of new ideas and aspirations was bound to be slow, partial and perhaps garbled – and none of the cases described here suggest that anything we could call 'enlightenment' had reached into village life. But independent reasoning and common sense were not the exclusive preserve of an educated elite, and it did not take much, especially in societies where landowners were themselves increasingly uncertain of their role, for new points of view to take root. As the French Revolution would soon show, there was no shortage of dynamic potential at all levels of society; harnessing that potential, however, was bound to prove far more difficult given the widespread lack of political experience.

Religious observance and beliefs

Historians have for many years exploited the rich sources which illuminate both the abstract theological emphases and the administrative practices of the main churches. Analysing the theology on its own seems valid enough, since we are dealing with an age in which Protestants emphasised justification by faith, where faith was regarded as an internalised mental process. Yet the social historian will not find such material satisfactory as a basis for analysing the outward and collective manifestations of religious behaviour and religious communication. For that we need to know what kind of people remained regular attenders at religious services, and why; what the participants saw in rituals and processions; how they interpreted what they heard; why they conformed to common standards of decorum and reverential behaviour; and how far religion reached beyond superficiality to provide daily life with convincing and relevant meaning.

Descriptions from many parts of Europe suggest that for a great number of church-goers religion consisted of a mixture of assorted fragments of memorised catechism, combined with simple (sometimes almost animistic) values not far removed from paganism. Divine favour could be bought or ensured through the performance of certain rituals, and everyday events were readily interpreted in terms which the *philosophes* would come to regard as pure superstition. Religious celebration went hand in hand with festive sociability, and to many parishioners morality may have been primarily a matter of benefit or retribution. Especially in rural communities, superficial

conformity (particularly in matters of sexual conduct) was ostensibly reinforced through the aggressive vigilante tactics of gangs of local youths –
otherwise rarely renowned for their religious fervour. To address moral
laxity, and ensure greater uniformity and conformity, churches had long
since had recourse to tactics such as regular episcopal visitations. However,
such inspections seem increasingly to have become matters of routine,
carried out unsystematically and without much thoroughness – perhaps
because of growing apathy amongst those career administrators or members
of the elite who increasingly dominated the leading ecclesiastical offices of
the established churches in Europe.

In order to bring some semblance of order to popular religion, and to
rekindle religious enthusiasm of a kind more congenial to church reformers,
most churches continued their missionary work both in urban and in rural
parishes. Within the Roman Catholic church, notably the Jesuit and Capuchin orders developed impressive techniques of itinerant preaching, but the
durability of their impact in rural communities was increasingly questioned.
The suppression of the Jesuit order in 1773 did not bring an end to mission
activity, but greater emphasis came to be placed on in-depth educational and
pastoral work conducted in a simpler language accessible to all. During the
second half of the eighteenth century the Catholic church also followed
Protestant precedent in placing increasing reliance on catechisms and prayer
meetings to try to improve popular religious orthodoxy. Precisely how much
impact this really had, anywhere in Europe, remains difficult to ascertain.
Economic and social change was bound to bring different expectations,
which in turn were certain to challenge the church as a stabilising framework
or as a forum for effective communication. Yet, particularly in rural society,
the priest or pastor retained his long-established and widely accepted social
functions; and even in urban communities, social and religious traditions
seem readily to have co-existed with newer forms of rationality and enlightened pragmatism.[7]

So we cannot simply assume that enlightenment brought inexorable
secularisation, or for that matter a significant relaxation of common religious intolerance. Nevertheless some general conclusions can be drawn on
the basis of work done so far. It is clear that, at least by the later eighteenth
century, regularity of attendance at meetings of religious worship seems to
have varied enormously even in those countries, like France and the Scandinavian monarchies, where there was a relatively high degree of nominal
religious conformity. In France, the striking regional variations highlighted
during the Revolution (for example in the varying rates of allegiance to the
Civil Constitution of the Clergy, and, later, in the confrontations over de-
christianisation) almost certainly pre-dated these upheavals by several

7 L. Châtellier, *The Religion of the Poor: Rural Missions in Europe and the Formation of
  Modern Catholicism, c. 1500–c. 1800* (Cambridge, 1997), 187–219; see also N.M. Hope,
  German and Scandinavian Protestantism 1700–1918 (Oxford, 1995); and C. Brown, *Reli-
  gion and Society in Scotland since 1707* (Edinburgh, 1997).

generations. Failure to fulfil major religious obligations, like Easter communion, seems to have become significantly more common during the eighteenth century, especially amongst urban males. If we are to believe stereotypes, women hung round the church for gossip, whilst male sociability increasingly shifted from church to the local tavern – a shift borne out by the staggering increase in turn-over in the drinks trade over much of Europe during the eighteenth century. A pattern of generally high church adherence in Brittany, parts of Normandy, much of the west and south-west, those areas of the Massif Central where Protestantism was perceived as a threat, and in a narrow belt along the north-eastern border down to Franche Comté, can be contrasted with levels of particularly low adherence in and around Paris, in parts of Languedoc, and some other areas. Perhaps we need to be cautious with evidence relating to peripheral issues like dwindling testamentary bequests to charity, falling monastic admissions and confraternity participation, or the growing frequency of illegitimate births and pregnant brides, yet such evidence also seems to point in the same direction.[8] In Britain, the lack of religious unity inherited from the seventeenth century means that evidence on popular religious observance is virtually impossible to use, whilst in the German lands the impossibly complex mosaic created by the post-Reformation struggles has hampered efforts to reach quantitative conclusions that can be regarded as representative. In both regions church discipline was gradually relaxed; however, it is possible that continuing denominational diversity, and fear of disorder, may in some areas have helped to strengthen rather than weaken traditional observance and loyalty.[9]

That said, it is clear that amongst the educated the established churches would have needed to be quite effective communicators to stand up to mounting intellectual criticisms after mid-century. If we were to go by La Mettrie's *Man a Machine* (1747), David Hume's *Essay on Miracles* the

8 O. Hufton, 'The French church', in *Church and Society in Catholic Europe of the Eighteenth Century*, ed. W.J. Callahan and D. Higgs (Cambridge, 1979), 13–33, esp. 20–31; M. Venard, 'Popular religion in the eighteenth century' in the same volume, 138–54; J. McManners, *Church and Society in Eighteenth-Century France*, vol. 2: *The Religion of the People and the Politics of Religion* (Oxford, 1998), 94–118 and 189–220; whilst O. Chadwick, *The Popes and European Revolution* (Oxford, 1981), 3–95, surveys popular religious beliefs in Catholic Europe as a whole. On traditional charitable bequests, see C. Fairchilds, *Poverty and Charity in Aix-en-Provence, 1640–1789* (Baltimore, 1976), 133–6; and C. Jones, *Charity and 'Bienfaisance': The Treatment of the Poor in the Montpellier Region, 1740–1815* (Cambridge, 1982), 82–7.

9 D.A. Spaeth, *Parsons and Parishioners in Wiltshire 1660–1740*, forthcoming; J. Albers, ' "Papist traitors" and "Presbyterian rogues": religious identities in eighteenth-century Lancashire', in J. Walsh, C. Haydon and S. Taylor, eds., *The Church of England c. 1689– c. 1833* (Cambridge, 1993), 317–33; and W.R. Ward, 'The eighteenth-century church: a European view' in the same volume, 285–98. On Germany, see for example M. Scharfe, 'The distances between the lower classes and official religion: examples from eighteenth-century Württemberg Protestantism', in *Religion and Society in Early Modern Europe 1500–1800*, ed. K. von Greyerz (London, 1984), 157–74; and the review of recent work in J.F. Harrington and H.W. Smith, 'Confessionalization, community and state building in Germany, 1555–1870', *Journal of Modern History* 69 (1997), 77–101.

following year, Voltaire's campaign against institutionalised religious bigotry (summed up during the Calas affair in his *On Tolerance* of 1763), the
baron d'Holbach's materialist–atheist tract *System of Nature* of 1770, or the
de-christianisation campaign in France in 1793, we might well conclude that
religious belief was liable to be severely undermined by enlightenment
rationality. For all of these writers, any system of personal beliefs had to be
compatible with reason. There were too many disagreements within Christianity, and too many unverifiable alternative value-systems in the world, for
the claims to universal truth within any one church to seem plausible. John
Trenchard, in his *Natural History of Superstition* (1709), bluntly suggested
that most established religious systems preyed on popular credulity. By
1770, d'Holbach felt able to risk an outright condemnation of the intellectual legerdemain and blackmail perpetrated by the church. In one of many
striking passages he noted:

> Man has no more rapport with God than stones do. But if God owes
> nothing to mankind, if he is obliged to show them neither justice nor
> goodness, mankind for their part cannot owe him anything either. . . .
> Yet it is on the relationships existing between man and his god that all
> religious worship is founded. All the religions of the world are based on
> a despotic god; but is despotism not an unjust and unreasonable
> power? . . . Is there anything more dreadful than the immediate
> consequences one might draw from these repulsive ideas given us about
> their god by those who teach us to love, serve, imitate and obey him?
> Would it not be better to depend a thousand times on blind matter, on
> a nature deprived of intelligence, on chance or on nothingness, on a god
> of stone or of wood?[10]

Others argued that the accrued corruption and degeneration in the established churches could be purged, to reveal a basic ethics of 'natural' religion
(deism) compatible with individual reason. In a way, this approach was
merely an updated and rationalised version of the search for Christian
fundamentals which had produced such astonishing religious radicalism in
England and other parts of Europe in the mid-seventeenth century. But the
deism of the eighteenth-century French *philosophes* and of the English
intelligentsia was unemotional. They detached themselves from divine revelation and providence, and even, as in Voltaire's *Candide* (1759), tried to
confront philosophically the problem of evil inherent in human society. Few
followed d'Holbach into atheism or materialism – and carefully concealed
their tracks if they did. Rather, Hume's efforts to demystify religion (*Natural
History of Religion*, 1757), together with the many other rationalist writings

---

10 Paul-Henry Thiry, baron d'Holbach, *Système de la nature, ou des lois du monde physique et
du monde moral* (1770), vol. 2, ch. 1 (pp. 23–6 in the Paris 1821 edition, reprinted
Hildesheim, 1966). Needless to say, the work was published anonymously, and was
amongst the most sought-after illegal books in late eighteenth-century France.

on the subject, found dynamic outlet in the campaigns against popular superstition and for religious tolerance (see below, p. 133).

For those of a less iconoclastic disposition, especially in Protestant Germany but eventually also in the west, variants of non-conformism and evangelical revivalism provided a more attractive route. Whilst deism was too individualist for historians to map its significance, there is no doubt that communitarian revivalist movements gained enormous popular appeal during the eighteenth century. Within the Lutheran church from the 1690s, for example, the Pietists, apart from launching educational reforms to which we shall return (p. 51), also initiated lay prayer meetings and conventicles intended to strengthen personal faith and devotional commitment. Although fundamental issues of theology were not questioned, Pietism did challenge the conservative and often staid leadership of the Lutheran church by demanding reform and revitalisation from within.

Other revivalist movements were much less disciplined and coherent. In 1722 Count Zinzendorf established on his Berthelsdorf estate in Lusatia a safe haven for Protestant refugees from Bohemia and Moravia, but he soon found his Pietist and ecumenical beliefs overwhelmed by the engrained traditions of the Moravian Brethren who arrived. By 1727 the settlement at Herrnhut came so close to disintegration that a set of strict statutes had to be imposed. These broke with family traditions by endorsing a communal structure, based on rigidly hierarchical groups or 'choirs' of followers. Their emotional and often anti-rational religious devotions soon attracted more enthusiasts than the estate could support. The Herrnhut settlement faced not only financial and economic problems, but also the critical hostility of neighbours and provincial administrators. Although some of the pressure was eased after new colonies of Moravian Brethren were established in Denmark, England and the American colonies, the movement remained volatile and unstable.

The picture is even more complicated in Britain. Not only did Scotland have a different established religion from that in England, but each was riddled with tensions which recurrently added to the complexity. A number of non-conformist Protestant groups survived from the great upheavals of the mid-seventeenth century, notably the Baptists, Congregationalists, Quakers and Presbyterian Unitarians. Within the Anglican church itself some major revivalist movements also appeared during the early eighteenth century, less intellectual than the earlier dissenting churches, but very effective at mass communication. The most significant of these was Methodism, which gained momentum from the 1730s onwards under the leadership of Whitefield, the Wesley brothers and other populist evangelical preachers. Like the Pietists, they were primarily concerned with personal devotion and methodical adherence to a Christian way of life – hence the gradual adoption of the term 'Methodists' to describe what was for decades a very loose and informal network of evangelical supporters. John Wesley was particularly effective as a preacher in communities neglected by the established church, as a populariser of devotional texts, and even (from 1778) as editor of a devotional journal. Common to both Methodists and the German Pietists was a determination to uproot what they saw as sinful popular entertainment (notably drink and games), and to help others achieve a reformed moral life. In the eyes of critics, such campaigns might seem at least as dictatorial, morally self-righteous and potentially divisive as the preachings of the zealots of earlier times – and quite incompatible with the supposedly rational/liberal value-system of enlightenment. But their popular appeal is irrefutable, and by the time the Methodist church split from Anglicanism after Wesley's death in 1791 it may have had nearly 60,000 supporters (compared to around 80,000 in the Catholic church). There were innumerable other but much smaller splinter groups, which, typically of Protestantism, were liable to infinite subdivision: thus when followers of the mid-century Swedish Lutheran visionary philosopher Emanuel Swedenborg established the New Jerusalem Church in London in 1787, it soon split into two rival factions. In Scotland, too, the church was troubled by substantial secessions after 1733 and again in 1761 – though not for purely devotional reasons, but rather because of controversies regarding the post-1712 rights of patronage of landowners in the appointment of ministers.

Judging at least from the Protestant world, the so-called Age of Reason seemed to fuel rather than dampen bitter feuding and sectarianism. Religious intransigence had many outlets, and when mixed with jingoism it could also explode into vicious xenophobia. A common form of this was anti-Semitism, endemic to many of those European cities that had substantial Jewish communities (including London and Hamburg). In England, the press, the clergy and some government authorities also deliberately fanned the recurrent outbreaks of popular anti-Catholic hysteria, particularly during the Jacobite crisis of 1715 and the rebellion of 1745. Even though these crises effectively demonstrated that most Catholics were increasingly disinclined to support the Stuart pretenders, Catholics were still branded as 'outlandish' (alien) and readily targeted – most spectacularly during the Gordon Riots in London in 1780. In short, there were no signs of religious exhaustion and few glimmers of tolerance.

Religious beliefs, however, were not invariably divisive, and could enhance a sense of identity within particular communities. A particularly striking, if oblique, illustration of this is provided by the many charitable hospitals set up in England, including Guy's Hospital in London in 1725, the Bristol Infirmary of 1737, the London Foundling Hospital of 1741, and more than 20 others set up over the next decades. In the absence of specific central government involvement, they were often the result of local initiatives motivated by a great variety of factors, ranging from religious charity and municipal self-help to local power politics and patronage. Although managed quite differently from earlier institutions, the new hospitals based their fund-raising initiatives on familiar and well-established religious–moral principles certain to attract donors. The history of these hospitals, however, also demonstrates the extent to which practical priorities changed in the course of the eighteenth century: rapid adaptation occurred to meet evolving views on population growth, labour discipline, morality and (towards the end of the century) a preference for out-patient assistance to encourage self-help. Similar views gained ground in later eighteenth-century Hamburg, notably in the work of the Medical Relief of 1778. These kinds of municipal initiative clearly reveal the baffling complexity we face in coming to grips with a society whose forms of expression are different from our own: can we determine the genuine motivations amongst administrators and subscribers? – can we take at face value what contemporaries said about the strengths and weaknesses of their own community, about its spiritual aspirations, and about the effectiveness of these initiatives in the face of threats posed by factionalism and by economic instability?[11]

Strictly speaking, 'good works' could not be regarded by rigorous Protestants as a means to salvation, but in practice religious phraseology was central to the promotion of eighteenth-century philanthropy and community work. Such language was used to justify other institutional developments, from the new workhouse initiatives of the 1740s to the prison reform movement spurred on by John Howard in the 1770s and 1780s (see below, p. 155). It would be easy to dismiss the moral phraseology used in these campaigns as a smokescreen covering quite different motivations – such as self-promotion of the organiser and donor, or collective hostility towards deviants and the unruly. But in the mind of many potential supporters and contributors religion and social commitment were inseparable, and we would risk misunderstanding the value-system of the eighteenth century if we failed to recognise that.

The dynamic strength that could be derived from essentially religious wellsprings, throughout most of the eighteenth century, is apparent even in Paris itself. Those who could not stomach *philosophe* attacks on the institutional weaknesses of the Catholic church might well gravitate instead towards Jansenism. Originally, Cornelis Jansen, in his work *Augustinus* of 1640, had raised a number of complex theological issues that took him in the direction of Calvinist beliefs in predestination, but he and his followers

---

11 There is a growing literature on hospitals and other voluntary/charitable foundations during the eighteenth century, but for the aspects considered here see notably R. Porter, 'The gift relation: philanthropy and provincial hospitals in eighteenth-century England', in *The Hospital in History*, ed. L. Granshaw and R. Porter (London, 1989), 149–78; A. Wilson, 'Conflict, consensus and charity: politics and the provincial voluntary hospitals in the eighteenth century', *English Historical Review* 111 (1996), 599–619; M.E. Fissell, *Patients, Power and the Poor in Eighteenth-Century Bristol* (Cambridge, 1991), 75–93 and *passim*; D.T. Andrew, *Philanthropy and Police: London Charity in the Eighteenth Century* (Princeton, 1989); D.T. Andrew, 'Two medical charities in eighteenth-century London: the Lock Hospital and the Lying-in Charity for Women', in *Medicine and Charity before the Welfare State*, ed. J. Barry and C. Jones (London, 1991), 82–97. On Hamburg, see M. Lindemann, *Paupers and Patriots: Hamburg 1712–1830* (Oxford, 1990). See also S. Cavallo, *Charity and Power in Early Modern Italy: Benefactors and their Motives in Turin, 1541–1789* (Cambridge, 1995) for a southern European perspective.

insisted on remaining within the Catholic fold. After a period of severe repression in the last years of Louis XIV's reign (culminating in the papal condemnation summarised in the bull *Unigenitus* of 1713), Jansenism re-emerged in the 1720s and 1730s as a puritan campaign for moral reform and spiritual revival similar to the evangelical movements of the Protestant world. Although Jansenism was barely coherent enough to be described as a 'party', let alone a sect, it had a dedicated journal, the *Nouvelles ecclésias-tiques* (1728–98), remarkable both for its longevity and for its success in raising complex religious issues for debate. Jansenism provided a common framework for those who resented the power of the Jesuits, and for those who wanted to further Gallican self-government within the Catholic church in France against papal and hierarchical authoritarianism. This old blend of religion and politics was crucial in the renewed ferocious confrontations of the 1750s, when Jansenists unwilling to accept *Unigenitus* might be refused the last rites by a conformist priest, who in turn might be arrested by the Parlement of Paris for dereliction of duty. Theology certainly mattered; but as David Garrioch has recently argued, the Jansenist cause won widespread support amongst lay parishioners because it favoured a more participatory and non-authoritarian style of parish administration. Those who supported the Jansenist cause may not have understood all the intricacies of predestina-tion theology; but they were unwilling to surrender control of parish affairs, poor relief and charitable work, schooling, confraternity management, and the many other local activities that bound the community more closely together. By appealing to the Parlement, they turned the controversy into a national one. Significantly, both the Jesuit order and the French monarchy itself were ultimately the losers, and the expulsion of the Jesuits from France in 1764 contributed significantly to the process which culminated in the total suppression of the order worldwide in 1773.[12]

If we needed further proof that religious beliefs were anything but a dead letter in eighteenth-century Europe, it is surely found in music. Widely accessible both through institutional and domestic use, much less exclusive than painting or architecture, enormously powerful yet entirely subjective in both its emotional impact and substantive interpretation, its significance here can hardly be overstated. One has only to listen to François Couperin's astonishingly expressive *Leçons de ténèbre* of 1714 (on the Lamentations of Jeremiah), or experience one of Johann Sebastian Bach's 200 extant church cantatas or two Easter Passions, to realise that religious faith continued to reach far beyond mere conformism. These works served specific liturgical

---

12 D. Garrioch, 'Parish politics, Jansenism and the Paris middle class in the eighteenth century', *French History* 8 (1994), 403–19; J. Swann, *Politics and the Parlement of Paris under Louis XV, 1754–1774* (Cambridge, 1995), 87–155; whilst J. McManners, *Church and Society in Eighteenth-Century France*, vol. 2: *The Religion of the People and the Politics of Religion* (Oxford, 1998), 345–561 provides a fuller discussion of the Jansenist–Jesuit controversy. For the longer-term perspective, the best guide is D. van Kley, *The Religious Origins of the French Revolution: From Calvin to the Civil Constitution, 1560–1791* (New Haven, 1996), ch. 3.

purposes, and so their likely impact on an audience is slightly easier to imagine than that of such unconventional and personal statements as the huge B-minor Mass which Bach compiled over the period 1724–49. But to those of a musical disposition, such textless chamber music of the period as Marin Marais' lament at the death of one of his children (the Tombeau in Book V of his *Pièces de viole* of 1725) or Mozart's late string quartets also have an overwhelming emotional and spiritual power which, then as now, defies all denominational boundaries.

Processions, festivals and the use of open space

Traditionally, market towns and cities had a rich civic life in which the officials of the town hall, the law courts, the educational establishments, the church and other institutions took prominent part. Collective identity was regularly affirmed by means of processions, festivals, receptions for visiting dignitaries, and other forms of public celebration. Whilst peace festivities and official receptions might well be fully stage-managed by the authorities, other events, like guild and trades fairs, had room for greater spontaneity. Religious celebrations could involve a mixture of both. In Catholic France, for example, major religious festivals like Corpus Christi (June) focused on carefully orchestrated processions through decorated streets, whereas Carnival (February) tended towards rather more exuberant and temporarily subversive manifestations of crowd participation. In Protestant Europe there were fewer annual religious celebrations, but the Lutherans marked important centenaries in the history of the Reformation – up to and including the bicentenary of the Peace of Augsburg, celebrated with great pomp in 1755 in for example Hamburg. That, however, was the last of its kind, and the increasing scepticism amongst some enlightened observers and officialdom in Protestant Europe seems to have brought a decline in public religious celebrations in the last decades of the century.

Some secular pre-revolutionary public spectacles have attracted attention, if only because of attendant disasters – as when, during the wedding celebrations for the Dauphin and Marie Antoinette on 30 May 1770, an official fireworks display in the Place Louis XV went wrong, causing a fire and a stampede during which reputedly 133 people were killed. Less spectacular events may have been common during the eighteenth century, but contemporary evidence is often too scanty to sustain substantial study. Only with the outbreak of the Revolution in France do public spectacles appear to have regained their central role as vehicles for official propaganda and the formation of public opinion. The first major one of its kind in Paris, the Festival of the Federation (14 July 1790 and annually thereafter) was a staid and seemingly rather stilted occasion, as were the processions marking the elevation to the Pantheon of Mirabeau and Voltaire (April and July 1791). The Legislative Assembly instructed its Committee of Public Education to plan a fuller series of events that could consolidate civic identity and cohesion, but its work was overtaken by the sudden developments of the summer of 1792. It was only in 1793, on the anniversary of the fall of the monarchy on 10 August, that a new festival programme was launched. Some official uncertainty (or downright scepticism) persisted, and the emphasis on precedents and symbols from antiquity became indispensable to ensure that as much as possible of the religious heritage of the *ancien régime* was effaced. In practice, this meant that most of the festivals in revolutionary Paris were heavily stage-managed, and, by 1794, sufficiently stilted to produce mixed reactions amongst onlookers. However, it is possible that at least some of the numerous revolutionary festivals outside Paris, especially those that involved a more pragmatic synthesis of old and new elements, were more convincingly successful.[13]

Civic pride and urban entertainment could complement each other more durably, and on the whole less controversially, by means of long-term building projects and urban planning. Some spectacular disasters helped such projects on their way. The Great Fire of London in 1666 had shown the potential for redevelopment – though in the event it also demonstrated how difficult it was to achieve tangibly unifying results in the face of complex property rights and the understandably overwhelming pressures for a speedy return to 'normality'. Nevertheless, London became something of a model for provincial English towns, in terms of wider streets with harmonious stone-built frontages, uniform and symmetrical squares, and the lay-out of parks and fashionable walks. Such developments became relatively common in the eighteenth century: Bath (from 1727) and Edinburgh (New Town built from 1767) stand out in terms of the scale and elegance of their new developments, but the evidence of lesser projects can readily be found in many other cities, notably York, Warwick after its fire in 1694, or the emergent spa towns. A characteristic feature was often the addition of an assembly room for balls and other social events amongst the leisured elite – where possible complemented with public parks and promenades. Assembly rooms, literary societies and social clubs could maintain fairly strict social segregation by imposing membership restrictions and charging appropriate admission fees – as to a lesser extent did fashionable 'secret' societies like the Freemasons. Such differentiation, however, was less tenable out of doors, or in the coffee-shops, tea-rooms, taverns, inns and wine-shops springing up in the livelier urban centres all over Europe. In places such as the Palais Royal in Paris and the Vauxhall Gardens in London, social mixing was no longer as avoidable in certain contexts as it had been in the seventeenth century. But what effect such social contact had, in terms of conversation and exchange of views, is uncertain.

13 The standard work on festivals in revolutionary France is M. Ozouf, *Festivals and the French Revolution* (Cambridge, Mass., 1988). See also L. Hunt, *Politics, Culture, and Class in the French Revolution* (Berkeley, 1984).

In the more centralised continental monarchies the scope for coordinated urban development was less dependent on private funds and local coopera- tion. A substantial fire in Copenhagen in 1728, for example, triggered not only some redesigning of the inner city, but also concerted efforts by central government to impose minimal building quality regulations and some stan- dardisation of façades. By 1749, when a large plot of land north of the old part of the city was released for development, owners had to build in accordance with a strict scheme around the handsome Amalienborg Square. In 1768 a magnificent equestrian statue of Frederik V was erected at the centre of the square. This statue, cast under the supervision of the French sculptor Saly, and financed by the Asian Trading Company, was an obvious counterpart to that of Louis XV erected in the Place Louis XV (later Place de la Concorde) in Paris just five years earlier. Just how potent a communicative symbol such a statue could be is illustrated by the fact that the French one was soon the target of derision, disfigured by graffiti, and eventually knocked down during the Revolution, whilst the Danish one has survived in virtually unchanged surroundings to the present day.[14]

It was again the French Revolution which produced the most striking projects for innovatory use of urban space and buildings. The range and scope of these projects illustrate how far visual symbolism might contribute to the political culture of the Revolution – even though rapidly shifting political and ideological priorities often prevented their realisation. Public squares, theatres, celebratory monuments and eventually churches all became the focus of attention. But above all, after the government was relocated from Versailles to Paris in October 1789, it was the urgent need for an assembly hall which fired the imagination of contemporaries. Such a project not only had to represent the new political culture visually, but also had to symbolise the organic link between government, the city and its people. Étienne-Louis Boullée, already known for his grandiose designs of the 1780s, submitted proposals along with Louis Combes, Jean-Baptiste Lahure and many others. They mostly envisaged a central amphitheatre surrounded by suitably imposing building complexes on classical models, to be situated either on the vacant site of the Bastille, in the Tuileries area, or in other central Parisian locations which could be redeveloped to create the right kind of setting. When financial problems made such plans unrealisable,

14 Formal statues, intended to glorify rulers (and hence the state with which they identified themselves) were a common attribute of urban redevelopment in continental Europe. The project for Louis XV, however, was singularly unfortunate both in timing and in the monarch that it attempted to glorify – see S. Rombouts, 'Art as propaganda in eighteenth- century France: the paradox of Edme Bouchardon's Louis XV', *Eighteenth-Century Studies* 27 (1993–94), 255–82; and for the follow-up, A.M. Wagner, 'Outrages: sculpture and kingship in France after 1789', in *The Consumption of Culture 1600–1800: Image, Object, Text*, ed. A. Bermingham and J. Brewer (London, 1995), 294–318. On the theories and comprehensive projects of urban planning developed in France by Pierre Patte and others, see A. Picon, *French Architects and Engineers in the Age of Enlightenment* (Cambridge, 1992), esp. 192–204.

other architects, like Armand-Guy Kersaint, suggested more modest rede-velopment of existing buildings to incorporate a suitable semi-circular assembly hall. It was not until May 1793, however, that a suitable conver-sion was finally completed, arguably too late to help soften the increasingly bitter and destructive polarisation of parliamentary politics. That this hall was located in the Tuileries, rather than on the ruins of the Bastille, was perhaps not just a matter of expediency and financial stringency, but also an indication of how far the Revolution was steering clear of its populist foundations.[15]

Street life, public entertainment and the theatre

Eighteenth-century society was one of extremes, both in the contrasts between rural and urban, and within urban society itself. In May 1770 Elizabeth Percy, duchess of Northumberland, an experienced traveller famil-iar with Paris, described a key area of the city as follows:

> In the Evening I went to the Old Boulevard where I was always pleased with the chearfulness & whimsical variety of the spectacle, the confu-sion of Riches & poverty, Hotels & Hovels, pure Air and stinks, people of all sorts & conditions, from the Prince of the Blood to the *Croche-teur*. The common people in their sprucest dress walking or junketting, fine Equipages, dirty Fiacres with five or six people squeezed into them ... The Sides of the Walks are almost cover'd with Prints & border'd with women selling Eggs, Loaves, Apples, Nosegays, Cakes, &c, others of both sexes running about among the Voitures, & mounting on the Steps of them, offer for Sale Fans, Oranges, Sweetmeats, Dogs, &c.[16]

That the streets of large and economically buoyant cities had a noisy energy and irrepressible vitality, almost resembling a continuous fair, was part of their attraction. All needs could be met: from tooth-pulling to alcoholic refreshments, from purchase of quack medicines to sale of stolen goods – not forgetting showing off the latest fashions, catching the latest rumours or just making new friends. The bustle started at first light, especially for those seeking casual labour or engaged in seasonal work, and went on well into the night, when prostitutes and other marginals were most active. Those higher up the social scale could afford to start later, and, given the scarcity of street-lighting, would be sure not to move about alone after dark. But even if the

---

15 The best discussion of revolutionary plans for urban redevelopment is J.A. Leith, *Space and Revolution: Projects for Monuments, Squares and Public Buildings in France 1789–1799* (Montreal, 1991).
16 Elizabeth Percy, duchess of Northumberland, *Diaries of a Duchess*, ed. J. Grieg (London, 1926), 105, cited in J. Lough, *France on the Eve of Revolution: British Travellers' Observations 1763–1788* (London, 1987), 212.

nature of street life changed with the time of day, it always offered something for those on the loose.

Amongst the many forms of entertainment, a few deserve to be singled out in the present context. One was the street-singer and pedlar who sold flysheets with topical texts set to a commonly known tune (vaudeville). Texts satirising prominent individuals, or narrating current scandals or events, could be printed overnight, and were sufficiently successful in most capital cities to be deemed worthy of police action, prosecution and raids. Their communicative effectiveness naturally depended on insider information supplied by courtiers and well-placed individuals, but since power struggles at most courts by the later eighteenth century routinely involved efforts to win over public opinion, there was no shortage of informants.

In Paris, such satires became particularly strident and irrepressible during the final years of Louis XV's reign (in connection with the king's mistress, Madame du Barry, as well as during the Maupeou crisis). They were no less obtrusive later on, in connection with the dismissal of Necker in 1781 or the Diamond Necklace affair (1785) which was used to damage Marie Antoinette's own reputation. In Copenhagen, the Struensee ministry was stung into reprisals against the flood of scurrilous flysheets and songs triggered by its relaxation of censorship controls in 1771. In England there was an even stronger tradition of lampooning public and socially prominent individuals, from Lord Bute to the duchess of Devonshire. Satirical songs and flysheets (and the more extended equivalents presented in fair and tavern theatres) were certainly nothing new – and almost invariable ephemeral – but judging from the reaction both of the perpetrators and their targets, such satires were a highly effective if often unedifying way both of fuelling rumours and of pillorying prominent individuals.

One of the most remarkable centres of such entertainment, free thought and ultimately political subversion was the Palais Royal just north of the Louvre in Paris. The palace itself was not large or particularly elegant; but it housed a very substantial art collection, and the garden behind had become a fashionable promenade for the better-off. In 1781 the then duke of Chartres (who in 1785 became duke of Orléans) started major development of the site, building elegant terraces with shops round the perimeter, and providing extensive facilities for ad hoc theatre, bazaars, exhibitions, restaurants, wine-shops and other forms of entertainment. The whole project was self-financing, largely through the high rentals paid by the up-market shops in the terrace arcades (eventually including 40 jewellers, 14 silk merchants, 8 bookshops, and many others). By the late 1780s the compound attracted everyone from the fashionable to aspiring journalists and soap-box orators, from prostitutes and pickpockets to gossips and the idle elite. Because of the terms on which the estate had been handed over by the crown to the Orléans family, the Palais Royal was under separate jurisdiction, effectively beyond the reach of the Paris police. As Orléans himself, especially after the king's disastrous confrontation with him in the Parlement de Paris in November

1787, gained a reputation as a free-thinker and political progressive, the Palais Royal also became a haven for hot-heads, political activists and reformers, and arguably a key centre in the early stages of the Revolution itself in 1789.[17]

This mixture of high and low, pretentious and enthusiastic, artistic and crude, could also be found in the theatres and playhouses of urban Europe. In Paris, the licensed opera (Académie Royale de Musique) and the Comédie Française still ostensibly promoted high culture, but apparently with dwindling success in terms of audience appeal. By contrast, the more volatile and earthy attractions of the developing boulevards became increasingly fashionable. For example, from 1769 Audinot's venture in simple comic acts and small plays, the Ambigu-Comique, to which tickets cost as little as 8 sous, attracted audiences from all walks of life. In the early 1780s the Comédie tried to suppress the Ambigu-Comique on the grounds of licence infringements, but Audinot had too many influential supporters and continued his productions until retirement in 1795. As in other aspects of boulevard entertainment, it seems that popular culture was taking over elite culture, not the other way round.

The London stage was not markedly different. The Licensing Act of 1737 placed the London theatres under a form of (primarily political) censorship and regulation which contrasts with the relative freedom of the British press (see below, Chapter 5). Not only were the licensees naturally keen to ensure that no unauthorised competitors emerged, but they also had to be as careful as their counterparts in Paris to avoid causing controversy through politically sensitive material. The Enabling Act of 1788 was designed to legalise theatrical productions in provincial English towns, but did not ease restrictions for the London stage. Nevertheless, as in Paris, there was a great deal of cross-fertilisation in genres and styles from the more serious performances of Italian opera (catching on from the 1720s), through the sometimes rowdy plays and pantomimes in the licensed theatres in Drury Lane and Covent Garden, to the earthy and stereotyped shows in taverns and inns which evaded licensing regulations. As in Paris, official regulation and monopolies in no way dampened the rowdy enthusiasm of a public which, though stratified, ranged across a broadening social spectrum – from the rich in their boxes (or, until the 1760s, even on stage) to those wage-earners able to pay 1 shilling for a seat in the upper gallery.

There was such a diversity in eighteenth-century theatre, both in content-matter and tone, that it is difficult to pinpoint shifts in social orientation and political consensus. The most famous example of a playwright bridging the gulf of social division amongst his audience was Beaumarchais, but his *Marriage of Figaro* of 1784 was wholly exceptional. Beaumarchais was

17 For short descriptions of the Palais Royal, see R. Isherwood, *Farce and Fantasy: Popular Culture in Eighteenth-Century Paris* (Oxford, 1986), 217–49, and *passim* for the Parisian context; and D.M. McMahon, 'The birthplace of the Revolution: public space and political community in the Palais Royal', *French History* 10 (1996), 1–29.

himself a bundle of contradictions, having made his way up from a fairly humble background (his father, like Rousseau's, was a watchmaker). He experienced great wealth as well as bankruptcy, served both as courtier and spy, and tried his hand at a variety of enterprises ranging from arms-dealing to publishing. His *Barber of Seville* (1775) had made his literary reputation, but it was the universality and social relevance of Figaro that attracted huge crowds. The play's irrepressible humour and dazzling effectiveness on stage won it many enthusiastic supporters, not just among the relatively impecunious and rowdy *parterre*, but even amongst those aristocratic circles that it pilloried. Since Beaumarchais had used his connections at court to win over prominent individuals (including Marie Antoinette), Louis XVI's efforts to have the work banned merely resulted in the postponement of the first performance. This in itself greatly increased public enthusiasm, fuelled by belated criticism from some members of the conservative elite. In reality *Marriage of Figaro* was not especially radical by the standards of contemporary non-fictional writing. Yet in the context of the Paris (and the many other cities where Figaro played to full houses) of the 1780s it illustrates how far contemporary attitudes had changed towards acceptance of freer social relations and freer forms of expression.[18]

By then, the theatre-going public had almost certainly increased substantially by comparison even with the mid-eighteenth century. The launching of new theatres and companies in many provincial towns in north-western Europe corroborates the admittedly very incomplete figures we have on growing attendance in the capitals. A recent study suggests that there were five times as many theatres in Paris in 1793 as there had been in 1750. With a seating capacity of 700–2,500, and occasionally up to five performances per day during the Revolution, the theatre could not be ignored by the authorities. Deregulation of the stage in 1791, whilst consistent with other legislation by the revolutionary government, brought very severe competition and commercialisation. The spectacular box-office success of plays like *Paul et Virginie* (based on Bernardin de St Pierre's novel of 1788, and over three years from January 1791 running to 68 performances with 78,000 tickets sold) was exceptional, and most authors found it as difficult as ever to live off their earnings. Significantly, some of the most successful plays were ones written before 1789, and in terms of thematic content the revolutionary theatres offered no obvious break of tradition. At least until 1793 programmes were dictated primarily by the demands of the volatile and vocal public. Not even the restrictive political and educational agenda of the Terror government, first outlined on 2 August 1793, had more than a passing influence on the nature and type of plays expected by the Parisian public. The opera (formerly the Académie Royale de Musique, from 1792 the Opéra

18 The best work in this area is still J. Lough, *Paris Theatre Audiences in the Seventeenth and Eighteenth Centuries* (Oxford, 1957), 178–226, and his *Writer and Public in France from the Middle Ages to the Present Day* (Oxford, 1978), 218–25 and 258–74.

National) was inherently amongst the most up-market stage shows of the period, and had to adapt rather more to political change and the disappearance of its aristocratic patrons after 1792 – but it too continued to flourish during the revolutionary period.[19]

It seems fair to assume that the eighteenth-century urban public saw more of a sliding scale than a clear demarcation line between street entertainment and more formal theatrical productions. Both forms had enormous potential for amusement as well as for social–political satire; and at least in the major cities, both appear to have been patronised by a socially diverse public. But we should probably be cautious in ascribing major innovatory (let alone revolutionary) potential to these forms of expression. Particular plays, like some prints and paintings, had qualities which caught the imagination and encouraged real debate. But all forms of public entertainment depended ultimately on public demand, the direction of which was difficult to influence and almost impossible to control.

* * *

The eighteenth-century city was a place of extreme contrasts, from the palatial to the slum, the picturesque to the sordid, the dignified to the violent. Reactions of visitors were usually mixed. In 1732, Rousseau wrote the following:

> How much the first view of Paris contradicted the idea I had formed of it. I had imagined a city as beautiful as it was great, of the most imposing appearance, where one would see only the most magnificent streets, palaces of marble and of gold. Coming in through the Faubourg Saint-Marceau, I saw only dirty and stinking alley-ways, hideous black houses, everywhere dirt, poverty, beggars, carters, menders, women selling tea or old hats. All this hit me so forcefully, that none of the real magnificence that I have seen in Paris since then has been able to erase that first impression.[20]

As historians of something as elusive as the enlightenment, we need to try not to be blinded by what we want to see, at the expense of the dirt and drudgery, the frustratingly static continuity, of everyday existence. The indications of peasant awareness that we observed earlier in the chapter, the varied forms

---

19　E. Kennedy, M.-L. Netter, J.P. McGregor and M.V. Olsen, *Theatre, Opera and Audiences in Revolutionary Paris* (Westport, Conn., 1996), 3–58 and *passim*, provides a comprehensive analysis of theatre repertoire and management. On aristocratic patronage of the opera in both capital cities, with a clientele arguably equivalent only to the upper end of the spectrum of theatre audiences, see W. Weber, 'L'institution et son public: l'opéra à Paris et à Londres au xviiie siècle', *Annales* 48 (1993), 1519–39. During the revolutionary period the opera probably had furthest to go in terms of adapting to a new audience with different interests: see also M.E.C. Bartlet, 'The new repertory of the Opéra during the reign of Terror: revolutionary rhetoric and operatic consequences', in *Music and the French Revolution*, ed. M. Boyd (Cambridge, 1992), 107–56.

20　Jean-Jacques Rousseau, *Confessions*, book 4 (published posthumously from 1782): translation based on text in Garnier-Flammarion edition, vol. 1 (Paris, 1968), 196f.

of religious revivalism, or the potential for radical social comment in the expanding world of street entertainment and theatre – none of these can be regarded as conclusive, or even necessarily entirely persuasive, in the light of overall continuity or inertia.

Nonetheless, some points stand out. The argument that an elite, driven by fear or disdain, somehow 'acculturised' and gradually suppressed the burlesque rudeness and semi-pagan deviance of an identifiable popular culture seems quite inappropriate at least for the eighteenth century. In any case, if a distinct popular culture ever existed, we shall probably never be able to see it in anything like an authentic form. In an age of ideological and religious ferment, of continuing high geographic mobility, of increasing social mixing both formally (in public places) and substantively (in step with economic development), cross-fertilisation and assimilation was inevitable. Two important conclusions may follow from this. First, if we acknowledge that 'common culture' was in reality a great pot-pourri of mutual influences and subtle contrasts, depending on many forms of communication other than the printed word, then its muddied reflection in the great range of disparate sources that survive may be less inadequate than we first thought. Second, if we accept the view that innovation, transmission of ideas and social activism could take many forms, only the narrowest and most abstract definition of the enlightenment would allow us to ignore the social and cultural layers below the educated elite. The enlightenment was socially diverse, highly complex and at times self-contradictory: to suggest otherwise would be to miss its essence.

|3|

Broadening the horizon: ways and means

Visual, verbal and other forms of communication that do not depend on the written word are a crucial and very complex part of every human civilisation. In so far as such forms of communication are amenable to historical analysis at all, they appear governed by continuity (or deliberate play on such continuity), gradual adaptation of existing traditions, and reliance on age-old symbolism: indeed their effectiveness as means of communication depends to some extent on long-accepted 'standard' interpretations.

Against that relatively static backdrop, we can now identify forms of communication and social interaction which underwent distinctive and sometimes intended change during the eighteenth century. This chapter will look at some of the most obvious of these: the growth in literacy, the diversification of educational strategies, the evolution of new forms and forums of communication, and the kinds of environments that encouraged such change. Most of the issues tackled in this chapter have been debated vigorously by historians in recent years; but because of the difficulties of interpretation, the evidence regarding changing patterns of literacy has proved particularly controversial. The eighteenth century undoubtedly saw a rapid shift in some parts of Europe towards mass reading skills, but there is little agreement on how or why it came about.

Literacy

In an age lacking other means of mass communication, access to the printed word was crucial. Such access was determined by a number of obvious factors: ability to read and the incentive in terms of interest, relevance and utility, as well as the more external factors of cost, supply and distribution of printed material. Subsequent chapters will deal with the external market determinants for books and newspapers; here our main concern will be the growth of basic literacy.

Literacy and numeracy, like many other personal skills, are not absolutes which a person either has or does not have. At one extreme, basic literacy may involve the ability to read an already familiar text (like the Bible, or the various catechisms often used to test parishioners during church visitations in early modern Europe). Such reading skills may not be sufficient to cope adequately with a previously unseen text, and, in the early modern period in particular, were often taught at least partly through memorisation rather than on unseen texts. Reading and writing were not taught together: the reinforcement achieved in learning to write was often left until later and hence in effect reserved for more select pupils. Accordingly, we should not assume that the acquisition of basic reading skills necessarily led to habitual reading.

Beyond basic reading might come actual numeracy, for those who needed it for professional and occupational purposes; high-quality writing skills for those entering clerical professions; fluency in rhetoric, Latin and philosophy for those who had intellectual aspirations; additional language skills for those wanting to succeed in eighteenth-century salon society; or familiarity with appropriate local dialects for those wanting a career in public administration and the church. From a list such as this it will be apparent that the skills we now associate with normal literacy could in fact easily be regarded as specific to individual occupations, and therefore hardly universally desirable. In practice, however, all the skills from basic reading ability to comprehensive literacy formed a stepless gradient. If we had sufficiently reliable evidence, we could almost certainly establish persuasive correlations between various levels of reading and writing ability on the one hand, and on the other a whole range of factors including social status, economic and family background, social and occupational aspirations, community norms, religious traditions and educational provision, as well as institutional, social and political strategies at local and national level. There is, accordingly, no simple answer to why individuals might go to the trouble of learning to read. It might be out of a vague recognition that someone unable to read was increasingly vulnerable in all kinds of daily relations, involving everything from wage payments, accounts and inventories to contracts and lawsuits. It might be out of religious curiosity, or out of personal interest. Or the incentive might come from social and family expectations, snobbery, career potential, eagerness to take part in community and parish life, or out of growing political awareness. Learning to read was not yet a social skill that could be taken for granted; but its utility does seem to have been widely recognised.

Few of the stages towards literacy can be quantified at all reliably by historians. Most research on literacy has relied either on prepared reading skills as measured in church visitations, or on basic writing skills as measured by the ability to sign marriage or other contracts, petitions or other formal documents. The former, in addition to the problems already mentioned, suffers from being highly contingent on particular religious and educational contexts, so that comparisons across different parts of Europe would be doubtful even where consistent visitation records exist. Ability to sign, however, is not much better: signing one's name is no proof that one can write anything else, especially given occasional evidence that the signatory was guided by someone else, or perhaps even had someone else write his name on his behalf. And given that reading and writing were taught separately, hesitant signing gives us no reliable indication of the level of fluency in reading that the person may or may not have had.

That said, the broad historical trend is not in dispute: literacy, by whatever standards it is measured, increased significantly almost everywhere for both men and women during the eighteenth century. Average male literacy (measured by signature) increased in France overall from 29% in 1690 to 47% in 1790, that of women from 14% to 27%. In England as a whole the male rate increased from 30% in 1642 to 60% in the later eighteenth century. For Lowland Scotland we have evidence that reading skills of some kind were nearly universal amongst both men and women even in rural areas, whilst the ability to write was around 70% for males and could be as low as 10% amongst the women there; overall, therefore, the average mid-eighteenth-century male literacy rate in the Lowlands of around 65%, measured by signature, almost certainly significantly underrepresents actual reading skills. Overall, literacy in the Scottish Highlands (by whatever measurement) lagged significantly behind. In north-western Europe as a whole, urban literacy (as measure by signature) could be very high: 92% for men and 74% for women in central London in the mid-eighteenth century, 85% for men and 64% for women in Amsterdam in 1780. But some rural districts also did very well: in many parts of Sweden the catechism reading test, included since 1726 in a system of annual pastoral household visits, was passed by nearly all parishioners (male and female) by the late eighteenth century. The predominantly rural Normandy had an average literacy of 80% by the 1780s; and even in East Prussia the proportion of male peasants who could sign their name increased dramatically from 10% in 1750 to 25% in 1765 and 40% in 1800.[1]

These figures, however, give only part of the story. In reality, the pattern of change was very uneven, even erratic. Every generalisation entails important qualifications. For example, rural literacy, as we would expect, usually lagged behind that of larger urban centres. But whereas central and wealthier urban districts naturally did well, poorer urban parishes and suburbs with

1 These statistics are derived from a wide range of regional and national studies: for an overview, see P. Burke, *Popular Culture in Early Modern Europe* (London, 1978), 252f; R.A. Houston, *Literacy in Early Modern Europe* (London, 1988), 130–54; R.A. Houston, *Scottish Literacy and the Scottish Identity: Illiteracy and Society in Scotland and Northern England 1600–1800* (Cambridge, 1985), 56–7 and *passim*; T.C. Smout, 'Born again at Cambuslang: new evidence on popular religion and literacy in eighteenth-century Scotland', *Past and Present* 97 (1982), 114–27; R. Chartier, D. Julia and M.-M. Compère, *L'éducation en France du xvie au xviiie siècle* (Paris, 1976), 87–109; and L. Stone, 'Literacy and education in England 1640–1900', *Past and Present* 42 (1969), 69–139.

high proportions of migrant or unskilled labour, or with heavy dependence on non-diversified proto-industrial production (for example in cloth-oriented Amiens and Lille) were often less literate than neighbouring rural communities. Rural society itself varied enormously, as we can readily illustrate from within France: by the late eighteenth century, the pattern in modernised and prosperous regions like the Paris basin, Normandy and parts of the north-east was totally different from those parts of Aquitaine, Provence and the northern Massif Central where male literacy (measured by signatures) remained persistently low and female literacy was negligible – not to mention *départements* such as Cher where literacy actually declined during the enlightenment period.[2] It may well be that the overall far higher literacy rates of north-western Europe (including northern France) compared with the Mediterranean and east-central Europe – probably in the order of at least two to one, possibly more – are in the first instance related to the relatively high levels of economic prosperity across much of society in these regions.

Discussion of regional variation, however, needs to take into account an additional and critical factor – that of linguistic barriers. Southern France was significantly disadvantaged, in terms of literacy and education, because Provençal and other variants of the *langue d'oc* spoken there had no established written form and was rarely seen in print, whilst the written dialects closer to French used in Provence for official purposes and taught in schools were not common currency. An even more extreme case of linguistic isolation was the Scottish Highlands: knowledge of English was very limited or non-existent in much of the north-west, and the profusion of phonetic spellings in Scottish Gaelic ensured that the use of print was hampered to the point of near non-existence. More damaging, however, was the reaction of the Lowlands to the cultural distinctiveness of the Highlands, especially its Jacobitism and Catholicism. From the 1690s onwards concerted efforts were made to impose English and Protestantism on the Highlands, backed (especially after the 1745 rising) by military force. The missionary activities of the Lowlands church, and of special organisations like the Scottish Society for Promoting Christian Knowledge of 1709, were at least until the later eighteenth century implacably directed against Gaelic culture, and there was a strict ban on the teaching of reading in Gaelic. Unlike the Irish and Welsh,

2 On the basis of the comprehensive information collected by the nineteenth-century education-alist Louis Maggiolo, and to some extent confirmed by later local studies, historians see France fairly clearly divided into a high-literacy area north-east of a line drawn from St Malo in eastern Brittany to Geneva just south of Franch-Comté, contrasting with the much less developed south-west. In the 1780s literacy in the north-east averaged 71% for men, 44% for women, against 27% and 12% respectively in the south and west. For a full assessment of Maggiolo's results in the context of more recent research, see F. Furet and J. Ozouf, *Reading and Writing: Literacy in France from Calvin to Jules Ferry* (Cambridge, 1982), 5–57. The signing of marriage contracts was expected in Amsterdam from the sixteenth century and in France from 1686, but did not become a requirement in England until 1754, and in Scotland and many other European countries until the nineteenth century.

Scottish Gaelic speakers did not even have a Bible in their own language until the New Testament translation of 1767 and the Old of 1801. The inevitable result was that very few learned to read, and whole communities lived in virtually total isolation from ideas from outside.[3]

By comparison with this, the linguistic isolation of Brittany was much less acute, but the spread of reading skills there nonetheless lagged seriously behind that of, for example, neighbouring Normandy. Although comparable evidence is not available, it is likely that Finland and northern Norway will also have suffered from the fact that printed texts were mostly in a language substantially different from that of everyday speech. All told, linguistic barriers – and the discrimination, cultural paternalism and potential for educational imperialism that often went with them – were of far greater significance in early modern Europe than we usually recognise today. Of course the effects were not all negative, and the experiences of Belgium and the Swiss Confederation suggest that language and dialect could add a richness of its own. But in the present context it is worth reminding ourselves that the culture of print was in many parts of Europe genuinely in a foreign language.

The gender imbalance observable all over Europe requires less comment. Social norms, and the reluctance to educate women beyond what their position was deemed to require, explain why we find fewer women signing their marriage contract than men, both in England and in France. In rural and remoter areas female literacy (by whatever measurement) was often half that of men, or worse. The gap was naturally smaller in urban society, and growing literacy amongst men there seems often to have triggered a similar improvement amongst women. What is more difficult to explain, however, is the fact that French evidence seems to suggest that the time-lag between comparable increases in male and in female literacy diminished significantly towards the end of the eighteenth century – in other words, female literacy (measured by ability to sign) increased proportionally faster than that of men across different social groups. This may at least in part have resulted from the fact that reading and writing were taught separately: the gap in basic reading skills between males and females was generally becoming smaller (as already

---

3 F. Furet and J. Ozouf, *Reading and Writing: Literacy in France from Calvin to Jules Ferry* (Cambridge, 1982), 107f, and R.A. Houston, *Literacy in Early Modern Europe* (London, 1988), 138–40, rightly emphasise the importance of regional language barriers and dialect differences as serious obstacles to the diffusion of printed material. The complex mixture of cultural pressures and tensions in such instances is well illustrated in C.W.J. Withers, *Gaelic in Scotland 1698–1981* (Edinburgh, 1984); whilst V.E. Durkacz, *The Decline of the Celtic Languages* (Edinburgh, 1983), 6–80, stresses how reluctant both church and secular authorities in Lowlands Scotland were to allow any growth in Gaelic literacy, even when the policy of teaching in English proved demonstrably ineffective. In France the Revolution brought increased awareness of linguistic diversity (as in the Grégoire survey of 1790, showing that less than half of all Frenchmen spoke recognisable French), but by late 1793 linguistic policies had become politicised, and the government had become much more determined to achieve uniformity: see P. Higonnet, 'The politics of linguistic terrorism and grammatical hegemony during the French Revolution', *Social History* 5 (1980), 41–69.

noted in the catechism results for Sweden), whereas notions of a more substantial education for girls did not begin to gain ground until the late eighteenth century.

Did Protestantism generally foster greater reading skills than Catholicism? Given the emphasis in most Protestant churches on scripture reading and on the responsibility of the individual for his or her own spiritual progress, the answer would seem obvious. Certainly, the areas heading towards mass reading ability, towards dwindling gender differences, and towards high functional literacy mostly coincided with the areas of consolidated Protestantism: England, the United Provinces, southern Scotland, Scandinavia and Protestant northern Germany clearly stand out compared with southern or eastern Europe. Economic incentives aside, those north-eastern parts of France that had comparably high levels of literacy were exposed to Protestant influences, and were arguably less bound by the pressures of Catholic conformism. Within southern France, despite its low literacy generally, the Huguenot communities were also usually more literate than neighbouring Catholic ones. Despite all this, however, we should be wary of jumping to conclusions about causality, especially since religious minorities often stood out in ways other than just their faith. In the case of the Huguenots, we know that relative economic prosperity, distinctive community structures and strong family ties may have been as much of an incentive to advanced literacy as their religion no doubt was. The Huguenot communities that had settled in the Protestant part of the Netherlands and in Scandinavia continued to be distinctive in their new environment. So did the Quakers in eighteenth-century England, and indeed many other close-knit minorities. The need to avoid simplistic analysis is even more obvious in the case of the Irish Protestants, whose greater literacy and dominant political, social and economic status were all part of a self-reinforcing attitude towards the Catholic majority.

The impact of Protestantism on reading skills was in fact not quite what it may seem at first sight. A convincing case has recently been made, on the basis of German evidence, that the early Lutheran leaders were not whole-hearted enthusiasts for popular education.[4] They quickly recognised that unsupervised Bible reading was far too dangerous and potentially subversive: various scrupulously edited versions of the catechism came to be regarded as much safer alternatives in the struggle against the abysmal ignorance of basic

4 R. Gawthrop and G. Strauss, 'Protestantism and literacy in early modern Germany', *Past and Present* 104 (1984), 31–5; and G. Strauss, 'Lutheranism and literacy: a reassessment', in *Religion and Society in Early Modern Europe 1500–1800* (London, 1984), 109–23; on the more conflicting evidence from Scandinavia, where Sweden and Norway had to rely on ambulatory schools and home instruction, see L. Guttormsson, 'The development of popular religious literacy in the seventeenth and eighteenth centuries', *Scandinavian Journal of History* 15 (1990), 7–35. Both provide fuller references to the research literature. On other aspects of Pietist reform, see R. Wilson, 'Pietist universal reform and care of the sick and the poor', in *Institutions of Confinement*, ed. N. Finzsch and R. Jütte (Cambridge, 1996), 133–52.

Christian beliefs so often displayed by parishioners during visitations. By the late seventeenth century, however, the context had changed. Genuine religious understanding may not have been much better, but the fear of social insubordination was receding: apathy and sterile formalism seemed more of a problem than radicalism or heresy. The Pietists around Spener and Francke could by the 1690s openly campaign for more genuine educational reform and even individual Bible study. Spener explicitly recommended that everyone read the entire Old and New Testaments regularly, and to this effect persuaded notably the government of Brandenburg-Prussia to launch what was eventually to become pervasive school and teacher-training reforms. After Spener's death in 1705, Francke ensured that a special press was set up in 1711 to print cheap editions of the Bible, and by 1727 it had produced 400,000 copies of the Bible and the New Testament.

Since the Prussian example of an efficiently integrated Pietist ideology proved its worth in the course of the century, other northern European states came from the 1720s onwards to appreciate the potential value of a devout, loyal and modestly literate population. Religious-based education seemed to provide an effective means of securing social stability and economic efficiency, cementing the long-standing Lutheran tradition of close cooperation between church and state. One of many illustrations of this partnership is found in the Danish law on Confirmation of 1736, which required candidates for Confirmation to satisfy significant educational criteria. That this was not an empty formality was emphasised by the imposition of a minimum age limit of 14–15 on those presenting themselves for Confirmation; and, at the other extreme, by the use of significant penalties (including even documented stints in the workhouse) for individuals who neglected the preparatory education required for Confirmation. Naturally, results were neither immediate nor spectacular; but we are surely justified in emphasising the significance of educational reforms pursued by church and state in tandem as part of a coordinated strategy.

Education

The Pietist approach to primary and secondary education, as developed by Francke around Halle, and later by his follower Hecker in Berlin, involved a number of ingredients that help explain why both secular authorities and parents found it attractive. For a start their curriculum emphasised practical vocational training in the vernacular, with a number of *Realien* or real-life practical subjects like geography and natural history prominent in the secondary school (at the expense of Latin and philosophy). They also inculcated a strong work ethic, encouraging group discipline and deliberately contrasting classroom concentration with scheduled free breaks. Corporal punishment was meant to be used solely for misbehaviour, not for failures of understanding, but attendance was compulsory and, in boarding schools, contact with the outside world and with the family strictly regulated. The overall aim was to cultivate an inward self-discipline so strong as to remove any risks attached to personal autonomy; but the way to achieve that was by moulding a child's will to the service of God. In the Lutheran tradition, service to God also meant subservience to the state. Seen in this light, it will be clear why Pietist educational policies held great appeal even outside Lutheran northern Europe – for example in the educational reforms initiated in the mid-1770s by Maria Theresa's advisor Felbiger after the Jesuits were removed.

Although the Pietists, and in particular their conventicles (lay meetings), were at first viewed with suspicion by religious traditionalists, the success of Francke's and Hecker's schools in attracting pupils added momentum to calls for government-driven school reforms in many parts of Europe from the second quarter of the eighteenth century. Pietist experiments, building on the long-standing educational experience of other religious groups, also influenced higher educational establishments, including the new universities of Halle and Göttingen. Nevertheless, there were serious obstacles to rapid implementation. For a start, there was an acute shortage of qualified teachers, which was not readily remedied even when attempts were made to improve teacher-training facilities. Teaching was seen as a career with little status and meagre earnings, attracting individuals whose only qualification might be religious conformism and perhaps some elementary reading ability. Parental support was far from universal: given the labour value of even younger children, schooling in many parts of Europe could at best be undertaken only during the winter months, and – in areas with domestic industry – with increasing difficulty even then. Where schooling provision existed at all, attendance rates varied enormously, running as high as 50% or more of eligible children in major old urban areas, but often much lower in rural communities. Many factors played a part: some urban charity schools, for example, were so successful that they were usurped by children of the well-to-do, whilst less well-endowed institutions might subject the children to a régime little different from that of the poor in the workhouse, with labour quotas designed to help cover overheads.

The problems of institutional financial backing were severe everywhere. In much of Europe governmental intentions were sincere, but the means always lacking. For this reason, above all others, the ambitious Brandenburg-Prussian school edict of 1717 was quite unrealisable, and the improvements that might have resulted from the provision of state funds from 1736 were largely nullified by the two subsequent wars. In Denmark-Norway, the substantial school ordinance of 1739, itself partly triggered by the Confirmation requirements mentioned earlier, paved the way for comprehensive local schools taxes to supplement the funding to be provided by landowners. However, the economic context was anything but good, and landowner resistance soon ensured this ordinance would remain a dead letter – as the crown itself recognised in the revised regulations issued the following year. In practice, serious efforts at implementation in much of central and northern Europe were delayed until after the return of peace in 1763 – in Denmark effectively until the major Schools Commission of 1789 had collected detailed information and could begin to make practical recommendations.

Further north in Scandinavia, sparse populations separated by formidable geographic barriers made organised schooling virtually impossible. According to an official national educational survey in 1768, 2,216 parishes in Sweden (apart from Stockholm and the island of Gotland) had just 165 fixed schools, with around 100 peripatetic teachers spending a few weeks every year in some of the other areas. By 1802 the number of fixed schools had merely increased to 240. The fact that basic reading skills were nonetheless widespread in rural Sweden not only explains why the peasantry were often reluctant to finance new schools, but also warns us that schools were not necessarily a precondition of growing literacy. In Sweden, reading ability had come to be part of that broader social and religious education provided by the family and the community – mostly without conventional schooling at all.[5]

In other parts of Protestant Europe, like Scotland, England and the United Provinces, there was no tradition of centralised educational provision and hence little scope for policy coordination or implementation. In England, the Society for Promoting Christian Knowledge (founded 1699) provided some standardisation across the new charity schools created during the following decades, but how much they achieved beyond inculcating deferential piety is open to doubt. Private provision effectively dominated English education at all levels, with perhaps two-thirds of all children educated in schools wholly reliant on fees, and many more dependent on philanthropic individuals, private organisations and the like. Contrary to long-held belief, the situation was probably not very different north of the border: charitable funding was probably available only to what a historian has recently described as 'a tiny minority of attenders at Scottish schools', and the rest would have had to pay, with all the social selectiveness that that implies.[6] In the Netherlands, too, there was little effective reform until the creation of the Batavian Republic in 1795 paved the way for some reforms based on current European ideas.

In Catholic Europe several religious orders had traditionally, and especially since the reforms of the Counter-Reformation period, taken a lead at various stages in the educational process. At primary level, the Capuchins (amongst others) were still prominent as organisers and providers of free education. Higher up, and especially in the advanced grammar schools and

5 H.A. Barton, 'Popular education in eighteenth-century Sweden', *StVEC* 167 (1977), 523–41, esp. 529.
6 R.A. Houston, *Scottish Literacy and the Scottish Identity: Illiteracy and Society in Scotland and Northern England 1600–1800* (Cambridge, 1985), 119; and the critical overview presented by R.D. Anderson, *Education and the Scottish People 1750–1918* (Oxford, 1995), 1–21.

seminaries, the Jesuit order provided the best and most sophisticated education. The successive measures of expulsion of the Jesuits from different parts of Europe, in the years before the formal suppression of the order in 1773, left serious shortfalls in the educational system – and created a particular opportunity for those rulers, like Frederick II of Prussia, who was sufficiently tolerant or far-sighted to appreciate the qualities of the best Jesuit teachers. As we have already noted in the case of Maria Theresa's policies in the Austrian lands, the suppression of the Jesuits ensured that state involvement in educational reform in most of Catholic Europe became a matter of urgent necessity.

In France central legislation was not lacking – witness the call for universal primary education in 1694, and the follow-up decrees of 1700 and 1724 – but as with so many other reforms the French government basically delegated funding matters to local fiscal authorities, with predictably limited results. The Jansenist controversy of the 1750s and the campaign leading up to the expulsion of the Jesuits from France in 1764, though primarily focused on other issues, helped revive serious debate about national reform and possible secularisation of education. The publication of Rousseau's influential *Émile* of 1762 helped widen the agenda further, whilst the physiocratic case for the public utility of genuinely universal education was made notably by Turgot, and in such works as Le Mercier de la Rivière's *De l'instruction publique* (*On Public Education*) of 1775. The Jansenists and others also called for elementary mass education, and found more supporters when the economic crisis of 1770–75 had revealed the potential instability of urban society. Yet, with the exception of Condorcet, most of the writers of the enlightenment (including Diderot and La Chalotais) continued to insist that education should correspond to social status – in other words, that women and the poor should not be educated beyond rote learning of basic moral and religious principles. In any case, radical reform was scarcely practicable as long as the church retained its dominance over most areas of education.

The French Revolution was at one level crucial in this respect, in that the oath of loyalty demanded on 22 March 1791 from every schoolteacher (as from clergymen) potentially changed his status from that of an assistant of the church to a functionary of the state. The importance attached to popular education by the republican régime was clearly visible in the Constitution of 1793 and subsequent legislation. Jacobin leaders like Saint-Just expressed confidence that, even if the Revolution was not a complete success at the moment, it would become so once the next generation grew up – in other words, education was the key to long-term republican virtue, political consolidation and patriotism. But here, as in so many other respects, revolutionary theory parted company with practical reality. Confiscation of church property had already significantly undermined what little material security teachers had had under the *ancien régime*, and nothing satisfactory was put in its place. The extreme penury and appalling lack of professional standards of state teachers became evident in the survey of 1791–92, and the detailed enquiries of Year II and Years VI–VII. Even more alarming for revolutionary optimists and central administrators was the gradual realisation that parents especially in rural communities imposed their own will, either by using financial means to force teachers to toe the line, or by opting out of the state system altogether. By 1798, the number of teachers supported privately was in some areas ten times the number officially employed by the state, whilst basic public education for those who could not afford such options had declined significantly compared with the last years of the *ancien régime*.

There is no shortage of anecdotal material from all over Europe identifying the shortcomings of what schooling did exist, particularly in rural areas. Although absenteeism reduced the size of classes, grouping pupils of all ages together in one class, under a single often seriously underqualified teacher, can hardly have been an exciting experience. Rigidly traditionalist teaching methods, dreary rote-learning, and corporal punishment would have combined to ensure that a winter or two would be as much schooling as many would want. In context, such inadequacies are not surprising: *ancien régime* notions of functionality, efficiency and accountability were very different from our own, and financial shortfalls plagued all social services. However, the inadequacy of much formally constituted primary schooling suggests that improvements in basic reading skills were almost certainly achieved, at least in part, by other means. It was not just in revolutionary France that parents grouped together and resorted to hiring private tutors. Such informal arrangements were not necessarily the preserve of the rich either: in Ireland and to some extent in the Catholic Scottish Highlands, so-called 'hedge schools' seem to have been a quite common but illegal alternative to the official Protestant and anglicising schools. Similar arrangements, often known in towns as adventure schools or *Winkelschulen* (corner schools), flourished all over the continent, either in protest against official religious conformism, or as a remedy to inadequate provision. In Bremen one reckoning in 1716 counts no less than 39 such establishments, though how their total enrolment compared with the official parish schools is unclear. Some of these establishments flourished precisely because they experimented with innovative educational methods. A few even adopted the ideas of reformers such as J.H. Basedow (1723–90) and J.H. Pestalozzi (1746–1827), emphasising child-centred learning and non-scholastic subjects popular with certain middle-ranking parents.

Most primary education was of very short duration, yet those having the means and desire to proceed further might choose from a bewildering range of options and substantial differences of quality. Increasingly, the traditional higher curriculum was recognised as being in urgent need of change in favour of the natural sciences, arithmetic and vocational subjects; and teaching methods in need of modernisation. But reform of post-elementary education was very difficult all over Europe because of the diversity of institutional framework, engrained conservatism, and lack of adequate funds. Outright state intervention was again most readily achieved in Lutheran Europe, as happened in the modernisation of the Latin schools in Denmark in the 1730s and especially through new directives in 1775; and in Copenhagen University in the late 1780s. In western Europe higher educational policy was often left to educational entrepreneurs and philanthropists, or to municipal and trade initiatives. Newer institutions with a reasonable catchment of fee-paying students might diversify in response to demand at different levels – as teacher-training colleges, adventure and grammar schools, colleges and academies, evening schools for apprentices, and even as new technical schools like the École des Ponts et Chaussées established in Paris in 1744. Although the first chaotic years of the French Revolution achieved little practical educational reform, the Thermidorian Convention did bring to fruition plans for additional technical education in the form notably of the École Centrale des Travaux Publics (soon the École Polytechnique), which started teaching in December 1794 and which had clear roots in enlightenment thinking.[7]

The older advanced institutions, the universities, largely failed to respond to the changing environment. They continued to provide traditional scholastic tuition (emphasising the classics, dialectics and rhetoric) for those pupils whose social status pointed towards careers in law and the church. However, with an antiquated curriculum, retention of Latin as the medium of instruction, and generally a total lack of research-based work, most universities had increasing difficulties identifying a clear educational role for themselves. French and English universities, in particular, were little more than social clubs for the sons of the rich – perhaps a relatively cheap alternative to the grand tour, but hardly an educational experience designed or intended to encourage critical understanding and independent thinking. In Germany, the total number of students declined significantly in the course of the century, except within the successful reforming universities like Halle and Göttingen. The Scandinavian universities continued to function primarily as seminaries for Lutheran clergymen, despite a slight broadening of the curriculum. The role of the universities in Scotland was traditionally slightly different, in that pupils were often admitted in their early teens, and treated as if they were at boarding school. With reform of the 'regenting' system and the curriculum from the 1730s onwards, however, Edinburgh and Glasgow universities (and to a lesser extent Aberdeen) experienced a period of considerable intellectual development, enhanced by some outstanding teaching staff whose reputation attracted students from abroad.[8]

7 See the illuminating article by J. Langins, 'Words and institutions during the French Revolution: the case of 'revolutionary' scientific and technical education', in *The Social History of Language*, ed. P. Burke and R. Porter (Cambridge, 1987), 136–60.
8 On numbers in German universities (apparently *c.* 9,000 in 1700, falling to 6,000 by 1800), see C.E. McClelland, 'German universities in the eighteenth century', *StVEC* 167 (1977), 169–89, esp. 170. On the Scottish universities, see R.L. Emerson, 'Scottish universities in the eighteenth century', *StVEC* 167 (1977), 453–74; and D.J. Withrington, 'Education and society in the eighteenth century', in *Scotland in the Age of Improvement*, ed. N.T. Phillipson and R. Mitchison (Edinburgh, 1970), 169–99.

The proportion of pupils proceeding beyond elementary schools to academies, colleges and universities remained low throughout the eighteenth century. The figures for France are probably typical of the most economically developed parts of Europe: with altogether some 50,000 places in *collèges* and other higher institutions, there was in effect about one place for every 50 males aged 10–18 – a provision which nearly all commentators (including those of the revolutionary government in 1793) found satisfactory. Many institutions had high drop-out rates, but precise figures are unobtainable because of the irregular paths taken by many students, particularly those not intent on a particular career. As usual, social exclusiveness was enhanced by costs: studying at Oxford could cost £75 or more per annum, whilst more thorough tuition could be had at Edinburgh or Glasgow for less than one-tenth of that cost.

As will be clear, post-elementary education was only rarely accessible to girls. The assumption that girls and boys had to be segregated as early as possible often provided a convenient excuse for abandoning the former. Nearly everyone agreed that girls, like the boys of poorer and artisanal families, would not be well served by being educated 'above their status'. Eighteenth-century society was conservative and hierarchical, and in education as in most other aspects of life there was no assumption that equality of opportunity was a goal worth striving for.[9] Once beyond the most basic religious instruction, therefore, education for girls frequently amounted to little more than needlework and comportment. Gender discrimination was eventually challenged by a few radicals towards the end of the century (see p. 211), but results remained nearly imperceptible for generations.

What provisional conclusions can we draw, from this discussion of literacy rates and educational provision, about the potential for what Kant described as a process of 'enlightening'? We would have to recognise that a significant proportion of the observed growth in different forms of literacy during the eighteenth century was at a basic level: perhaps functional, but hardly sufficient to support habitual reading. Clearly, painstaking ability to read the Bible is not inevitably a first step towards enthusiastic reception of the enlightenment. Indeed Pietists and enlightened reformers in conservative Lutheran Europe were not alarmed by a potential conflict of purpose in their campaigns for better education – perhaps rightly so, since so much primary schooling aimed at religious indoctrination and rote-learning rather than at imparting transferable skills.

In the second half of the century, increasing discussion of the proper purpose and substance of different levels of education may have been constructive at a theoretical level. But it is also clear that actual conditions

---

9 See for example P. Petschauer, 'Eighteenth-century German opinions about education for women', *Central European History* 19 (1986), 262–92, which suggests there was some debate, but within very cautious limits. Mary Wollstonecraft was the first person to address this issue in some detail, in her *Vindications of the Rights of Women* of 1792.

everywhere fell far short of the ideal: what we know about formal educational provision suggests it was extremely patchy, chronically underfunded, often of poor quality and (especially in the countryside) beset by so much structural inertia that reform would have required huge resources. Even if funds had been available, many writers and government officials agreed that too much education might be dangerous. Judging from what we know of actual elementary education in many parts of Europe, it is likely that many who acquired literacy skills of some kind or other did so on their own initiative rather than in school. This may help to explain why some historians have been pessimistic about genuine reading patterns: in later eighteenth-century France, for example, it has been argued that out of a total population of over 25 million, there may have been six million potential readers, half a million who actually read one or two books a year, and a habitually reading elite of just 30–50,000 or so.[10]

There are undoubtedly grounds for caution, but two points are worth emphasising. First, the evidence that we have regarding the book and newspaper industry (to which we shall return in Chapters 4–5) suggests that demand for printed material really did undergo explosive growth during the eighteenth century, with or without the help of formal education. Equally, the desirability of being able to read was sufficiently widely appreciated to ensure that a significant (and growing) number of men and women made the effort to learn on their own, outside the controlled environment of the classroom – so much so that by the late eighteenth century reading skills of some kind are likely to have been nearly universal amongst adults in urban society in north-western Europe. But in addition, we should also remind ourselves that access to new ideas – and to information which might make people capable of 'rational' independent judgement – was not necessarily, at least initially, contingent on the ability to read well. As we know from contemporary comment, reading aloud remained common in the households, salons, inns and other meeting places of eighteenth-century Europe, amongst literate as well as illiterate people. Habits of discussion, changing evaluations of community needs and ideals, or the growth of at least basic political and social awareness – all these could thrive even in environments where only a few had literacy skills or contacts with the outside world. We should not assume that the predominantly oral culture discussed in Chapter 2, and the literate culture discussed here, worked in totally distinct worlds, without overlap or mutual interaction.

---

10 Such estimates are largely guesswork based on a variety of conflicting data. This one, cited in *Histoire de l'édition française*, vol. 2: *Le livre triomphant 1660–1830*, ed. H.-J. Martin and R. Chartier (Paris, 1984), 391, is based on the work of D. Roche and H.-J. Martin. A more optimistic estimate for England is offered by J.P. Hunter, *Before Novels: The Cultural Contexts of Eighteenth-Century English Fiction* (New York, 1990), 65f.

Prints, pictures and the eye of the beholder

All over Europe there was a long-standing tradition of using visual imagery to reinforce the message of the printed word – especially in churches and in other frequented places where the impact might be greatest, and where money and effort could therefore be spent to maximise the communicative effect. Hogarth's biblical scenes painted in the stairwell of St Bartholomew's Hospital (1735–36), or the Old Testament paintings donated in 1746 by various artists to Thomas Coram's controversial Foundling Hospital in London, are good examples of the use to which moral imagery was put outside actual church buildings. Apart from such public or semi-public locations, however, a visual message was not readily disseminated except in the form of woodcut or copper-plate engraving. Woodcuts were relatively inexpensive and hence frequently used on flysheets and as illustrations in cheap books; but they did not allow high levels of precision or detail. Engravings, on the other hand, permitted a far greater range of detail and nuanced effects, but were more costly to produce and therefore less likely to attain wide circulation even when (as often happened) they were sold as single sheets rather than as part of a book.

Copper-plate engraving was commonly used all over Europe for maps, up-market book illustrations and quality music printing; and, since the seventeenth century, had even on occasion been used for political propaganda and social commentary. Any discussion of its increasing popularity in the eighteenth century, however, must start in London, and more specifically in the workshop of William Hogarth (1697–1764). Apprenticed as a decorative silver engraver, Hogarth had by the 1720s turned to painting and illustrative engraving. His reputation was confirmed with *The Harlot's Progress*, a series of six prints sold by subscription in 1731. Hogarth did both the prototype paintings and the actual engraving work himself, so the success of the series (possibly as many as 1,240 sets sold at 1 guinea per set) was a personal breakthrough. Subsequent series, like *The Rake's Progress* (1733–34) or the *Four Stages of Cruelty* (1750–51), as well as such striking individual prints as *The Sleeping Congregation* (1736) or *Enthusiasm Delineated* (1759–60), not only established Hogarth as the leading satirist of the age, but also helped consolidate a growing market for this kind of highly communicative, socially sensitive and potentially subversive material.

Hogarth established an important precedent in freeing himself from individual patronage. This not only gave him greater thematic and stylistic independence, but also enabled him to participate more freely in current debates. His print *Gin Lane* (1751), especially when set against the jovial prosperity of his corresponding *Beer Street*, is regarded as influential (alongside the work of his friend Henry Fielding) in the campaign which led to the Gin Act of that year. Similarly, his series on *Election* (1758), although not issued until long after the elections which they were designed to illustrate, were a valid commentary on parliamentary electoral practices generally. Yet, with the exception of the demonic *John Wilkes* (1763) – which apparently sold several thousand copies in a few weeks – he largely avoided confrontational politics. Judging from his own record, and that of a growing number of lesser print-makers, a reliable market existed for social satire directed against obvious targets: not just general problems such as drink, immorality and violence, but also more specific and widely recognised evils like the corruptness and cupidity of lawyers, doctors, clergymen and other professionals. Although the Wilkes affair did bring about an increasing use of personalised caricature for political purposes, full-scale satirical scrutiny of Westminster politics did not develop until the later 1780s, at the hands of the greatest caricaturist of the age, James Gillray.

It is easy to recognise the outstanding satirical and artistic genius in the work of Hogarth, Rowlandson and Gillray, but rather more difficult to assess the overall impact of their work and that of their more routine contemporaries. It has been argued, on the basis of incomplete data regarding initial and subsequent revised editions of isolated works,[11] that Hogarth's prints could reach an audience comparable to that of great periodicals like the *Spectator* (see below, p. 109). There are also indications that he made his mark across widening social circles: not only did he produce smaller cheap versions of some of his work, but others found it sufficiently worthwhile producing pirated imitations of *The Rake's Progress* that Hogarth was obliged to help implement the legislative copyright protection for original prints embodied in the Engravers' Act of 1735. Yet how frequently did individual images achieve such success? Did the satirical print have an audience significantly different from that of the newspapers, plays and works of moral philosophy to which we shall turn later? Was there really a significant demand for prints outside the wealthy elite? Was Gillray's message, let alone that of his less gifted contemporaries, sufficiently universal to make any impression at all on political and social consciousness outside the narrow circles of Westminster? And if so, what sort of impression?

The answers to such questions are far from obvious. The quantitative work done on books and periodicals, to which we shall return, has not yet been replicated for political and popular prints. We know that a copper-plate engraving or etching might yield up to at most 1,500 copies before it was so worn as to require substantial touching up. Newspaper advertisements at times indicate second and third editions of quite recent prints, a fact that may be taken to mean that the plates concerned had already been worn to this extent. Commonly, however, initial print-runs may well have been much smaller – explaining the care with which Hogarth and others stored their

---

11 R. Paulson, *Hogarth*, 3 vols. (Cambridge 1992–93), notably vol. 1, 310; vol. 2, 45; and *passim*. See also L. Lippincott, *Selling Art in Georgian London: The Rise of Arthur Pond* (Yale, 1983), esp. 126–59, which emphasises that not everyone shared Hogarth's success. On social satire generally, see P.J. Corfield, *Power and the Professions in Britain 1700–1850* (London, 1995), 42–69; and N.K. Robinson, *Edmund Burke: A Life in Caricature* (New Haven, 1996).

plates for years, in case reprinting or revision might become viable. Some of the more specific and context-sensitive political prints may have been too esoteric and allusive to reach beyond a small and exclusive clientele – an exclusiveness probably reinforced by the customary pricing policies of the later eighteenth century, often between sixpence and a shilling per medium-sized sheet, more (as we have noted with Hogarth) for special sets or large formats, and usually at least double for coloured versions. It seems likely, therefore, that the print was not an alternative to the newspaper as a means of communication, but rather a decorative supplement, bought to be hung on the wall by those who had money to spare for such purposes. This may indeed go some way towards explaining why in the 1790s in England the great majority of political prints appeared to be hostile to all forms of radicalism – and hence especially hostile to Tom Paine and the French, a connection where jingoism could be given free reign.[12]

On the continent, engravers seem to have been slower to realise the potential of the satirical and socially relevant print. Just like the newspaper, the art of the caricaturist thrived on social change, the commercialisation of leisure, scandal, oppositional party politics and, ultimately, increasing consumerism. In later eighteenth-century Paris many of these conditions were met, but censorship restraints were still significant, and crown politics mostly out of bounds. Whilst French engravers were thus unable to respond adequately to growing demand, the scurrilous imagery of English prints was much appreciated on the Paris black market. As soon as censorship collapsed in France in the summer of 1789 both the newspaper press and the graphic printing industry diversified rapidly. Engravings, however, were more expensive to buy than newspapers, and many print-makers found their traditional elite clientele dwindling. Although some periodicals (notably *The Acts of the Apostles*) began including prints and illustrations of great complexity and sophistication, the speed of political change pushed many engravers in the direction of relatively obvious political imagery. Typically, radical prints attacked privilege in general and *émigrés* in particular, the papacy and church, and ultimately the whole royal family; whilst those intended for a more conservative market concentrated on mob violence and barbarity. Although images of great detail and caricatural power were produced in the period 1790–92, freedom of expression effectively ended with the fall of the

---

12 For a critical evaluation of how far presently available evidence can reliably take us, see E.E.C. Nicholson, 'Consumers and spectators: the public of the political print in eighteenth-century England', *History* 81 (1996), 5–21; and R. Porter, 'Seeing the past', *Past and Present* 118 (1988), 186–205. On types of prints and changing patterns of demand, see S. Nenadic, 'Print collecting and popular culture in 18th-century Scotland', *History* 82 (1997), 203–22. It is worth noting that the production of engravings was technically quite complex, and hence rare outside the major capital cities of western Europe. On circulation more generally, see also D. Donald, *The Age of Caricature: Satirical Prints in the Reign of George III* (New Haven, 1996), 19–21.

monarchy, and visual imagery was harnessed to the propaganda needs of the state.[13]

If it is too early to draw fully satisfactory conclusions about the growth and impact of satirical and political prints during the later eighteenth century, it will nevertheless be clear that there is a great deal of historical potential in this kind of material. Significantly, as Hogarth himself had acknowledged, the success of the print-maker often depended on imagery inspired by both popular and literary motifs of earlier generations, as well as by a host of other expressive traditions ranging from Renaissance grotesques to puppet and peep shows. By contrast, when we turn to interior decorations, paintings, painted artefacts and other one-off durable creations intended for permanent display, we might expect to find greater conformity to the expectations of decorum and convention. But even here we need to be cautious in imposing tidy demarcations between elitist and popular art on the basis of cost, qualitative content or impact. Is, for example, the fairly uncomplicated imagery of painted shop signs really significantly different from the loving pictures of prize farm animals executed by unknown artists on behalf of members of the lesser gentry in eighteenth-century rural England? Indeed quite often the fluidity between elite and popular art was reflected in the careers of the more adaptable painters themselves – perhaps nowhere more clearly than in the case of Watteau (1684–1721), rising from hack assembly-line painter of devotional pictures to the highly prized creator of those delicate pseudo-rustic *fêtes galantes* which won him admission to the Royal Academy in Paris, and which were enthusiastically sought (and imitated) in the art centres of Europe.

In the case of paintings, however, material success and breadth of audience often tended to be inversely related. Those artists that made a reputation – either because they played particularly successfully to current fashions, or because their work was controversial and open to multiple interpretations – might find themselves constricted by the elite public they served. For most of the eighteenth century significant earnings could only be made within the patronage system, where the demands of patron or collector were paramount, and where a picture would be seen just by the buyer's family and his visitors. Moreover, the demand for specific types of painting was often dictated more by social convention and fashion than by intrinsic artistic or interpretative significance. In England, for example, convention placed great weight on portraiture, forcing many artists to earn their living producing stereotyped and idealised representations of those who were keen to consolidate the status of their families. Elsewhere there was some creative and imaginative scope in small-format biblical and moralising motifs, still-lifes and landscapes, where potential buyers had fewer preconceptions. In France,

---

13 See *French Caricature and the French Revolution* (Grunwald Centre for the Graphic Arts, 1988), 41–54 and *passim*; see also A. de Baecque, *La caricature révolutionnaire* (Paris, 1988), and C. Langlois, *La caricature contre-révolutionnaire* (Paris, 1988).

there was a significant if widely fluctuating demand amongst the elite for grand history painting. But generally speaking, throughout the early modern period, the artist was at the mercy of a fickle and snobbish art market.[14]

It is hardly surprising that the greatest richness and variety in pictorial art in this period was found in France, where a discerning public increasingly made itself felt outside the circle of rich consumers, art dealers and speculators. Like so much else in *ancien régime* France, artistic life was supposed to be regulated by the complex grants of privilege that had evolved over a century or more. These had been intended to ensure bureaucratic control and exclusiveness at least at the higher end of the market, but eighteenth-century growth and diversification inevitably made the system prone to disputes and contradictions. Just as the Comédie Française was becoming increasingly concerned about the rivalry of fair theatres in the 1720s and 1730s, so the Royal Academy of Painting became increasingly conscious of perceived infringements of its monopoly. One of the threats came from a long-established art exhibition held every year in the Place Dauphine in Paris to coincide with the Corpus Christi procession. Originally much of the art there had consisted of devotional images and artisanal work, but by the eighteenth century the Place Dauphine display had become much more varied, attracting substantial public interest. It was partly in response to this that in 1737 the Academy relaunched the official exhibitions of new art which had been held sporadically during the reign of Louis XIV.

The Salon (as the Academy's exhibition was known, from its location in the Salon Carré of the Louvre) became a major biennial event. Lasting each time between three and six weeks, it was publicised in the various guides and critical reviews that proliferated in response to growing demand. Because admission was free and unrestricted, the Salon attracted viewers from across a quite broad social spectrum, leading not only to unprecedented public shoulder-rubbing amongst unequals, but also to lively debate regarding the identity of that 'public opinion' which artists and critics were attempting to address. The Academy itself was run along fairly strict lines of rank and social differentiation (as illustrated in the subordinate place given for example to the painter Chardin), and it continued to see its function in terms solely of elite art for the educated. Yet the bureaucracy which managed the official state patronage network around the Director of Buildings and the Academy inevitably became conscious of the fact that artistic policy could no longer

14 Consumer aspects of the art market have been the object of much study in recent years. See for example D.H. Solkin, *Painting for Money: The Visual Arts and the Public Sphere in Eighteenth-Century England* (New Haven, 1993), 137–56; S. West, 'Patronage and power: the role of the portrait in eighteenth-century England', in *Culture, Politics and Society in Britain, 1660–1800*, ed. J. Black and J. Gregory (Manchester, 1991), 131–53; and *The Consumption of Culture 1600–1800*, ed. A. Bermingham and J. Brewer (London, 1995), notably L. Lippincott, 'Expanding on portraiture', 75–88, and J. Brewer, ' "The most polite age and the most vicious": attitudes towards culture as a commodity, 1660–1800', 341–61. On what art critics at the time made of new works, see M. Fried, *Absorption and Theatricality: Painting and Beholder in the Age of Diderot* (Chicago, 1980).

simply be dictated unilaterally. So whilst private aristocratic patronage continued to support the titillating and self-indulgent canvasses which earned Boucher (1703–70) as much as 50,000 livres a year around mid-century, and which continued to support Fragonard (1732–1806) until the Revolution, the Salon helped pave the way for shifts in both style and content. With unrestricted public access, the exhibition became a crucial forum for artists such as Greuze to attempt a more socially conscious type of work in the 1760s, and for others to relaunch the grand historical genre which David (1748–1825) adopted with such self-promotional flair in the 1780s. No less significantly, the Salon provided a focus for increasingly voluminous and often highly controversial critical review, which (given the official status of the Academy) could be read as a surrogate criticism of the old order itself. Not until the first anniversary of the fall of the monarchy (10 August 1793) was the Louvre officially opened as the nucleus of a permanent national public art gallery.

In imitation of the French, the London Academy also launched its series of art exhibitions in 1769. By then, the artistic scene both there and in Paris was diversifying. The private development and commercialisation of the Vaux-hall Gardens in London, and the garden and galleries of the Palais Royal in Paris, provided attractive and fashionable centres which artists, satirists and hawkers could exploit more freely. It would be rash to claim, on evidence such as we have seen in this section, that pictorial art was becoming a vehicle for greater social and political awareness; as with ornamental gardens, country house architecture, or even funerary monuments, we may know what the patron wanted, but cannot be sure how the finished object was interpreted by outsiders of lower rank. Yet as public interest became suffi-ciently widespread for collectors and connoisseurs to make significant profits from admission charges and exhibitions, the potential for a socially more diverse public definitely grew.

Venues of contact, conversation and debate

Inherent in all early modern thinking regarding the structure of society were assumptions of inequality and segregation. Even though the finer details of rank might at times be disputed, an essentially immutable overall hierarchy was taken for granted, built on dependency, deference and patronage. Accordingly, informal social contact across barriers of wealth and status were not encouraged. Even places of refreshment – ranging from coffee-houses, taverns and innumerable alehouses to the down-market brandy and dram shops – were in practice often patronised by quite distinct social layers. In Paris, for example, the Café Procope was a place for the elite (including eventually some famous leaders of the Revolution), whilst the seedier estab-lishments on the boulevards catered for a cheaper clientele. Mercier seems to underline this distinction when he notes that in Paris there are some six or seven hundred cafés. They are the usual refuge for idlers, and an asylum for the poor, where they can warm themselves in winter to save on firewood at home. In some of these cafés academic discussions are held, where authors and plays are judged.[15]

Coffee-houses and taverns were not an invention of the eighteenth century, but it does seem that they became a far more common and lively part of the urban scene. Whilst the fashion for companionable coffee-, tea- and chocolate-drinking contributed to this growth (particularly in the later decades of the eighteenth century), it was the consumption of alcohol outside the home that increased most dramatically. Smuggling and home brewing make excise figures on spirits somewhat unreliable, yet such figures suggest that alcohol consumption increased tenfold in Britain over the period 1690–1750, with even faster rises in gin and rum. By 1730, in addition to a generous provision of coffee-houses, metropolitan London probably had around 6,000 alehouses. It would be hard to sustain the argument that alcohol consumption, sociability and the exchange of news all increased in proportion to each other; yet there can be little doubt that some coffee- and alehouses came to be regarded as important meeting places. Equally, the nearly 200 inns in London, and especially those at the ends of provincial coach and carrier routes, acquired a natural function of communication and entertainment for the relatively better-off.[16]

The rich had their own networks. In provincial England spas and so-called assembly rooms were built to provide facilities for those with leisure. But fashionable eighteenth-century life ultimately centred on the unofficial weekly soirées and studiously informal dinners sometimes referred to as salons, admission to which was a prized social privilege achieved through introductions and connections. Salons of a kind became fashionable every-where in enlightened Europe by the later eighteenth century, but the most sophisticated examples were in Paris, where they provided a mainstay of elite intellectual life. Amongst the most famous salons were those hosted by Mme Geoffrin, Mlle Lespinasse, Mme Necker and Mme Helvétius. But, like Mme Roland and Mme de Staël during the early revolutionary years, these women did not themselves take a real intellectual lead, preferring to use their salon as a coordinating and self-educative framework within their own control. Conventionally, the lively and witty conversation which was the focal point of these evenings, the play on imaginative superficiality and sensibility, appears to have been dominated by the male participants. The baron d'Holbach was unusual for being both the male host of an important salon and at the same time a major author and intellectual in his own right.

---

15 L.-S. Mercier, *Tableau de Paris*, vol. 1 (Hamburg, 1781), 102.
16 P. Clark, *The English Alehouse: A Social History 1200–1830* (London, 1983), 44, 306–26; J. Brewer, *The Pleasures of the Imagination: English Culture in the Eighteenth Century* (London, 1997), 34–50; see also T.E. Brennan, *Public Drinking and Popular Culture in Eighteenth-Century Paris* (Princeton, 1988).

Inevitably, efforts were made to combine the studied informality of the salon with the more systematic approach of organised societies. An interesting example of such innovation is the *musée* set up by Pahin de la Blancherie in Paris in 1777. A *musée*, in the sense current at the time, was a voluntary and free association of men (and sometimes women) with intellectual aspirations, unrestricted by the need for letters of introduction, and not bound by the unspoken rules of the aristocratic salon. La Blancherie's was based on his journal, *Nouvelles de la république des lettres* (*News from the Republic of Letters*). He encouraged its readers not only to use its pages as a forum for debate, but if possible to make such exchange more sociable by using the network of subscribers and, above all, by coming in person to weekly open discussions held at his editorial office in Paris. These weekly meetings, at which new books and objects of interest were on display, were in effect open to anyone who subscribed to the journal – enabling subscribers to come to know each other personally without formal introduction. Thanks in part to la Blancherie's skills of unobtrusive intellectual sociability, the meetings were such a success that they had to be moved to larger premises. But the journal was eclipsed, and, in seeking a firmer financial footing through patronage, la Blancherie inevitably succumbed to pressures for exclusiveness and regulation, and eventually had to close in 1785.

In France, any effort to create an association or society was bound to trigger formal complaints from existing privileged corporations and organisations. The old order was built on restrictive practices sanctioned by government regulation. Any unauthorised assembly was likely to be investigated by the police authorities – culminating with the order in 1786 to suppress all clubs and societies. Even if efforts of this kind were in the long run ineffective, threats were far from empty, and many individuals found themselves vulnerable. Just as la Blancherie had become the target of an official investigation (which in the event approved what he was doing), so others trying to go beyond the restraints of the established royal academies in Paris and the provinces had to tread very carefully. When Pilâtre de Rozier established his Musée de Monsieur in 1781 he aimed to get round these problems by seeking the highest patronage (that of the king's brother, known as Monsieur). This seemed to work, in that Pilâtre encountered few obstacles, and even won the support of the Académie Française and several other official bodies. His *musée* had two distinctive features: it concentrated on practical empiricism (combining wide-ranging instruction with actual experiments by members using equipment provided by the organisers); and it admitted women (albeit in a subsidiary role). By the mid-1780s the *musée* was allowed to open up gradually under collective management (which helped it to survive the death of Pilâtre himself in a balloon crash). In the words of one contemporary, the Musée de Monsieur came to see itself explicitly as a 'living *Encyclopédie*'.[17]

17 D. Goodman, *The Republic of Letters: A Cultural History of the French Enlightenment* (Ithaca, 1994), 242–80, esp. 266.

The specific examples cited here were part of a growing awareness in the last decades before the Revolution of the need for new ways of using social space – going well beyond the traditional community of scholars (the 'republic of letters') and beyond the polite salon into novel educative and enlightening territory, at times close to the limit of what the *ancien régime* as a system could accommodate. Although some of the royal academies were still trying to function as institutions of intellectual discussion and practical scientific investigation, in practice they had by the later eighteenth century often become very bound by tradition, by the socially exclusive expectations of their lay members, and by the restrictive agenda imposed by those who mediated official policies. Condorcet, perpetual secretary of the French Academy of Sciences from 1774, was keen to promote his own agenda for scientific work in the provincial academies. Not surprisingly his centralist approach met with strong opposition. The provincial academies had built their own identities, and often saw their remit in broader but more conventionally conservative terms than the Parisian institutions. There is little evidence that they had the adaptability required to meet changing expectations. Perhaps the most useful contribution made by the academies in later eighteenth-century France was in the form of the regular public prize essay competitions which many of them supported, encouraging public debate on a range of broad questions whilst at the same time providing opportunities for aspiring writers and reformers.

Elsewhere in Europe debating societies and social clubs appear to have developed with only sporadic obstruction from the authorities. London was exceptional in fostering several public debating societies from the mid-eighteenth century, each of which offered oratorical entertainment and lively discussion of current social and moral issues to any members of the public prepared to pay for admission at the door. In most other cities, clubs and societies generally continued to restrict attendance through annual membership criteria. One of the most distinguished of these privately run societies was the Select Society of Edinburgh, which flourished in the decade 1754–64, and included amongst its members many of the leading figures of the Scottish enlightenment. In its debates it covered a broad range of moral, philosophical, economic and social questions, usually treated in the rational and empirical (rather than speculative) way characteristic of an elite with strong connections to the law and professions, the landed establishment and the more liberal wing of the church. Through its well-connected membership, the Select Society could directly foster agricultural improvement, educational reform and the raising of awareness of other public issues.[18]

Similar more or less formal organisations flourished all over Europe. One

18 R.L. Emerson, 'The social composition of enlightened Scotland: the select society of Edinburgh, 1754–1764', *StVEC* 114 (1973), 291–329. There is every indication that literary and philosophic societies of various kinds flourished in the provincial cities of Britain and France: see for example D. Roche, *Le siècle des lumières en province: académies et académiciens provinciaux (1680–1789)*, 2 vols. (Paris, 1978).

of the most important was the so-called Mittwochsgesellschaft ('Wednesday society') in Berlin, meeting fortnightly or monthly from 1783 to discuss broad issues of current social and political concern, including legal reform, censorship, education, and the persistence of superstition and credulity. To preserve its freedom of speech and unrestricted agenda, the Mittwochsgesellschaft remained a secret society until it disbanded in 1798: although it published summaries of some of its debates in the highly influential enlightenment journal *Berlinische Monatsschrift* (*Berlin Monthly*), no mention of its actual existence was ever made in print. The society served as a highly innovative and unfettered forum of debate for around two dozen intellectuals and senior civil servants, including Kant, the writer and publisher Nicolai, the jurist Justus Möser, the philosopher Moses Mendelsohn (grandfather of the composer), Christian Garve, the royal librarian Johann Erich Biester (editor of the *Berlin Monthly*), several liberal clergymen, and Frederick II's physician Karl Wilhelm Möhsen. Individuals with hereditary noble titles were debarred from membership, but with the membership it had the society was clearly well placed to influence public policy at the highest level.[19]

In Copenhagen and Stockholm debate was less lively, but the overall trend similar. Some societies acquired their own permanent library, so that genteel discussions could be held in an environment not unlike that of the new subscription libraries. Again, membership was elective and subject to an annual fee. During the 1770s discussions often concentrated on literary, linguistic, moral and national issues, running parallel to the practical agrarian and economic discussion fostered by the academies and official learned societies. As if to emphasise this conservative role, a police order of 10 May 1780 in Denmark imposed some restraints on club membership, and suggested that the preferred chairman be a person who already held public office, or was a man of established reputation. The few surviving membership lists indicate a small and respectable clientele, without women: even though we lack precise information, we would almost certainly be entitled to assume that these societies represented moderate enlightened values compatible with those of the establishment.

Across Europe, a rather different impetus was provided by the Freemasons. Emerging in the seventeenth century from origins that are still disputed, the order was consolidated in London in the period 1717–23, from where it spread to the continent. French lodges were established in the later

19 G. Birtsch, 'Die Berliner Mittwochsgesellschaft', in *Über den Prozess der Aufklärung*, ed. H.E. Bödeker and U. Herrmann (Göttingen, 1987), 94–112; E. Hellmuth, 'Enlightenment and freedom of the press: the debate in the Berlin Mittwochsgesellschaft, 1783–1784', *History* 83 (1998), 420–44; J. Schmidt, 'The question of enlightenment: Kant, Mendelsohn and the *Mittwochsgesellschaft*', *Journal of the History of Ideas* 50 (1989), 269–91; B. Nehren, 'Aufklärung – Geheimhaltung – Publizität: Moses Mendelsohn und die Mittwochsgesellschaft', in *Moses Mendelsohn*, ed. M. Albrecht *et al.* (Tübingen, 1994), 93–111; S. Lestition, 'Kant and the end of the enlightenment in Prussia', *Journal of Modern History* 65 (1993), 57–112.

1720s, with separate provision for women attempted around 1737 and again from the 1760s. The order soon gained firm footings in the Netherlands and Protestant Germany, and (despite papal condemnations in 1738 and 1751) also in Catholic central and southern Europe. Quantification is necessarily difficult, but the order seems to have expanded rapidly and quite openly in most major cities during the later half of the eighteenth century. Contemporary estimates suggest that there may have been 50–100,000 Freemasons in France by 1789, distributed over at least 600 lodges. They were undoubtedly very active in the intellectual and charitable life of the old régime, from the 1770s openly encouraging debate on a wide range of public issues. But despite advocating a brotherhood of equals, and admitting a large number of commoners from a range of backgrounds, most lodges were in practice led by a few individuals of high social standing. Initiation into or promotion within the order was dependent on an elaborate hierarchy of tests and symbolic acts which were almost certainly less subversive of the social order than has sometimes been argued. Admission was in most lodges quite expensive, with fees often around 24 livres in France early on, rising to at least twice that by the time of the Revolution. The mystique was enhanced by secrecy, and by the promotion of a complex (perhaps in part deliberately impenetrable) symbolism strongly influenced by ancient Egyptian mythology. Although the Masons did promote international and cross-social contacts which were essentially non-religious and broadly in agreement with enlightened values, they can hardly be described as a major radical or reformist network in their own right. Many prominent individuals of the age were members, ranging from Montesquieu and Benjamin Franklin to Mozart, Frederick II of Prussia, abbé Sieyes and Dr Guillotin – but each had a wide range of other contacts as well. There is no reason to assume that Freemasonry was more influential than so many other eighteenth-century societies and networks in the promotion of sociability and new ideals.[20]

There has been significant recent debate regarding the extent to which social exclusiveness was relaxed more effectively in the case of special interest groups, for example those promoting music. We noted earlier (p. 63) how pictorial art became accessible to a broader public thanks to prints, free exhibitions and cheap mass-production of images. Given persistent traditions of amateur music-making both at the French court, in fashionable London, and in provincial towns, it would seem likely that some social mixing would be natural, and that individual artistic quality or technical ability might to some extent compensate for lower birth and standing. In

20 The Freemasons have been the subject of a great number of studies, not all equally informative or reliable. For a good review of recent work, including the controversial research of M.C. Jacob, see S.C. Bulloch, 'Initiating the Enlightenment?: recent scholarship on European Freemasonry', *Eighteenth-Century Life* 20 (1996), 80–92. On the subordinate role of women Freemasons, see D. Goodman, *The Republic of Letters: A Cultural History of the French Enlightenment* (Ithaca, 1994), 253–9. It is clear from contemporary comment that Freemasonry was not in most eyes regarded as incompatible with active church membership.

Paris, concert promotion outside court and private aristocratic circles, first seen in the middle of the seventeenth century, remained sporadic until Philidor in 1725 launched the *concerts spirituels* – concerts designed specifically for holy days (when the opera was closed). Yet these concerts remained very exclusive, held in sumptuous surroundings in the Tuileries and sustained by high ticket prices. Other subscription series began to appear in the 1770s, but the audiences were not significantly more mixed. As Mozart discovered when as a child prodigy he was paraded round the Paris salons, the level of attentiveness was sometimes not much above that at the opera – whose fashionable clientele were there to chat and be seen, rather than to listen seriously. For a while, music was dismissed simply as entertainment, with little emotional or expressive potential. Only in the 1780s, following Gluck's efforts to create a more authentic and persuasive style of opera in the 1770s, was the artistic power of music once more recognised – a trend which composers like François-Joseph Gossec succeeded in using to good effect by composing for a broader audience during the revolutionary period itself, especially after the *concerts spirituels* ended in May 1790.

At first sight one might expect London, with Stuart patronage gone, to have provided the right environment for socially more diverse music gatherings. Ever since John Banister's public concerts of 1672, sporadic efforts had been made to organise relatively inexpensive events, and by the early eighteenth century subscription series seem to have been fairly common ventures amongst musicians like Loeillet, Geminiani and others. When Vauxhall Gardens were redeveloped in the 1730s, informal concerts were organised which, with deliberately low ticket prices, were intended to attract a socially diverse audience to popular and lively programmes. More esoteric were the meetings of the Academy of Ancient Music of 1726, which over the next decades performed music ranging over a century and a half, from Handel right back to Tallis, and which encouraged gifted amateurs to take part alongside professionals. There are many other signs of musical activity at all levels, from the unpretentious music-making of the wealthy commercial and financial circles of the City, who in 1766 formed a dinner club known as the Anacreontic Society, to the more affordable concert series organised by respectable music societies in some of the City's more prosperous taverns from mid-century onwards. Large-scale oratorio performances and other celebratory musical events in theatres and churches created further opportunities not only for listening but also at times for participation. But despite this promising diversity, concert management in the trend-setting west end of London seems over time to have tended towards commercialisation, with more famous (often foreign) performers, more expensive subscriptions and tickets, and more scope for domination by rich patrons. During the second half of the century economic success seems to have encouraged conscious social grading in the arts, and, with it, sharper segregation of professional musician from audience and amateur enthusiast.[21] Whilst a renewed appreciation of the intrinsic expressive potential of music gradually became apparent – witness the Handel commemoration of 1784, and the boost to modern music provided in the early 1790s by Salomon's sensational concert series featuring Haydn – there is no clear evidence that music helped the communicative processes which are our main concern here.

Political radicalism in the 1790s

Some forms of cultural activity, then, were slow in crossing social barriers; but perhaps it is in the study of popular political activism that we shall see most clearly both the growing dynamism and the persistent barriers in eighteenth-century society. In recent years, historians have devoted much attention to the prominent outbursts of popular feelings, in the form of riots, demonstrations and labour disputes; in the process, however, less dramatic forms of communication have also been unearthed. Urbanisation and the concomitant changes in social and economic organisation from the 1760s onwards seem to have encouraged a growth in social and political consciousness amongst artisans and skilled wage-earners in some of the more rapidly developing urban areas. In London, for example, public and quite democratic debating societies had become well established by 1780, and their success encouraged imitations in other cities like Birmingham and Norwich. In crucial distinction to most other organisations with intellectual aspirations, these debating societies were genuinely open, admitting anyone prepared to pay the entrance fee (often sixpence) at the door. In London, by the early 1790s, audiences of up to 650 were attracted each week through public advertisements. Professional managers brought in gifted speakers like John Thelwall to ensure a lively evening, but anyone (women as well as men) could speak from the floor. Catering for a socially broadly based public in which artisans, shopkeepers, printers and lesser professionals may have been predominant, the debating society managers chose questions ranging from religious and moral issues to subversive social and political questions of direct current relevance. By the autumn of 1791 the advertised debating topics covered comparisons of the British and French constitutions, reopened discussion of the need for parliamentary reform, and analysed actual instances of ministerial tyranny in British politics – often from a point of view sympathetic to reform (see below, p. 211). Not surprisingly, the government perceived such a growth in political consciousness amongst middling and

---

21 S. McVeigh, *Concert Life in London from Mozart to Haydn* (Cambridge, 1993), 11–27 and *passim*, is the most helpful study of these issues; but see also W. Weber, *The Rise of Musical Classics in Eighteenth-Century England: A Study in Canon, Ritual and Ideology* (Oxford, 1992) and J.H. Johnson, *Listening in Paris: A Cultural History* (Berkeley, 1995). On Mozart in Vienna, see notably D. Beales, 'Mozart and the Habsburgs' (Stenton lecture, University of Reading, 1993).

lower sorts as a clear threat. Unlike more formal organisations of the time, such as the London Corresponding Society of 1792 (to which we shall shortly return), the debating societies depended on public advertisement and open admission for survival, and were hence more vulnerable to police infiltration and sabotage. By 1792, fearing the loss of control apparent in Paris, the London authorities increasingly resorted to intimidation against both the managers and against the landlords from whom appropriate premises were hired. The proclamation against seditious meetings (May 1792), though primarily aimed at Tom Paine, could also readily be used with the help of planted trouble-makers as a means of closing down meetings. Over the next few years the government acted intermittently to quell any resurgence in popular debating societies. Despite more draconian legislation in 1795, some cautious debating societies continued to meet sporadically until they were definitively destroyed by the government in 1799.[22]

In Paris, London and a few other major cities, the upheavals of the 1790s also fostered a range of more organised political clubs and societies. All over France, the calling of the Estates General for 1789 entailed electoral meetings and the drawing up of *cahiers de doléances* which brought politics into the life of a wider range of people than ever before. Amongst the privileged, pressure groups rapidly formed to steer the new assembly in the direction of moderate 'patriotic' reform – notably the Society of Thirty formed already in November 1788, and the Breton club which from April 1789 provided the nucleus for what would later become the Jacobin club. But as indicated by the exclusive membership, and in the case of the Jacobin club by its high admission fee, these were not intended to be remotely democratic. Rather, it was the unusual election procedures in Paris itself that led to the emergence of a more broadly based political consciousness in the city's 60 district assemblies. Most famous was the Cordeliers club, whose low admission fee and persistent radicalism made it an important centre of popular politics well beyond its original base, enabling it to survive the replacement of the districts with reorganised sections in May 1790. The Cordeliers admitted both men and women of what might be called the middling ranks of society, from lawyers and professionals to printers, artisans and shopkeepers. As popular political activism in Paris increased from 1791, other popular societies were formed: the re-organised Société fraternelle des deux sexes (Fraternal Society

---

22 M. Thale, 'London debating societies in the 1790s', *Historical Journal* 32 (1989), 57–86; M. Thale, 'Women in London debating societies in 1780, *Gender and History* 7 (1995), 5–24; and D.T. Andrew, 'Popular culture and public debate: London 1780', *Historical Journal* 39 (1996), 405–23. On the emergence of political consciousness, see also the classic work on the subject, E.P. Thompson, *The Making of the English Working Class* (London, 1963); A. Goodwin, *The Friends of Liberty: The English Democratic Movement in the Age of the French Revolution* (London, 1979); H.T. Dickinson, *The Politics of the People in Eighteenth-Century Britain* (Basingstoke, 1994), 221–86, which surveys both the radical and conservative tendencies; and for source editions, M. Thale, *Selections from the Papers of the London Corresponding Society 1792–1799* (Cambridge, 1983), and G. Claeys, ed., *The Politics of English Jacobinism: Writings of John Thelwall* (Philadelphia, 1995).

for Men and Women); the remarkable Société de citoyennes républicaines révolutionnaires (Women's Republican Revolutionary Society) of May 1793, soon with a membership of several hundred; various networks around some of the more active Parisian sections; as well as the loose groupings supporting extremists like the *enragé* Jacques Roux, or the opportunist newspaper editor Hébert. None of these fared well under the Jacobin Terror, and their political priorities were abandoned before or during the reaction that followed; yet the mould of elitist politics had been broken.

In Britain, similar organisations were not slow to appear, but most remained far more moderate in their aims and inspiration. One of the most successful was the Sheffield Society for Constitutional Information, which had a membership of 2,500 by June 1792. Like the London Corresponding Society (formed in January 1792) and similar groups which appeared at this time in many other major English cities, the Sheffield Society had roots in the sporadic parliamentary reform movements of the previous decades. But political radicalism was now clearly attracting more substantial followings further down the social scale. At its peak in 1795, the London Corresponding Society had weekly attendances of up to 3,500 between its various divisions across the city, mostly from among artisans, tradesmen, printers and professionals. Its supporters, in paying a regular membership fee, were probably more committed than the audiences at the public debating societies, but the political orientation was similar. The London CS and the Sheffield SCI encouraged detailed discussion of important radical works like Paine's *Rights of Man*, and established regular postal contacts with similar societies across the country. In Scotland, criticism of the self-protective corruption of Parliament was enhanced by the even more urgent need for reform of the self-perpetuating oligarchies of burgh government. Associations of Friends of the People proliferated all over the Lowlands, leading to several Constitutional Convention meetings in Edinburgh in 1792–93. Whilst we should not exaggerate the scale of this spread of political radicalism amongst the middling ranks of British urban society, nor underestimate the strength of popular loyalist and anti-Jacobin feelings as anti-French war hysteria built up from November 1792 onwards,[23] there is no doubt that the government became extremely concerned. Repression was initially most effective in Scotland, where the rigged trials of Thomas Muir and Thomas Fyshe Palmer in September 1793 resulted in sentences of transportation to Botany Bay, just at the time when the British Convention to promote parliamentary reform was about to assemble in Edinburgh. Despite the ease with which anti-

---

23   Ann-Carolin Albert, 'The Impact of the French Revolution on Local Activity in West Central Scotland in 1792 and 1793 in connection with Reports of France', unpublished M.Phil. dissertation (University of Glasgow, 1998), 30–81, emphasises both the moderation of the reform movement and the extent of the loyalist response, noting that most of the press reporting of activity of either kind was concentrated in the period from the late summer of 1792 to the spring of 1793. See also N. Rogers, *Crowds, Culture and Politics in Georgian Britain* (Oxford, 1998), 176–214.

French feelings could be exploited during wartime, the London movement proved more difficult to crush. When a group of key radical activists were charged with treason during the autumn of 1794, including John Thelwall, John Horne Tooke and the founder of the London Corresponding Society, Thomas Hardy, the juries rejected government allegations and secured a spectacular string of acquittals in November 1794. But for the London Corresponding Society, the Sheffield Society and their like the respite was only temporary: as with the public debating organisations, the government adopted a range of tactics, including repressive legislation, to drive popular political consciousness underground.

* * *

It would be difficult, on the basis of the evidence discussed here, to deny that the 'public sphere' – or at least the range of associations, meeting places, institutions and forms of collective expression that facilitated the formation of 'public opinion' – developed enormously during the eighteenth century. Of course 'public opinion' in some form or other has existed in every organised society, from antiquity onwards, and seeing it as essentially a product of the age of enlightenment is historically misleading.[24] Nevertheless, it may well be appropriate to regard the eighteenth century, and perhaps particularly the second half, as a time when public opinion acquired a far more tangible identity and role. At the end of this book we shall look more closely at the ways in which contemporaries began to identify a universal public opinion (in contrast to the many contradictory opinions of individuals) – in France ultimately producing an intoxicating enthusiasm for the universal tribunal of 'the people' and its supposed egalitarianism. In the present context, however, we might simply note the key factors that fell into place in the course of the century: literacy (the effects of which we shall study more closely in the next two chapters), and the creation of a whole range of new forms of sociability and communication across urban society. London and Paris were undoubtedly in a league of their own, but, as in so many other respects, these cities did not lack imitations elsewhere.

24 For full references to the historical debate, see pp. 197–9. An approachable overview of the subject, taking in the seminal works by Habermas (1962), Koselleck (1959) and others, is provided by J. Brewer, 'This, that and the other: public, social and private in the seventeenth and eighteenth centuries', in *Shifting the Boundaries: Transformation of the Languages of Public and Private in the Eighteenth Century*, ed. D. Castiglione and L. Sharpe (Exeter, 1995), 1–21; A.J. la Vopa, 'Conceiving a public: ideas and society in eighteenth-century Europe', *Journal of Modern History* 64 (1992), 79–116; see also the fuller discussion in Chapter 8 of this book.

|4|

Books and readers

As we have already noted, there was more to the enlightenment than a range of innovative ideas presented through printed texts. Nevertheless books, pamphlets and other printed material are bound to remain an essential part of any study of the dissemination and communication processes of the period. Books were themselves often used as a symbol of enlightenment in the paintings and illustrations of the later eighteenth century; appropriately enough, Étienne-Louis Boullée's project of 1785 for a new building to house the Royal Library in France is little short of a vast classical temple of learning. This chapter will look at some of the obvious factors affecting the production, distribution and use of books and pamphlets, and will discuss some of the evidence regarding the expansion of the market in the second half of the century. It will also attempt to identify what sorts of books mattered most, and for whom: we cannot assume that works which we might now regard as particularly important were necessarily seen in the same light when they were first published.

It is worth emphasising at the outset that books remained, throughout the eighteenth century and beyond, relatively expensive to acquire. In the absence of bulk manufacturing techniques, costs of production were high. Fonts and paper were expensive; and even if the printing presses of the day tended to be fairly simple pieces of technology, a skilled labour-force was indispensable if satisfactory results were to be achieved. All but the most affluent readers were therefore likely to find that well-made books might be beyond their financial reach; and, conversely, most of the publishing and bookselling sector had to survive primarily on pamphlets or cheap editions in paper covers. But cheap publications are inherently less likely to survive, and any conclusions we can draw from inventories and private book collection catalogues may therefore be skewed. Using other types of evidence to create a profile of the book market is just as problematic: the records of official censorship administrators clearly tell us nothing about the clandestine trade;

police records from seizures are often only part of the story; and the few publishers' records that survive provide only limited context. Establishing exactly who read what during the enlightenment period is therefore not an easy task.

However, the quantitative side of the book market is not the only difficulty. There has been much debate in recent years about how readers actually approached particular texts – how they read. Given prices and accessibility, books were for most of the century probably read more intensively or thoroughly than is the norm today. Contemporary illustrations often show books being handled by solitary readers in a contemplative environment – just as news-sheets (see the next chapter) are commonly shown in the context of the coffee-house or the street scene.[1] But are these distinctions based on factual reality, or simply on pictorial conventions? If the latter, for whose benefit? Whatever the answer to these questions, we need to be aware of the fact that some readers might treat the printed word very differently from what we would normally expect today.

Book production and distribution

Traditionally, much printing and bookselling had been done on a small-scale basis, with a master printer overseeing not only his journeymen and apprentices operating a few fairly simple presses, but also working closely with authors and contributors, and even to some extent overseeing distribution and sale of the finished product. Of the various stages in book production proper, only the binding process was normally totally separate, a reflection of the fact that most books were sold unbound, at the discretion of the buyer. The power of the bookbinders' guilds, and their claims to control part of the retail book trade, could at times be a problem – in Sweden, publishers had to fight until 1752 before they won the right to sell bound books – but noticeable market growth often paved the way for the gradual erosion of guild restraints.

Even if a good part of the work of many printers continued to consist of 'jobbing' or ephemera with rapid turn-over and small overheads, the efficient production of more significant lengths of text required heavier investment. The greatest capital expense was likely to be in the large quantity of type

---

1 During the eighteenth century, some educationalists still recommended that solitary reading should be done aloud, in order to intensify the experience. For discussion of intensive/extensive reading habits, see notably R. Engelsing, *Der Bürger als Leser: Lesergeschichte in Deutschland 1500–1800* (Stuttgart, 1974), 182–215 and *passim*. However, this may be a simplistic view, and it is more likely that divergent ways of reading (and of treating printed material generally) simply becomes more obvious with increased availability, as argued notably by R. Darnton, 'Readers respond to Rousseau: the fabrication of Romantic sensitivity', in his *The Great Cat Massacre* (Harmondsworth, 1985), 209–56, esp. 242f. See also R. DeMaria, 'Samuel Johnson and the reading revolution', *Eighteenth-Century Life* 16 (1992), 86–102.

required, especially since it was vulnerable to damage and wear. Of the consumables, ink was rarely a problem since it was often made on the premises; but paper depended on erratic supplies, and invariably constituted by far the biggest single expenditure for any printing firm.

The printing press itself remained in all essentials unchanged until the early nineteenth century. Commercial presses were large wooden structures, heavy but not particularly expensive (in England typically £15–18 new). Techno-logical refinements were made during the century, particularly to enhance reliability and accuracy, but basic production methods remained unchanged. Assuming a 10-hour work day, a press manned by two strong operators could produce 10–18,000 single-sided printed sheets per week, depending on labour discipline and efficient organisation. These technical restraints remained virtually unchanged until the first experiments with new types of presses at the very end of the century. Accordingly, throughout our period, the only way of increasing overall output was to acquire additional presses and operate them simultaneously. By 1790, the official Imprimerie royale housed in the Louvre in Paris had a total of 44 operational presses, with a staff of well over 100 men to deal with typesetting, paper handling, sorting and dispatch.[2]

A relatively static technology, however, was no obstacle to certain refine-ments entirely characteristic of the period. Anyone who has used the original editions will be well aware of the dramatic changes in lay-out and typeface design which transformed the visual appearance of the printed page in the course of the century. In Scandinavia this was demonstrated most dramat-ically in efforts to replace the Gothic or black-letter *Fraktur* types with the more cosmopolitan Roman type: the first Danish book in Roman type appeared in 1723, and in 1740 the Swedish Academy of Sciences switched to Roman type for its publications. However, the change was not universally accepted, and *Fraktur* remained in common use in Scandinavia in the nineteenth century, and in Germany until more recently.

Less fundamental, but just as important, were the meticulous experiments with clearer page lay-out and redesigned typefaces. From 1741, the Foulis brothers in Glasgow, for example, produced high-quality books whose title pages and design reflect a classic preference for simplicity and clarity (an austerity that was not adopted in France until the revolutionary period). John Baskerville, working in Birmingham (1757–75), took this further with his redesigned typefaces and his meticulous attention to paper quality and the visual aspect of the printed page. His work was recognised by the best contemporary typographers on the continent, notably Didot and Fournier in

---

2 An overview of the technical aspect of paper manufacturing and printing is found in *Histoire de l'édition française*, vol. 2: *Le livre triomphant 1660–1830*; ed. H.-J. Martin and R. Chartier (Paris, 1984), 34–61.

France, and Bodoni in Italy.[3] The search for clarity and ease of use led to a whole range of minor changes, ranging from the gradual elimination of the long 's' (easily misread as 'f') to the systematic use of paragraphing and headings in both books and newspapers. Publishers also experimented with different formats, sometimes seeking to attract less affluent readers by means of small cheaper editions (like the pocket-size duodecimo format) alongside the more upmarket octavo or even quarto formats intended for wealthier collectors.[4]

The visual transformation of the page may well have contributed to the genuine popularisation of reading during the eighteenth century, to which we shall return shortly. But a growing market may also have encouraged specialisation within the trade. In particular, publishers became increasingly distinct from the printers, often with a managerial shift in the direction of the former – though complex associations continued to keep demarcations fluid. The role of the bookseller also diversified, ranging from the small-scale multi-purpose dealer of the provincial town to the large-scale wholesaler in London or Paris. Some firms grew very substantial in the course of the century: already in 1730 Tonson's publishing business in London involved a staff of 50, and many other great firms (for example Longmans, or Vandenhoeck and Ruprecht) became well established during this period. For long-distance marketing and overseas exports wholesalers had traditionally relied on the great international book fairs (formerly Frankfurt, but after mid-eighteenth century Leipzig), but might also turn to the illegal trade designed to circumvent trade restrictions[5] and censorship. However, whilst the fair remained important for specialised works, commonly sold books were increasingly traded by means of more sophisticated networks across Europe.

A variety of trade directories reveal how extensive this network was by the time of the American War of Independence. A Parisian directory lists not just the 400 printers and booksellers in France (roughly half in Paris), but also

3 For a summary of such developments, complete with illustrations, see N. Barker, 'Typography and the meaning of words: the revolution in the layout of books in the eighteenth century', in *The Book and the Book Trade in Eighteenth-Century Europe* (*Wolfenbütteler Schriften zur Geschichte des Buchwesens*, vol. 4; Hamburg, 1981), 127–65.

4 The biggest normal format, the folio, was made up from large (but not standardised) sheets of paper folded only once; quarto, octavo and duodecimo sizes involved two, three and more folds for each sheet, and hence a smaller final size of book. But the real economy was achieved in the size of print, for the smaller formats were often printed very densely, so that a duodecimo edition need not consist of many more pages than an octavo. Paper quality, proof-reading standards, and optional bindings also varied, so that a novel in the 1780s might sell in Paris at less than 2 livres, roughly the same sum of money (significantly less if one allows for inflation) as a similar text in larger format might have cost half a century before.

5 See J. Feather, 'The commerce of letters: the study of the 18th-century book trade', *Eighteenth-Century Studies* 17 (1983–84), 405–24. On the British international book trade, see G. Barber, 'Books from the old world and for the new', *StVEC* 151 (1976), 185–224; and W. McDougall, 'Scottish books for America in the mid-18th century', in *Spreading the Word*, ed. R. Myers and M. Harris (Winchester, 1990), 21–46. The book trade was heavily regulated by legislation and protective tariffs, but these, too, were systematically evaded.

gives details of 72 in London, 30 in Leipzig, 22 in Venice, 20 in Geneva, and nearly as many in the other major European cities – not a comprehensive list by any means, but an indication of what a Parisian book trader needed to know. Distribution was becoming a specialised occupation, requiring financial and managerial skills different from those of the printer and even of the publisher. Indicative of the complexity and size of the market is the list of current books in German drawn up by the Berlin bookseller Friedrich Nicolai in 1787: his total of 5,072 titles were available from 101 different places of publication and altogether 282 different publishers – not counting any foreign publications at all.[6] We should not exaggerate the extent to which specialisation subdivided the book trade; but it is a feature of the later eighteenth century that press barons like Charles-Joseph Panckoucke (1736–98) could deal in copyrights and newspaper titles, move in high society, and contemplate enormous publishing ventures (like the *Encyclopédie méthodique* launched in 1782) without much experience of actual printing.

Copyright and profits

Early modern Europe afforded the prospective author very few rights or material rewards. Traditionally, the support of a patron had been virtually indispensable not just for material comfort but also to limit the scope for open piracy of published work. During the eighteenth century, however, the first tentative steps were taken towards defining and protecting literary rights in national (and ultimately international) law. This was motivated not so much by concern for the authors themselves, but out of a desire to protect a publisher's investment in a particular title.

In Britain, the need for controls had become acute following the lapse of the Licensing Act in 1695 and the consequent disintegration of the control mechanisms hitherto exercised by the Stationers' Company. Accordingly, a Copyright Act was drafted in 1709 and implemented the following year. It went some way towards defining literary rights as a kind of 'property' on which others could not encroach (for example by issuing a reprint) without paying a compensatory fee to the publisher or author. As a piece of legisla-

---

6 G. Barber, 'Who were the booksellers of the enlightenment?', in *The Book and the Book Trade in Eighteenth-Century Europe* (*Wolfenbütteler Schriften zur Geschichte des Buchwesens*, vol. 4; Hamburg, 1981), 211–24, esp. 212f; P. Raabe, 'Der Buchhändler im achtzehnten Jahrhundert in Deutschland', in the same volume, 271–91. On Nicolai personally, see H. Möller, *Aufklärung in Preussen: der Verleger und Geschichtsschreiber Friedrich Nicolai* (Berlin, 1974).

tion, the Act left much to be desired both in terms of precision and in terms of enforcement mechanisms within England (let alone Scotland or Ireland).[7] Nevertheless, norms of copyright protection for books did in practice become fairly well established amongst major publishers, supervised by the so-called 'Conger' (a group of cooperating booksellers) and by subsequent London booksellers' associations. Their copyright claims over old best-sellers caused some confusion in law after 1732, and their demand for perpetual rights was not finally quashed until a House of Lords ruling in 1774. But in practice piracy within the British bookmarket seems to have remained fairly marginal, and the overall increase in demand in the later eighteenth century ensured sufficient prosperity within the book trade to dampen tensions over copyright privileges.

On the continent, copyright protection did not become the subject of general legislation until much later. Instead, authors and publishers continued to rely on particular grants of exclusive rights for individual works, like the *privilèges* (official permissions) issued by the French monarchy. Since they were usually without time limit, such grants increasingly led to complaints from provincial booksellers and printers who were unable legally to respond to their readers' demand for the kinds of devotional literature, older texts and reference works which the Paris printers were now allowing to go out of print. In response, the crown in 1777 restricted publishers' *privilèges* to the lifetime of the author or ten years; after the lapse of a *privilège*, any printer could apply for permission to reprint, subject to a fee payable to the crown. In reality, however, the situation was much more complicated than such a reform might suggest, for none of the regulatory legislation could be enforced effectively. Books that sold well, whether they had a *privilège* or not, were widely pirated either within the kingdom or across the border. One publisher alone produced 11 pirated editions of Rousseau's best-seller, *La nouvelle Héloïse*, in the 30 years after its first appearance. Only in 1793 did the French revolutionary government finally produce legislation defining the complex issues of literary property and the 'public domain', and by then enforcement had become very difficult.

In the German lands, similar grants of exclusive publishing rights were totally unenforceable outside the particular principality in which they were

---

7 Until 1732, there was in theory a monopoly on printing in Ireland (restricted to a single printer in Dublin) and this, coupled with import controls and other regulations, ensured that neither the Copyright Act of 1709 nor the Stamp Act of 1712 applied there (a Stamp Act was implemented in Ireland in 1774). In practice, however, the Dublin monopoly was no longer enforceable by the early eighteenth century, and the unauthorised reprinting of English publications became quite common. For the consequences of this, see M. Pollard, *Dublin's Trade in Books 1550–1800* (Oxford, 1989), esp. 66–109. On the broader consequences of the English copyright principles as they emerged between 1710 and 1774, see H. Amory, '*De facto* copyright? Fielding's Works in partnership, 1769–1821', *Eighteenth-Century Studies*, 17 (1983–84), 449–76; T. Ross, 'Copyright and the invention of tradition', *Eighteenth-Century Studies*, 26 (1992–93), 1–27; and M. Rose, *Authors and owners: the invention of copyright* (Cambridge, Mass., 1993).

issued. Attempts at general copyright legislation were made in Saxony in 1773, and in Prussia and elsewhere in the early 1790s. Although there was much debate during those decades both for and against comprehensive copyright protection, there was no means of implementation at imperial level. More seriously, many states within the Empire actively encouraged book piracy at their neighbours' expense. The Habsburgs themselves sanctioned large-scale piracy, notably by helping firms like Johann Trattner produce a long list of cheap classics pirated from other German publishers. The decision in 1773 to ban such pirated imprints from the prestigious Leipzig book fair seems to have had little effect. Southern Germany as a whole became a copyright jungle in the later eighteenth century, seriously undermining the financial basis for scholarly and innovative publishing, and thereby depriving authors of solid grounds for negotiating better fees. The international market was just the same: many English-language books were printed in Germany, many French books in England, the Netherlands or Switzerland (to say nothing of the highly profitable market for translations in all directions) and none of these ventures were controllable by political means. Increasingly in the second half of the eighteenth century, there was a truly multilingual market for books in north-western Europe, on a scale that was quite unprecedented.

The ineffectiveness of most domestic copyright protection, and the total absence of international agreements, help to explain why most writers, perhaps making a virtue of necessity, claimed not to be interested in material profits anyway. In the smaller markets of the Scandinavian and Dutch languages, authors invariably had other sources of income (frequently from public office or inheritance). Even in the bigger markets, authors often had to subsidise production costs out of their own pockets. Surviving by your pen alone was both very difficult to achieve and, until late in the century, liable to be perceived as demeaning or mercenary. Fulsome dedications to potential patrons remained the socially acceptable norm, not freelance professionalism.

Nevertheless, market growth during the eighteenth century, and the additional publicity afforded through shorter pieces published in the periodical press, did enable some writers to become financially independent. In England, Alexander Pope (1688–1744) and Samuel Johnson (1709–84) secured themselves in this way. Although copyrights for short pamphlets and journalism remained unenforceable even in England, the market value of bigger works did begin to rub off on authors: Fielding is said to have earned £700 for his *Tom Jones* of 1749 (but nothing for its foreign translations), William Robertson nearly as much for his *History of Scotland* of 1759, and a staggering £4,000 for his *History of Charles V*. Johnson was paid £1,575 for his eight-volume *Dictionary of the English Language* (1755), David Hume £3,450 by his Scottish publisher Millar for his six-volume *History of England* (1754–62). Samuel Richardson had already built up a successful career as a printer before he became an author; but on his death his substantial fortune of £14,000 owed much to the success of his two most successful moral novels, *Pamela* (1740) and *Clarissa* (1747–48).

Only a single well-known writer of the eighteenth century was really wealthy, namely Voltaire. He was in any case exceptional in that he had set about systematically amassing so substantial a fortune (mostly from income unrelated to his literary activity) that he became totally independent both of patrons and of publishers. His reputation remained such that, shortly after his death, the author and publisher Beaumarchais bought the rights to a complete collected edition for 300,000 livres: with type bought from John Baskerville's widow, Beaumarchais then produced the 70-volume complete edition of Voltaire during the years 1781–87. No other single French writer attracted speculation on this scale, but there were nevertheless reasonable earnings to be made. Publishers often paid fees in the range of 1,000–2,000 livres for first editions of promising manuscripts – Laclos' *Dangerous Liaisons* (1782) earned him 1,600 – but subsequent income was unpredictable because of the certainty of illegal piracy. Playwrights had even greater difficulty securing any reasonable fees for plays that ran successfully over a period of time – Beaumarchais was quite exceptional in earning nearly 60,000 livres for his *Marriage of Figaro* (1784), which was so phenomenal a success with the public that not even the Comédie Française could pretend otherwise when settling with him.

We need to be wary of generalising from exceptional instances, and there are plenty of complaints from impoverished authors in later eighteenth-century France. Although by the later eighteenth century patronage and pensions were fairly free (with for example the Orléans household alone supporting 12 writers in 1787), younger authors and those without an established market encountered great difficulties. Even Diderot decided to sell his library to Catherine II for 16,000 livres, admittedly on very favourable terms, in order to raise money for his daughter's dowry. For basic everyday existence, only those with established reputations seem to have had a reasonable chance of managing one way or another on their literary earnings. Rousseau was paid 2,160 livres for the first edition of *La nouvelle Héloïse* (4,000 copies, with a wholesale value of 8 livres each, on which his publisher made 10,000 livres), but was also immediately the potential beneficiary of a pirated edition. In the end it seems that the author was paid three times over for this work, effectively doubling his initial fee. Since his main Amsterdam publisher had been undercut because of this, Rousseau felt sufficiently guilty to reduce his fee for *The Social Contract* from 3,000 to 1,000 livres (for a print-run of 5,000 copies). *Émile* earned him 6,000 livres – which he regarded as sufficient to cover his own living expenses for four years, at an annual level of expenditure which in fact equalled that of a Paris university professor. A complete edition of Rousseau's works after his death gave his heirs 24,000 livres.

Neither German authors nor their publishers had any real copyright protection, so freelance writing was virtually impossible there. Lessing

(1729–81) found it so precarious that he accepted appointment as librarian at Wolfenbüttel in 1770; and Schiller (1759–1805), who fled from a particularly restrictive form of patronage in Württemberg after the success of *The Robbers* of 1781, accepted an aristocratic pension elsewhere 10 years later. In Scandinavia, the market was too small to support any writers full-time, so most literary activity depended on officeholding or other earnings. It seems that publishers had a better chance of doing reasonably well. The German publisher Wendler made a great deal out of publishing the work of the popular writer Christian Gellert (1715–69), selling the remainder of his stock in 1786 for 10,000 thaler – whilst Gellert himself had spent most of his life in very modest circumstances. However, publishers had to take the risks, and it is salutary to remind oneself that the first complete edition of Goethe's works produced by Göschen (1787–90) was a failure, attracting only 602 subscribers for a print-run of 5000. As in later periods, contemporary fame and posthumous reputation did not always go together; but as these scattered figures suggest, authors *could* if they were lucky do quite well out of the growing demand for books in the later eighteenth century, and publishers with a gift for speculation could make a fortune.[8]

Censorship before the reforms

Although experiments with the abolition of censorship became an important part of government reform programmes in some parts of Europe in the last decades before the Revolution (see below, pp. 142–6), pre-publication control of printed material was until then the norm in Europe. Most states had a long tradition of such controls, often dating from shortly after the development of basic printing technology itself, or at least from the period of the Reformation. The controls had originally been implemented to protect orthodox religious views against heresy, but, as the publishing industry diversified, material deemed subversive of morality or of the security of the

8 R. Birn, 'Rousseau and his publishers, 1754–1764', *StVEC* 304 (1992), 1041–4; and more fully as 'Rousseau et ses éditeurs', *Revue d'Histoire Moderne et Contemporaine* 40 (1993), 120–36; J.E. McEachern, 'A French pirate's editions of Rousseau', *StVEC* 304 (1992), 1038–41. It is significant that when Rousseau was in England in 1766 he was rumoured to have received 800 guineas for two volumes of his works: the English copyright system had evidently secured far better income for authors than in France. For a good overview of the income of authors and playwrights in France, see J. Lough, *Writer and Public in France from the Middle Ages to the Present Day* (Oxford, 1978), 199–238; whilst the classic survey of the difficulties of writers is R. Darnton, 'The high enlightenment and the low-life of literature in pre-revolutionary France', *Past and Present* 51 (1971), 81–115. On large-scale ventures, see G. Barber, 'The financial history of the Kehl Voltaire', in *The Age of the Enlightenment: Studies Presented to Th. Bestermann*, ed. W.H. Barbour *et al.* (Edinburgh, 1967), 152–70; and P.H. Muir, 'The Kehl edition of Voltaire', *The Library* 5 (1948), 85–100. On authors' and publishers' fees in Germany, see M. Woodmansee, 'The genius and the copyright: economic and legal conditions of the emergence of the "author"', *Eighteenth-Century Studies*, 17 (1983–84), 425–48; and A. Ward, *Book Production, Fiction and the German Reading Public 1740–1800* (Oxford, 1974), 132–4 and *passim*.

state was also consistently suppressed. By the seventeenth century, censorship was a natural adjunct of every strong and stable state: the brief collapse of controls in France and England during the 1640s, and the resulting flood of unauthorised and subversive publications, had merely emphasised the necessity. The renewed consolidation of central power in many European states after 1660, helping to concentrate most printing in capital cities (and a few privileged universities), effectively postponed any significant growth of provincial printing businesses until the early eighteenth century, and ensured that manuscripts continued to serve as an important medium of communication throughout the century.

Two significant parts of Europe, however, gradually came to form exceptions to this general pattern of regulation – exceptions caused more by accident than design. One was the United Provinces of the Netherlands, where much political authority had devolved during the seventeenth century to municipal and local government, and where, as a result, religious conformity and control of the printing industry were unenforceable at national level and highly variable at local level. Just as religious toleration had come about by default, so the printing industry benefited from local self-government and from the absence, most of the time, of any single political interest sufficiently dominant to enforce censorship in most areas of the book industry. For most of the eighteenth century, when Dutch politics were relatively static and stable, the book trade there could continue to serve the interests of foreign writers whose works were banned or controversial at home: Amsterdam and Leiden became the familiar (if not always true) imprints on foreign books whose authors felt vulnerable.

In the case of England, the disappearance of pre-publication censorship was less gradual but equally unplanned. Various control mechanisms were maintained in the second half of the seventeenth century, by means for example of the Printing Act of 1662, which was renewed as late as in 1693. However, the system whereby the Stationers' Company of London had supervised all output from the 20 licensed master printers and their workforce ended in 1695, when Parliament failed to renew the Licensing Act. Indirect restraints, exercised for example through the Stamp Act of 1712 (see below, p. 111), were not very effective. Instead, a complex and disputed interpretation of libel and seditious libel came to serve as the most commonly applied legal restraint on published work. The narrowly circumscribed role of juries in such prosecutions caused serious controversy in the early 1730s and again during the Wilkes crises of 1763–70, and critics of the government remained very vulnerable in this respect until the clarifications in the Libel Act of 1792. However, apart from the stage (see above, p. 42), statutory pre-censorship was never re-introduced, and publishing became much less complicated than on the continent. Books such as Bernard Mandeville's *Fable of the Bees: Private Vices, Public Benefits* (1714, extended edition 1723), its satirical analysis of contemporary hypocrisy vehemently denounced as amoral and cynical, might well not have appeared under an older system of censorship – indeed its French translation in 1740 was immediately banned by the authorities there.

How a regular system of pre-publication censorship could operate is most clearly visible in the traditional Scandinavian monarchies and, on a much bigger scale, in France. By the eighteenth century, the French system involved the workings of a substantial bureaucracy around the Chancellor (*Chancelier de France*) and the Lieutenant General of Police. These two authorities had fundamentally different roles and policies. The Chancellor, or his delegate the *Directeur de la Librairie* (Director of the Book Trade), dealt solely with the vetting of new texts intended for publication; whilst the police authorities (responsible to the often rather illiberal Parlement de Paris) were more concerned with infringements of regulations, and with the ubiquitous pamphlet and newspaper press working on the margins of the law. At times, overlapping appointments blurred this distinction, just as the provinces offered several variants on this system; but the essentials remained unchanged until 1789.

In principle, every new manuscript in France intended for printing (unless accepted by the crown's own Imprimerie royale) had to be submitted to the *Directeur de la Librairie*, who in turn allocated it to a reader from an official list of more than 100 unpaid censors.[9] The censor might check and initial every page of the text, and return it to the *Directeur* with recommendations for specific deletions or emendations in those texts otherwise deemed worthy of a *privilège* (official authorisation and copyright combined). While an author might be fortunate enough to have a say in the choice of censor for his work, and might even negotiate over details, there was no guarantee of either consistency or even fairness in the vetting procedures. As a result, many of the texts that were rejected (around 10–30% of the total) might well have passed unscathed if read by a different censor. Equally, texts that were passed might still cause both controversy and trouble: Helvétius' authorised but irreligious *De l'esprit* (*Essay on the Mind*) of 1758, for example, caused such outcry that the Parlement de Paris took up the case, banned the book, forced Helvétius to recant some of his views, and secured both his and the careless censor's dismissal from their court offices. The repercussions from this were so severe that the *privilège* for the equally controversial *Encyclopédie* was withdrawn soon afterwards, in mid-production.

Such famous disasters apart, the operation of the pre-publication censorship system was not especially oppressive during the second half of the century, starting with the tenure of Malesherbes as *Directeur de la Librairie* (1750–63). Malesherbes was a well-known sympathiser of the enlightenment, and a distinguished and respected intellectual in his own right. He allowed a significant growth in the use of the so-called *permission tacite*, a

---

9 The role of the censors, and the fact that they were themselves part of the 'republic of letters', contributing to journals as literary reviewers, has recently been emphasised by A. Goldgar, 'The absolutism of taste: journalists as censors in eighteenth-century Paris', in *Censorship and Control of Print*, ed. R. Myers (Winchester, 1992), 87–110.

kind of registered permit which withheld official approval but protected the publisher and author against reprisals – typically for works that were deemed fairly harmless, but which were supposed to look as if they had not been printed in France (and were therefore often given a false place of publication). The *permission tacite* was a characteristic *ancien régime* compromise, and had the disadvantage of sanctioning what to the general public must have seemed like an increasing law-enforcement failure. But it had several advantages: the books concerned were not given the publicity arising from outright ban, the censors themselves did not have to put their name to a doubtful work, and economic losses resulting from forcing parts of the book trade out of the country were limited. The *permission tacite* had some very distinguished beneficiaries: the *Encyclopédie* itself from volume 8 onwards, a collected edition of Montesquieu, and works by Hume, Condillac, Diderot, Voltaire and others.

Failing either open or tacit permission, a work might be given a *permission clandestine*, a *permission de police*, or just a plain *tolérance*, a totally unregistered verbal promise that prosecution or police raids would be initiated only with advance warning. Such 'understandings' were so precariously close to the edge of the law that anonymity and false imprints were essential, together with all kinds of manoeuvres from time to time to hide or move stocks. Malesherbes himself was on this account in deep trouble in 1762 over Rousseau's *Émile*, whose illegal publication within France he himself had encouraged, but which (once again) the Parlement de Paris was not prepared to tolerate. Not surprisingly, as some censors became more relaxed, police repression became more frequent: Malesherbes's tenure coincided with a major religious confrontation within the established church, between the Jesuits and the Jansenists, and this was the cause of several of his problems.

It was primarily in cases of infringement or apparent evasion of the censorship regulations that the police authorities and the courts became involved. The result might be one of a wide range of penalties for authors, printers and booksellers alike. In practice, fines, confiscation of stock and presses, or forced closure of premises were all relatively common. Already issued *privilèges* could also be revoked, as we noted in the case of the *Encyclopédie* in 1759. Some authors and publishers suffered actual imprisonment in the Bastille or the Vincennes prison, including amongst them Diderot and Voltaire as well as the journalists Fréron and Linguet.[10] Others,

---

10 A tally of imprisonments in the Bastille resulting from book-related offences indicates that authors were themselves highly vulnerable, especially in the period 1750–80: but printers and their work-force were also hit, as were the very vulnerable vendors who constituted the largest number of prisoners overall. The Bastille housed on average more than 100 book-related offenders per decade from the 1720s until the controls began to disintegrate in the 1780s: in the 1770s, there were 121 such imprisonments, out of a total number incarcerated in the Bastille of just 296. See summary in *Histoire de l'édition française*, vol. 2: *Le livre triomphant 1660–1830*, ed. H.-J. Martin and R. Chartier (Paris, 1984), 87, also cited in R.

like La Mettrie and the abbé Raynal, preferred to go into voluntary exile in order to escape prosecution, but if they did so their publications might subsequently come under the scrutiny of the officious Parlement de Paris either as foreign works or for some technical infringement of the law – as happened to Raynal's *Histoire philosophique* (*Philosophical History*) in 1782, and also to d'Holbach's anonymously published materialist tract, the *Système de la nature* (*System of Nature*). Similarly, Beaumarchais' decision to publish his complete edition of Voltaire from Kehl (on the German side of the border, near Strasbourg) saved him from direct prosecution; but he was badly affected when, at the insistence of the archbishop of Paris, his edition was formally banned from France in 1785.

Clearly, the crown was far from powerless, and the generosity of individuals like Malesherbes did not rub off on those authorities whose primary concern was with already published 'bad' books – the Parlement and the police. It was primarily the Parlement that used the Jansenist crisis and the aftermath of the attempted assassination of the king in 1757 to pave the way for new draconian legislation against the illegal book trade. The Parlement itself enjoyed exemption from pre-publication censorship, and later used that privilege for its own ends during the political crisis of 1771–74; but, characteristically, it had no desire to extend such rights to others. Most ministers of the crown probably agreed: in 1776, when Turgot proposed sweeping guild deregulation, he explicitly excluded the book and printing industry on the grounds that liberalisation there would be too dangerous. The following year, a set of new decrees was published to consolidate and modernise the regulatory system. To help ensure better enforcement, the total number of independent printing works was to be reduced to around 300 for the whole kingdom, significantly below the level counted in 1701. In 1783, Vergennes also tightened the inspection system for imported books – partly no doubt at the request of Panckoucke and other domestic publishers anxious about their profit margins, but also in the hope of bringing the illegal book trade under control.

It seems the battle for control was not yet lost. Nevertheless, demand for print was growing so fast that the authorities had little hope of achieving consistency, or even avoiding confusion. The number of applications for *privilèges* increased over the century, from an annual average of 200–400 in the early years of the eighteenth century to over 1,000 by 1780, and the increasing use of the *permission tacite* by Malesherbes and his successors was partly an attempt to deal with this flood of new works. But the illegal book market undoubtedly increased faster still: by definition it is difficult to quantify, but most historians agree that more than half the books sold in

Darnton and D. Roche, eds., *Revolution in Print: The Press in France 1775–1800* (Berkeley, 1989), 24. On the activities of the police, see R. Darnton, 'A police inspector sorts his files: the anatomy of the Republic of Letters', in his *The Great Cat Massacre* (Harmondsworth, 1985), 141–83; and A. Williams, *The Police of Paris 1718–1789* (Baton Rouge, 1979), 212–21.

France by the later eighteenth century were illegal. Malesherbes himself explicitly recognised that it was pointless to try to control the market in detail: all the state could do would be to deal with some of the worst abuses, and hope that in doing so it did not attract too much unpopularity with the public at large.

Major legislative reform of the censorship system was attempted in various parts of Europe from 1766 onwards, but as we shall see (below, p. 142) such policies did not often have quite the intended effects. In much of Europe, it seems, reading habits, choice and availability were to a considerable extent independent of government policy. In the more buoyant markets the profit-making book had, for better or for worse, a life of its own. Louis-Sébastien Mercier no doubt spoke at least for some when, in his 1771 best-seller *L'an deux mille quatre cent quarante* (*The Year 2440*), he described how mankind had, by some miraculous consensus, condensed all useful information into a small library, and dealt conclusively with all the rest:

> Unanimously, we gathered together on a huge plain all the books that we judged frivolous, useless or dangerous, and piled them into a huge pyramid which in height and width resembled a great tower: assuredly a new tower of Babel. Newspapers crowned this bizarre edifice, covered on all sides with episcopal edicts, *parlement* remonstrances, indictments and funeral orations. For the rest it was made up of five or six hundred thousand commentaries, eight hundred thousand volumes of jurisprudence, fifty thousand dictionaries, one hundred thousand poems, one million six hundred thousand travel stories, and one billion novels. We set fire to this appalling pile, like an expiatory sacrifice to truth, good sense and true good judgement.[11]

Changing demand for books

Historians are inherently prone to looking for change rather than continuity, and nowhere more so than in the enlightenment. In respect of books, a preoccupation with the novelties and diversification of the major urban intellectual centres may tend to overshadow the fact that the great bulk of the European provincial population stuck to their traditional, often very limited, reading habits. Even if we restrict our search just to that small minority who engaged in habitual reading, we are likely to find that conservative tastes predominated. Provincial France, for example, supported a book trade that was so modest that real concern was expressed after 1763 about the economic viability of the provincial printing and bookselling industry. The government decision of 1777 to limit the duration of certain types of

---

11 Louis-Sébastien Mercier, *L'an deux mille quatre cent quarante*. This quotation is taken from ch. 30 of the 1786 edition (revised and reprinted in Paris in 1793).

privilèges was partly in response to such concerns. Over the next decade, provincial printers accordingly reprinted some older books – mostly devotional and pious works (nearly two-thirds of all reprints), with only a modest share of fictional literature, and even less of the sciences and arts, law or history. Demand for manuals and basic works of reference grew, but there is little indication of an active enthusiasm for critical or provocative 'grub-street' work, least of all in the more tradition-bound southern and western parts of the kingdom.[12] The vast bulk of innovative works in French were clearly printed either in Paris itself, or abroad. It has been estimated that the total average annual output of French books and pamphlets increased from around 1,000 titles in 1720 to around 3,500 in 1770, including illegal and foreign publications; but how much of this was made up from new titles, and what kinds of work they represented, is probably impossible to determine because of the large illegal trade.

In England, contrasts between provincial and city demand may have been rather less pronounced than in France, partly no doubt because London did not foster the kind of radical and philosophically orientated salon society that sustained the Parisian literary market. The English provincial book trade seems to have thrived on demand for elementary educational material, practical works (on subjects such as law, accounting and housekeeping), religion (including the revivalist writings of the Methodists and other groups), history, and of course fictional literature from the popular novel down to traditional chapbooks. That the provincial market was economically worthwhile is demonstrated by the number of advertisements which London publishers placed in provincial papers, by the demand for subscription publications, and by the apparent provincial interest in sales of second-hand books and collections. For less wealthy purchasers, booksellers adopted various marketing strategies, including the serialisation of larger works like Defoe's *Robinson Crusoe* into short regular instalments or 'number books'. Other popular books, like *Moll Flanders* or *Gulliver's Travels*, suffered more or less ruthless abridgement, but classics like Bunyan's *Pilgrim's Progress* continued to be viable in both full and shortened illustrated versions. Newspaper editors often doubled as agents for London publishers to ensure an efficient and relatively cheap distribution service. The rapidly expanding provincial newspaper press also allowed an explosive growth in verbose doggerel verse, pompous moral commentary and other now virtually unreadable efforts.

Since there was no need in Britain for systematic and organised illegal book trading, it is easier to gain a reasonably accurate overall impression of the true state of the market there. There are various ways of attempting to

---

12 The register of applications for such permissions has been analysed by J. Brancolini and M.-T. Bouyssy, 'La vie provinciale du livre à la fin de l'ancien régime', in *Livre et société dans la France du xviiie siècle*, vol. 2, ed. M.-T. Bouyssy *et al.* (Paris, 1970), 3–37. See also R.L. Dawson, *The French Booktrade and the 'Permission Simple' of 1777: Copyright and Public Domain*, StVEC 301 (1992).

estimate overall book production in this period, notably by using contemporary library and auction catalogues, reviews, fragments of publishers' data, and other sources. For an overall impression, however, a simple title count can be done using reliable modern aggregate lists such as those derived from major national collections. Table 4.1 summarises data from the English-language Short Title Catalogue, regarding four important English-language publication centres in the eighteenth century. The actual numbers are less important than the overall trend, since the annual totals include small or ephemeral items. Equally, not all items were new publications – in fact the eighteenth-century printing industry depended to a very great extent on cheap reprints of older best-sellers. But since initial print-runs generally remained small throughout the century (usually 500–1,000 copies for a first printing, with 1,500–2,000 commonly being the largest technically and economically viable print-run even for well-established titles), the frequency of reprints may provide a good clue to the popularity of individual works.[13]

As Table 4.1 shows, there was a significant increase in the total number of items published in the second half of the eighteenth century. Until mid-century, London accounted for over 80% of the total English output, just as Edinburgh and Dublin dominated the respective Scottish and Irish markets. This dominance was slightly weakened in the second half of the eighteenth century. In England there were some shifts: thus the output of Oxford increased only slightly (from an annual average of 35 items at the start of the century to 45 at the end), but other centres like York and Cambridge trebled their output. In Scotland, the accelerating economic and demographic growth of Glasgow, and the reform of its university, help to explain why its publishing industry made significant inroads into the market from the early 1740s, with an average of 55–60 items produced each year from then on. But all over Britain lesser provincial towns also acquired a growing share of the general market, notably during the period of the Seven Years War and from the later 1770s onwards. Despite fluctuations, the overall trend everywhere was clearly upwards, with striking accelerations around mid-century and

13 The ESTC (English-language Short Title Catalogue), a development of the Eighteenth-Century Short Title Catalogue, is compiled from the holdings of the British Library and other major collections, and is still being extended (so the averages given here will all be revised in an upwards direction). Because of variant titles, problematic imprints and the common practice of several printers sharing the printing of a single work, the true number of distinct publications is somewhat smaller, but proportionally comparable (except for a possible slight over-representation in the case of London). For a brief description of what conclusions can be drawn from the ESTC database, see C.J. Mitchell, 'Provincial printing in eighteenth-century Britain', *Publishing History* 21 (1987), 5–24. There is unfortunately no equivalent database of French-language publications. For a discussion of various alternative types of evidence, see J. Raven, *Judging New Wealth* (Oxford, 1992), 31–41; F. Donoghue, *The Fame Machine: Book Reviewing and Eighteenth-Century Literary Careers* (Stanford, 1996), together with his chapter on 'Colonizing readers: review criticism and the formation of a reading public', in *The Consumption of Culture 1600–1800*, ed. A. Bermingham and J. Brewer (London, 1995), 54–74; and, for Germany, H. Möller, *Aufklärung in Preussen: der Verleger und Geschichtsschreiber Friedrich Nicolai* (Berlin, 1974), 199–208.

Table 4.1: Average annual output of new and reprinted works in English (books, pamphlets and smaller items) in key cities in the British Isles

	London	Dublin	Edinburgh	Glasgow
1710–19	1,705	114	160	12
1720–29	1,378	162	144	11
1730–39	1,446	160	147	12
1740–49	1,345	157	214	41
1750–59	1,567	216	201	65
1760–69	1,693	209	379	58
1770–79	2,038	195	249	55
1780–89	2,434	247	207	53
1790–95	3,472	374	316	90
Mid-century population in thousands	675	90	57	24

during the 1780s and early 1790s. The same trend in English-language publications is apparent in North America, where Boston, and to a lesser degree Philadelphia and New York, led the way.

Equally striking are changes in the kinds of works produced both for metropolitan and provincial markets. Until mid-century, provincial demand favoured collections of sermons, acrimonious works relating to church secessions and the accompanying partisan politics, devotional literature, elegies, ballads and short stories (including the life histories of criminals executed for murder). Most were pamphlets and very short texts. In Glasgow, for example, less than one-quarter of the output before 1742 was more than 50 pages long; but from then onwards the growth in scholarly printing by the Foulis brothers and others resulted in a marked shift towards much more substantial books. By 1792 Glasgow firms offered a comprehensive range: works on the slave trade and on canal building, an edition of John Quincy Adams' *Observations on Paine's Rights of Man*, and proclamations of the newly formed Glasgow branch of the Friends of the Constitution and of the People. Also included were new editions of Chaucer, John Bunyan's ever-popular *Pilgrim's Progress*, works by Allan Ramsay and Alexander Pope, a set of lectures on government by John Millar (Professor of Law at the University), and a single publication in Gaelic. Glasgow's book industry, like that of many other thriving provincial cities in Britain and on the continent, had clearly come of age: its local output of printed material had changed out of all recognition since the start of the century.

The German book market, fragmented and unencumbered by any widely enforceable regulation, provides some of the clearest evidence on changing demand during the later eighteenth century. A number of cities, including notably Frankfurt and Leipzig, held book fairs two or three times a year, at which booksellers would exchange new titles and evaluate overall demand. Some years ago Albert Ward completed a study of the trade catalogues produced for the Leipzig book fairs, especially those held at Easter and at

Michaelmas (late September). His analysis shows that, whilst the market was relatively constant in the century up to 1740, the next 60 years produced some striking changes. The huge overall growth in demand is demonstrated by the fact that the 2,500 titles offered at the Leipzig fair in 1800 were more than treble the total number available in 1740. The emphasis on certain types of books changed just as dramatically. Whereas theology still dominated the market in 1740 (with nearly 40% of the total), by 1800 it was down to 14%. Demand for scientific, philosophic and historical writing remained fairly level, but there was growing interest in medicine, mathematics, natural and applied science, agriculture and industry. By far the most significant upsurge, however, occurred in imaginative literature, particularly the novel. That sector had remained fairly constant at about 5–6% of the total market up to 1740, but grew to over 21% by 1800.[14]

No less significant was the rapid decline in the proportion of books printed in the international language of scholars, Latin – a decline which had already begun in the seventeenth century, and which reduced the Latin share to 27% in 1740 and to a mere 4% by 1800. Most of this shift was taken up by German-language works, but it is interesting to note that a significant part of it was made up of translations from French and English. *Robinson Crusoe* (1719) had had an immediate impact on the German market, with no less than three different translations appearing within a year, followed by a number of German derivatives over the next decades – the most important of which was Schnabel's four-volume *Insel Felsenburg* (*The Island of Felsen-burg*) (1731–43). *Gulliver's Travels* (1726) made nearly as big an impact: German readers might understand its political allusions in their own way, but would certainly enjoy its social satire. When the composer Telemann published his imaginative set of chamber music, *Der getreue Music-Meister* (*The Trusty Music-Master*), in Hamburg two years later, he included a *Gulliver Suite*, complete with a Lilliputian Chaconne notated in the shortest possible note values ever printed, and a Brobdingnagish gigue with absurdly long bars of 24 breves each – a visual joke which, appropriately enough for music intended for the domestic market, would be apparent only to the performer, not to a passive listener.

The appeal of Defoe, Swift, Fielding and Richardson to a wide northern European Protestant readership is not surprising: these tales of moral strug-gles, of individuals with whom the reader could readily identify, of providential benevolence mixed with exotic adventure, were accessible at widely different levels. Significantly, however, the translations also helped pave the way for a native German fictional literature which appealed at least as much to women readers as to men, and to as broad a social spectrum as in England. Scholarly and philosophical translations also made significant

---

14 For full explanation of these and the following quantitative summaries, as well as the overall background, see A. Ward, *Book Production, Fiction and the German Reading Public 1740–1800* (Oxford, 1974), 30–58 and *passim*. Less detailed work on other markets suggests that the German trend is typical of most of Europe, except for Russia.

inroads in northern Germany, especially those of the Scottish philosophers such as Adam Ferguson.[15] Significantly, the German market could in due course sustain a significant proportion of foreign books either imported from source or reprinted in their original language, especially French, Italian and English. William Remnant opened an exclusively English-language book-shop in Hamburg in 1788, and he continued to offer a comprehensive and fast import service until his death in 1810. Copenhagen also acquired no less than two specialist French-language bookshops in the second half of the eighteenth century. No doubt these ventures relied on the custom of a fairly small well-educated elite, but their very survival would have been unthink-able half a century earlier.

The social diffusion of books and other reading material anywhere in Europe is necessarily very difficult to determine. Purchase of new books by subscription or mail order, sale of book collections by auction, and discus-sion of newly read works, are all activities where the elite would be heavily over-represented. But incidental comments by many writers suggest that reading was becoming socially more widespread. Voltaire expressed concern about his books being read by people without sufficient understanding, whilst Mercier commented in his *Tableau de Paris* that 'people are certainly reading ten times as much in Paris as they did a hundred years ago'.[16] But, while observing that contemporaries found such enthusiasm for reading worthy of comment, what legitimate conclusions can we draw? Was the growth in reading really that great? What social groups might be affected, and which parts of the bigger cities? Was something similar observable in provincial towns?

To elucidate these questions, a group of French historians including Daniel Roche have tried to analyse wills and inventories after death. Not all the conclusions point in the direction we would expect. For example, the proportion of inventories that mention books seems higher in the provincial towns of western France in mid-eighteenth century than in Paris itself; equally, in some provincial towns (not in Paris), and amongst the lower social orders, the mention of books becomes noticeably less, not more, frequent in the last decades before the Revolution. More predictably, book ownership is very common within the social elite and amongst professional families, rather less common amongst traders, tradesmen and artisans, with usually only the better-off in each social category managing to collect a significant number of books. Interestingly, book-ownership amongst domes-tic servants and Parisian 'bourgeois' was quite significant by mid-century, and reached 40% for domestic servants by 1780. The types of books also

15 On the problems of translation in the enlightenment period, see above, p. 4. See also F. Oz-Salzberger, *Translating the Enlightenment: Scottish Civic Discourse in Eighteenth-Century Germany* (Oxford, 1995).

16 Louis-Sébastien Mercier, *Tableau de Paris*, vol. 12, 151f, quoted by D. Roche, *The People of Paris* (Leamington Spa, 1987), 198; on Voltaire's attitude to popular education and the spread of knowledge, see below, p. 196.

changed: we might note that theology occupied a dwindling share in the collections of the upper clergy towards the end of the century – perhaps for the same reason as might account for the relative scarcity of law books in the collection of the law officer, censor, and government official Malesherbes: lack of relevance and intellectual interest. Throughout French society, fiction ranked high; but it is clear that individual choice of books became genuinely more diverse in the course of the century.[17]

The evidence from French wills and inventories summarised here suggests some patterns; but it also raises a number of uncertainties. Did books become so commonplace that those who drew up the inventories might not bother to mention them? Are the samples of inventories used necessarily representative of the total population? Can we draw at all meaningful conclusions about the kinds of books read amongst the less well-off, where inventories sometimes just make passing mention of 'a bundle of books'. Is book-ownership at death necessarily representative of lifetime interest? And, perhaps above all, is ownership itself an indication of great significance, at a time when (as we shall see) it became increasingly possible to borrow from libraries and friends?

Clearly, it is not easy to reach tenable conclusions about changing demand for different types of books during the enlightenment: each type of evidence seems to raise as many problems as it provides answers. Yet, despite all these reservations, we can probably make some valid generalisations that few would dispute. Clearly, provincial France, Scotland and Scandinavia continued to a support a fairly traditional book industry, where a steady demand for devotional, moral and mostly edifying literature was met by small-scale printing and bookselling businesses, supplemented by some postal ordering and subscription services for those who could afford it. By contrast, Paris, London, Hamburg and other bigger cities supported a diversifying book trade spilling over into whole regional hinterlands in northern Germany and parts of England. This market nourished a growing appetite for innovative and foreign books, and was marked by a decline in the relative numeric significance of traditional scholarly works in Latin. The novel held sway, but there was a continuing interest in narrative history, biography, some popular science, and other types of easily accessible non-fictional reading. Judging from sales, there was evidently also some support for the more innovative kinds of work usually associated with the enlightenment, ranging from Rousseau and Johnson to Schiller and Diderot.

With this last category of books we reach one of the most difficult problems facing the historian of the enlightenment. We may accept the overall picture outlined so far, but can we demonstrate the impact of books

17 D. Roche, *The People of Paris* (Leamington Spa, 1987), 211–17; R. Chartier, *The Cultural Uses of Print in Early Modern Europe* (Princeton, 1987), 183–239; see also the short overview in *Histoire de l'édition française*, vol. 2: *Le livre triomphant 1660–1830*, ed. H.-J. Martin and R. Chartier (Paris, 1984), 403–10, with references to the detailed work of Marion on Paris, Queniart on western France, and others.

likely to encourage independent ways of thinking? What books should the historian of the enlightenment *really* be concerned with? As long ago as 1910, Daniel Mornet tackled this question. Famously, his thorough search of the auction catalogues of private book collections of the period 1750–80 revealed just a single copy of Rousseau's *Social Contract* out of a total of 20,000 identified titles. But auction catalogues were themselves censored, and in any case Mornet's sample was by definition not socially representative. Equally serious reservations have been raised about quantitative conclusions drawn from the main review journals, or from the records of the regulatory bureaucracy itself.[18]

On the other hand, the work of Robert Darnton, particularly in the archives of the Société typographique de Neuchâtel just across the French border, has demonstrated how much we have yet to learn about booksellers and readers in eighteenth-century France. Amongst the real best-sellers of the illegal trade he has found some works of recognised quality, like d'Holbach's *System of Nature* (1770), Raynal's *Philosophical History* (1770), several of Voltaire's and Restif's more controversial writings, and above all Mercier's futuristic utopian vision *The Year 2440* (1771). But no less important in the trade, Darnton argues, is the work of now often forgotten younger writers, trying (but often failing) to make a career in a cut-throat and fickle market. The aggressive and unedifying grub-street literature by which some of them sought to make an impression was often euphemistically described as 'philosophical books', ranging from outright pornography like *Thérèse philosophe* and *Venus in the Cloisters* to political libels like *Anecdotes Regarding Madame la Comtesse Du Barry*. The latter, provocatively describing the sordid intrigue surrounding Louis XV and his mistress at the end of the reign, will have done nothing to revive the tarnished image of that particular ruler, or enhance the divine stature of the monarchy as an institution. Other works on the lists were equally unacceptable because of their explicit or implicit attacks on the Catholic church and its corrupt clergy, their portrayal of decay and corruption at the higher levels of society, or, in the case of *Thérèse*, even their moral relativism or hedonism – all good reasons why they could only ever be traded secretly, hidden in the bottom of trunks or concealed unbound amongst the pages of orthodox religious texts.

This perspective on reading habits and trading methods has made a major difference to our understanding of late *ancien régime* France in particular, and the enlightenment in general. The contrast between 'grub-street' and the fêted salon culture of later eighteenth-century Paris may in the long run turn out to be less stark – and Darnton's own work has helped clarify just how

18 For a summary of these problems, see R. Darnton, 'Reading, writing and publishing', in his *The Literary Underground of the Old Regime* (Cambridge, Mass., 1982), 167–82, with references notably to F. Furet, 'La "librairie" du royaume de France au 18e siècle', in *Livre et société dans la France du xviiie siècle*, ed. G. Bollème *et al.* (Paris, 1965), 3–32; and J. Ehrard and J. Roger, 'Deux périodiques français du 18e siècle', in the same volume, 33–59.

complex and multi-layered the book market really was. We should also remember that some of what did go into print legally (including press reports of the American revolt, and the proceedings of controversial lawsuits) could in fact be highly significant to an attentive and careful reader.[19] But overall we now have a much more comprehensive view of who might read what. The 'great' authors have not disappeared – Rousseau's *Collected Works* figure prominently, as do many other writers whom we can readily recognise today – but they have been placed in the context of a lively, irreverent and lucrative literary culture capable of reaching a far wider audience than was once thought possible. This complex market created employment not just for printers and booksellers trying to cater for all tastes without being caught out, but also for carriers, smugglers, insurers and agents within France and across its borders. The grey and illegal markets often operated by means of personal networks, fuelled by a common system of bartering of printed unbound sheets between publishers (often with differential rates for danger-ous texts), and maintained by means of clandestine catalogues and extensive postal contacts couched in oblique language. Covering all tastes – from the titillating to the socially and philosophically radical – the trade encompassed large-scale reputable firms outside France as well as smaller enterprises inside the kingdom. Just how large-scale the underground market was, and how many could afford to buy its products, is still uncertain. What is clear, however, is that demand for print was growing so rapidly that the traditional regulatory machinery increasingly looked ridiculous. Malesherbes himself recognised as much in his memorandum of 1788–89 advocating a compre-hensive reform towards freedom of expression.[20] Soon, however, his recommendations were overtaken by events, in that the loss of political control by the crown in the summer of 1789 entailed amongst other things a *de facto* collapse of the old regulatory system.

19 R. Darnton, 'The forbidden books of pre-revolutionary France', in *Rewriting the French Revolution*, ed. C. Lucas (Oxford, 1991), 1–32; his *The Forbidden Best-Sellers of Pre-revolutionary France* (New York and London, 1996); and his *The Corpus of Clandestine Literature in France 1769–1789* (New York and London, 1995), which offers a checklist of 720 forbidden texts handled by the publishing firm Société Typographique de Neuchâtel, or seized by the Paris police and customs officials. Darnton's work over the last 30 years has generated a very lively debate. Key contributions can be found in H.T. Mason, ed., *The Darnton Debate: Books and Revolution in the Eighteenth Century*, *StVEC* 359 (1998) – notably those by Jeremy D. Popkin, Daniel Gordon and Elizabeth Eisenstein, 105–77, and the response by Darnton, 251–94. See also J. Lough, 'The French literary underground reconsidered', *StVEC* 329 (1995), 471–82, emphasising the need not to exaggerate either the socially divisive or politically subversive potential of the literary world in the last years before the Revolution. For a survey of writings by some of the opponents of the *philosophes* – often defenders of the church and of traditional values, but some of them (like Fréron in his *Année littéraire*) more independent-minded – see D.M. McMahon, 'The counter-enlightenment and the low-life of literature in pre-revolutionary France', *Past and Present* 159 (1998), 77–112.
20 R. Birn, 'Malesherbes and the call for a free press', in *Revolution in Print: The Press in France 1775–1800*, ed. R. Darnton and D. Roche (Berkeley, 1989), 50–66, gives an overview of his ministerial role and private views up to the revolutionary period.

Libraries and book clubs

As we would expect from the discussion so far, large-scale book-collecting became more widespread during the eighteenth century amongst secular institutions and private individuals. Few could match aristocratic biblio-philes like the Danish count Otto Thott, who had amassed 140,000 volumes by the time of his death in 1785 (when a large part was bought to supplement the Royal Library in Copenhagen, itself opened to the public in 1793). Thott was generous in allowing access to scholars, but many great book collections remained inaccessible behind elaborate regulations or the over-zealous unfriendliness of some librarians. Only the privileged few could access the major state collections themselves, such as the formally constituted British Museum (British Library) of 1753. More surprisingly, severe restrictions were also applied in many university libraries, often accessible only to the teaching staff. A significant exception was the magnificent collection of the new University of Göttingen (founded in 1736), whose library staff also had close contacts with the prestigious and cosmopolitan literary review, the *Göttingische Anzeigen von gelehrten Sachen* (*Göttingen Journal of Learned Matters*). Later in the century, however, the idea of genuinely public libraries began to catch on. One prominent episcopal collection in Grenoble was bought communally by means of public subscription, and opened for the benefit of all in 1774.

However, not all cities were as corporately minded as that, and most ordinary readers had to have recourse to other options. An innovative feature of the eighteenth-century book market was the proliferation of commercial or circulating libraries run by booksellers – where any reader could borrow a book in return for a small rental fee. The origins of such commercial libraries probably lie a century or more back, but by the eighteenth century they had become common not just in big cities (Allan Ramsay started a circulating library in Edinburgh in 1726, London saw several ventures in the 1730s, The Hague one in 1750, and Glasgow had John Smith's from 1751), but also in smaller towns (such as Carmarthen by the 1780s). Swedish printers may not have been alone in fearing that such ventures would undercut their sales, but they were the only ones to take their hostility so far as to secure legislation (in 1787) which restricted the lending activities of booksellers solely to foreign publications, thereby limiting the growth potential for commercial libraries. Elsewhere commercial book-lending grew apace: the selection may have been much smaller than in those institutional and ecclesiastical collections accessible to the public, but was potentially much more responsive to the interests of ordinary readers.

More important in terms of the diversity of available material, however, were the reading societies, subscription libraries and book clubs formed in many parts of Europe in the second half of the century. Their scope and organisation varied enormously, but they usually relied on a regular subscribing membership, who might meet annually to elect their executive office-bearers, decide on admissions of new members, and determine priorities for acquisition of new books. Many reading societies naturally tended to be socially exclusive (controlled through admission fees and annual subscription); but since there were no limits to who could form them, these ventures certainly helped provide cheap access to books, and might foster an environment for sociable discussion. Judging from current knowledge, their spread seems in fact to have been very uneven. In France, a modest 49 new *cabinets de lecture* have been identified for the period 1759–89, of which 13 were in Paris itself. A study of reading societies in Germany (*Lesegesellschaften*) suggests a far greater profusion, with as many as 500 by the end of the century, the majority of them in Protestant northern Germany, and most of them dating from the 1780s and 1790s.[21] Their acquisitions policies naturally reflected their membership, but would usually include subscriptions to reviews and political journals, as well as standard reference works and major books on biography, travel, history, law and contemporary politics. Interestingly, reading societies on the whole bought relatively little fiction, suggesting that the market for the latter was largely pitched at the individual private buyer.

The impact of the book: two case studies

We noted earlier that it may be highly misleading to see the enlightenment in terms of key works that later generations have rated highly. As Darnton has argued so persuasively, it is virtually impossible to establish what eighteenth-century readers really did read most, let alone what they made of it all. For some, reading Rousseau produced a trance-like state of almost religious devotion; others preferred the titillations of grub-street, with or without a veneer of social comment; whilst some salons engaged in earnest discussion of literary, philosophical and ultimately also political issues. The enlightenment was different things to different people even at the time, just as it has

---

21 C. Jolly, ed., *Histoire des bibliothèques françaises*, vol. 2: *Les bibliothèques sous l'ancien régime 1530–1789* (Paris, 1988), 415–21. Almost certainly, this tally is not exhaustive. As Mercier noted at the time, many small *cabinets* were attached directly to bookshops, perhaps more akin to commercial libraries, where the bookseller could boost business by allowing patrons to read on the premises (perhaps in return for a 'membership' fee) or borrow books on a rental basis. New works in great demand, like *La nouvelle Héloïse*, might even be split into sections and hired out by the hour (L.-S. Mercier, *Tableau de Paris*, vol. 5 (1783), ch. 377). See also M. Stützel-Prüsener, 'Die deutschen Lesegesellschaften im Zeitalter der Aufklärung', in *Lesegesellschaften und bürgerliche Emanzipation: ein europäischer Vergleich*, ed. O. Dann (Munich, 1981), 71–86. Information on borrowings from individual libraries and reading societies, however, is fraught with problems of interpretation, and no clear profile of readers' interests has so far emerged. Overall, however, books were by the later eighteenth century clearly becoming readily accessible (by some means or other) even for the less well-off: see for example the overview in J. Brewer, *The Pleasures of the Imagination: English Culture in the Eighteenth Century* (London, 1997), 176–90.

been ever since. Yet, provided we try to distance ourselves from simplistic stereotypes of 'typical' readers or 'great' works of enlightenment, we may nevertheless gain some understanding of the role of the book by looking at a few publication histories.

The *Encyclopédie ou Dictionnaire raisonné des sciences, des arts et des métiers*, edited principally by Denis Diderot but with the assistance of around 160 other outstanding writers and *philosophes*, must be regarded as one of the great book-publishing achievements of the enlightenment. Originally conceived in 1745 as a revised translation of Chambers' two-volume Cyclopedia of 1728, the project soon grew. When Diderot and his main publisher, Le Breton, launched the bid for subscriptions in 1750, they promised completion of the planned 10 volumes by 1754, at a total subscription price of 280 livres. In the event, the last of altogether 17 volumes of text did not appear until 1765, and the accompanying 11 volumes of plates ran on until 1772 – by which time the total subscription price had become 980 livres.

Diderot's *Encyclopédie* was not the first large-scale compendium of information. Zedler's 64-volume *Grosses Universal Lexicon* appeared in Halle and Leipzig between 1732 and 1750, and to French-speaking scholars such smaller works as Pierre Bayle's two-volume *Dictionnaire historique et critique* of 1694 remained indispensable. The new *Encyclopédie* had already attracted 1,400 subscribers by the time the first volume appeared in June 1751; immediate controversy and the publicity of an unenforced ban early in 1752 ensured that the print-run had to be raised substantially, reaching 4,225 by the time the fourth volume appeared in 1754. But by volume 7, late in 1757, the climate had changed. Confrontation between the Jansenists, the Jesuits and the Parlement of Paris had become open, and the attempt in 1757 on the life of Louis XV (the Damiens affair) was used as an excuse for repression. A ban on supposedly subversive writing was applied not only to Helvétius (above, p. 86), but also to Diderot's co-editor d'Alembert. Early in 1759 Malesherbes himself had to order the suppression of the *Encyclopédie* and the withdrawal of its *privilège*. However, Diderot and his publishers had friends at court, so Malesherbes could arrange for him to continue the editorial work, under the discreet cover of the rather less controversial volumes of plates. To minimise further outcry, the remaining 10 volumes were released all together in 1765, and under a false imprint. Even so, the chief publisher, Le Breton, did not escape a token week in the Bastille.

The success in publishing terms was outstanding: pirated editions were attempted almost immediately, and a sequence of legitimate reprints in different formats ensured that a total of around 25,000 copies of the *Encyclopédie* were distributed over the next decades. Diderot himself earned a mere 2,600 livres yearly during the long period of production, though possibly more at certain times; his faithful assistant Jaucourt, author/editor of an estimated 17,000 articles (out of the total of 72,000) was paid virtually nothing. The original publishers, however, did very well, and Panckoucke (who bought out Le Breton in 1768) made a fortune on the reprints and their Supplements. He was so encouraged that he launched the even more ambitious new *Encyclopédie méthodique* in 1782 – its staggering 160 volumes eventually completed by his widowed daughter-in-law in 1832.[22]

Diderot's *Encyclopédie* aimed to be a dictionary, a historical encyclopedia and a general encyclopedia all in one. Who its original subscribers were is not known, but evidence on the circulation of the cheaper octavo editions of the 1770s, selling at prices as low as 240 livres, indicates that it had a very wide appeal amongst the elite, the officeholders, professionals, upper clergy, army officers and salon society of France and elsewhere, even finding its way into some *cabinets littéraires*.[23] Despite Diderot's own misgivings over the final text, it immediately established itself as a symbol of the French enlightenment, complete with all its contradictions and ambiguities. As stated clearly in d'Alembert's *Preliminary Discourse*, and reiterated in Diderot's own entry for '*Encyclopédie*', they aimed to present a compendium of philosophical, historic and practical knowledge, organised solely according to rational principles, emancipated from preconceptions and irrational beliefs. That not all articles lived up to such high expectations, and that readers occasionally had to use their imagination to find what they needed, did not pacify its critics. It was seen by many as both a deeply subversive and a deeply anti-religious work: a text which actively sought to encourage critical and rational evaluation of all aspects of human existence.

The *Encyclopédie* could without exaggeration be described as the most prominent reference work of the French enlightenment, practical and informative in intent; but there were many other ways of presenting new ways of thinking to the reading public. This chapter has already referred to a number of key fictional works, from *Robinson Crusoe* to *La nouvelle Héloïse*, which clearly caught the imagination of readers across Europe by speaking in a powerful language, uncontrived, true to personal experience. Many case studies could be chosen from the diverse list of eighteenth-century best-sellers, but just one more will be sufficient: *Die Leiden des jungen Werthers* (*The Sorrows of Young Werther*). This novel by the great German writer and scholar Johann Wolfgang von Goethe (1749–1832) was first published in 1774, and substantially revised by him in 1787. It immediately became controversial, and in many parts of Europe was promptly censored. It was translated into French within a year of publication, and went through

---

22 There is a very large literature on both the original *Encyclopédie*, its precursors, and its later offshoots. Amongst the best are J. Lough, *The Encyclopédie* (London, 1971); R. Darnton, *The Business of Enlightenment: A Publishing History of the Encyclopédie, 1775–1800* (Cambridge, Mass., 1979); C.P. Braunrot and K.H. Doig, 'The Encyclopédie méthodique: An Introduction', *StVEC* 327 (1995), 1–152; and F.A. Kafker, *Notable Encyclopédies of the Late 18th Century*, *StVEC* 315 (1994). On Diderot's collaborators, see also F.A. Kafker and S. Kafker, *The Encyclopedists as Individuals: A Biographical Dictionary of the Authors of the Encyclopédie*, *StVEC* 257 (1988).

23 See R. Darnton, *The Business of Enlightenment* (Cambridge, Mass., 1979), 287–319 and 520–9.

16 editions in English between 1779 and 1794. *Werther* remained a key work which nearly overwhelmed many of its readers – including Goethe himself, when he came to write a preface for a celebratory re-issue half a century later, in 1824.

Why did *Werther* have such an immediate and lasting impact? The novel adopts the popular epistolary form already used by Richardson in his strikingly successful *Pamela* (1740) and by Rousseau in *Héloïse*, but all the letters are written by a single person. The story is hardly promising by modern standards: it is the account of an over-sensitive youth who falls hopelessly and tortuously in love with a married woman, and eventually works himself up to a suicide which, an intervening editor confirms, brings lingering and painful death. There is not much broader social commentary, except for the fact that we learn that Werther (a commoner) is rejected by the aristocracy of a minor German court, and feels a loser. Tension and stress pervade the entire text: its heavy *Empfindsamkeit* (sentimentality, cult of sensibility) has much in common with Rousseau, and is a complete denial of the rationality and common sense of the *encyclopédistes*. Here, perhaps, is a key to its importance: *Werther* represented a rejection of both Pietist and rational norms, turning instead towards an inward focus on moral (psychological) tensions, a dark contemplation of the meaningless futility of life – where suicide, traditionally regarded as a crime (or sign of insanity) becomes a symbol of true relief. Particularly important to many contemporaries was the fact that the story was based on real life: on Goethe's inward struggle and emotional entanglements, and on the suicide of someone whose predicament the author understood. The book becomes a public testimony to the incompatibility between outer and inner worlds hitherto rarely revealed. Alongside other highly emotional works like Schiller's *The Robbers*, it represented a break from traditional enlightened thinking, towards a far more fraught and frank self-analysis.

It will be apparent that the historian wishing to understand the enlightenment, or wishing to read between the lines of the *Encyclopédie* as Diderot told his readers to do, has to try to understand the many different (and sometimes incompatible) contemporary strands of writing in the later eighteenth century. The reasons for Rousseau's growing alienation from Diderot and the other *philosophes* is much more intelligible once we are aware of his fictional writings. Similarly, the anti-rationalist reaction of the German pre-Romantics (like Schiller and early Goethe) begins to fall into place as a legitimate part of the enlightenment. In fact such apparent contradiction is visible within Diderot's own writings: his fiction, hardly any of which he allowed to be published during his lifetime, demonstrates how little of his true complexity we see in the pages of the *Encyclopédie*. None of this needs further explanation, given the circumstances of publishing in eighteenth-century Europe; but it reminds us that there is more to the enlightenment than merely pragmatism and reason.

Pamphlets and politics

The pamphlet – a short topical book intended for a wide audience – was the natural outlet for individuals wishing to contribute to a current debate or controversy. Unlike newspapers, pamphlets were inherently one-off ventures, and could therefore more easily be published clandestinely and distributed surreptitiously. Without pre-determined deadlines, the pamphleteer could make do with a simple mobile press, and if his work was not too lengthy he could afford to do successive small print-runs according to demand. But since pamphlets rarely had any predictable long-term commercial value, they were less attractive to professional printers and publishers. Accordingly, even though individual pamphlets may not be of great significance on their own, more protracted campaigns which can be followed through sequences of pamphlet contributions can provide us with insights into areas of public debate not driven primarily by editorial or commercial interests.

Given the restraints on freedom of expression in France, it is hardly surprising that the political pamphlet became an established genre there well before the Revolution. Significant already during the Jansenist crisis of 1750–57, the pamphlet had made a real impact during the Maupeou crisis of 1771–74, when Chancellor Maupeou and his ministerial colleagues used skilled pamphleteers (including Voltaire himself) in defence of their drastic reforms of the *parlements*. Since especially the Parlement de Paris was already accustomed to publishing accounts of some of its proceedings, the French public was treated to a full-scale battle of words touching on some of the central institutions of government.

The role of the political pamphlet in France became even more critical during the run-up to the meeting of the Estates General in May 1789. The Assembly of Notables had triggered some pamphleteering already in 1787, but on 5 July 1788 the crown had invited written suggestions regarding procedural aspects and historic precedents for that meeting. Proposals were to be sent to the Guard of the Seals, but in practice many contributors took the opportunity of going into print uncensored. The result was a flood of pamphlets. Judging from the holdings of the Bibliothèque Nationale, only a few dozen pamphlets appeared annually in the early 1780s, rising to 217 in 1787; but the total for 1788 is 819, and that for 1789 an impressive 3,305. Of these, 2,000 or more appeared during the period of elections to the Estates, between January and April 1789 – which, if the average print run was 1,000, would on a conservative estimate make a total of 2 million pamphlets in four months.[24] Varying in length, style and substance, these

24 R. Birn, 'The pamphlet press and the Estates General of 1789', in *The Press in the French Revolution, StVEC* 287 (1991), 59–69; see also D. van Kley, 'New wine in old wineskins: continuity and rupture in the pamphlet debate of the French pre-revolution, 1787–89', *French Historical Studies* 17 (1991), 447–65; and A. de Baecque, 'Pamphlets: libel and

tracts addressed a much wider range of issues than what the crown had originally intended, including matters of finance and government reform.

Amongst them was abbé Sieyes' famous piece entitled *What is the Third Estate?*, first issued in January 1789 and reprinted at least three times over the next few months. Not short by the standards of some pamphlets, it nevertheless clearly belonged to that genre in terms of its combative and polemical tone, as shown in the very opening:

> The plan of this work is quite simple. We have three questions to ask ourselves.
>
> 1. What is the Third Estate? – EVERYTHING.
> 2. What has its role been so far in the political order of things? – NOTHING.
> 3. What does it demand? – TO BE SOMETHING.
>
> We shall see whether these answers are right. Until then, it would be wrong to dismiss as exaggeration truths whose substantiation has not yet been examined. We shall then study all the means so far tried, and the measures that should be taken, in order that the Third Estate become in reality *something*. We shall therefore recount
>
> 4. What the ministers have tried to do, and what the privileged orders themselves propose.
> 5. What *ought* to have been done.
> 6. Finally, what *remains* to be done in order for the Third Estate to assume the place that it is due.

We shall return later to the substantive social and political issues raised by works such as this (below, p. 194), but the present extract will suffice to show how its direct style might well have helped focus wider public opinion on an agenda which the crown itself seemed incapable of putting across.

We know that Sieyes had a significant (if only temporary) impact on national politics; what is more difficult to demonstrate is his influence beyond the relatively select society of lawyers and officeholders to which he himself belonged. The size of the print-run and the number of reprints must indicate some popularity, but tells us nothing about who actually read it. Such evidence is rarely available in this period; but the exceptional track record of Tom Paine's *Rights of Man* may serve as an illustration that fundamental political and social debate was not necessarily beyond the reach

political mythology', in *Revolution in Print*, ed. R. Darnton and D. Roche (Berkeley, 1989), 165f. The years from 1789 saw a slight decline, partly because it now became much easier to launch newspapers (see below, p. 128), but even so the annual total did not fall below 500 until 1796. Since, however, the Bibliothèque Nationale holdings are not complete, the real output is likely to have been higher, arguably much higher: H. Chisick, 'The pamphlet literature of the French Revolution: an overview', *History of European Ideas* 17 (1993), 149–53 and *passim*, who also argues that the print-run of some pamphlets was much higher than indicated here, exceptionally even over 10,000 copies.

of ordinary readers. Published in two parts (early in 1791 and 1792 respectively), as part of a long-running confrontation between conservatives and radicals (see below, p. 209), the *Rights of Man* was reputed at the time to have sold several hundred thousand copies. Initial demand for both parts of the work exceeded 10,000 copies per week, and cheap editions were bought in bulk by enthusiasts for free distribution. Part II went through five editions within a month, with extensive sales also in America and in translation in France. By 1802 Paine estimated (perhaps over-enthusiastically) that total sales were upwards of half a million. No less important, local groups shared and debated copies of the work: a cabinet-maker in Perth shared his copy with a dozen friends, since he could not 'do a greater service to my country than by making such principles known'.[25] As part of a pamphlet debate that eventually ran to many titles and drew contributions from outstanding figures like Mary Wollstonecraft and Joseph Priestley, the gist of the argument can hardly have been unknown to anyone who took any interest at all in politics in England at the time, whether they sympathised with the radical cause or not.

* * * *

If a reader in 1710 had been able to look forward to the 1790s, he would hardly have recognised the world of print that he would see. The diversity of titles and subject matter that had appeared in the intervening years, the availability of cheaper editions, the erosion of much of the official regulatory machinery, and the growth of commercial and even public libraries, all contributed to an unprecedented growth in the accessibility of the printed word to those who could read. To those as yet inexperienced in the art of reading, the novels of mid-century and the pamphlets of the last decades of the eighteenth century provided short and stimulating challenges, often couched in language designed for the widest possible appeal. If there was ever an age where the value of literacy suddenly became widely recognised, surely the later eighteenth century was it.

25 Quotation and numerical estimates are from G. Claeys, *Thomas Paine: Social and Political Thought* (Boston and London, 1989), 111f.

| 5 |

The press

Well before the eighteenth century, journals, pamphlets and news-sheets had become firmly established as media for the diffusion of ideas, information and commentary. Printing technology was efficient and adaptable, and the capital overheads required to swap between different types of printing (say from book production to news-sheets) was low – particularly so since eighteenth-century newspapers were done in small format, mostly printed in continuous prose without headlines, and thus virtually indistinguishable in appearance from unbound books. As literacy became more common, the market was bound to expand. Although the characteristics of this market could be assessed only by trial and error, the industry was well suited to the task. For a printer or editor to abandon a serial that was poorly supported did not have to result in major losses, and a new venture could be launched virtually overnight.

The enormous political potential of the printing press had become clear both in England and in France during the unstable 1640s, and the return to stability in 1660 did not induce collective amnesia – even if efforts by governments all over Europe to restore effective control of the press meant that writers and publishers often had to go to great lengths to cover their tracks to escape serious censure. If the background to single substantial works by recognised intellectuals like Locke or Fénelon is difficult to unravel, it is hardly surprising that the history of less illustrious publications raises even more uncertainties – sometimes about the identity and purpose of the author and publisher, and almost certainly about editorial policies, market role, the size of print-runs, means of distribution and circulation, and range and size of readership – to say nothing of feed-back from readers, and (in the case of longer-running serials) any editorial responsiveness there may have been to public opinion generally.

For the early modern period, it is difficult to attempt even a definition of the types and genres of publications that we are dealing with. A modern reader may readily distinguish different forms of printed material currently available (from up-market newspapers and tabloids to scholarly journals, from commercial magazines to mail-distributed advertising); it is much more difficult to reconstruct the equivalent reactions of eighteenth-century readers to the growing range of occasional publications which they might come across. For practical purposes, however, we shall confine the subject of this chapter to printed publications appearing reasonably frequently and sequentially, and providing information or debate intended to be of topical relevance. Such information might include what we would today recognise as news (based on events), but more often in the eighteenth century included review-type and anecdotal material, moral essays, poetry and other material strung together (often, it seems, at random) by the editor. Accordingly, rigid distinctions between newspapers, journals, reviews, literary miscellanies and other periodical material seem inappropriate for this period.

Easiest to identify, perhaps, are the specialised learned journals: they were often just formalised versions of the network of contacts and correspondence which had sustained the international community of scholars since before the Renaissance. Like the durable academic periodicals of today, some were, and remained, venerable institutions with a reliable but exclusive readership. By the eighteenth century, however, there was a widening market in salon society for lighter scientific–philosophical journals. In France, for example, the *Journal des sçavans* (*Scholars' Journal*) of 1665, although a state-designated paper protected by a *privilège* (exclusive right to publish), thus came to face increasingly severe competition from lesser publishers trying to exploit the enthusiasm for popular science and debate.

Rather different in content, but also fairly easy to identify, are the news-sheets and newspapers that survived for any length of time. All news, and especially domestic news, was regarded as highly sensitive, and was normally channelled through a single controlled outlet with monopoly rights. Government-sponsored papers like the *Gazette de France* (from 1631) or the London *Gazette* (founded in 1665) thus gained a permanent niche as purveyors of official but uncontroversial and unexciting political news summaries. And while other papers, in the absence of enforceable copyright restrictions,[1] adapted or lifted material from such official sources, they could not readily verify the information, and could not easily take an independent

---

1 In Britain, the Copyright Act of 1709 (see p. 80) applied only to books, and seemed relatively effective only because of the market monopolies maintained by the booksellers' syndicates. By contrast, the persistent copying between serials and papers was actively defended by some, on the grounds that it ensured a wider circulation for material of general interest. Ireland was not subject to the 1709 Act, and its applicability to Scotland was disputed. On the continent, authors and publishers often tried to protect their literary property by means of an official grant of exclusive rights (like the *privilèges* granting French publishers exclusive rights over a book or the market-sector of a journal), but enforcement was often left at least partly up to the beneficiary. The political and judicial decentralisation of the German lands and the Netherlands made such enforcement even more problematic (see p. 83).

view. Accordingly, well into the eighteenth century much news remained derivative and carefully filtered.

Beyond such established forms, however, was a great wealth of more experimental and often more ephemeral output, ranging from one-off pamphlets by hopeful writers and journalists, to more sophisticated attempts to launch new advertisers, reviews and journals with a broader appeal. Very different in appearance, size and content from their modern counterparts, these periodicals defy generalisation. Where should we place complex ventures like the *Gentleman's Magazine* (launched 1731), which introduced parliamentary reporting and mixed news alongside its literary material, or the up-market manuscript journal *Correspondance littéraire* edited from Paris by the German *philosophe* Grimm from 1754? Can we really put side by side two so utterly different literary reviews as Fréron's personalised and belligerent *Année littéraire* (*Literary Yearbook*), and the long-lived and much more conventional *Kiöbenhavnske Lærde Efterretninger* (*Copenhagen Learned Review*, 1720–1810)? And how do we classify the bewildering and idiosyncratic array of one-man ventures that sprang up at the time of the French Revolution, such as Mirabeau's influential *Letters to his Constituents* of 1789, or Marat's blood-curdling and sweepingly non-factual *L'ami du peuple* (*Friend of the People*)? In an age where humour, euphemism, self-deprecation and self-censorship were standard tools of survival for writers of all kinds, where the ownership and editorial networks behind each publication are often unclear, and where state repression was a real threat at most times, can we ever be sure that we even understand what we read?

None of these questions are readily answered. We cannot even gauge reader response reliably, for devices such as letters to the editor were (and still are) hardly representative. The business records of most papers of the period have long since vanished, so success in satisfying either investors or potential buyers can rarely be measured in any way other than in terms of how long a paper actually survived. But in spite of all these difficulties, the study of the news and periodical industry, and not least its spectacular development in the last decades of the eighteenth century, has enormous potential in terms of clarifying the nature and diffusion of new ideas and new debates. We can examine not only shifting editorial agendas, but also the evolution of linguistic metaphors, the moulding of common phrases and words, and the gradual adoption of journalistic techniques designed to hold a reader's interest – ranging from the use of outlines and headings, to more subtle context-sensitive appeals either to sensationalism or to social preservation. More elusive than the book, and often to the modern reader infuriatingly superficial, imprecise, non-committal or verbose, eighteenth-century papers and journals nonetheless command our respect as source material which may have greater potential than the single works of great authors.

The *Tatler* and the *Spectator*

By the early eighteenth century, the London press was the richest and most diverse in Europe. This is hardly surprising, considering the city's enormous growth in size and buying power since the middle of the seventeenth century, coupled with the effective (if unintended) abandonment of pre-publication censorship resulting from the lapse of the Licensing Act in 1695 (see p. 85). What these changes meant in practical terms, however, is best illustrated by means of two serials which effectively set the tone for at least one genre of enlightenment journalism.

The *Tatler* was launched anonymously in April 1709 by Richard Steele, appearing three times weekly, and costing one penny per issue. It carried a selection of material, most importantly a series of reports by the fictional Mr Isaac Bickerstaff, ostensibly from different London coffee- and chocolate-houses. As explained in the first issue, these venues provided a classificatory framework: 'St James's Coffee-house', for example, headed sections dealing with foreign and domestic news. Other journalistic devices, including letters from readers (genuine as well as editorially conceived), were used as pegs on which to hang witty, good-natured and brilliantly readable commentaries on a wide range of issues of contemporary interest, from moral reform, decorum and good manners, public affairs and international relations, to religion, literary criticism and review of the arts. The tone was always moderate and reasonable, appealing to what a later age would call 'middle-class values', but in an independent-minded and illuminating way. Various imaginary contributors were introduced along the way, including a woman, Jenny Distaff; but the true identity of the editor was not revealed until Steele voluntarily brought the *Tatler* to an end with issue no. 271 (January 1711).

Analysis of its printing has shown that the *Tatler* achieved very rapid popularity, and that by issue no. 118 (when two simultaneous print-runs on different presses were required to meet demand) its circulation must have exceeded 3,000. Each issue remained quite short, averaging around 1,700 words (densely printed on both sides of a single sheet of paper, slightly larger than modern A4), but the use of different typefaces allowed quite significant variations from that norm, also accommodating a variable number of advertisement-notes, without any change in overall format. Although the *Tatler* was not totally innovatory in style or substance – Defoe's successful bi-weekly *Review* (1704–13) and other journals were attempting to tap similar markets – it clearly deserves its reputation both in terms of quality and elegance. Its rapid reprint in book form, and the open praise it earned even from its competitors, leaves us in no doubt that from the start it was seen as a model of its kind.

Steele had substantial previous journalistic experience as editor of the official London *Gazette*, and of course good contacts in government circles – including the patronage of the Lord Treasurer, Robert Harley, thanks to whom he held a sinecure as one of the Commissioners for the Stamp Duties. This may at times have created difficulties, both in the handling of the news sections (where there was overlap with the official *Gazette*), and in the level of criticism of public affairs that he could risk. But whatever the reasons for the sudden termination of the *Tatler*, Steele's imagination had clearly not yet been exhausted. Within a few months he and his collaborator Joseph Addison launched a new daily, the *Spectator*, which, despite its different editorial practices, continued the format and tradition of its predecessor.

Whilst Addison had clearly helped Steele with the *Tatler*, the new serial became a genuinely collaborative effort for the duration of its first series (555 issues, from March 1711 to December 1712). Although a daily, it carried less political news and commentary than its predecessor, and lacked its sectional structure. The continuity, so vital for maintaining reader support, was assured through a tighter thematic organisation sustained through a single extended essay in each issue. The *Spectator* was thus quite distinct from its predecessor, often more soberly reflective; but it too achieved normal print-runs estimated at 3,200–3,400, with a readership that might well have been ten times that number.[2]

If imitation is the sincerest form of flattery, Steele and Addison could be well satisfied. Within months of the launch of the *Tatler*, Benjamin Bragge started a derivative entitled the *Female Tatler*, which also appeared three times a week and openly exploited Steele's distinctive inclusion of material of particular interest to women. After Steele's termination of the *Tatler*, others attempted to continue it, but without lasting success. When the first series of the *Spectator* ended in December 1712, Addison inaugurated a second series on his own which lasted from June to November 1714. Over the next decades the *Tatler* and the *Spectator* were translated into French, Dutch and German, and countless national imitations appeared all over Europe, from Italy to Russia, often under titles which clearly echoed the originals.

The *Spectator*, more so perhaps than its predecessors, firmly established a new genre, quite distinct either from the scholarly journal or the bald official news-sheet. Equally important, however, these experimental papers demonstrated, for all to see, that there was a varied market for both informative and imaginative journalism, and that such journalism need not pose a threat

---

2 R.P. Bond, *The Tatler* (London, 1971), 39; A. Ross, *Selections from the Tatler and the Spectator* (Harmondsworth, 1982), introduction, 53; J. Dwyer, 'Addison and Steele's *Spectator*: towards a reappraisal', *Journal of Newspaper and Periodical History*, 4 (1987–88), 2–11; and M.L. Pallares-Burke, 'The *Spectator* abroad: the fascination of the mask', *History of European Ideas* 22 (1996), 1–18. Estimating total readership for any publication is impossible: some historians have accepted a factor of 10 (an average of 10 readers per copy) for the eighteenth century, based on assumptions regarding individual lending, family reading and coffee-shop availability, but this can only be guesswork. When the *Spectator* in 1711 claimed a readership of 20 for each copy printed, or worried critics feared a readership of 40 per copy of the subversive *Craftsman* in 1732, they remind us that average readership per copy was higher than nowadays, but we are no nearer reliable quantification: see M. Harris, *London Newspapers in the Age of Walpole* (London, 1987), 48.

either to the social establishment or to the government. Where to draw the line between what could acceptably be discussed in print, and what could not, was a matter of running controversy from now on.

The growth of press output and readership

As the Spanish War of Succession and the Great Northern War wound down between 1712 and 1721 – in some instances (notably in Britain, France, Spain and Sweden) accompanied by a settlement of dynastic difficulties or by major change in the form and style of government – some relaxation of wartime restraints was inevitable. Such a relaxation is particularly clear in France, where the death of Louis XIV in 1715 inaugurated what would evidently be a long regency; and in Britain, where the Hanoverian succession in 1714 confirmed a long spell of Whig domination at the expense of Jacobites and Tories. The scale and impact of war during the last years of Louis XIV, however, ensured that these changes were of interest beyond the narrow circles of the political elite. The change of political mood in the years around 1715 may help account for the increasing demand for information and for more open debate reflected both in the book trade and in the press – initially most obvious in London, Hamburg and other thriving and relatively free urban centres, but each fostering wider provincial dissemination through national postal services and other distribution networks like booksellers and hawkers. As we shall see, quantitative and qualitative comparisons are very difficult to make, but there is little doubt that the English and Protestant north German press led the way. Curiously, both the Dutch and the Scots were much slower in developing a press that went beyond the merely derivative. The centralised monarchies seem to have been rather quicker in recognising the potential of the press as a political adjunct well before 1789. We thus find significant and perhaps unexpected developments both in France and, more peripherally, in the Scandinavian kingdoms. In the case of France, despite the maintenance of press controls right up until the Revolution (to which we shall return), the number of new papers launched on to the market increased steadily through the century, with more than 100 new titles appearing in the decade from 1750, and 148 new titles in the decade from 1770. Even though many of these did not survive, we can be in no doubt about the perceived growth potential of the market.[3]

In Britain, the Stamp Act of 1712, creating new levies on all news-sheets and pamphlets, also helped produce the first contemporary estimates of total circulation. Like so much eighteenth-century legislation, the Stamp Act was

---

3 J. Sgard, ed., *Dictionnaire des journaux, 1600–1789* (Oxford/Paris, 1991), vol. 2, 1179–90 and his summary in *Histoire de l'édition française*, vol. 2, ed. R. Chartier and H.-J. Martin (Paris, 1984), 200–5. Although some of the titles counted here were printed outside France, the majority were domestic.

intrinsically ambiguous (notably in its failure actually to define news-sheets and pamphlets) and, at least until the revised legislation of 1743, the levies were relatively easy to circumvent. Many papers had a short life, others mutated under different titles and formats, so all quantification must be tentative. That said, the Stamp Act returns show 12 London-based newspapers in 1712 (ranging from dailies to weeklies), with a total weekly output of around 50,000 copies. By mid-century the number of titles had not increased, but the total number of stamps sold every week had trebled – no doubt in part because of better enforcement. The upward trend continued: by 1783 there were 9 London dailies and around 10 bi- or tri-weeklies, and by 1790 the number of dailies had risen to 14. The first Sunday paper appeared in 1779, even though it was in breach of sabbatarian legislation. The newspaper industry outside London was handicapped by communications, but by mid-century Dublin, Edinburgh and Glasgow offered some choice, whilst provincial weekly papers in many smaller towns built up a durable existence by offering distribution and courier services for a considerable area of hinterland. Total circulation was also up: in 1776, if we are to believe the estimate by Lord North and the Stamp Act returns of that year, more than 12 million copies were issued in Britain per annum, or on average nearly a quarter of a million per week (for a total population including Scotland of not quite 9 million). Supposing that London accounted for around half of the total newspaper market at the time, then in effect one paper was sold there daily for every 24 persons aged 15 or over – a remarkable achievement equalled only in a few independent cities like Hamburg.[4]

This dramatic growth in circulation was far from universally welcomed. Everyone condemned excessive licence, but there was no agreement on how to safeguard limited freedom. Some had hoped that the Stamp Act itself, although intended primarily for fiscal purposes, would dampen demand for news-sheets, as indeed it did for a short period. By the 1720s, even some printers were expressing open resentment against growing competition from cut-price popular papers which successfully exploited the absence of copyright protection by undercutting established titles. It was partly thanks to this that the Stamp Act was tightened in 1725. Coffee-house keepers, too, resented the proliferation of titles because it forced them to take out more

---

4 Such an average of course does not take into account that some readers may have bought more than one paper, but nor does it allow for multiple readership of a single copy. The circulation figures are based on J. Black's summaries, in *The English Press in the Eighteenth Century* (London, 1987), 14 and 105: see also his footnote references to more detailed studies, and the survey in B. Harris, *Politics and the Rise of the Press* (London, 1996), 10–28. On the provincial press, see also R.M. Wiles, 'The relish for reading in provincial England two centuries ago', in *The Widening Circle*, ed. P.J. Korshin (Philadelphia, 1976), 87–115. For Ireland, see R. Munter, *The History of the Irish Newspaper 1685–1760* (Cambridge, 1967). The Scottish press has not been so well served: there is no adequate modern study to fill in the outline provided by works like M.E. Craig, *The Scottish Periodical Press 1750–1789* (Edinburgh, 1931).

subscriptions: in the late 1720s they even tried to set up a protective cartel with its own news system. In the 1730s, and especially at the time of the Stage Licensing Bill of 1737, there were renewed fears that the press might once more be subjected to licensing.

In the absence of any other restraints, both private individuals and the government had recourse to the libel laws, which became a key tool for post-publication control of potentially subversive or dangerous material (above, p. 85). Use of the libel laws was always bound to be rather selective, and, when initiated by ministerial action, occasionally so politically biased as to be self-defeating. But even the threat of prosecution, combined where necessary with harassment (workshop searches, confiscation of stock or of printing equipment, temporary imprisonment during investigations) could be an effective means either of ruining papers that were financially unsteady, or at least of keeping in check printers who, like the Jacobite Nathaniel Mist in 1721, or the outspoken editor of the *Craftsman* in 1729, Francklin, were regarded as a threat to the establishment. A generation later, Wilkes' highly scurrilous *North Briton*, and its particularly violent attack on the crown in issue no. 45 (April 1763), triggered a renewed controversy over press control. The crown's recourse to a general warrant (a warrant without specific names) could now be portrayed by Wilkes and his supporters as a questionable and repressive tactic. The newspaper industry had gained another firm foothold in the volatile politics of later eighteenth-century Britain, and over the next years press criticism of the government at times became extraordinarily vicious, as in the hands of pseudonym journalists like Junius (1769).[5] But the libel laws themselves remained functional, and – bolstered by extensive patronage and ownership interests in the press – ensured that public political debate at times seemed more like a savage war of factionalised and personalised satire than a genuinely 'public' debate fostered by principles of liberty of expression. Accordingly, it is hardly surprising that freedom of the press faced recurrent threats – notably in the 1790s, when British fears of French radicalism led to renewed repression.

Elsewhere in urban Europe, too, newspapers and serials flourished as best they could. One of the most remarkable centres was the city of Hamburg, which, perhaps because of its vigorously defended political autonomy, and certainly because of its impressive economic achievements, had become a leading cultural innovator in the later seventeenth century. By the early

5 For a survey of this debate, see E. Hellmuth, ' "The palladium of all other English liberties": reflections on the liberty of the press in England during the 1760s and 1770s', in *The Transformation of Political Culture: England and Germany in the Late 18th Century*, ed. E. Hellmuth (Oxford, 1990), 467–501; and K. Wilson, *The Sense of the People: Politics, Culture and Imperialism in England, 1715–1785* (Cambridge, 1995), 29–54 and *passim*. On the background, see also G.C. Gibbs, 'Government and the English press, 1695 to the middle of the eighteenth century', in *Too Mighty to be Free: Censorship and the Press in Britain and the Netherlands*, ed. A.C. Duke and C.A. Tamse (Zutphen, 1987), 87–106. There is a vast literature on the Wilkes movement: amongst more recent contributions, see P.D.G. Thomas, *John Wilkes: A Friend of Liberty* (Oxford, 1996).

eighteenth century several literary and printing ventures made a significant impression on a wider northern European reading public. One was *Der Patriot* (*The Patriot*), a periodical produced by the Patriotic Society (founded in 1724) for the promotion not just of *Spectator*-like moral commentary, but also for practical reform within the city itself. Unlike much English journalism, *Der Patriot* preached both loyalty and tolerance as essentials for the preservation of a prosperous and stable community. Although the periodical ceased after a few years, it had established a precedent which was revived a generation later with the new Patriotic Society of 1765, whose published proceedings (its *Verhandlungen und Schriften*) became a model in Protestant Europe for critical yet constructive debate of practical reform. The Society became important in Hamburg not just for its contribution to the actual development of the city's institutions, but also for its deliberate efforts to widen its own membership and foster social cohesiveness. But Hamburg was not alone, and readers in northern Germany arguably had both the widest choice and the best overall quality of journals and papers available anywhere, ranging from literary reviews such as the prestigious *Göttingische Anzeigen von gelehrten Sachen* (*Göttingen Journal of Learned Matters*, founded 1739) and Friedrich Nicolai's famous *Allgemeine deutsche Bibliothek* (*General German Library*, founded 1765), to a growing number of papers with explicitly reformist enlightened aims.[6]

As regards more factually informative newspapers, Hamburg also provided the right kind of environment. In 1721 Hermann Holle had founded a paper which in 1730 moved to the city and became known as the *Zeitung des Hamburgischen unpartheyischen Correspondenten* (usually abbreviated as *The Hamburg Correspondent*). Exploiting the city's extensive maritime communications network, Holle and his successors established regular and reliable news links which made the *Correspondent* one of the most dependable papers in Europe. Although a moderate and factual reporting of international news was (as its full title proclaimed) one of its primary strengths, the paper also contained literary reviews. Initially a bi-weekly with two supplements, each normally of four sides, the paper by 1730 had a circulation of around 1,600 and a solid financial base. Despite occasional difficulties, the paper expanded over the next decades, and by 1800 required 12 concurrently operating presses to meet its staggering circulation of upwards of 30,000 copies – at least three times greater than the most successful London paper. The *Hamburg Correspondent* may have been the most successful of all European papers of its time, but was not alone: a study of the political press in the German lands identifies 92 papers for the period 1745–50 and no less than 151 in the year 1785. By then a variety of German-

6 F. Kopitzsch, *Grundzüge einer Sozialgeschichte der Aufklärung in Hamburg und Altona* (Hamburg, 1982), 269–94. The diffusion of the first *Patriot* is difficult to estimate, but it was sold through agents in many north German cities, and (like the *Tatler* and the *Spectator*) was reprinted repeatedly in book form over the next decades. Hamburg also acted as an important continental contact-point with the London literary market.

language current affairs publications had established a firm international reputation, including von Schirach's monthly *Politische Journal* (*Political Journal*, started in Altona in 1781) and August Ludwig von Schlözer's prestigious but more discursive quarterly *Staats-Anzeigen* (*State News*, which by the late 1780s had a circulation of over 7,000). Aggregate newspaper print-runs in northern Germany by then suggest that upwards of half the adult male population may have had regular access to a paper, as readers or listeners if not necessarily as actual subscribers. In the context of Europe as a whole, the German press built on remarkably solid traditions: Hamburg had opened its first coffee-house in 1677, and the easy availability and socialising importance of newspapers in such locations had been remarked upon already a few years later. By at least the 1720s, journals and papers were also routinely incorporated into the school and university curriculum. Clearly the serial and newspaper industry in northern Germany had two great assets: a discerning public, and a level of political decentralisation which made attempts at regulation difficult to implement and easy to evade.[7]

In the light of the Hamburg experience, and the steady growth elsewhere in northern Europe, one might have expected the Dutch news and periodical press to have achieved great success during the eighteenth century. Why this did not quite happen is still a matter of debate, but several factors may have played a part. In the later seventeenth century Dutch printers had prospered by serving those sectors of the European book market hampered by domestic censorship and other restraints; a century later the European market had become freer and more competitive, with enterprising firms in the Rhineland and the Swiss cantons catering for much of the French and German market. Dutch intellectual life itself also appeared less vibrant, relatively speaking, than a century before: arguably its most distinguished institution, the University of Leiden, had become a backwater compared with reforming universities like Göttingen, Halle, Edinburgh and Glasgow. The Dutch press remained substantial and diversified by the standards of most of Europe, but its contribution was arguably less distinctive than in the past. It is also worth emphasising that, despite the lack of central controls in the United Provinces, local restrictions on the newspaper industry, especially at times of political

---

7 M. Welke, 'Gemeinsame Lektüre und frühe Formen von Gruppenbildungen im 17. und 18. Jahrhundert: Zeitungslesen in Deutschland', in *Lesegesellschaften und bürgerliche Emanzipation*, ed. O. Dann (Munich, 1981), 29–53; M. Welke, 'Die Legende vom "unpolitischen Deutschen": Zeitungslesen im 18. Jhrh. als Spiegel des politischen Interesses', *Jahrbuch der Wittheit zu Bremen* 25 (1981), 161–88; B. Tolkemitt, *Der Hamburgische Correspondent: zur öffentlichen Verbreitung der Aufklärung in Deutschland* (Tübingen, 1995); J. Whaley, 'The Protestant enlightenment in Germany', in *The Enlightenment in National Context*, ed. R. Porter and M. Teich (Cambridge, 1981), 106–17; J. Whaley, 'New light on the circulation of early newspapers: the case of the "Hamburgischer Correspondent" in 1730', *Bulletin of the Institute of Historical Research* 52 (1979), 178–87; J.D. Popkin, 'Political communication in the German enlightenment: Gottlob Benedikt von Schirach's *Politische Journal*', *Eighteenth-Century Life* 20 (1996), 24–41.

crises in the 1740s and again in the 1780s, could be enforced quite severely.[8]

In Scandinavia, not surprisingly, Copenhagen and Stockholm were the two totally dominant printing centres. The early eighteenth century brought durable new papers there, notably *Kiöbenhavns Post-Rytter* (*Copenhagen's Postal Courier*, originally launched in both a Danish-language and a German format in 1698, still published in the 1790s), the Danish *Berlingske Politiske og Avertissementstidende* (*Berling Political and Advertising News*, founded 1749 under a variant title, still published today), *Stockholms Gazette* of the 1740s, and other general-purpose news and advertising papers. Literary journals also proliferated – in Denmark notably the influential literary weekly *Lærde Efterretning* (*Copenhagen Learned Review*, 1720–1810); and in Sweden the substantial Stockholm *Lärda Tidningar* (*Learned News*), produced from 1745 by the printer Lars Salvius, in rivalry with its more volatile competitor from 1755, Gjörwell's *Den swenska Mercurius* (*The Swedish Mercury*). The ending of pre-publication censorship in Sweden in 1766 temporarily encouraged free discussion of social and political issues in the press, and facilitated the launch of some new titles. None of the Scandinavian papers, however, was particularly innovative, and their print-runs rarely exceeded 1,000 copies until late in the century. Even the new and controversial Danish liberal paper *Minerva*, launched in 1784, reveals in its published list of subscribers an initial circulation of just 496 copies, which increased only very slowly over the next few years. Nevertheless, the proliferation of durable titles is a clear indication that Scandinavia had a modest but growing market for topical debate and for reliable reviews of new (especially French and German) publications. What quantitative evidence we have regarding distribution points in the same direction, and a recent assessment suggests that by 1800 the Danish press may have been read by as many as 10% of the adult population.[9]

8 Some contrasting views of the Dutch press can be found in *The Dutch Republic in the Eighteenth Century: Decline, Enlightenment and Revolution*, ed. M.C. Jacob and W.W. Mijnhardt (Ithaca, 1992); G.-J. Johannes, 'A small-scale culture: Dutch eighteenth-century periodicals and the paradoxes of decline', *Eighteenth-Century Studies* 31 (1997), 122–9; and more controversially, in S. Schama, 'The enlightenment in the Netherlands', in *The Enlightenment in National Context* (Cambridge, 1981), 54–71, and in his earlier *Patriots and Liberators: Revolution in the Netherlands 1780–1813* (London, 1977), 68–74 and 79f. For a case study, see W.R.E. Velema, *Enlightenment and Conservatism in the Dutch Republic: The Political Thought of Elie Luzac* (Assen/Maastricht, 1993). On the uneven nature of censorship controls in the United Provinces, see A.H. Huussen, 'Freedom of the press and censorship in the Netherlands 1780–1810', in *Too Mighty to be Free: Censorship and the Press in Britain and the Netherlands*, ed. A.C. Duke and C.A. Tamse (Zutphen, 1987), 107–26.
9 T. Kjærgaard, 'The rise of the press and public opinion in 18th-century Denmark-Norway', *Scandinavian Journal of History* 14 (1989), 215–30, and especially 223. His estimates are based partly on post office distribution lists, and on the assumption that every copy would be read by an average of 10 readers. See also T. Munck, 'Absolute monarchy in later eighteenth-century Denmark: centralized reform, public expectations and the Copenhagen press', *Historical Journal* 41 (1998), 201–24; and M. Nyman, *Press mot Friheten* (Uppsala, 1988), 75–81.

The French-language press before the Revolution

One of the exceptions to the apparent lack of resourcefulness in the Dutch press was the bi-weekly *Gazette de Leyde*. Founded around 1677 by French Huguenot refugees settling in Leiden, it was from 1738 until the French invasion of 1795 in the hands of the Luzac family of printers, and rose to become the most distinguished of several French-language *Gazettes* published in the Netherlands. It is important in the present context for several reasons. Firstly, whilst the *Gazette* established itself as a reliable source of information on the proceedings of both the British Houses of Parliament and the French Parlement of Paris (at a time when neither allowed free reporting of their debates at home), it did not provide its readers with a comparable summary of Dutch politics – confirming that even in the United Provinces domestic news was still in the later eighteenth century regarded as more dangerous than foreign material. Secondly, again from a local Leiden perspective, the *Gazette* reminds us that French was very much the international language of culture and enlightenment in eighteenth-century Europe, and that a Dutch printing firm might have a better chance of financial success by denying local and popular cultural traditions, and by ignoring Dutch ambivalence towards French cultural imperialism.

But there is another dimension to the history of the *Gazettes* which clearly illustrates the complexity of studying the impact of the press within *ancien régime* France itself. There was a long tradition within the kingdom of substantial restrictions on what could be printed and published in serial, newspaper, pamphlet or book form, and all printed output – papers and pamphlets as well as books – was supposed right up until 1789 to be cleared by the censors before it was released to the public (see p. 86). In the case of books, we have already noted that some of the best work of the French enlightenment was printed outside the borders of France, or at least with an imprint purporting to suggest that it was printed abroad. Publishing and distributing one-off pieces illegally became big business in France; but a serial, which necessarily required a business address, a firmer schedule and a reliable distribution mechanism, was much riskier. Yet submitting to the unpredictable schedule of the official censors did not make for steady business either. One solution was that of publishing from an autonomous enclave, as did the *Courrier d'Avignon* (*Avignon Courier*) from 1730.[10] Rather safer was to publish from across the border: remarkably, those who did might even manage to use the French royal mail to distribute their paper openly within the kingdom, provided certain niceties were observed.

10 Avignon, as a papal enclave, was exempt from domestic French censorship regulations. Although dependent on the good will of the French monarchy, and hence cautious in all matters of policy that might cause friction, it was well placed to exploit the French-language market in Provence and the Dauphiné. On this basis the *Courrier d'Avignon* attained quite a high circulation of over 3,000 in the 1770s, and could keep its subscription price within France (18 livres per annum by post), around half that commonly charged for the Dutch *Gazettes*.

The *Gazette de Leyde* made the most of these apparent contradictions. The Jansenist crisis in France in the 1750s led the *Gazette* to provide detailed coverage of constitutional confrontations between the crown and the Parlement of Paris. From then on, no doubt in part because of demand from the strong Huguenot emigrant community in the Netherlands, the paper built up a reputation for systematic, accurate and impartial reports on domestic French news – far more convincing than anything the official *Gazette de France* could offer. This reputation was consolidated by Jean Luzac, chief editor from 1772, a multilinguist and historian, professor at Leiden University, and committed supporter of the American colonists. Significantly, however, the reports carried in the *Gazette de Leyde* were, especially after the change of government in France in 1774, based to a large extent on material compiled in Paris itself, by various well-placed individuals. Amongst these was Pascal Boyer, enjoying the direct protection of none less than the French foreign minister from 1774 to 1787, the comte de Vergennes. Although (as we shall see shortly) such semi-official 'leaks' inevitably dried up from time to time, the silence never lasted for long. The political life of France was no longer regarded as just the crown's private affair, and the many ministerial and *parlementaire* confrontations of the 1770s and 1780s ensured that participants openly used whatever channels were available for communicating their points of view, even if doing so was technically illegal. The crown, unable (and probably unwilling) to risk more draconian restrictions against the foreign French-language press, preferred accurate leaks to misinformation: a full ban would merely have resulted in the papers being imported illegally, and would have removed any incentive for publishers to keep on the right side of the government. Besides, there were enough realists in the French government to appreciate that some appearance of freedom of debate could be politically beneficial, if only to shift responsibility away from the narrow inner circle of government.

Like so much else in eighteenth-century France, then, the large grey area between formal press restrictions and practical reality – the jungle of tacit connivance and informal understandings, pragmatism and personal contact – in many ways made the whole system more, rather than less, stable. Aspiring journalists inside France may have found it frustrating to read the most detailed domestic news in foreign papers, yet the French crown, just like its British counterpart earlier in the century, had difficulty contemplating positive emancipatory legislation. In a pluralistic society which feared disorder and instability, ambiguity was a virtue, and absolutism a convenient formal construct.

For the historian of pre-revolutionary France, however, the consequences are real enough. For a start, no assessment of public opinion or growing political awareness before 1789 can rely simply, or even primarily, on domestic French publications. Individual foreign papers like the *Gazette de Leyde*, with a circulation within France probably fluctuating between 1,500 and 2,500 in the later 1770s and 1780s, might not appear a major threat against the estimated 7–12,000 copies distributed by the official *Gazette de France* at the same time. But the cumulative effect of a number of foreign papers giving alternative (and more detailed and credible) versions of events to that carried by the official French press was bound, especially in the uncertain political climate of the later 1780s, to raise deeper political questions. That the foreign papers were deemed dangerous is demonstrated by recurrent attacks on them by ministers and government officials.[11]

At the same time, the non-official domestic French press itself was far from dormant. Because many papers were published either clandestinely or through informal understandings with the censors, quantification is again difficult. From the scattered information we have, it seems that print-runs for individual titles often remained fairly low, mostly ranging, as in England, from a few hundred to a few thousand. But Jack Censer has recently argued, on the basis of a systematic study of those general serials after 1745 that were sufficiently successful to survive for three or more years, that the total number of titles available in France (including cross-border ones) increased no less than fivefold, to more than 80, over the period 1745–85. The domestic contribution to this increase was naturally strongest amongst the advertisers, the *affiches*, but the internal French contribution to the growth in literary–philosophical serials was also very strong. Only amongst those papers that can best be classified as primarily political in content did the French market continue to be dominated by foreign imports – partly, no doubt, because this sector was more vigilantly controlled, but partly also because the official news monopoly came in the 1770s and 1780s to be dominated by the press entrepreneur Charles-Joseph Panckoucke, who went to great lengths to protect his privileged position against rivals.[12]

---

11 By the 1785 the total circulation of the *Gazette de Leyde* (including those taken in France) is estimated at 4,200 or more, and it was deemed influential enough to be targeted by Brienne and Lamoignon in 1788, and by d'Eprémesnil in the Estates General on 24 June 1789. See C. Joynes, 'The *Gazette de Leyde*: the opposition press and French politics, 1750–1757'; and J.D. Popkin, 'The *Gazette de Leyde* and French politics under Louis XVI', both in *Press and Politics in Pre-Revolutionary France*, ed. J.R. Censer and J.D. Popkin (Berkeley, 1987), 133–69 and 75–132 respectively. The other Dutch-based *Gazettes*, especially that from Amsterdam, also had significant sales in France.

12 Jack R. Censer, *The French Press in the Age of Enlightenment* (London, 1994), 6–12 and *passim*. Panckoucke was not interested in probing for loopholes in the French control system. On the contrary, he built up a system of contacts and 'friends' within government circles. He responded readily to ministerial pressure, for example in 1776, when he agreed to sack Linguet, the gifted editor of his *Journal politique* (founded 1774, also known as the *Journal de Bruxelles* even though it was in fact Paris-based). In 1778 he acquired control of the old literary weekly *Mercure de France* (founded 1672), and in 1787 even added the *Gazette de France*. Panckoucke became the most powerful press baron in the 1780s through a combination of factors: shrewd editorial appointments (like La Harpe on the *Journal politique*, and Mallet Du Pan on the *Mercure*), systematic buy-outs of competitors, and exploitation of his official contacts to enforce his rights against rivals. Getting control of papers that held a *privilège* entitled you to compensatory payments from rival papers that were deemed to be encroaching on the market defined by your *privilège*, so this strategy lent itself very well both to making money and eliminating competition. See also S. Tucoo-Chala, *Charles-Joseph Panckoucke et la librairie française 1736–1798* (Paris, 1977); and R. Darnton, *The Business of Enlightenment* (Cambridge, Mass., 1979), 66–75 and *passim*.

Recent work indicates that the development of the domestic press in France was as unsteady as the overall political environment itself seemed to be. Rather than looking for a uniform pre-revolutionary trend, historians are recognising that each distinctive period (often ministry) has to be seen in its own terms, with journalists sometimes enjoying comparative freedom, sometimes having to retrench again under renewed regulation. Such a tightening of control had been experienced already in the lead-up to war in 1740, but we noted earlier how the *Gazette de Leyde* exploited the Jansenist crisis in the early 1750s to expand its French news. In fact both the domestic and the foreign press benefited from the generally benign attitude of Malesherbes, the director of censorship from 1750 to 1763, and from the liberal views of the powerful foreign minister of France from 1759 to 1770, Choiseul. The last years of Louis XV, however, were marked by the major political confrontations of the Maupeou crisis (1771–74), aggravated by serious economic instability. The crisis centred on the fundamental historical and political role of the crown and the sovereign law courts (*parlements*): effective use of the press, especially by the Parlement of Paris, triggered renewed efforts by the crown to stifle debate in print. From then on, ambivalence and uncertainty were key characteristics of crown policies. The succession of Louis XVI brought a mood of reconciliation and optimism ushered in with the ministerial appointment of the physiocrat Turgot (1774–76) and his old friend Malesherbes. Another change of ministry produced a clamp-down in the later 1770s, but the American war encouraged Vergennes (foreign minister from the start of the reign until his death in 1787) gradually to give 'reliable' agents of the press, like Panckoucke, more scope. However, debates concerning the rights and constitutional principles of the American conflict had an obvious bearing on French absolutism as well, and this helps explain why press policies in the 1780s seem so unsteady.

The changing use to which the complex regulatory system was put is reflected in the chequered history of individual publications. Some journalists managed to steer an independent course whilst staying within the system – such as the conservative editor of the *Année littéraire* (*Literary Yearbook*), Fréron, who in 1754 secured a *permission tacite* (see p. 87), and who suffered only a few brief detentions in prison during the two decades he kept his review very much in the public eye. But many others were less adept, as the remarkably rapid turn-over in current titles during this period clearly reveals. The unpredictability of the regulatory system may itself help explain why a daily paper took so long to appear: the *Journal de Paris*, launched in 1777, was the first such, and under Garat's editorship remarkably managed to survive well into the Revolution.

In many respects, the 1770s can probably be regarded as a watershed in the development of new styles of communication in France between journalists/authors and the reading public. Many examples of this process have now been identified, ranging from the *Journal historique* edited by

Pidansat de Mairobert from 1771 to 1776, to the *Journal des dames* re-launched by Louis-Sébastien Mercier in connection with a literary–political 'fronde' in 1775. Common to many of them was a new realism in language and content (even when discussing politics), expert use of structured argument to emphasise particular points of view subtly, combined with an obvious ideological partiality far removed from the studied neutrality of the *Gazettes*.[13]

· Most famous amongst the innovative papers, perhaps, is Linguet's outspoken *Annales politiques, civiles et littéraires* (*Political, Civil and Literary Annals*) from 1777, which briefly reached sales which contemporaries estimated at 20,000 in 1780 (including pirated editions). Although this paper was launched from London, Linguet allowed its sporadic issues to be vetted by the censors in order to ensure their unhindered circulation in France, and he later even moved his press to Brussels. Linguet's *Annales* was volatile and provocative. In 1784, in connection with the controversial parliamentary election in England, he noted that:

> it seems to me that there is something noble and consoling for the *English* in being able to claim, at least every seven years, a right which all the rest of the human race has lost: [the right] to designate for the sovereign magistrate assistants who must guide him in the name of the *People*; [the right] to provide moderators to power, create mouths which will not only carry the vow, the desires of the nation, to the foot of the throne, but if necessary, will force the prince to listen to them, to comply with it.[14]

Despite his idiosyncratic belligerence (sometimes verging on paranoia), Linguet seems to have been valued by the French government itself as a potent antidote to more fashionably liberal papers, and as an admittedly unpredictable spokesman for authoritarian reform. Indeed Linguet often attacked the *philosophes*, and deliberately cast himself as a kind of journalists' Rousseau, an image no doubt enhanced by his imprisonment in the Bastille (1780–82). Remarkably, his paper survived until 1792, and in its

---

13 J. Popkin, 'The prerevolutionary origins of political journalism', in *The Political Culture of the Old Régime*, ed. K.M. Baker (vol. 1 of *The French Revolution and the Creation of Modern Political Culture*, Oxford, 1987), 203–23; Popkin's more specific study of Le Maitre and other Jansenist/*parlementaire* publishers, in 'Pamphlet journalism at the end of the old régime', *Eighteenth-Century Studies* 22 (1988–89), 351–67; N.R. Gelbart, ' "Frondeur" journalism in the 1770s', *Eighteenth-Century Studies* 17 (1983–84), 493–514, and the same author's *Feminine and Opposition Journalism in Old Régime France: 'Le Journal de Dames'* (Berkeley, 1987). It is worth stressing that Mairobert's *Journal historique* may initially have appeared in book rather than periodical form, since there appear to be no references to it before the 1774 'reprint', when Mairobert was himself appointed royal censor by the new government. Both he and Mercier, however, were in trouble by 1779, Mairobert committing suicide and Mercier having to flee abroad – no doubt colouring the latter's rosy view of freedom of expression in London, as expressed in his *Parallèle de Paris et de Londres* (unpublished until the edition by C. Bruneteau and B. Cottret, Paris, 1982).

14 Cited in translation in D.G. Levy, *The Ideas and Careers of Simon-Nicolas-Henri Linguet: A Study in Eighteenth-Century French Politics* (Urbana, 1980), 208.

determined iconoclasm and fierce independence can be regarded as a clear precursor of the revolutionary press.

The journalists of pre-revolutionary France were important in testing, at times almost to destruction, the viability of the regulatory machinery itself. But they did much more than that. Unlike the British press, they largely abstained from direct assaults on the monarch and his ministers. Yet in probing the whole spectrum of politics in France in the 1770s and especially the late 1780s, they encouraged a diversification of viewpoints fundamentally at odds with the myth of unanimity on which French absolutism was built. In addition, the more radical press not only revealed how changeable and unpredictable crown policy really was, but also gave prominence to an innovative vocabulary which included potentially volatile terms like 'patriot', 'nation', 'rights', 'citizen' and 'the people' (see p. 197). Even the *Gazette de France* could no longer restrict its domestic reporting to a summary of the king's engagement calendar. In short, the explosion in print that occurred with the collapse of censorship in France in 1788–89 did not come out of the blue: many journalistic techniques were already well practised, and the public appetite whetted on a whole range of political, cultural and social issues.

The press, enlightenment and change

Clearly, the press made a distinctive contribution to the eighteenth century not just quantitatively but also qualitatively. Its growing diversity and its resilience against attempted restrictions were nourished by rapidly growing public interest in a wide range of topical issues ranging from philosophy and ethics to gossip and politics. But how far was this potential realised? As in the case of books, identifying entertainment value is not a substitute for trying to demonstrate practical impact on habits, prejudices and ways of thinking. There are several ways of clarifying how significant the press really was, and where its impact might be most noticeable. Historians have commonly adopted two particular approaches: examining the detailed contents of the press itself (just as they might study the contents of other printed texts) as evidence of the diffusion of new patterns of thought and communication; and collating external but usually anecdotal contemporary evidence about the observable impact of the press at specific (usually critical) junctures. Neither approach is fully satisfactory, but both can lead to interesting conclusions.

Content analysis itself is not easy: the often chaotic editorial practices of the day, multiplied across the many serial and daily publications that came and went during the eighteenth century, makes sampling very difficult. In the unfettered British market, in particular, many papers had to change their approach in order to survive. Serious material was diluted with news and entertainment, gossip, advertisements and bought insertions. Some papers turned more to practical information relating to trade, prices, markets, overseas developments and shipping matters, for which demand increased with the expansion of the British colonial empire after 1740.[15] As communications improved, regular daily papers containing a miscellaneous range of news, commentary and advertisements became increasingly viable. The *Daily Advertiser* had started in 1731 with nothing but advertisements: although it soon added news and other information to attract other types of readers, it was one of several papers demonstrating not just that advertisements and personal inserts were crucial for financial viability, but that this type of ephemeral material could become an end in itself, a fashionable form of communication amongst readers. The enthusiasm for this kind of novelty spread rapidly to the provinces: by the end of the century, the total fiscal revenue from newspaper advertisements was as great outside as within the London area.

Some papers did, however, acquire more specific editorial profiles relevant in the present context. The British press again provides some obvious examples of specialisation, aided by the overall increase in readership and by the relative absence of severe restraints.[16] For the reader with literary interests, the *Gentleman's Magazine* or the *Scots Magazine* popularised a well-meaning and sober genre of review. Those with a more irreverent streak might go for the *London Evening Post*, which mediated its sharp political views by means of colourful and scurrilous verse, often playing on some of its readers' worst instincts for scandal and intolerance. A harder hitting opposition paper like the London *Craftsman* (started in 1726 as a bi-weekly, later just weekly), combining short lively political essays with other types of material designed to increase topical awareness, relied on the skills of provocative contributors like the Tory opposition leader Lord Bolingbroke to achieve print-runs that sometimes exceeded 10,000 copies. In the face of such pressure, successive administrations – most famously Walpole's – were sufficiently alarmed to go to the trouble of subsidising rival papers, as well as attempting substantial buy-offs and bribes to tone down independent papers when public opinion seemed in danger of becoming too hostile. In theory such diversification, supported by the income from sales as well as from advertisements and personal columns, could have paved the way for a healthy independent press. But in practice the tone of especially the London press from the 1770s had a tendency to lapse into superficialities, scandal and ferocious attacks on what we would now call corruption or sleaze. The general elections of 1784 and 1788 demonstrated the extent to which money

15 See the discussion by K. Wilson, 'Empire of virtue: the imperial project and Hanoverian culture c. 1720–1785', in *An Imperial State at War*, ed. L. Stone (London, 1994), 128–64.
16 For a brief overview of emerging typologies, see notably G.A. Cranfield, *The Press and Society from Caxton to Northcliffe* (London, 1978), chs. 1–3. A slightly different approach, applied to France, is adopted by Jack R. Censer, *The French Press in the Age of Enlightenment* (London, 1994), 7 and 15–118.

could be used to manipulate the press for personal ends, often at the expense of constructive or responsible political debate. It is not easy to establish how far this tendency was the product of market demand, or whether it was a natural reflection of a society where the better-off were, by European standards, relaxed and self-confident. Distinguished journalism was not lacking; but perhaps Britain had less need for high-minded idealism and penetrating debate than those continental states whose political and social structure might appear less adaptable.

On the continent, the varied demand for political, cultural, commercial, agricultural, entertaining and other material was also met, but not in quite the same way. As we have already noted, the French press, somewhat more so than the British, worked under fluctuating pressures that directly affected its contents. Provided allowance is made for such political constraints, however, genuine comparative content analysis across frontiers is potentially very fruitful. A few years ago a group of scholars in America attempted a comparison of the British and French press, based on a sample of papers from the decade 1755–64. That the French press was less dynamic in terms of the reporting of contemporary political debate is hardly surprising. But it was, significantly, also more socially exclusive – apparently mostly edited by and for the elite, and thus either constrained by, or reinforcing, the relatively slower spread of literacy down the social spectrum which we noted earlier (see p. 49). Coffee-house subscriptions to leading newspapers appear to have been less common than in England, and may not have become widespread until the revolutionary period. Commercial and personal advertising was slower in developing, too, and even the property sections tended to concentrate on the needs of the elite. Coverage of commerce and manufacturing increased less rapidly than in the British press, and discussion of social issues like poverty and criminality tended to be even more patronising or superficial. By contrast, the French press was strong on literary, artistic and philosophical matters: appropriately, it tended to address these matters in a tone fit for the salon rather than for the coffee-house. Even obituaries, both in coverage and tone, seem to reflect the exclusiveness of the mid-century French press.[17]

Much more work of this kind is needed before firm conclusions can be drawn. For a start, it is likely that samples from the 1770s or the 1780s might have produced significantly different results. More fundamentally, as recent work in France has suggested, the technical obstacles to systematic and reliable content analysis are very great even within one language and culture, let alone across two or more. Nevertheless, such an approach may help to identify differences in the markets for which individual or groups of papers

17 S. Botein, J.R. Censer and H. Ritvo, 'La presse périodique et la société anglaise et française au xviiie siècle: une approche comparative', *Revue d'Histoire Moderne et Contemporaine*, 32 (1985), 209–36. For a somewhat different perspective on the provincial *affiches*, see C. Jones, 'The great chain of buying: medical advertisement, the bourgeois public sphere and the origins of the French Revolution', *American Historical Review* 101 (1996), 13–40.

were intended, and hence their likely impact across different parts of the social spectrum. In this instance it seems that the British press around mid-century was more broadly based than the French, although perhaps at the expense of subtlety; it is also possible that the British press accurately reflected the more pragmatic, but less introspective and analytical, nature of public debate compared with that in France.

In addition to overall content analysis of the press, we also need to consider observable political impact. From hindsight, we might argue that the eighteenth-century press could have been significant in several ways: (i) by influencing those in positions of authority; (ii) by influencing public opinion to exert various kinds of pressure on those in positions of authority; or (iii) by allowing those in power themselves to influence public opinion. All three variants are plausible, and, given the nature of eighteenth-century society and government, probably overlapping. But to those familiar with early modern source material or contemporary fictional literature it will come as no surprise that contemporary references to, or comments on, such causal relations are rare and often too vague to be helpful.

In any discussion of the impact of the press, we need to be careful to distinguish between, on the one hand, a natural interest in information regarding domestic political developments, and on the other, any potential for turning such information to practical interactive use. The case of parliamentary reporting in Britain is a clear illustration of this distinction. Strong reader demand for parliamentary news provided newspapers with a recurrent incentive to circumvent the well-entrenched ban on all parliamentary coverage. The *Gentleman's Magazine*, for one, tried publishing summaries during the summer recess, and, when the Commons in 1738 renewed the ban, even resorted to the tactic of reporting the proceedings of the Parliament of Lilliput. By the 1760s editors found it financially worthwhile simply to break the law – formal prosecution or harassment in any case tended to enhance the circulation and reputation of a paper. The situation was not clarified until 1771, when an attempt to reaffirm the ban against a group of publishers, whilst technically successful, was perceived as unreasonable and in effect nullified by the concerted defiance of the publishers themselves and the City of London authorities. In a way, market demand had made the ban unenforceable. Yet important as this development undoubtedly was in securing public access to information on parliamentary business, there was nevertheless still a long way to go. The unsystematic and quite unreliable summaries that were published may have made some observers more politically conscious, and more aware of the need for parliamentary reform. But such awareness in itself brought actual reform or political change no closer.[18]

18 On parliamentary reporting, and on the broader issues of the reliability of evidence on central politics, see D. Wahrman, 'Virtual representation: parliamentary reporting and languages of class in the 1790s', *Past and Present* 136 (1992), 83–113. For a clear overview of the 1771 debacle, see P.D.G. Thomas, *John Wilkes* (Oxford, 1996), 125–40.

It seems unlikely at first sight that the press could somehow directly influence those in positions of authority. After all, the *ancien régime* was an inherently closed system, with little or no sense of accountability outside the exclusive circles of power. The existence of parliamentary structures, as in Britain and Sweden, may have made these circles of power slightly more porous, but hardly made politics more transparent. Yet, if power remained a very exclusive prerogative, government nevertheless was no longer conducted in anything remotely resembling a vacuum. One of the reasons why Linguet was allowed to continue his *Annales politiques* so relatively freely was that Louis XVI was one of his avid readers. Similarly, of the 496 initial subscriptions to the Danish reformist journal *Minerva* listed in 1785, no less than 41 came from members of the royal family and their household. Some papers were clearly as well embedded as books in the fabric of high politics – read by those who ruled, and contributing to the informed practicality gradually and visibly spreading through the administrative corridors of later eighteenth-century Europe. The Maupeou crisis in France in the years 1771–74, the growing controversy in Britain in the later 1770s over the relationship with the North American colonies, or on a lesser scale the palace coup in Copenhagen in 1772 which toppled Struensee's administration – such confrontations, and many others, would have been unthinkable without the growing power and influence of the public press.

Could newspapers contribute to popular disturbances and other forms of direct pressure on government? For some time, historians have accepted that this happened in England in the Excise crisis of 1733, and again in connection with the difficulties experienced by Walpole before his fall in 1742, with the so-called Jew Bill of 1753, and, not least, with the 'Wilkes and Liberty' riots of the 1760s. It may be difficult to demonstrate that any of these campaigns alone produced changes of policy, but few would question that in each instance governmental room for manoeuvre was significantly curtailed as a result.[19] In the United Provinces, the domestic political crises of the 1780s revitalised domestic debate, allowing militant newspapers like the Utrecht *Post van Neder Rijn (Post from the Lower Rhine)* to become a crucial force in the emergent Patriot movement. In the case of France, the direct impact of the press on popular disturbances before the Revolution is less tangible: the Flour War of 1775, as its name implies, was triggered more by economic hardship than by press fall-out from the aftermath of the Maupeou crisis, and there is not much evidence that rioters were influenced by any press discussion of Turgot's new physiocratic policies. Generally speaking, because of the continued exercise of pre-censorship controls, the press could not really be an effective agitational tool in France before 1788. Other printing strategies, however, were already demonstrating what could

19 These issues are discussed notably by R. Harris, *A Patriot Press: National Politics and the London Press in the 1740s* (Oxford, 1993), 33–9 and *passim*; and B. Harris, *Politics and the Rise of the Press* (London, 1996), 37–52.

be done: Necker's unprecedented publication in 1781 of his *Compte rendu* (*Summary of State Income and Expenditure*), and the equally extraordinary public call to arms of Calonne's *Avertissement* of 1 April 1787, were both part of a struggle for political legitimacy which was no longer fought merely in the king's privy council, and which indeed assumed that political events could be directly influenced by the public.

There is not a large step from politicians using print as part of a defensive strategy to avert trouble, to governments exploiting the press pro-actively to influence public opinion. The substantial sums of money used by Walpole to subsidise papers and buy press support would suggest that he, at any rate, not only thought he could influence public opinion in this way, but deemed it worthwhile. Regarding the latter, naturally, many disagreed, and the drying-up of subsidies after the fall of Walpole suggests not just a reaction but also a different evaluation of the whole process. After 1763, however, press patronage became firmly established on the British political scene. In France, the Maupeou crisis can again be seen as a turning point, with the government hiring the services of writers as prominent as Voltaire in order to win public support for institutional reform, though mostly through pamphlets rather than existing papers.[20] By the 1780s, successful management of the press for political ends was an art which clearly not all governments had learnt – but it was increasingly becoming a necessary adjunct to contemporary politics.

To assess its impact, we would ideally need to know who exactly the 'public' of the pre-1789 press really was. Unfortunately, historians are unlikely ever to be able to answer this fundamental question at all satisfactorily. We have already noted that circulation figures in different parts of north-western Europe demonstrate a rapidly growing market. In the area of heaviest market penetration, London, the historian may be justified in talking in terms of a mass readership – where the sight (if not possession) of a paper would be commonplace for anyone who frequented a coffee-shop or was in daily contact with the bustle of urban life. Clearly, however, this was not the case everywhere. The scattered data we have on postal distribution, together with the few surviving subscription lists and advertisements for particular titles, suggest that in much of Europe (and particularly outside major towns) the majority of purchasers were the well-off – typically members of the political and social elite (including nobles, officeholders, clergy, lawyers and some other profession-als).[21] As we have seen, the impact of the press on these groups, whether

20 P. Hudson, 'In defense of reform: French government propaganda during the Maupeou crisis', *French Historical Studies* 8 (1973), 51–76; D. Echeverria, *The Maupeou Revolution: A Study in the History of Libertarianism, France 1770–1774* (Baton Rouge, 1985). The *parlements* had a long tradition of independence from the crown, going back before the reign of Louis XIV, but for a recent view of the period of Louis XV see J. Swann, 'Power and provincial politics in eighteenth-century France: the Varenne affair, 1757–1763', *French Historical Studies* 21 (1998), 441–74.

21 For an attempt to use such evidence systematically, see for example Jack R. Censer, *The French Press in the Age of Enlightenment* (London, 1994), 184–205. Other types of evidence seem to point in the same direction: even inventory data, which often demonstrate a spread of book-ownership down the social spectrum, fail to indicate similar trends for periodicals.

confirming their prejudices or goading them into re-evaluations and sometimes action, is beyond reasonable doubt. But what impact the press may have had beyond this elite before 1789 is much more difficult to document – not least because there was no scope in most of Europe for any mass participation in politics except in periods of crisis.

Revolutionary media

The collapse of the old order in France precipitated a period of political uncertainty which proved a significant turning point in the history of the newspaper. We have already noted that there was much experimentation and development within the domestic French press during the later years of the *ancien régime*. But it was the drastically shifting political ground of the Revolution that gave the press a key role in the rapid dissemination of news within the capital, and as the only effective tool for nationwide mobilisation. In an age without any other reliable means of mass communication, the press was vital for the propagation of a new political culture. As the Revolution became more radical, so new means of expression were adopted in the name of hitherto disenfranchised groups in the population – the formerly 'passive' citizen, the manual worker, the political novice, the army volunteer, the formerly domestic woman – presented in a language appropriate for those with little formal education. In claiming to speak for 'the people', papers like *L'ami du peuple* (*The Friend of the People*) and the several versions of *Le père Duchesne* (*Old Man Duchesne*) even tried to make Rousseau's vision of direct democracy appear plausible. Other journalists took up diametrically opposed positions, including (at least until August 1792) an outspoken and often sophisticated defence of the old monarchy, notably in the pages of *L'Ami du roi* (*The Friend of the King*) and of the brilliantly satirical *Les actes des apôtres* (*Acts of the Apostles*). Neither extreme was well integrated into the process of political change, and both were prone to personalised satire and venomously irresponsible rhetoric. But as successive municipal and central authorities failed to moderate or integrate the divergent social groups on which such papers fed, the extreme press on both sides magnified that corrosive factionalism which in the end irretrievably undermined all hope of coherent and stable reform.

The gradual collapse of censorship and copyright restrictions in the printing industry ensured an explosion of newspapers as soon as the Estates General met in May 1789. Some of the earliest unauthorised papers, like those of Brissot and Mirabeau, faced real government reprisals, but by July nationwide regulation had failed. The Paris municipal authorities continued to try to exercise control on their own, notably forcing the violently radical journalist Marat into hiding in October 1789, and continuing to use libel prosecutions and other threats the following year. But these measures were difficult to implement and anything but effective: by the end of 1789 at least 140 new titles had appeared in Paris alone, and in 1790 perhaps twice as many. Not all of these survived, but new ventures were launched whenever circumstances appeared favourable. As a result, the Parisian, who in January 1789 had had to rely on just one daily paper (the *Journal de Paris*), had by the end of the year a choice of 23 dailies and as many others appearing at least weekly. By 1791 there was at one stage a choice of 45 dailies, 27 bi- or tri-weeklies, and 31 weeklies.[22] Major issues, such as the debate over war early in 1792, encouraged demand for news, with even Robespierre himself briefly trying his hand as editor of the *Défenseur de la constitution* (*Defender of the Constitution*). After the fall of the monarchy on 10 August 1792, however, royalist papers were banned. Even moderate papers found their position threatened, and it is not unreasonable to regard the violent destruction of pro-Girondin presses on 10 March 1793 as a turning point towards renewed suppression of a politically independent press.

On the whole, lay-out and production changed little during the revolutionary period. Panckoucke attempted to introduce English-style presentational methods when he launched the *Gazette nationale* or *Moniteur* at the end of 1789. Printed in three columns on folio format, with separate headings for the National Assembly, events in Paris, and other categories of material, the *Moniteur* was unusual for its systematic and factual narrative. Such an approach required substantial staff resources, or, as in the case of the full parliamentary reports offered from 1791 by *Le logographe* (founded by four deputies), reliance on special note-taking techniques. Nearly all the other papers, however, continued in the traditional mould: small octavo format, occasionally with a rough thematic structure (as in Prudhomme's well-written and influential *Révolutions de Paris*), but more often consisting of highly contentious and rambling editorial fulminations which seemed more akin to the campaigns of serial pamphleteers than a balanced summary of the day's or week's events. The demand for political news and commentary was certainly the driving force behind the huge growth in press output during the years 1789–94; but the way such news was presented seems, by the standards of modern national papers, highly subjective and idiosyncratic. Amongst the more outrageous of these efforts was Marat's notorious *L'ami du peuple*, but the following quotation from Hébert's *Le père Duchesne* (summer 1793) will illustrate the style and approach of such papers:

> I don't know a better Jacobin than this brave Jesus. He is the founder of all popular societies. He did not want too many, for he knows that huge assemblies nearly always degenerate into a throng, and that sooner or later Brissotins, Rolandins and Buzotins slip in. The club he created had only 12 members, all poor *sans-culottes*; but even so a false brother

---

22 J.R. Censer, *Prelude to Power: The Parisian Radical Press 1789–91* (Baltimore, 1976), 8–10 arrives at a much higher estimate of total new titles in 1789 by including papers that did not survive for long, in contrast to C. Labrosse and P. Rétat, *Naissance du journal révolutionnaire: 1789* (Lyon, 1989), 19–22. The latter also discusses production, distribution and contents of the 1789 papers.

slipped in, called Judas, which in Hebrew means a Pétion. With these 11 Jacobins, Jesus taught obedience to the laws, preached equality, liberty, charity, fraternity; and made eternal war on priests and financiers.[23]

Distribution methods were slow in adapting to the growth of a mass market, and the growing provincial readership remained at the mercy of agents and postal services which, by 1793, were handling 80,000 papers daily out of Paris (probably slightly more than half the total production, with at least another 50,000 being sold daily in the capital itself). Deregulation of the press brought piracy of titles and manipulative control of subscription lists on an unprecedented scale. Even Marat found, on return from his London exile in May 1790, that his paper had been pirated, and after his assassination several competing journalists seized on the famous title. Most papers remained in the hands of an individual editor or publisher, printed on very tight overnight schedules by workers whose skills and training were as unregulated as everything else. Little wonder that publication schedules were unpredictable, quality and accuracy highly variable, and success dependent on sensationalism and brass neck. Only a few editors were able to capture important bulk markets, such as that of the growing provincial network of affiliated Jacobin clubs, or, better still, the bulk deliveries to the armed forces undertaken in 1793 to help unify the disparate professional and volunteer regiments. But even for those who had to survive on the open market, earnings could be raised vastly above what had been the norm before 1789. Linguet and Mallet du Pan had been quite exceptional in their earnings of 6–10,000 livres per annum before the Revolution; by 1790 the latter was probably making 20,000, while Loustallot was reputedly paid 25,000 on the *Révolutions de Paris*. In the cut-throat business of revolutionary newspapers, deals might even include income protection in case of arrest, secretarial costs, sales-related bonus schemes, and retirement schemes.[24] Whole reputations could be built on a newspaper – and in the case of Marat, with the help of the Cordeliers club, even martyrdom and revolutionary canonisation.

* * *

This chapter has tried to convey some of the diversity and vitality of the growing eighteenth-century press. In much of Europe (but no longer in

---

23 *Je suis le véritable père Duchesne, foutre*, vol. 277 (1793), 5–6, in the version reproduced in *The French Revolution Research Collection* (Oxford, 1989–96), Section 1/3A.

24 H. Gough, *The Newspaper in the French Revolution* (London, 1988), 10f, 174f and 210–12. On the profession, see also W.J. Murray, 'Journalism as a career choice in 1789', in *The Press in the French Revolution*, ed. H. Chisick *et al.*, *StVEC* 287 (1991), 161–88; J.D. Popkin, *Revolutionary News: The Press in France 1789* (Durham, N.C., 1990, 39–78; and W.J. Murray, *The Right-Wing Press in the French Revolution: 1789–92* (London, 1986), 30–88. It is worth emphasising that the average size of print-runs probably did not surpass what had been normal before the Revolution, namely a few thousand copies. Contemporary technology ensured that print-runs of 10–15,000 – apparently reached by the *Feuille villageoise* (*Village News*) – had to be done in three or more separate printing operations: in other words, unit costs did not drop uniformly with higher circulation, and many publishers were prepared to charge fairly high prices in order to keep circulation within a set number.

London), the bulk of newspaper production remained traditional in terms of format, lack of headlines and lack of illustrative material to relieve the dense print. Yet visual conformity conceals a bewildering variety of styles, and an increasingly vociferous clash of views on all kinds of subject matter. Ranging from literary debate and philosophy to advertisements, gossip and politics, eighteenth-century journalists proved increasingly versatile and effective in tapping a rapidly growing market. In England, the press grew increasingly irreverent, some papers thriving on an unrelenting style of gutter journalism the likes of which did not exist anywhere else. In France the press helped make nonsense of censorship regulations before the Revolution, became a key tool of politicisation from 1789, and probably contributed directly to the destabilising extremism of 1791–93. In Germany and Scandinavia the press remained more restrained and deferential, but nonetheless made significant contributions to the creation of an informed public opinion. In effect, newspapers and journals had become the most flexible and attractive source of up-to-date news and ideas. And since provincial papers relied heavily on material printed in the national capital, the press also helped to foster a gradual process of national and cultural–linguistic integration.

We can usually only guess at total circulation, but the figures we have suggest that in later eighteenth-century London and Hamburg, at least, newspapers were widely and easily accessible for anyone who was interested – by loan if not by purchase. In France this did not happen until the Revolution; but by 1793 Paris appears to have produced one newspaper for roughly every eight adults. Although the French press did not retain its complete political freedom for long, it had acquired a critical role in terms of mass communication. Evidently, this was not effective over the whole of France: penetration was very uneven both in social and in geographic terms. But where literacy rates were low, or the number of purchasers limited, the common practice of reading papers aloud in cafés and clubs still ensured widespread dissemination of some kind in the more heavily populated areas. More so than the book, and perhaps now also more so than the pamphlet, the regular newspaper (whether daily or weekly) was becoming part of everyday urban life. No less important – if potentially disastrous for long-term political continuity – was the fact that the reporting of political and social debate in both the London and the Paris press had acquired some autonomy from the unchallengeable assertions made by those in power.

|6|

Reason and the dissolution of certainties

It will be clear from the previous chapters that a number of mechanisms were in place by the second half of the eighteenth century which could help spread information of one kind or another, facilitate discussion and sociability, foster public comment, and to some extent even create expectations of variety and entertainment which had not existed on a comparable scale before. Growing economic prosperity clearly encouraged a rapid increase in demand not just for consumer goods including prints, books and news-papers, but also for the attractions of coffee-houses, debating societies and elementary schooling. We should resist the temptation to treat all of this – or perhaps even any of it – as genuinely innovatory *per se*; but equally it would be absurd to deny that, taken overall, the terms of reference and the outreach of debate had changed, often beyond recognition, since the start of the century.

That said, what kinds of substantive issues generated most public interest? Were there elements of a common agenda shared by intellectuals, by salon society, by those in positions of political influence, as well as by this wider public? Or, conversely, were there enough contradictions and inconsistencies in contemporary trends to allow the elite and those in government to ignore demands for change, or at least exploit divisions of opinion? Can we in any case be certain that the issues that we identify are also ones that con-temporaries would have placed high on a list of priorities? Much of what went into print may nowadays at first sight seem ephemeral, gossipy or light-hearted. Yet the eighteenth century is remarkable for the way some core structural and ideological assumptions that it inherited were taken up for re-examination – albeit sometimes superficially, sometimes obliquely, and sometimes with studied cynicism. The next three chapters will address these issues from different angles. In this chapter we shall focus on issues of long-standing significance in public affairs: matters of religious belief, the efficacy and legitimacy of institutions of authority (religious and secular) which maintained ideological constructs and discipline, and the collective response to crime and disease.

State legislation on toleration

Inherent in the growing debate of the eighteenth century was an erosion of certainty, in religious matters as much as in other areas. Yet governments that took steps which might be construed as tampering with inherited value-systems (doctrinal or social) ran a considerable risk of violent popular reaction. Such a risk was most dramatically illustrated in the widespread hostility confronting Joseph II both after his decrees of 1781–83 extending some measure of toleration to most Protestant, Greek orthodox and Jewish minorities, and again during his closure of around a third of Austria's monastic houses and redistribution of their resources. His younger brother Leopold was more cautious in northern Italy, but still not immune to popular resistance to religious reform, as shown by the riots in Tuscany after his departure in 1790. In most other parts of Catholic Europe the state steered well clear of such controversial measures. In Protestant Europe, too, conventional piety was massively buttressed by an uncompromising rejection of non-conformity, and by an instinctive obsession with anything that might be construed as blasphemy.

The question of peaceful co-existence of different religious denominations went back a long way, but acquired new prominence during the seventeenth century when it became increasingly obvious that interminable conflict was unlikely to produce any clear geographical separation, resolution or even containment of the bewildering variety of sects. In England and in the United Provinces a measure of religious toleration evolved *de facto* in the later seventeenth century, not really by intent, but because of stalemate disagreements between leading political interests. The political upheaval in England in 1688–89 was about religious co-existence as much as anything else, and marked a turning point not just there but for Europe as a whole. It stimulated renewed radical writings, including Locke's *A Letter concerning Toleration* (1689) and his *The Reasonableness of Christianity* (1695). No less controversial was the Irishman John Toland's *Christianity not Mysterious* (1696), which argued that religious mysticism was a clerical invention merely obstructing the application of reason to all religious beliefs. In a different style, Pierre Bayle's *Historical and Critical Dictionary* (also 1696) became a standard work of reference for European scepticism. But there was a broader interest in such matters, as shown by the staggering success of Montesquieu's *Persian Letters* (1721), which brought refreshing cultural comparison to a range of fundamental questions about ethics and religious beliefs.

By mid-century intellectual debate in this field was wide-ranging and vigorous, encompassing David Hume's rationalist essay on miracles published with his *Philosophical Essays concerning Human Understanding* (1748), Voltaire's two influential contributions (*On Tolerance* of 1763, and *Questions regarding Miracles* of 1765), as well as several expositions of outright materialism such as La Mettrie's *Man a Machine* (1747), d'Holbach's *Christianity Revealed* (1767) and his *System of Nature* (1770). Such extreme forms of scepticism and materialism hardly penetrated the innately conservative Lutheran traditions of Germany and Scandinavia, and remained highly controversial even amongst intellectuals in France and Britain. But less extreme forms of pragmatism, rationality and emotional detachment appear to have had a growing appeal. The systematic challenging of the church's monopoly on truth arguably reached a point of no return in 1751 with the launch of the *Encyclopédie* edited by Diderot and d'Alembert. The chequered publication history of this huge work has already been discussed (above, p. 100), and it is not difficult to see why its opponents were so determined to have it stopped. Diderot may secretly have been an atheist, but of course carefully covered his tracks partly by means of irony and apparent self-contradiction, partly by scattering some of the more controversial statements in unlikely entries. Even so, the *Encyclopédie* was littered with remarks calculated to make the reader think twice about many aspects of church administration and religious beliefs. Diderot defined intolerance (in the article under that keyword) as a 'ferocious passion that leads one to hate and persecute' those who hold religious views other than one's own. Listing all the evils of intolerance, he argued that the ruler of an intolerant state was no more than an executioner in the pay of priests.[1] In an earlier volume, the article on '*Dragonnade*' (billeting of troops) had explicitly condemned the repressive policy of Louis XIV against the Huguenots, whilst the article on 'Refugees' lamented the loss to France caused by the subsequent Revocation of the Edict of Nantes. Other entries were even more certain to cause trouble. The article on 'Preacher', written by none other than the baron d'Holbach, was a broadside against clerical abuse of power. Superstition was depicted as worse than atheism, since it did more damage to natural ethics, morality and the law. But here, as in so many other entries, caution prevailed in terms of providing specific examples. Thus no reference was made to specific French incidents such as the 'miracles' and convulsions which had attracted huge crowds to the tomb of a clergyman in Saint-Médard in 1731.

The *Encyclopédie*, then, provided ample grounds for censorial condemnation by theologians: it was placing firmly in the public domain whole areas of discussion which hitherto had been strictly confined. The decision in 1765 to turn a blind eye to the publication of the remainder of its text would suggest, therefore, that attitudes to religious beliefs amongst a significant part of the

---

1 *Encyclopédie*, article '*Intolérance*' (intolerance), vol. 8 (1765), 843; but characteristically contradicted, on the basis of Rousseau's *Social Contract*, by the article on '*Tolérance*' written by a Genevese pastor, Romilly, for vol. 16.

French elite were becoming quite relaxed. Recently, one aspect of the enlightenment in England has been described as 'first and foremost a movement to preserve civilised society against any resurgence of religious enthusiasm and superstition, that is to say, of evangelical Protestantism and Counter-Reformation Catholicism'.[2] Despite differences of circumstance, the *encyclopédistes* clearly shared such concerns.

Yet nowhere in Europe did actual toleration come about either naturally or amicably. The unsatisfactory Act of Toleration of 1689 in England was a characteristic case of compromise by exhaustion: it was to have been just part of a larger settlement of the deep ideological divides that had persisted since the civil war in the 1640s, but the complementary legislation was never ratified. In the event a fairly narrow Anglican viewpoint prevailed in the definition of what constituted 'dissent', and whilst the Act eventually ensured some moderation of penal legislation on religious uniformity, dissenters were excluded from full civil rights. In the course of the eighteenth century a growing leniency in the interpretation of the legislation allowed many groups of Protestant dissenters to gain practical recognition. Yet repeated efforts after 1787 to win a repeal of notably the Test and Corporation Act all failed. Popular hatred of religious non-conformists readily erupted into violence, spontaneous as well as manipulated – as in the Gordon Riots of 1780 and the Priestley riot in Birmingham in 1791.

Scotland attained limited *de facto* religious toleration as an indirect result of the Act of Union of 1707. Partly in reflection of English practice after 1689, kirk sessions in 1712 lost control over Scottish Episcopalians, and by extension (though much more gradually) also over individuals following other recognised non-conformist tendencies. Inevitably, doctrinal rigidity within the Church of Scotland itself began to appear old-fashioned, and by the 1750s the increasingly influential group of Moderates (William Robertson amongst them) helped from within to steer the church away from some of its more austere Calvinist strictures. As churchmen themselves turned to less inflammatory scholarly pursuits, open conflict over the fundamentals of religious belief became rare. However, other issues continued to cause bitter factionalism – above all the power (patronage right) exercised by some Anglicised landowners in Scotland to appoint a local minister, precipitating open conflict and secessions from the church in 1733 and again in 1761. After 1770 the situation was further complicated by the growth of Irish immigration and hence of Catholicism. By 1778, when the British government began to remove some of the more draconian restrictions on Catholics in England and Ireland, several Scottish factions helped inflame public resistance. Despite the efforts of the Moderates in favour of compromise, there were such serious 'No Popery' riots in both Edinburgh and Glasgow in February 1779 that the government was forced to withdraw its proposals.

2 K. Haakonssen, ed., *Enlightenment and Religion: Rational Dissent in 18th-Century Britain* (Cambridge, 1996), 2, citing the work of J.G.A. Pocock.

These anti-Catholic disturbances may have provided a model for the Gordon Riots in London the following year.

In the more conservative climate of German-speaking central Europe the church was less vulnerable to criticism, but the difficulties of sectarian co-existence were for historic reasons even more acute. One possible solution was that adopted after 1740 by Frederick II for Brandenburg-Prussia. Perhaps as a result of influences from the French enlightenment, for which he had very high regard, Frederick was personally a non-believer. He ensured that religion was as far as possible side-lined in central government, and sought not only to ignore Christian sectarianism but also to grant partial toleration for Jews in 1750. In all parts of Europe, conceding even limited civil rights for settled Jews was likely to bring out long-engrained anti-Semitic popular prejudices; but the admission and naturalisation of immigrants from other countries was liable to provoke more openly xeno-phobic reactions. Brandenburg-Prussia experienced some of each, but at least avoided the kind of outright rioting which in 1753 forced the British government to withdraw altogether its modest bill dealing with Jewish immigration. It took another generation before more constructive debate on Jewish rights could emerge, first in some of the German principalities in the 1770s and 1780s, then in the later 1780s in France.[3]

In Brandenburg-Prussia, the massive law codification initiated in mid-century by Samuel von Cocceji, and finally brought to fruition with the publication of the Code in 1794, regulated church–state relations in great detail, and consolidated state administration of the church with regard to secular matters (buildings, civil registration, clerical careers). It also con-firmed religious freedom for the individual citizen – but within the strict parameters of a state which since the later seventeenth century had sought to prosper on the principle of peaceful co-existence between Lutheran, Calvi-nist and eventually also significant Catholic populations. Inevitably there was some slippage after the death of Frederick II in 1786, when Brandenburg-Prussia reverted to a more conservative line. An edict of 1788 re-affirmed religious censorship and strengthened the authority of a con-servative clergy within each of the recognised religious denominations, and this legislation was not neutralised in the subsequent Code. The French Revolution merely served to endorse stricter vigilance against enlightened ideals.

The free city of Hamburg, with a long tradition of political independence and deliberate admission of religious minorities for economic gain, might reasonably be expected to have avoided the worst manifestations of intoler-ance. By eighteenth-century standards it did, but there were nevertheless serious incidents. In 1719, an authorised Catholic chapel was destroyed by a

3 On the status of Jews, see R. Liberles, 'From toleration to *Verbesserung*: German and English debates on the Jews in the eighteenth century', *Central European History* 22 (1989), 3–32, which discusses significant German writings around the time of Lessing's play *Nathan the Wise* (1779), portraying Jews in a new light.

Lutheran crowd following alleged mutual provocation, and the precarious equilibrium was shaken again in 1742. Similarly, there was an anti-Semitic outburst in 1730. By the 1760s, although the city government was taking a more relaxed view both of Catholics and of Jews, popular opinion barely tolerated any formal concessions on either count. Predictably, it was the Reformed Huguenot community which made the first gains by negotiation, helped by the Patriotic Society and other groups within the Hamburg intelligentsia. Even so, it took much campaigning before formal toleration of Calvinists and Catholics was finally approved by law in 1785.[4]

In the rest of Europe, the gradual relaxation of religious uniformity was equally problematic and controversial. Governments in Lutheran countries generally had slightly more room for manoeuvre than in Catholic areas, but even so change had to be very cautious and gradual. In the Scandinavian kingdoms, excommunication was abandoned as a tool of control, and by the second half of the century strict supervision of the spiritual lives of parishioners had eased in other respects too. Denmark had opened its doors to carefully circumscribed Protestant non-conformist groups in the later seventeenth century, but took no further legislative steps. Since the late sixteenth century Sweden had been less secure in its religious balance, and hence more cautious, but limited concessions to other Protestants were introduced in 1741. More substantial measures were debated in the Swedish Riksdag (parliament) after 1779, resulting in controlled freedom of conscience and worship for all Christian denominations by 1781, and a rather restrictive formalisation of admission procedures for Jews in 1782.

Clearly, throughout Scandinavia, all this amounted to no more than a limited and very partial tolerance, from which not even fellow-Protestants gained full civil rights. The state-controlled church hierarchy seemed nearly unshakeable in its role as strict and omnipresent defender of both the letter and the spirit of Lutheran orthodoxy. Denmark had some contact, through northern Germany, with moderate new ideas there; but in both countries the more radical views of the French enlightenment remained suspect and potentially subversive in the eyes of theologians and censors. Even the revision of the statutes of Copenhagen University in 1788, including a widening of the curriculum beyond the specific needs of the clergy and towards a broader functionality, led to heated public controversy.

France was the last state to attempt major legislative relaxation of religious uniformity. For some time there had been signs of change. The question of civil liberty for Protestants had been raised occasionally ever since the Revocation of the Edict of Nantes in 1685, and, thanks to the efforts of Turgot and Malesherbes, became a real possibility after the accession of

---

4 J. Whaley, *Religious Toleration and Social Change in Hamburg 1529–1819* (Cambridge, 1985), 145–68 and *passim*. See also M. Lindemann, *Paupers and Patriots: Hamburg 1712–1830* (Oxford, 1990). Popular hostility to non-conformist religious views was still in the 1770s fuelled by some of the Lutheran establishment, including the utterly inflexible and belligerent first pastor in Hamburg, Johann Melchior Goeze.

Louis XVI in 1774. By then most *parlements* had abandoned any attempt at enforcing existing penalties against Huguenot marriages. Yet hostility to Protestantism remained strong, and the issue cut across the political divides of pre-revolutionary France. In 1787 a proposal for civil rights for Protestants was spearheaded by a Jansenist *parlementaire* magistrate, Robert de Saint-Vincent, with the backing of Lafayette and members of the Assembly of Notables. The final edict, as drafted yet again by Malesherbes, survived discussion in the Parlement de Paris and eventually became law in January 1788 – at a time when both the Parlement and members of the church hierarchy were taking obvious exception to other initiatives from the crown.[5] However, full religious toleration, including freedom of worship, had to await the Declaration of the Rights of Man of 26 August 1789. Protestants won the right to hold public office in December 1789 – not long before the whole machinery of the Catholic church was subjected to public scrutiny and secular administrative control through the Civil Constitution of the Clergy in the spring of 1790. It took until September 1791 before Jews became entitled to vote as active citizens, by which time all aspects of religious beliefs and church life were beginning to be questioned.

All these instances of hesitant state reform suggest that, on the surface, the established churches had retained a very strong position. But cautious public legislation can hardly be regarded as a good reflection of what happened on the ground. Equally, it is difficult to assess the impact which enlightened debate may have had on the real beliefs of individuals. We might simply note that, nearly a decade before the implementation of legislation in France, an observer of Parisian life reminded his readers that official policies and practical reality did not necessarily match – not even in the monarchy that prided itself on its Catholic orthodoxy. Mercier, writing in 1781, noted that:

> religious freedom is possible to a very large degree in Paris. No one will ever ask you to account for your beliefs. You can live for 30 years in a parish without setting foot in its church, and without recognising the face of your priest. But you will nonetheless take care to ... have your children baptised there, if you have any, and to pay the tax for the poor ... The priest no longer visits anyone other than the poor, for that class have no doorman.[6]

5 For a discussion of the background to the French toleration edict of 1787, see notable D.K. van Kley, *The Religious Origins of the French Revolution* (New Haven, 1996), 341–4; G. Adams, *The Huguenots and French Opinion 1685–1787* (Waterloo, Ontario, 1991), 265–306; C.H. O'Brien, 'The Jansenist campaign for toleration of Protestants in late eighteenth-century France: sacred or secular?', *Journal of the History of Ideas* 46 (1985), 523–38; and J. McManners, *Church and Society in Eighteenth-Century France*, vol. 2: *The Religion of the People and the Politics of Religion* (Oxford, 1998), 644–57.
6 Louis-Sébastien Mercier, *Tableau de Paris*, vol. 1 (Hamburg, 1781), 292f.

The churches under scrutiny

There may, then, have been a more rapid relaxation of urban conformity than official policies would suggest – but the absence of reliable evidence on church membership and attendance probably makes it impossible to draw firm conclusions about overall religious observance. As we noted earlier (p. 33), the proliferation of revivalist groups everywhere should warn us against assuming there was a pervasive loss of interest in spiritual values. Equally, atheism or outright denials of spiritual beliefs were rare – even amongst those who took a lead in open debate, criticised the established church, or scrutinised recent biblical and other scholarship. What is clear is that systematic critical reasoning and the espousal of humanist ethical values amongst many of the French *philosophes* made their writings deeply suspect in the eyes of conventional religious minds. No doubt some of these writings helped to pave the way for slightly greater toleration in matters of fundamental beliefs. But many observers may have had a more tangible interest in the practical and critical scrutiny of the actual institutional and managerial framework of the church. If rejection of Christianity was rare in enlightened Europe, anti-clericalism was not.

The established churches everywhere did face a number of problems which had the potential of damaging their image and provoking criticism. In Catholic Europe critics – including those associated with a revived Jansenism and with the attack on the Jesuit order – increasingly targeted the wealth of the church, its lack of accountability in terms of management of resources, and its apparent failure to fulfil traditional pastoral expectations. Inertia and inefficiency in the Papacy itself ensured that, even in such Catholic strongholds as Italy and the Habsburg lands, anti-clericalism grew significantly after the 1760s. Some of the problems raised were real enough. In France, for example, clerical income differentials created an unbridgeable gap between the small upper clergy (around 5% of the French clergy had annual incomes over 10,000 livres) and the underpaid and overworked parish *curés* on an annual income of a few hundred livres that barely distinguished them from skilled workers. All the 139 bishoprics of late eighteenth-century France were held by nobles, and some could expect annual revenues up to 200,000 livres for what was essentially an administrative and managerial role rather than spiritual leadership – and as Loménie de Brienne (archbishop of Toulouse) and others demonstrated, you did not have to be a believer at all in order to qualify for the highest offices in the church. Amongst the parish clergy, education and training were not always adequate to meet the increasingly wide-ranging demands placed on the incumbent with regard to local poor relief, elementary education, civil registration and even secular administration.

The richly endowed cathedral chapters and regular monastic orders attracted particularly unfavourable attention in some quarters. Kaunitz, one of the most astute ministers appointed by Maria Theresa, displayed a pragmatism characteristic of contemporary opinion in France when he condemned monasticism outright as economically damaging, unhelpful in religious terms, and, given the vow of celibacy, 'very disadvantageous to the propagation of the human race'.[7] If we are to believe contemporary gutter literature, this last factor seems not to have applied to all French houses. However, more reliable evidence suggests that some male monastic orders in France (notably the Benedictines and Franciscans) were suffering dwindling rates of new admissions, leaving some houses half empty and poorly disciplined – in marked contrast to many female houses, which continued to integrate themselves successfully in the local community by providing voluntary staff in hospitals and orphanages. Only in the Habsburg lands, and especially through the initiative of Kaunitz, was a serious programme of monastic reform initiated, designed to transfer resources from 'redundant' houses to new medical and educational services – in the process more than halving the number of men and women in orders and closing 530 monastic houses in the central Habsburg lands.

Overall, the research completed so far suggests on the one hand that the institutional problems in the French church were not all as great as some contemporaries made them out to be; but on the other that changing lay expectations, compounded by a growing awareness of imbalance or misuse of tithes and other income, put the established church on the defensive. Already in 1750, Voltaire had raised some key issues when he argued that:

> In France, where reason gains a firmer foothold every day, this very reason tells us that the church should contribute to the costs of the state in proportion to its revenue ... Reason tells us that the ruler must be absolute master of all matters relating to good order in the church, without restriction of any kind, because such good order is part of government; and, just as the head of the household prescribes for his children's teacher the hours to be spent in learning, the nature of the studies, and so on, so the prince can prescribe to all churchmen, without exception, all that which has the least relevance to public order.[8]

A few years later, in the *Encyclopédie* article on '*Fondations*' (foundations), Turgot openly criticised the inefficacy of church-administered poor relief (see below, p. 182), and his comments appeared to be borne out during the economic crises of the early 1770s and the later 1780s. Others more sweepingly blamed the church for what appeared to be increasing moral laxity and social disorder. It will be obvious that not everyone shared these views – and indeed there is plenty of evidence suggesting a continuing and adamant popular adherence to the rituals, elaborate processions and colour-

---

7 T.C.W. Blanning, *Joseph II and Enlightened Despotism* (London, 1970), 127.
8 Voltaire, *La voix du sage et du peuple* (1750), cited in *Dictionnaire de la pensée de Voltaire par lui-même*, ed. A. Versaille (Brussels, 1994), 389.

ful imagery of the church. But amongst the better-read and more influential levels of French society doubts might extend to the very fundamentals of belief, especially after such intercessions as Voltaire's celebrated and withering denunciation of the bigotry associated with the Calas affair (a case of serious miscarriage of justice, 1762–65). If we add to these problems the deeply divisive confrontation, culminating in the 1750s and 1760s, between the powerful and rich Jesuit order and the more puritanical and reformist Jansenists (above, p. 36), it becomes possible to understand why support for the church in France could no longer simply be taken for granted. These differences of opinion became deep and bitter in response to not only the administrative reforms imposed by the revolutionary government in 1790, but above all to the more violent de-christianisation campaign in the autumn of 1793.

As far as most of Protestant Europe is concerned, we still lack the detailed social histories of the church on which to base a more precise assessment of its response to changing needs and expectations. In Lutheran areas criticism remained muted, but comparative silence is no proof of a relative absence of problems. More likely, the close alliance between the Lutheran churches and secular government in northern Germany and Scandinavia ensured a more effective repression of criticism – as illustrated in the conflicts over Pietistic influences early in the eighteenth century, and the conflicts over religious censorship later on, to which we shall return. In any case public opinion there was far more cautious and less developed than in France.

The more detailed work done on England suggests that whilst problems may have been less acute than in France, there are similarities which bridge the confessional divide. One such area is the question of earnings differentials within the church hierarchy. The most prominent bishops earned well over £1,000 per annum (the archbishop of Canterbury £7,000), whilst in 1736 half the parish clergy were classified as below a poverty line of £50 per annum (and about 10% were in livings worth less than £10). Many of the latter were curates standing in for a parson holding several benefices. Pluralism (which may have affected between one-third and half the parishes in many parts of England) was an obvious way of trying to avoid the poverty trap, but non-residence also readily led to criticism and complaints from parishioners. Evidence on each of these aspects is conflicting. Economic growth in some parts of England clearly increased the yield from tithes, tithe-commutations and other sources of income, and standards of clerical education also seem to have improved. On the other hand, the undermining effect of dissent and of revivalist splinter groups like Methodism, even if numerically not very substantial, was bound to make the loyalty of parishioners less certain. It is perhaps significant that late seventeenth-century support for voluntary religious organisations to improve lay education and social discipline, notably the Societies for the Reformation of Manners (from 1691) and the Society for Promoting Christian Knowledge (the SPCK, founded 1699), clearly lost impetus in the second quarter of the eighteenth century. Overall, the Anglican church remained fairly tranquil until the 1790s; but worries about latitudinarianism within, as well as non-conformism, dissent, deism, irreligion and amorality outside it, suggest that some degree of erosion was taking place, unquantifiable though it is.[9]

There are similarities between the impact of Jansenism in France and that of at least some forms of dissent in England. Both tendencies exerted an influence well beyond their numeric and institutional importance, both had puritanical intellectual tendencies, and both touched a raw nerve within the respective established church. Although Jansenists by the eighteenth century had a less clear historical and ideological identity than the dissenters in England, both still stood clearly apart from other more radical contemporary forms of religious non-conformism such as deism (belief in God but not in divinely revealed religion). Neither Jansenism nor dissent, however, encouraged the kind of critical free-thinking associated with David Hume or with the sceptical deism of the French *philosophes*. Intrinsic or latent deism in the radical enlightenment is precisely what caused the greatest anxiety to churchmen, censors and self-appointed guardians of public morality or political stability. As deism appeared to spread amongst the better-educated and literate sections of both countries, enlightenment and traditional religious faith seemed set on a collision course. The by-product of such a confrontation was bound to be greater freedom and openness for those who were undecided regarding the many interrelated issues of the day. Criticism of the institutional church and its failings thus formed part of a wider agenda which included doctrinal non-conformity, toleration and censorship.

Censorship reform and state hesitations

We observed earlier (p. 85) how in Britain and the Netherlands the mechanisms for formal pre-publication censorship had lapsed before 1715; and how even in France censorship was in practice significantly relaxed after mid-century. French evidence has also confirmed how difficult it was for *ancien régime* authorities to enforce those book-publishing and distribution controls that remained: market demand seems increasingly to have found ways round all kinds of restrictions. It may therefore be justifiable to see the dramatic gestures of censorship reform, which we shall examine in this section, as having primarily symbolic rather than real value. That this may have been so seems to be corroborated by the fact that the first formal

9 Little comparative work has been done on the established churches across eighteenth-century Europe, but a helpful start for much of Europe can be made on the basis of W.J. Callahan and D. Higgs, eds., *Church and Society in Catholic Europe of the Eighteenth Century* (Cambridge, 1979), notably with O. Hufton's chapter on 'The French church', 13–33, and Callahan's own on 'The Spanish church', 34–50; O. Chadwick, *The Popes and European Revolution* (Oxford, 1981) on Catholic Europe, notably ch. 2; J. Walsh, C. Haydon and S. Taylor, eds., *The Church of England c. 1689–c. 1833* (Cambridge, 1993), particularly 4–29; and N. Hope, *German and Scandinavian Protestantism 1700–1918* (Oxford, 1995).

relaxation of pre-publication censorship came in the Scandinavian monarchies – in other words in areas which remained on the periphery of
innovative enlightenment thought even after liberalisation.

It was the Swedish Riksdag that took the lead in formally reducing pre-
publication censorship. Before 1766 the Swedish regulatory machinery,
organised round a chief censor responsible to the Chancery, had been one of
the most effective in curtailing the circulation not only of unorthodox
printed material but even of manuscripts. The Swedish book-publishing
industry was still largely in the hands of a few entrepreneurs, mostly based in
Stockholm, and imports from abroad were subject to close scrutiny. But
substantial discussion in the Riksdag resulted in a quite dramatic decree of 2
December 1766, whereby censorship was abolished for all domestic publications except those dealing with matters of religion. All alleged attacks on the
church, the constitution and the state were henceforth to be dealt with in
accordance with normal legal procedures (including the libel laws). A number of areas were specifically listed as being open to publication, including
the non-secret part of the debates of the Riksdag and its committees.
Imported foreign books, however, remained subject to scrutiny, and any
book published anonymously within Sweden had to carry the name of the
publisher, who would be held responsible.

The result was a significant growth in the range of books published in
Sweden, including important contributions to the political debate surrounding the last years of the Age of Liberty. With the Gustavian coup of 1772,
however, some of these freedoms immediately came under threat. The
librarian and publisher Gjörwell was tried in February 1773 before the
Supreme Court regarding an article in a journal he edited, and other lawsuits
followed. In 1774 the king issued what appeared to be a confirmation of the
decree of 1766, emphasising the public value of a free press. But at the same
time he imposed changes of detail which in effect restricted debate not just on
religion but also regarding constitutional, political and foreign affairs. In
other words, the liberal aims of the decree of 1766 were now significantly
circumscribed. As intended, the number of book and periodical publications
on current affairs declined significantly in the following years – the independence of the public debate further curtailed where necessary either through
judicial pressure or through further legislation. Only the Riksdag of 1786
questioned growing press controls: its insistence on the continued publication of its own official reports provided the only substantial dissent against
the increasingly repressive policies of the crown.

Danish experiments with press freedom at first proved even less durable,
though for very different reasons. Because of the more heterogeneous nature
of its possessions, and especially the organic link to a more diverse political
culture through its north German possessions, the Danish-Norwegian crown
had become less anxious both about religious minorities and about moderate
social and political debate amongst the elite (for example at the privileged
Academy at Sorø). But without an Estates General or any other major

political institutions outside direct crown control, there were few signs of active political consciousness. The succession of the mentally unstable Christian VII in 1766 ushered in a period of greater tension, but also of greater possibilities. A reforming ministry headed by the German cameralist Struensee issued a brief decree on 14 September 1770 which unconditionally abolished all pre-publication censorship. As a news item in the European republic of letters this decree worked well: none other than Voltaire responded with enthusiasm, seeing it as an example to be followed by other governments. In practice, however, the results were disappointing: apart from a brief outburst of scurrilous attacks on Struensee himself, there were few signs of the more substantive domestic political debate which the unusual political circumstances clearly warranted. In fact the fall of Struensee in 1772 inaugurated a long period of reactionary regency government. Although the decrees on press freedom were not formally rescinded, public debate was effectively discouraged by other means.

Genuine public debate, using a more independent press and a growing publishing industry, only came in the late 1780s. In 1784, what amounted to a peaceful coup led to the removal of the entire regency government and its replacement by a reformist ministry in the hands of the crown prince – a kind of proxy absolutism on behalf of the now totally incapable monarch. In order to implement its cautious programme of reforms (eventually covering land tenure and peasant–landowner relations, education, poor relief, public health and banking), the new government took significant steps to win public support. A number of new papers and journals appeared, notably the monthly *Minerva*, which, though edited independently, included amongst its contributors several leading figures from within the government itself. *Minerva* printed regular news bulletins where domestic news was presented alongside quite full summaries of events in France and elsewhere. Some effort was also made by the government to provide open access to more detailed information on domestic affairs, notably in the unprecedented publication from 1788 of the full minutes of the meetings of one of its most important and controversial reform commissions, the Rural Reform Commission launched two years earlier. But, as elsewhere in Europe, the impact of the French Revolution on more radical political opinion in Copenhagen caused concern by 1790. A pamphlet of 1790 calling for a French-style Estates General in Denmark was immediately banned. No doubt deliberately, the press laws were never clarified in detail: an order of 1790 merely confirmed the general principle of press freedom whilst insisting on the independent role of the law courts in any eventual prosecutions. Over the next few years some satirical and subversive publications did in fact trigger police prosecutions, not always well-judged. But it has been argued that, within the parameters of an unchanged system of monarchical absolutism, the Danish government made increasing and effective use of moderate public opinion to consolidate its reform programme. Remarkably, given the European context, no formal restraints on press freedom were imposed until 1799.[10]

Few other major governments were prepared to follow even such a cautious course. Like the initial Danish efforts, Joseph II's dramatic censorship reforms of 1781 looked promising on paper, and indeed released a flood of pamphlets. But the liberal intent was soon side-tracked by the government itself, and by the later 1780s systematically undermined by Joseph's own chief of police, Pergen. Not even Frederick II, despite both his own early protestations and some constructive debate in the press from the later 1770s, allowed political freedom of the press in Brandenburg-Prussia. After his death, what practical flexibility had existed was further curtailed through the edict on censorship of December 1788. In 1794 Nicolai noted that Berlin had had 81 active presses before the censorship restrictions of 1788, but that the number had shrunk to 61 by 1792.[11] Conditions were usually no more liberal under the other princely governments in the German lands, many of which imposed additional restrictions after the outbreak of the Revolution in France. Nonetheless, given the political mosaic, it remained quite easy to avoid restrictions in one state by publishing in another.

As with religious toleration, the last experiment with a free press came in France. This delay is surprising, given that the unenforceability of the existing system had been openly recognised by mid-century (p. 87). Voltaire put the case for a free press succinctly in 1765:

> Some five or six thousand pamphlets were printed in Holland against Louis XIV, but not one contributed to making him lose the battles of Blenheim, Turin or Ramilles... I know many books that have annoyed me, but I don't know any that have caused real harm ... If some new book comes to your attention containing ideas that jar with yours – assuming you have any ideas – or whose author belongs to a different faction from yours, or, worse still, belongs to no faction, then you cry 'Fire!' – a scandal, a great commotion in your little corner of the world ... What for? – for five or six pages that no one will remember after three months. If a book displeases you, then refute it; if it annoys you, don't read it.[12]

10 For a fuller discussion, see T. Munck, 'Danish absolutism in the later eighteenth century: centralised reform, public expectations and the Copenhagen press', *Historical Journal* 41 (1998), 201–24.
11 H. Möller, *Aufklärung in Preussen* (Berlin, 1974), 213. Nicolai may have been one of the few intellectuals in Brandenburg-Prussia supporting genuine freedom of the press for the whole population, according to E. Hellmuth, 'Enlightenment and freedom of the press: the debate in the Berlin Mittwochsgesellschaft, 1783–1784', *History* 83 (1998), 420–44. For the more pragmatic views of the majority of the Berlin intellectuals, see also E. Tortarolo, 'Censorship and the conception of the public in late eighteenth-century Germany: or, are censorship and public opinion mutually exclusive?', in *Shifting the Boundaries: Transformation of the Languages of Public and Private in the Eighteenth Century*, ed. D. Castiglione and L. Sharpe (Exeter, 1995), 131–50.
12 Voltaire, *Nouveaux mélanges* (1765), cited in *Dictionnaire de la pensée de Voltaire par lui-même*, ed. A. Versaille (Brussels, 1994), 779f.

Yet, despite specific proposals for reform such as that by Malesherbes in 1788–89 (p. 97), the old system of censorship broke down more by accident than intent. Most historians see a turning point in the government's decision of 5 July 1788 to consult 'educated persons' regarding the forthcoming calling of the Estates General. Few contributors bothered to send their text as required to the Keeper of the Seals, preferring to go straight into print. Rearguard action by the Parlement de Paris and other institutions failed to stem the resulting flood, and by 29 August 1789 the Declaration of the Rights of Man, clause 11, established the right of every 'citizen to speak, write and publish freely, subject to the penalties for the abuse of such freedom established in law'. In the upheavals of that year, the whole legal framework for the printing industry disintegrated; the Paris guild of book traders and printers held its last meeting, to no effect, in May 1791. Media ownership, monopolies on official news, copyrights (including journal titles) and authors' rights all crumbled. Even legal definitions of libel and sedition were overshadowed by confusion over what legislation was still valid. Efforts by both the National Constituent Assembly and the Paris Commune to clarify some of these issues (including an author's right of ownership) were drowned by more urgent priorities. The press and book trade, in effect totally deregulated by 1791, lost any last semblance of order with the fall of the monarchy on 10 August 1792. The creation of a republic, however, also brought the first demands for censorship of the right-wing press. The destruction of the main Girondin printing press on 9–10 March 1793 marked a symbolic stage in the return to politically motivated control of the press: in this as in other respects the liberal provisions of the remarkable Constitution of 1793 remained a dead letter.

The judiciary and the law

If concern about the proper role of the church, and about attitudes to religious belief, were central to the French enlightenment, so was the emphasis on the need for a fair and consistent legal system in order for society to function satisfactorily. In France and elsewhere, many features of such a system were recognised – notably the need for a simple and standardised body of law intelligible to all, for reasonably clear jurisdictions to avoid undue delay, for a well-trained judiciary, for a legal profession whose income should not depend on corruption or the interminable prolongation of lawsuits, and for safeguards to ensure that the outcome of a lawsuit would not be too obviously dependent on the social status of plaintiff or defendant. In criminal matters, a scale of punishments was needed that might seem 'reasonable' according to the (often contradictory) impulses of deterrence and humanitarianism. Following the European-wide impact of works like Montesquieu's *The Spirit of the Laws* (1748) and Beccaria's *Of Crimes and Punishments* (1764), other issues were gradually tackled, including demands for the removal of torture from the process of judicial enquiry, and for a judiciary that should be reasonably independent of the political executive (the state).

It must be stressed that in the context of the eighteenth century this amounted to a truly formidable agenda. Implementation of reform would require drastic curtailment of those interminable demarcation disputes amongst the myriad and chaotically overlapping jurisdictions that made most of Europe a lawyer's paradise and a litigant's nightmare. Not surprisingly, such changes were liable to provoke resistance and prevarication amongst the many corporate bodies and officeholding interests. Ultimately, however, serious reform of the legal system might well also bring into question the very principles of deference, hierarchy and social inequality which were the bed-rock of pre-revolutionary society. Glaringly overdue though it might appear to be, such reform could therefore be regarded as one of the most difficult challenges facing eighteenth-century Europe.

Law standardisation and codification might be a first step. Achieved in Denmark already in 1683, in the Austrian lands in several stages from 1766–69 to 1787, and in Prussia in 1794, codification was not likely to have dramatic immediate results, but did in the long run undoubtedly improve accessibility for laymen. France manifestly needed reform of this kind, since it had widely different legal systems (and hence institutional practices) in various parts of the kingdom. Although few real steps towards standardisation were taken until late in the day, there was no shortage of writings by individual lawyers suggesting overall change of one kind or another – including suggestions by Chancellor Henri-François d'Aguesseau (from 1725, but unpublished) for national standardisation of the law and reconstruction of the court system, and schemes by the marquis d'Argenson (from the 1730s) for law codification and more radical political restructuring. A great deal more was written over the next half-century on this and related subjects. What was needed above all, according both to the *philosophes* and to virtually all the great legal minds of the age, was a visible consistency and fairness (if not yet equality) in the application of the law. That depended not so much on the law itself – though there was indisputable need for reform there too, notably of the brutal ordinance of 1670 on criminal procedure – but above all on its functionaries.

As in all other European countries, the lawyers and judges of eighteenth-century France have not had a good press. Many historians, following contemporary reformers like John Law (1717–20) and Chancellor Maupeou (1771) – and reflecting the most common of contemporary literary stereotypes, the ignorant and corrupt lawyer – have focused particularly on the French system of venality (private purchase) of offices. Private hereditary ownership of offices might at first sight readily account both for the very uneven professional standards and the insufferable self-interest of the legal profession there. Yet venality in one sense gave the *parlements* and other courts some degree of immunity against political manipulation by the government, if not quite in the way intended by purists. Challenging the security of tenure of officeholders would require either massive financial compensation by the state, which few ministers could even contemplate; or, as had been tried in the past, a major political confrontation, the outcome of which was far from assured. The risks involved in either approach were bound to increase as fiscal reform became more urgent, and as the *parlements* increasingly claimed to speak on behalf of the nation against a supposedly despotic government.

This is not the place to rehearse the arguments surrounding the confrontation between the upper law courts and the French crown in the last decades before the Revolution. Suffice it to say that recent work has shown beyond reasonable doubt that the legal profession itself was not invariably as blinkered and self-interested as has sometimes been assumed. The crown must take a significant share of the blame for the failure to realise durable reform of the legal system – and in particular of the arcane complexities of the intermediary and lower courts, so often amounting to an absolute antithesis of simplicity, efficiency or fairness. The lucrative taxation of venal offices was a strong disincentive against significant restructuring. But in any case the most significant reforms of the period, those imposed by Maupeou in 1770–71, were seriously mismanaged and in some important respects ill conceived. Whilst the ensuing debate was both vigorous, far-reaching and unprecedentedly public, the abandonment of the reforms in 1774 as a gesture of good will on the accession of Louis XVI left nearly all the problems unresolved. The upper levels of the legal profession, deeply divided by the traumas of this bitter confrontation, became more politicised than ever before. The political stakes were raised again in the late 1780s, culminating in the bold judicial reform proposals of Lamoignon in 1788. Significantly, however, the specific flaws in the legal system seemed increasingly to be overshadowed by a more general public spectacle in which an erratic and sometimes indecisive crown attempted to confront the self-conscious corporate identity of the *parlements* and the other superior courts. In the end, Lamoignon's efforts were swallowed up in the uncertainty of the Revolution.[13]

The English bar had even greater corporate autonomy than the higher levels of the legal profession in France. Through the mechanisms of the Inns

13 There is a very large literature on this subject, guidance on which will be found in J. Swann, *Politics and the Parlement of Paris under Louis XV* (Cambridge, 1995), B. Stone, *The Parlement of Paris 1774–1789* (Chapel Hill, 1981) and his *The French Parlements and the Crisis of the Old Régime* (Chapel Hill, 1986). The effects of the Maupeou crisis on the barristers themselves (including Linguet and Target) is cogently argued by D.A. Bell, 'Lawyers into demagogues: chancellor Maupeou and the transformation of legal practice in France 1771–1789', *Past and Present*, 130 (1991), 107–41, and in his book *Lawyers and Citizens: The Making of a Political Elite in Old Regime France* (Oxford, 1994). It is worth noting that Maupeou did tackle both specifics (like venality and exorbitant fees) and general issues (like the uneven jurisdictions); but that, like so many other ministers of the French crown, he relied more on tactics than a clear overall strategy, and was slow to grasp the implications of the publicity generated by his own measures.

of Court, a total professional monopoly was maintained which seemed nearly impervious both to political reform and to public accountability. No significant parliamentary regulation was ever attempted, except for legislation in 1731 to diminish the use of law-Latin, and an Act of 1729 subjecting aspiring attorneys and solicitors to rudimentary examination by a judge. Yet, as in France, training remained haphazard and ineffectual. The Inns of Court provided even less formal training than the English universities, and only those students who went on as articled clerks eventually acquired some knowledge of the law. The profession was strongly hierarchical, with only the lower levels of attorney or solicitor being relatively open (and hence of doubtful social status amongst the gentry). Above them, barristers maintained strict control of the admission procedure, and salaried judges were chosen from their ranks. Movement between the legal profession and office-holding or politics was common, but the predominantly conservative instincts of this elite ensured that change would be minimal. As in France, simplification of the law itself was consciously avoided, and public dependence on the legal profession thus maintained. According to a recent study, Jeremy Bentham decided in the 1770s not to enter the English legal profession because

> in his view the system was rotten to the very core; the interests of lawyers were in direct opposition to those of their clients and the general public. The greater the delay, obscurantism and injustice perpetrated by the courts, the greater would be their remuneration; it was a conspiracy against the public weal; the structure of the law sanctioned delays and denial of justice and covered its faults in a smug patina of mutual admiration.[14]

Although less cluttered by corporate tradition and institutional self-interest, Brandenburg-Prussia was hardly better off. Frederick II was legendary in Europe in his ruthless demand for efficiency and accountability in public service. His quest for a rational and fair administration of justice, however, was to some extent negated by the extraordinary influence of the military in all branches of the administration, including justice. Despite being directly under royal control, and paid by central government, the vast military apparatus was riddled with problems. Because of Frederick's habit of using the civil service as a pensioning system for supernumerary military officials, these problems spilled over into the civilian sector. Interminable delays, wrangles over overlapping jurisdictions, staff incompetence, persistent incompatibilities between the different legal systems of the scattered territories of the Hohenzollern inheritance – not to mention an interminable bombardment with sometimes contradictory royal decrees – all added to the confusion. Some real progress was made by Samuel von Cocceji, the legal advisor whom Frederick II inherited from his father. Amongst Cocceji's

14 J. Semple, *Bentham's Prison: A Study of the Panopticon Penitentiary* (Oxford, 1993), 21.

priorities was a proper salary system for the judiciary, to reduce corruption and dependence on fees; a better legal training scheme complete with a rudimentary exam; and regular scrutiny of the lower courts by more senior judicial staff. But Cocceji himself died in 1755, and many of his plans were undermined by the enormous strains of the Seven Years War. Frederick's own increasing impatience with bureaucratic niceties did not help, but above all the engrained resistance of the landowning elite (on whom the crown was utterly dependent) ensured that change was minimised. The work of Cocceji and his assistants was not all lost: the eventual completion in 1794 of the great law codification project, in simple and comprehensible German, was tangible proof of that. Equally, there is evidence that by the later years of the reign deference and cowed obedience could no longer invariably be taken for granted even in rural Brandenburg. Nevertheless, as Frederick himself had demonstrated, justice remained unpredictable or even crude.[15]

In short, the *ancien régime* seemed ill equipped for the task of law reform. There were too many vested interests, too much defensive immunity, for results to be achieved on a rational basis. Few if any governments had either the resources or the level of pervasive control required to ensure that changes were implemented effectively (or at all). If simplification of the law and reform of the judiciary were the sole standards by which we would wish to judge the track record of enlightened Europe, we would have to resign ourselves to disappointment. Ironically, this failure was not the result of lack of public interest. In the eyes of contemporaries, law reform and the work-ings of the justice system were anything but a matter of dry technicalities. It has recently been demonstrated that there was a rapidly growing market in France for *mémoires judiciaires* (summaries of lawsuits) describing the complex lawsuits and miscarriages of justice relating to the great and the infamous. Some of these summaries had print-runs that would have been the envy of most writers – in some instances as many as 10,000 copies. Although the success of this genre did rely to a large extent on public interest in scandal and intrigue, the cumulative effect may well have added to contemporary awareness of the problems in the system.[16]

Crime and punishment

Contemporary opinion also focused on the apparent inadequacies of the criminal system. The accusatorial methods conventionally used alongside

---

15 For a fuller discussion and instructive comparison with France, see C.B.A. Behrens, *Society, Government and the Enlightenment: The Experience of Eighteenth-Century France and Prussia* (London, 1985), 89–115, which includes a summary of the notorious Müller Arnold case from 1774, which Frederick personally turned into an embarrassing miscarriage of justice.

16 S. Mazah, *Private Lives and Public Affairs: The Causes Célèbres of Prerevolutionary France* (Berkeley, 1993), 120–31 and *passim*.

torture to secure criminal confessions had been questioned already in connection with the witch-craze in the previous century; now doubts were also
raised about the validity of certain forms of evidence, about specific barbaric
details of the criminal system (such as the treatment of suicide as self-
murder), and about the purpose of the death penalty itself for serious
offenders. Arguably the enlightenment period brought no major new arguments to light, but it did significantly sharpen public awareness and
sensitivity.

Least problematic was the phasing out of torture. Its utility was dwindling,
in a system where the responsibility for criminal prosecution was gradually
being transferred from the individual plaintiff to the state, and where criteria
of supposedly absolute certainty were being replaced by more pragmatic
judgements 'beyond reasonable doubt'. Confessions extracted under duress
were no longer supposed to be regarded as conclusive in many parts of
Europe. By the eighteenth century, torture was no longer explicitly sanctioned either in England or in the Netherlands. The formal ban on its use in
Brandenburg-Prussia in 1754 thus readily set an explicit precedent which
could be followed elsewhere over the next decades, for example in Saxony in
1770, in the Austrian lands in 1776, and in France (at least as a means of
extracting a confession) in 1780.

Frederick II, however, was also a pragmatic opponent of the death penalty
in civilian affairs (military discipline was different). Traditionally, early
modern law enforcement had relied on a brutal ritual of exemplary punishment. By age-old tradition kings had an undisputed prerogative of mitigation
or commutation of punishment – a right which rulers took care to retain even
when they personally distanced themselves from their presiding functions in
the highest courts of the land. In most of Europe it became quite common
during the later eighteenth century for capital sentences to be commuted into
less draconian (if hardly less harsh) sentences of forced labour, either in the
name of a magnanimous ruler or on the basis of local discretionary powers.
In England, perhaps as many as half those condemned to death ended instead
with a lesser punishment such as transportation – so that, apart from a brief
surge after the end of the American war (1783–86), the total number of
executions remained fairly constant throughout the eighteenth century
despite new categories of capital offence being added regularly. Such mitigation, however, in no way improved consistency or apparent rationality in
sentencing, and may indeed ultimately have helped draw attention to the
potentially extreme disparity between many categories of relatively minor
offences and the scale of punishments accorded in law.

It has long been recognised that the impact of Beccaria's tract *Of Crimes
and Punishment*, first published in 1764 in Italy and soon translated into
many other languages,[17] can be explained at least in part because it addressed

---

17 For example, by 1793 at least 14 English-language editions had appeared, including three in
    North America (based on ESTC evidence, see p. 91).

concerns already prevalent amongst both rulers and reformers all over Europe. But although the parts of Beccaria's succinct tract that attracted most contemporary attention had to do with the effects of capital punishment, cruelty and torture, his analysis was more far-reaching than that. He fundamentally questioned the link between sin and crime, arguing that the criminal system should devote itself solely to evaluating the economic or material significance of a breach of the law, both to ensure reasonable compensation and to emphasise that crime would not pay. From that point of view, as well as out of humanitarian concerns, the death penalty had no role to play: instead, forced labour was a more appropriate way for a criminal to make amends to society. In emphasising the gross unfairness in the actual distribution of wealth in contemporary society, however, Beccaria also seemed to make a case for greater equality, and even came close to legitimising revolt by the poor against their oppressors. The possible link between indigence (extreme poverty, involving failure to provide a living) and certain forms of criminality like theft seemed inescapable. This in turn took Beccaria well beyond questions of punishment, towards a challenge to the right of property itself – towards a position which one critic at the time actually described as 'socialist'. Understandably, Beccaria's tract was seen by many contemporaries as deeply subversive, blasphemous and dangerous. This no doubt enhanced his reputation amongst the French *philosophes*, notably Morellet (who produced the first French translation) and Voltaire.

Beccaria also highlighted a fundamental contradiction within the system of punishment itself – namely, whether it should aim to reform and improve the ways of the criminal, or whether by contrast it should seek to deter others and perhaps allay a thirst for revenge in the victim and in society at large. Capital sentences could obviously have only the latter purpose. Throughout the eighteenth century public executions continued to attract large and mostly unperturbed crowds. In the case of very prominent victims, executions could even be used to project a particular image of the state. This was demonstrated in 1757 at the ostentatiously gruesome execution of the failed assassin of Louis XV, Damiens, who was condemned to be torn apart by horses, and whose four hours of agony were demonstratively aggravated by means of assorted refinements inflicted by the executioners. Similarly, when Count Struensee was found guilty of *lèse majesté* in 1772, his execution outside Copenhagen (a hand cut off, followed by decapitation, his body then drawn and quartered) was used to consolidate a questionable regency on behalf of a demented king. But a gesture of mercy could be just as effective in terms of public relations: when a woman tried to stab George III in 1786, he interceded on her behalf and won enormous sympathy and public praise for doing so.

Only in the criminal code implemented by Archduke Leopold for Tuscany in 1786, however, was the death penalty unconditionally ruled out. Executions generally remained popular events; but they easily disintegrated into unedifying violence, as pickpockets, onlookers paying for good viewing positions, and perhaps the friends of the offender clashed. An unruly crowd could easily become a threat, and was at best liable to undermine the symbolic value of the ritual. This partly explains why, in 1783, the London authorities definitively abandoned Tyburn as the site for executions, moving to the front of Newgate prison itself, where the ritual could more readily be controlled. The trap door (or 'drop') which had occasionally been used since 1759 was now also made a permanent feature of the raised execution platform, to ensure more instantaneous death and hence minimise the chance of crowd intervention.[18]

For offences that fell short of the death penalty, or for which mitigation was allowed, punishment nonetheless remained highly public. It had to be, given the universal lack of effective mechanisms of control, and hence the dependence on deterrence and self-regulation. Punishments like the pillory or the stocks, whilst not intrinsically harmful, relied for their effectiveness on the mood of the crowd. An hour in the pillory for, say, someone found guilty of a homosexual act could be very dangerous, as the crowd often pelted the offender with stones. Conversely, punishment could seriously backfire on the authorities, if they misjudged the mood of the public. This happened in 1703, when Defoe was placed in the stocks for publishing a heavily ironic pamphlet concerning dissenters: the crowd was entirely on his side, the stocks were decorated with flowers, and Defoe was celebrated as a hero. In more extreme cases, a crowd could even threaten the whole system – though they rarely went as far as the Gordon rioters in London in 1780, who freed hundreds of prisoners from Newgate and burnt down the building itself.

Prisons, executions and other forms of punishment seem to have played an increasingly vivid role in the imagination of contemporaries. Newgate prison loomed very large in Defoe's novel *Moll Flanders* (1722), whilst Hogarth, Mandeville and Fielding devoted a great deal of their attention to analysing deviant behaviour, criminality and the effect of prisons and punishment both on society as a whole and on the individual offender. In France, too, the reading public seems to have become more sensitive to these issues, though via a different route: the theoretical arguments in Montesquieu's *Spirit of the Laws* were brought into renewed focus not just by the translation of Beccaria's much punchier tract, but also by French involvement in the struggle of the American colonists against what were regarded as British repressive tactics. As French opinion became more aware of the potential for domestic abuse of power by the government, publications dramatising *lettres de cachet* (unspecified warrants of imprisonment) grew significantly. So did the impact of sensationalist autobiographical prison stories – amongst them that of the enterprising Latude (a familiar of the Bastille and other prisons

18 R. van Dülmen, *Theatre of Horror: Crime and Punishment in Early Modern Germany* (Oxford, 1990) provides a brief survey of the whole early modern period. On England, see V.A.C. Gatrell, *The Hanging Tree: Execution and the English People 1770–1868* (Oxford, 1994), where the high rate of executions in England compared with other European countries is emphasised, 9.

from 1750 until 1784, whiling away his time making pets of the rodents), and the rather grimmer story of Linguet (incarcerated in the Bastille in 1780 for his publications, and psychologically more adversely affected by it).[19]

Changes in attitude, combined with the growing complexities of economic and social relations all over western Europe, may have helped to point up the need for finer gradations of punishment in between death, at one extreme, and symbolic public humiliation at the other. Such a gradation had been applied already for some time to beggars, vagrants and petty violent offenders, through the mechanism of the workhouse and forced labour schemes (below, p. 183). The dividing line between workhouses and prisons in early modern Europe was not altogether clear, and in many towns the same building might even serve both purposes.[20] But long-term prison detention was costly and its rationale far from obvious. In the eyes of most early modern authorities, prison was meant to be transient – typically for prisoners of war, debtors and felons awaiting deportation.

For those who did end up there, prison was a calamity in every conceivable way. For a start, a delay in coming to trial could spell disaster: detention on remand brought accumulated gaoler's fees which were not waived even if the outcome was a clear acquittal. A debtor paying to avoid the worst possible conditions in prison would obviously just add to his difficulties, especially if his family could not sustain his means of livelihood in his absence. Avoiding the worst conditions, however, could be a matter of life and death. A late eighteenth-century description of Wood Street prison in London may serve as a typical illustration: built in 1670, it had various quarters ranging from individual cells, for paying prisoners, to dungeons without bedding or straw, for felons. Of the two rooms for ordinary debtors,

> that for men, which is their day-room, night-room, and kitchen, with a copper, &c., is dark and dirty; about 35 feet by 18, and 16 high; far too small for the number of prisoners, many of whom sleep in 23 beds which are on three stories of galleries, or broad shelves. At one of my visits there were in this room 39 debtors: seven of them had their wives and children. The room swarms with bugs ... I learned [from the keeper] that in the beginning of the year 1773 his prisoners were sickly, and 11 died.[21]

---

19 J. Bender, *Imagining the Penitentiary: Fiction and the Architecture of Mind in 18th-Century England* (Chicago, 1987). For an overall analysis of the imagery of imprisonment in the last years of *ancien régime* France and after 1789, see H.J. Lüsebrink and R. Reichardt, 'La "Bastille" dans l'imaginaire social de la France à la fin du xviiie siècle', *Revue d'Histoire Moderne et Contemporaine* 30 (1983), 196–234.

20 P. Spierenburg, *The Prison Experience: Disciplinary Institutions and their Inmates in Early Modern Europe* (New Brunswick, 1991); and T. Munck, 'Forced labour, workhouse-prisons and the early modern state: a case study', Institute of Historical Research: Electronic Seminars in History, February 1997.

21 John Howard, *The State of the Prisons in England and Wales* (4th edition, London, 1792), 228–9.

John Howard, who wrote this, did more than anyone else to raise public awareness of prison conditions. In contrast to such bland theoretical digests as William Eden's *Principles of Penal Law* (1771), Howard set out to document in great detail exactly what was wrong in the prisons of Europe. Between 1773 and the mid-1780s he travelled over 40,000 miles to compile the material on which he based both his *The State of the Prisons in England and Wales* (first published in 1777) and *An Account of the Principal Lazarettos in Europe* (1789). Howard was a remarkable example of that new generation of reformer who believed that precision and cumulative detail was the best way to ensure a response. His *State of the Prisons* (which reached its fourth edition in 1792, shortly after his death in Russia from a highly infectious gaol fever) not only described virtually every detention centre in Britain in some detail, but also included comparisons with comparable institutions across much of Europe. Reading through its 500 pages, one cannot help being awed by the dogged determination of its author not only to document in detail the abject misery of so many of the inmates, but also to provide comprehensive recommendations for improvements ranging from relatively minor alterations (such as might ensure adequate ventilation in overcrowded cells, or improve water supplies and sanitation) to the planning and construction of complete new prisons along rational and more humane lines. Judging from passing observations, Howard had an intuitive instinct for observing what local authorities would have preferred him not to see. His return visits to particular institutions could lead to embarrassing revelations of change (or lack of it). But above all the sheer scale of accumulated comparative evidence, and the comprehensive range of dispassionate practical recommendations, ensured that this one-man crusade acquired an attentive audience across enlightened Europe.

In England, contemporary opinion was particularly receptive. Following the revolt of the American colonies and the consequent end of transportation (1775), an alternative way of handling convicted offenders was urgently needed. Stop-gap use of forced labour in the naval dockyards, or incarceration of convicts in old ships (the hulks), proved unsatisfactory. The Penitentiary Act of 1779 (in which Howard had a hand) envisaged the construction of new reformed prisons aiming at the moral regeneration of offenders: amongst the novel techniques proposed, particular emphasis was placed on the extensive use of solitary confinement. With this in mind Jeremy Bentham designed a comprehensive penal institution which he called the *Panopticon*, first proposed in 1786 and revised many times until 1813. It incorporated a system of individual cells encircling a central managerial observation tower: the guards themselves were to be monitored, and the whole institution open to public scrutiny. Central to its success, both as a penitentiary and as a business enterprise, was the routine of heavy labour around which everything revolved. Bentham, like so many workhouse entrepreneurs in earlier generations, regarded profit and moral reform of convicts as compatible. The Treasury, however, was not convinced, and disputes amongst the reformers meant that very little was in the end achieved. Instead, a new penal colony, founded at Botany Bay in Australia in 1787, encouraged a reversion to old policies.

Elsewhere in Europe, transportation was not the normal way of dealing with offenders who avoided the death penalty. Until 1748 France had, like other Mediterranean powers, allocated convicts to row the galleys used in coastal defence. As the military usefulness of these vessels declined, however, French convicts were re-allocated to forced labour in the naval dockyards (*bagnes*), especially those at Toulon, Rochefort and Brest. As in the older forced labour camps of the Netherlands, northern Germany and Scandinavia, convicts in the *bagnes* worked harsh sentences, often for life but sometimes for shorter periods of years. Chained at night and sometimes also while at work during the day, the convicts suffered such brutal discipline that at most half seem to have survived their term. Yet the later eighteenth-century records both of the French *bagnes* and of the Danish forced labour camps – incomplete and sketchy though they all are – demonstrate that the offences of which the inmates had been found guilty ranged from very serious violent crimes down to relatively minor cases of fraud or theft. Clearly early modern penal institutions still found it difficult to classify and segregate offenders according to even fairly basic criteria of whether they might be a danger to others, or whether there was a realistic prospect of rehabilitation.

Only the well-off could turn prison, if not to their advantage, then at least to a mitigated inconvenience. The marquis de Sade made his stay in the Bastille in the later 1780s more comfortable by bringing in a wardrobe full of clothes, paintings and wall-hangings, comfortable bedding, a desk and a substantial collection of books. Madame Roland, on her arrest in Paris in June 1793, paid her way to a small individual cell, away from what she saw as the vulgar and disreputable women around her. Like other better-off prisoners she had separate meals cooked for her, arranged for books and writing implements to be brought, and was allowed by the keeper's wife to install a fortepiano in their apartment for herself to play. But interesting though such cases are, the nature of extant source material makes it impossible even to guess at the overall characteristics of prisoners and their treatment. Equally, we have no means of assessing chances either of evasion or of escape. What is abundantly clear, however, is that prison, like other eighteenth-century institutions, distinguished fundamentally between rich and poor.

Treatment of the sick

Medicine, like the law, was a highly conservative and tradition-bound profession. At the top were the elite corps of physicians, whom few people could afford to consult, and whose knowledge was in any case more often based on long-established theories of illness than on direct practical experience. Surgeons, responsible for administering purges, treating injuries or wounds, and dealing with amputations and common ailments like bladder-stones, may have seemed more useful to most contemporaries, but they had less social prestige than physicians because of their proximity to the barber trade. Even closer to popular medicine were the pharmacists, druggists, toothpullers, midwives and sellers of quack remedies. Given the recurrent and potentially overwhelming health problems of the time, there was bound to be a ready-made demand for the services of each of these groups. Ointments, poultices and medicines were particularly sellable, and though some were based on well-founded folk remedies, many others appear from contemporary observation to have been useless or downright dangerous. Itinerant practitioners had considerable scope both in cities and at fairs in smaller towns, providing patients with plenty of choice and sometimes a little hope. Building up a successful non-itinerant practice, however, required more skill and confidence, combined with a medical track record that would appear at least plausible. Yet disease remained so unpredictable, and medical expertise so mysteriously arcane, that it was easy to find alternative explanations for unexpected outcomes.

Of all the medics and quacks relying on an unquenchable human fascination with medicine and popular science, the most famous was the Austrian physician Franz-Anton Mesmer (1734–1815). He developed (but never fully explained) a form of medical practice intended to restore the natural balance of cosmic fluid and 'animal magnetism' in the body – usually by means of group therapy using purpose-built equipment such as magnetic bars and special tubs, combined with a laying on of hands by the 'curer'. Mesmer set up practice in Paris in 1778, and despite the very sceptical reaction of the medical establishment soon had a large following from amongst the elite. With support from prominent Freemasons and from amongst Marie Antoinette's circle, Mesmer was offered a substantial court pension of 20,000 livres in 1782, but he turned it down and left. Some of his assistants, however, ensured that mesmerism remained in the headlines for some years. Even an official enquiry by the Academy of Sciences, dismissing mesmerism as a complete fraud, failed to convince the rich and gullible. Quackery, appropriately packaged, evidently had as much appeal amongst salon society as in the village fair.

Historians of medicine now accept that a linear view of the gradual triumph of a 'modern' rational system of enlightened medical expertise, gaining momentum from the later eighteenth century onwards, simply is not tenable. As with other branches of science, any tidy sense of progression rapidly evaporates once we recognise how many routes were sought down wonderfully imaginative but unsustainable blind alleys, and how many empirically effective cures were in fact based on long-standing misunderstandings of the causal factors of disease. Just as the supposed distinction between elite and popular culture vanishes on closer inspection (see Chapter

2), so there is really no conclusive way of distinguishing 'scientific' from popular medicine during this period. Superstition, quackery, folk remedies, obstinacy and ignorance were never far away from clinical, professional, supposedly progressive, rational and 'scientific' medicine. In some fields, such as midwifery, there appear to have been serious rivalries between traditional and supposedly 'professional' (male) practices. But contemporary academic medicine did not on the whole cope well with the range and diversity of actual medical needs, and its credibility was not necessarily greater than that of more traditional healing methods. Surgery may have had the benefit of more immediate practical knowledge, but even the most skilled surgical treatment was more often than not negated by the lack of elementary hygienic precautions. Patients of both high and low social standing often hedged their bets by trying a mixture of treatments, sometimes simultaneously. In the circumstances, this was probably a sensible approach. Rivalry between individual practitioners, as well as feuding over catchment areas or functional demarcations – accompanied by mutual accusations of 'quackery' – were as rife as in the legal profession. And, as Mary Lindemann has recently demonstrated, no amount of official regulation could standardise actual medical practices on the ground, or even ensure minimum educational requirements amongst the practitioners. The trained physician was likely to be pinned 'in the jaws of a vice composed of local interests on the one hand and the aspirations of central government on the other.'[22]

Medical training in western Europe, like other aspects of the educational system, was of very uneven quality. The most celebrated medical school at the turn of the century, that run at Leyden University by Herman Boerhaave (1669–1738), was based on tradition and systemisation rather than on innovation. Boerhaave was famous partly for his lectures, which in the words of one of his students helped 'digesting a huge Heap of Jargon and indigested Stuff into an intelligible, regular and rational System'.[23] He also took over the University Botanic Garden, with its medicinal herbs, and in 1714 became professor of clinical medicine on the basis of a 12-bed teaching ward. His teaching became legendary, the model for new medical schools founded in Vienna, Edinburgh and elsewhere. Yet, despite his attention to clinical observation, he seems to have remained deeply loyal to the theoretical framework he found in the old writings of established medical authorities from Hippocrates onwards. Accordingly, even though the patients admitted to his teaching ward were chosen for their typicality and treatability, verifica-

---

22 M. Lindemann, *Health and Healing in Eighteenth-Century Germany* (Baltimore, 1996), 75; this work also provides a succinct description of the medical policies of a north German state, and the difficulties of ensuring practical implementation, 49–65 and *passim*.

23 A description by James Houston, cited by Andrew Cunningham, 'Medicine to calm the mind: Boerhave's medical system, and why it was adopted in Edinburgh', in *The Medical Enlightenment of the Eighteenth Century*, ed. A. Cunningham and R. French (Cambridge, 1990), 41. On changes in French medical thinking in the eighteenth century, see L. Brockliss and C. Jones, *The Medical World of Early Modern France* (Oxford, 1997), 411–79.

tion of treatment procedures was not sufficiently objective or systematic to establish definitive cures of specific diseases.

Most hospitals in eighteenth-century Europe continued to place greater emphasis on care than on cure. But during the eighteenth century the age-old Christian priority of caring for the sick and the poor came into more obvious potential conflict (both in Protestant and Catholic Europe) with other practical considerations – such as the repression of begging or the containment of epidemic disease. In France, as elsewhere, the monarchy habitually responded to newly perceived social problems by sanctioning yet more institutions, even if these might overlap in function with existing ones. By the end of the *ancien régime* France had thus acquired, in addition to hundreds of surviving older charitable foundations, some 176 so-called *hôpitaux généraux*. A literal translation would render them as 'general hospitals', but from the later seventeenth century onwards both central government and local authorities came to regard these institutions as care (or detention) centres for beggars, vagrants, foundlings, lunatics and social misfits. Actual conditions in these institutions varied enormously, and we should not assume that all were equally grim. Nevertheless most general hospitals probably had a closer resemblance to a workhouse, or even a prison, than to a medical institution.

In France, the poor who really needed medical assistance preferred to go to the *hôtels-Dieu* situated in most bigger towns, where (except for lepers and syphilitics) conditions were generally more benign and treatment less punitive. The religious-oriented care provided in the *hôtels-Dieu* by nursing sisters and volunteers was gradually supplemented during the eighteenth century with the more academic medical attention of hired physicians. But here again it is perhaps not helpful to impose too clear a distinction between those with formal medical training and those without. The nursing sisters who worked in the French *hôtels-Dieu* performed a great deal of significant medical work, and were on hand far more of the time than the fleeting physicians and surgeons. What is clear, however, is that changes in medical practice came only very slowly. The military hospitals were often better at practical experimentation and training than their civilian religious counterparts – both because military needs were more specific, and because these institutions gave greater prominence to surgeons rather than the more conservative physicians.

Some medical establishments of the enlightenment period acquired a considerable reputation – amongst them the Royal Infirmary founded in Edinburgh in 1729. Like the other voluntary hospitals created around this time (see p. 34), the Royal started from very modest beginnings and continued to depend very largely on the generosity of its philanthropic subscribers. Yet by all accounts it came to serve the city well. John Howard stated that:

> I could not but admire the Royal Infirmary at Edinburgh. Few hospitals
> in England exceed it in airiness and cleanliness. Great attention is paid

to the patients, and their complaints are very accurately minuted: the students attend the physician in his round of the wards. The success of this institution is evident, from the few that die in comparison with the number admitted. The proportion of deaths to the number of admitted, from 1770 to 1775 inclusive, was one to twenty-five nearly ... The total number of patients admitted in 1780 was two thousand two hundred and twenty-eight, of whom seventy-six died.[24]

This was certainly an impressive record by contemporary standards, but it needs to be remembered that patients were admitted only if they were deemed curable. In any case, all British voluntary hospital foundations had to try to make their patient statistics look as good as possible in order to ensure continuing public support. In the Royal Infirmary the standard of clinical observation, the quality of student training, the level of staff expertise, and the standard of patient care all seem to have been good. But as a recent study of the institution has made clear, its success rate was probably at least as much the result of reasonable hygiene, nutrition and nursing, as a product of the actual medical treatment offered. As in other teaching hospitals, much emphasis was placed on detailed patient records, but even under William Cullen in the 1770s each case was expected to fit into a preconceived classificatory scheme of disease systems, and treated accordingly. If such treatment failed, autopsies were only rarely allowed (because of complicated restrictions), and if they were, the recorded results appear superficial and almost perfunctory. The procedures of the Royal Infirmary thus did not greatly assist in the critical assessment of the effectiveness of alternative treatments of specific illnesses – let alone in establishing convincing causal explanations.[25]

At governmental level, the scope for regulatory activity was considerable. Health boards had a long history (especially in dealing with outbreaks of the plague), and during the eighteenth century it was not uncommon for state

24 *The State of the Prisons in England and Wales* (4th edition, London, 1792), 199. Howard is here relying on the official statistics put out by the Royal Infirmary itself, according to which hospital mortality was within the range 3.0 to 6.5% every year during the period 1763–1800.
25 G.B. Risse, *Hospital Life in Enlightenment Scotland: Care and Teaching at the Royal Infirmary of Edinburgh* (Cambridge, 1986); and his 'Before the clinic was "born": methodological perspectives in hospital history', in *Institutions of Confinement: Hospitals, Asylums and Prisons in western Europe and North America, 1500–1950*, ed. N. Finzsch and R. Jütte (Cambridge, 1996) 75–96; see also C. Jones, 'The construction of the hospital patient in early modern France', in the same volume, 55–74, which suggests that French provincial *hôtels-Dieu* had a fatality rate at around 10–12%, probably less than half that of the Paris *hôtel-Dieu* (which housed around 1,000 of the capital's 20,000 patients in 1785, when it came under the more progressive direction of the surgeon Pierre Desault). On changes of attitude in the later eighteenth century regarding the role of hospitals, see L. Perol, 'Diderot, Mme Necker et la réforme des hôpitaux', *StVEC* 311 (1993), 219–32; and S.C. Lawrence, *Charitable Knowledge: Hospital Pupils and Practitioners in Eighteenth-Century London* (Cambridge, 1996).

governments – notably that in Brandenburg-Prussia – to seek to remove abuses amongst medical practitioners by means of regulatory guidelines. How effectively these were enforced is questionable. Many governments, however, also sought by mid-century to use their growing bureaucratic network to collate information, including vital statistics of the kind that had hitherto only been compiled in connection with plague epidemics. Encouraged by writers like John Arbuthnot (1733), Montesquieu (1748) and Boissièr de Sauvages (1754), many theorists and medical practitioners favoured using environmental data to help explain and control disease. Even though there was no clear understanding of the vectors of most diseases, resulting practical measures could have beneficial results. Thus the assumption that infection was related to noxious smells encouraged a range of improvements in urban sanitation, the search for better water supplies, the drainage of marshland, and improved ventilation in hospitals and other institutions – all of genuine medical benefit, if not for the reasons assumed at the time. Such apparent successes in themselves encouraged more state regulation, a notable example of which is found in the medical instructions compiled by the royal inspectors of hospitals and prisons in France in 1785, Jean Colombier and François Doublet. These instructions can be seen as an important stage in the legitimisation of empirical approaches to social medicine. Notably, they encouraged major improvement in the handling and selective treatment of the insane in the hitherto dreaded Bicêtre and Salpêtrière hospices in Paris.[26] By the early 1790s medical reform had become far more urgent: the Revolution had triggered massive institutional upheaval (such as the near-destruction of the religious nursing orders), and had imposed huge wartime strains on medical resources.

If the eighteenth century was thus not without some modest medical achievements, there was only one spectacular breakthrough – that of inoculation against smallpox, one of the worst killers of the time. A technique of inoculation with mildly infectious matter was known to have been used in the east, and was advocated by Lady Mary Wortley Montagu in 1718. The Royal Society discussed its possible application in 1720, and the procedure was tested successfully on six Newgate prison volunteers the following year. The treatment, however, carried significant risks, and there was understandable resistance both in England and in France to exposing healthy people to a treatment which not only entailed hospitalisation but also required isolation. The disease and its treatment continued to attract much attention throughout the century, and it was not until Jenner's discovery of

---

26　There is a growing literature on the treatment of insanity from the early modern period onwards, some of it in response to the seminal but controversial work of M. Foucault, in particular his *Madness and Civilisation* (New York, 1965) and his *Histoire de la folie* (Paris, 1972). On the commercialisation of asylum management during the eighteenth century, and efforts to improve treatment and institutional conditions from the 1790s onwards, see notably A. Scull, *The Most Solitary of Afflictions: Madness and Society in Britain 1700–1900* (New Haven, 1993), esp. 17–103; see also J. Andrews *et al.*, eds., *The History of Bethlem* (London, 1997).

the efficacy of cowpox vaccination (1796–98) that a safe immunisation programme could be initiated. Here again, as in the gradual taming of the bubonic plague some generations earlier, effective measures were based not on any real understanding of the nature of the disease itself, or its transmission, but rather on the effective use of some relevant but fortuitous environmental observations.

* * *

In terms of the issues discussed in this chapter, then, we have to be cautious in regarding the enlightenment as a decisive turning point. Few governments were genuinely keen on the idea of freedom of opinion, and the relaxation of censorship was frequently half-hearted. The spiritual environment of the great majority of Europeans was even more resistant to change. Policies on religious toleration did not remove religious bigotry, and the relative relaxation of religious discipline apparent in bigger cities in the second half of the century was not widely replicated in smaller towns or the countryside. All over Europe, not only the various churches but also other administrative machineries such as the law continued to fall far short of enlightenment ideals.

Yet we need to avoid judging the past by unrealistic (or anachronistic) standards. Recent work on the medical professions, in particular, has taught us not to look simply for 'rational progress' towards some pre-ordained empirically satisfactory or efficient outcome. Many contemporaries will have found social health policies depressingly ineffective, crime control a chimera, and both the church and the law corrupt. Given the inheritance from the seventeenth century, spiritual resignation and practical helplessness might have seemed an understandable reaction. Yet what is striking is that some of the fundamental certainties which had been accepted for so long without question were now more open to pragmatic re-valuation and public scrutiny – a process which was not necessarily always beneficial or consistent, and the results of which were not always worked through satisfactorily, but which at least had the potential for constructive re-engagement.

|7|

Property, the underprivileged and reform

Eighteenth-century society was built on assumptions of inequality. That inequality rested in part on a long-standing traditional belief, supported both by religious imagery and by secular justification, that every person had an allocated position and role in a 'great chain of being'. Such a belief was of obvious convenience for rulers, for the elite, and for anyone else of some social standing. None of the great writers of the enlightenment were remotely egalitarian, and not until late in the eighteenth century were some key social assumptions seriously questioned. Acceptance of the near immutability of the hierarchical order, deemed vital for the preservation of stability, was reinforced by a variety of means: by selective quotation from the Scriptures, by censorship of non-conformist or libertarian ideas, by political structures ensuring socially selective access to power, and above all by means of a panoply of legal and economic controls.

Central to this whole edifice was an all-pervasive ideal of the sanctity of property. Derived from classical and 'feudal' origins, notions of property were so embedded in early modern law as to be utterly fundamental to the very fabric of European society. The *Encyclopédie* is typical in basing its own definition on well-worn Lockian thinking:

> One of the principal aims of men in forming civil societies was to assure for themselves tranquil possession of the advantages that they had gained or might yet gain. They wanted no-one to be able to disturb their enjoyment of their possessions. It is for this reason that everyone has consented to give up a share, called taxes, for the preservation and maintenance of the whole of society ... However strong the enthusiasm amongst men for the sovereigns to whom they have submitted themselves, they have never pretended to give them absolute and unlimited power over all their property; they have never reckoned with

putting themselves under compulsion to work for anyone other than themselves.[1]

Several consequences seemed to stem naturally from such assumptions. Firstly, taxation was a natural part of civilised society, designed for mutual benefit and preservation rather than to pay for the whims of a ruler. Subjects and princes had mutual obligations and shared interests, and the preservation of property figured very prominently in both. Secondly, because of the inherent inequality in society (a subject on which the *Encyclopédie* does not provide any great insights) it might well be assumed that those in possession of greater wealth might also have a greater stake in the preservation of the social order – a stand-point that was taken for granted by Locke and later political commentators. The labour of each individual might therefore sensibly be valued not simply in terms of its utility, or in terms of supply and demand, but according to its place in the hierarchy. Similarly, the worth of each person could be rated not just in terms of his/her intrinsic qualities, but according to his 'natural' rank in the greater whole. These ideas fundamentally underpinned the way most contemporaries addressed matters of economic policy, agrarian and labour reform, poor relief, and the underlying issues of public versus private interests in society.

Taxation

Public concern for fiscal accountability, coupled with the expectation that taxation should be reasonable both in its incidence and in the purpose for which it was collected, is as old as taxation itself. During the first half of the seventeenth century disputes over the legitimacy of taxation had fuelled an interminable sequence of fiscal revolts all over Europe. In England, taxation had helped to legitimise the confrontation with Charles I. Fiscal accountability ultimately became one of the corner-stones of parliamentary power, and a permanent part of the unwritten British constitution from 1689 onwards. With it, not surprisingly, came a number of institutions providing regulatory and administrative back-up, notably the Bank of England (1694) and the Board of Trade of 1696. During the eighteenth century, the need to control the national debt naturally led to more detailed parliamentary reporting, to closer scrutiny of key branches of the revenue-collecting machinery (notably during periods of crises, as in the post-war reports of the Commissioners of Public Accounts 1780–86), and to a growing overall interest in the compilation and analysis of precise statistical information of various kinds. How far down the social ladder such information might have attracted attention is uncertain. But amongst the commercial and political elite state finances were of sufficient interest, especially in times of war, to

---

1 Article by unknown author on property ('*Propriété: Droit naturel et politique*'), *Encyclopédie*, vol. 13 (1765), 491.

support the publication of works such as Postlethwayt's monumental *The History of the Public Revenue* (1759).

On the continent, progress towards fiscal accountability was much more erratic, incompatible as it was with the ideal of unfettered royal power. Towards the end of the reign of Louis XIV, Fénelon compiled a catechismal self-examination for the expected heir to the throne, the duc de Bourgogne, in which he asked:

> Have you ever taken property from any one of your subjects, arbitrarily and against the rules? Have you compensated him, as a private person would have done, when you have taken his house, or enclosed his field within your grounds, or suppressed his office, or annulled his pension? Have you thoroughly examined the real needs of the state, in order to balance them against the drawback of taxes, before burdening your peoples? Have you consulted, for such an important issue, the most enlightened men, those most zealous for the public good, those most able to tell you the truth with neither flattery nor understatement? Have you ever described as necessity of state that which merely served to flatter your ambition?[2]

Such a pointed series of questions implied more than superficial or dismissive answers. But with the advent of a regency in 1715, and a prolonged period of relative peace, the issue of public fiscal accountability could be brushed aside. Despite renewed conflict around mid-century, it was not until the French intervention in the American Wars of Independence in the late 1770s that a change of approach became unavoidable. Necker's attempt in 1781 to provide a plausible public statement of accounts was thus, for all its deficiencies, a real landmark. By then a detailed system of economic and fiscal reporting had long since been implemented by the government for internal use, notably through the trusted *intendants* (the long-established agents of royal power throughout the kingdom). In the 1770s, successive administrations even considered setting up a full-scale statistical office to help the crown, and eventually, at the suggestion of the scientist Lavoisier, this idea was implemented by the new government in 1791.

Similar trends towards the compilation of more accurate economic and fiscal statistics, for government as well as for public use, can be documented for other parts of Europe during the later eighteenth century. We have already noted such information being used specifically for prison and hospital reform (above, p. 154). Yet we should also remind ourselves that information does not necessarily entail any real understanding: descriptive statistics do not by themselves explain demographic change, fluctuations in interest rates, customs and other revenue, investment and exchange rates,

---

2 François de Salignac de la Mothe-Fénelon, *Examen de conscience sur les devoirs de la royauté*, Art. III, paragraph 14, in *Écrits et lettres politiques*, ed. C. Urbain (Paris, 1920), 43f. The text was written for the instruction of the grandson of Louis XIV, Louis of France, duke of Burgundy (1682–1712), but first published in London and The Hague in 1747.

trade, or changes in domestic output and wages. Nor does the availability of information on these economic variables necessarily foster a more analytic approach to financial and fiscal policy generally, either inside or outside government. An obvious illustration of this can be found in connection with overseas trade and colonial development, which clearly caught the imagination of newspaper readers in early eighteenth-century Britain and France (above, p. 123). As the virtually concurrent speculative disasters in France (John Law's scheme of 1717–20) and Britain (the South Sea Bubble of 1720) clearly demonstrated, Treasury officials and private investors alike did not always put the available information to best use.

In the much more prosaic area of domestic taxation, systematic re-evaluation and analysis were also slow in coming. Various types of poll taxes (including variable-rate ones like the French *capitation* and *dixième*), land taxes and other direct impositions, though crude and often unfair, were not easy to change without considerable political risks. The threat of violent popular revolt against new taxes may have been less than during the early seventeenth century, but quiescence could not be taken for granted. With real power everywhere in Europe in the hands of a very small elite, no-one was likely to encourage such risk-taking. By contrast, indirect (value-added) taxation, customs and excise offered greater flexibility. Well tried and relatively easy to administer, such impositions remained a mainstay of public revenue. In Britain, the customs and excise service developed (at least by contemporary standards) a high degree of professionalism. Normally, the risks attached to indirect taxation were more limited – though the traumas of the Excise Crisis of 1733 and of the Stamp Act controversy in the American colonies after 1763 might suggest otherwise.

As we would expect given the exigencies of great-power status, the most innovative fiscal thinking of the period is found in French and British writings. In France in particular, the search for alternatives was made all the more urgent because of the relatively greater emphasis on direct taxes of various kinds, the prominence of the largely unaccountable private (tax-farming) sector, and the resulting disproportionately greater unpopularity of the whole fiscal régime there. The idea of a progressive income tax, where each would pay according to his earnings rather than on a flat rate, was aired already early in the century, notably by Boisguilbert in his *Le détail de la France sous le règne présent* (*Analysis of France during the Present Reign*) of 1707, and by the abbé de St Pierre in his *Mémoire pour l'établissement de la taille proportionelle* (*Memorandum on the Establishment of Proportional Taille Taxation*) first issued in 1717 and soon substantially revised and extended. St Pierre even suggested innovations such as a personal annual tax return, and pointedly emphasised the need for a permanent staff of professional tax officers who could operate the system fairly.

By mid-century, the *Encyclopédie* could incorporate a number of significant articles. Amongst them was Rousseau's on '*Économie*' (economy, published 1755), which, whilst emphasising the sanctity of property, also recognised that indirect taxation on luxury goods might have to be supplemented through direct taxation, to be levied in proportion to each person's means over and above what was needed for basic subsistence. Jaucourt's article on '*Impôt*' (taxation, published in 1765) also discussed a range of proportional taxes, emphasising that basic necessities of life should not be taxed, whilst luxuries should be subject to a geometrically increasing scale. Other articles dealt in general terms with related social aspects, such as '*Grains*' (grain), '*Manufacture*' (manufacture) and '*Privilège*' (privilege). By contrast, the very last article added to the end of the *Encyclopédie*, under the keyword '*Vingtième*' (twentieth tax), argued, rather illogically in an age supposedly critical of excess luxury, that only land was worth taxing. Such an approach, a keystone in physiocratic thinking (to which we shall shortly turn), only made sense if one could assume that all production ultimately depended on the agricultural base of the economy. That assumption was dismissed as absurd already in 1767, when Jean-Louis Graslin published his *Essay analytique sur la richesse et sur l'impôt* (*Analytical essay on Wealth and Taxation*). This was a precise and detailed explanation of how a truly progressive income tax might work – covering all forms of wealth generation in such a way as to ensure that higher earnings were taxed in 'constantly increasing proportion'. Graslin not only made a clear distinction between proportional and progressive taxation, but, in the words of a recent historian, gave 'meaningful fiscal expression to the social conscience of his age ... [implying] over time, a gradual process of "levelling", but not a direct attack on property as such'.[3]

It goes without saying that, before the Revolution, no finance minister could contemplate implementing anything as radical as this, and Graslin himself recognised as much. In the *Wealth of Nations*, Adam Smith bowed to contemporary British consensus in favour of indirect taxation, while stressing that the basic necessities of life should be exempt. Yet, if more complex schemes were dismissed as unviable, at least flat-rate direct taxation was being seriously questioned, and some form of graduated taxation increasingly seen as desirable. In Denmark, for example, a two-pronged proportional tax was imposed in March 1789 to pay for an unexpected defence crisis. It was levied at 5% on earnings over certain levels, dependent on occupation, but alongside a tax of 0.5% on wealth and capital over a certain amount.

In France, too, the 1780s and 1790s brought more open and increasingly painful debate. The proposals put before the Assembly of Notables by Calonne in February 1787 – to replace the unsatisfactory *vingtièmes* with a new land tax – was the most drastic reform ever tabled by the *ancien régime* monarchy, and also effectively its last. This is not the place to discuss whether his plans could ever have been viable. Suffice it to say that the idea

3 Jean-Pierre Gross, 'Progressive taxation and social justice in eighteenth-century France', *Past and Present* 140 (1993), 79–126, and especially 100f.

of replacing the existing fiscal base with a new comprehensive land tax was revived by the National Constituent Assembly once the old fiscal edifice had disintegrated in 1789, but as part of a three-stranded tax structure which would also cover movables and personal earnings. At the instigation notably of Condorcet, the Assembly repeatedly touched both on the right to subsistence and on the principles of progressively redistributive personal tax. Its actual implemented schemes, however, constituted a modest and not very workable compromise which had to be reviewed once more by the Convention from autumn 1792 onwards. The most intensive parliamentary debates on fiscal progression came in March 1793 when the Convention, repeatedly citing the traditional liberal views of Montesquieu and Adam Smith whilst at the same time ever more acutely aware of popular pressures and expectations, allowed local authorities to implement a variety of such schemes to help meet the wartime emergency.[4]

It is perhaps a measure of the European-wide impact of this kind of thinking that even the British government, despite fears of French-style 'levelling', adopted modest progression in some of its additional war taxes from 1798 onwards, including the controversial new income tax of 1799. Other governments had similar ideas at least to cover emergencies, as illustrated in the Dutch progressive income taxes implemented in 1797–98. All over Europe interest in 'top-heavy' taxation fluctuated in the 1790s in tune with changing political directions. But taking a long perspective, it seems justifiable to conclude that, in the course of the eighteenth century, fiscal policy evolved from a manipulative and secret art practised in the innermost recesses of government to something which in theory at least was slightly more open to public scrutiny.

Political economy, cameralism and the physiocrats

The burden of taxation affected most people; but the purposes for which it was collected (leaving aside its most obvious traditional application in paying for warfare) also had the potential to generate domestic debate.

4 There is inevitably a very extensive literature on the finances of pre-revolutionary and revolutionary France; useful guidance in English will be found in Jean-Pierre Gross, 'Progressive taxation and social justice in eighteenth-century France', *Past and Present* 140 (1993), 79–126; for the wider context, see also R.F. Bosher, *French Finances 1770–1795* (Cambridge, 1970); P. Mathias and P.K. O'Brien, 'Taxation in Britain and France, 1715–1810', *Journal of European Economic History* 5 (1976), 601–50; E.N. White, 'Was there a solution to the ancien régime's financial dilemma?', *Journal of Economic History* 49 (1989), 545–68; M. Kwass, 'A kingdom of taxpayers: state formation, privilege and political culture in eighteenth-century France', *Journal of Modern History* 70 (1998), 295–339; F.R. Velde and D.R. Weir, 'The financial market and government debt policy in France, 1746–1793', *Journal of Economic History* 52 (1992), 1–39; and K. Norberg, 'The French fiscal crisis of 1788 and the financial origins of the Revolution of 1789', in *Fiscal Crises, Liberty and Representative Government, 1450–1789*, ed. P.T. Hoffman and K. Norberg (Stanford, 1994), 253–98.

Political arithmetic (collection of numerical data relevant to government and political life) and political economy (the study of the production, distribution and consumption of wealth) were not new areas of enquiry, and both terms had been used for generations. In England, the decades after the Restoration had produced some remarkable works of political arithmetic, ranging from John Graunt's and William Petty's *Observations upon the Bills of Mortality* (1662) to Gregory King's *Natural and Political Observations* (1696). These were followed in the eighteenth century by the substantial work of John Arbuthnot, Joseph Massie and others. In the German lands, cameralism (the study of government and economic administration) evolved over the same period. It was based on traditional mercantilism, in part influenced by the English political arithmeticians; but it placed more systematic emphasis on administrative practices conducive to the maintenance of domestic stability and order, and sought to improve state revenues within the limitations of a utilitarian and fair fiscal structure. From its early versions in the writings of theorists like Johann Joachim Becher (1668) and Wilhelm von Schröder (1686), cameralism after 1721 became a formal subject taught at German universities. Classic textbooks of cameralism, including Johann Heinrich Gottlob von Justi's *Staatswirtschaft* (*State Economy*) of 1755, and Joseph von Sonnenfels's three-volume *Grundsätze aus der Polizey, Handlungs- und Finanzwissenschaft* (*Principles of Administrative, Commercial and Financial Science*) of 1765–76, created a central European norm of good administrative practice. There were many variants, but common to most was a recognition of the importance of government in fostering economic prosperity and responsible financial management, securing population growth, and collecting detailed information on which functional social policies could be based. Such sensible aims were fully compatible with the central European enlightenment, but also had significant appeal further afield. In Scandinavia it matched the ideological expectations of Pietism to perfection (see p. 52). Even in Italy similar views were put forward by some of the leading reformers of the day, notably Ludovico Antonio Muratori in his *Della pubblica felicità* of 1749.

Some of these ideas recur within a rather distinctive group of economic thinkers in mid-century France who came to be know as the physiocrats – a group headed by the physician François Quesnay (1694–1774) and including the maverick Victor Riquetti marquis de Mirabeau, Mercier de la Rivière, Du Pont de Nemours, and others. Quesnay made his reputation in part on the basis of an analysis of the total economic system, in his impenetrable *Tableau économique* of 1756–58, but he was also known for his contributions to the *Encyclopédie* under the keywords '*Fermiers*', published in 1756, and '*Grains*' of the following year. A defining characteristic of the physiocrats was their insistence on a universal land tax or *impôt unique* to replace all other forms of taxation (including indirect ones). They regarded agrarian production as fundamental to everything else, and recommended its consolidation through investment, free trade in agricultural produce, the prevention of 'hoarding', the limitation of 'sterile' luxury trades coupled with mercantilist restrictions on foreign trade, and government de-regulation of most other aspects of the economy. Revisions and refinements were added over the next decades, and in the hands of Turgot (an experienced *intendant* and later Controller General of French finances) physiocracy was widened to take other forms of wealth generation into consideration. Although some contemporaries (such as Galiani and Diderot) remained critical, physiocracy became a common point of reference for much economic debate in France in the last decades of the eighteenth century. In central Europe, blended with more traditional cameralist thinking, it likewise influenced both economic analysis and actual policy – not least in the government of Joseph II and of his younger brother Leopold in Lombardy and Tuscany.

Comprehensive political–economic analysis in the enlightenment period reached its most sophisticated form in Scotland, notably in the work of David Hume, James Steuart (Steuart-Denham) and above all Adam Smith. Hume did not aim at systematic coverage, concentrating instead on specific topics, notably in various essays published in his *Political Discourses* of 1752. Steuart, in his large-scale *Inquiry into the Principles of Political Economy* (1767), explicitly dismissed physiocratic system-building as simplistic and misleading. But both he and Smith were influenced by some of Quesnay's ideas – whilst being much more acutely aware than the physiocrats of the wider political and social ramifications which government policy on agriculture and manufacturing might have. Smith in particular, despite the selective interpretation that has been put on parts of *The Wealth of Nations* in recent years, was acutely aware of the need to avoid seeing apparently impersonal economic factors in isolation. He preferred to see the totality of social relations as an interconnected whole, in which government itself should fulfil

> the duty of erecting and maintaining certain publick works and certain publick institutions, which it can never be for the interest of any individual, or small number of individuals, to erect and maintain; because the profit could never repay the expence to any individual or small number of individuals, though it may frequently do much more than repay it to a great society.[5]

What evidence do we have of the actual impact of cameralism, physiocracy and systematic political economy on contemporary thinking? Later in this chapter we shall deal with some specific applications in relation to rural

5 Adam Smith, *The Wealth of Nations* (1776; this quotation from the Glasgow edition, Oxford, 1976), 687–8. For discussion and references to recent work on the changing perceptions of the economic role of the state during the eighteenth century, see notably J. Hoppit, 'Political arithmetic in eighteenth-century England', *Economic History Review* 49 (1996), 516–40; T. Hutchison, *Before Adam Smith: The Emergence of Political Economy, 1662–1776* (Oxford, 1988); P.K. O'Brien, 'The political economy of British taxation, 1660–1815', *Economic History Review* 41 (1988), 1–32; R. Bonney, ed., *Economic Systems and State Finance* (Oxford, 1995), 176–229.

reform and attempts to deal with poverty. But even if we make a broad comparison of the type and quality of records generated by later eighteenth-century governments, against those of a century earlier, we cannot help being struck by the vast increase in precision and detail that we find. In the continuing and no doubt self-interested quest for prosperity and stability, governments adopted significantly more ambitious strategies. Admittedly, as in the field of taxation, great ideas were not always matched by tangible achievements. But if we try to evaluate eighteenth-century reforms not by the absolute standards of seventeenth-century divine politics, nor by the theoretical and moral standards of the Victorians, we may well see this as a period where the domestic roles and responsibilities of government really came of age.

Before we turn to some major areas of reform, it is worth lingering for a moment on one particular illustration of this trend: the obsession with population growth. A steady increase in population had been regarded, even in traditional mercantilist thinking, as an obvious asset or resource. For the more discriminating eighteenth-century political arithmetician or cameralist administrator, however, it was not just a matter of overall numbers, but also of age distribution, health and occupational equilibrium. Clarity on such matters could be obtained only by means of a comprehensive census. Enumerating taxpayers, potential military recruits, the sick, or other specific groups had been common practice in early modern government for a long time, but the desire to survey the entire demographic resources of a whole nation was a far bigger administrative task. Many proposals to that effect were made in different parts of Europe around mid-century. Actual national registration of population statistics was initiated in Sweden in 1748 and in the Austrian lands in 1754. Even in Britain, less centralised than many continental monarchies, parliamentary bills were proposed in 1753 and 1758 to launch a nationwide compilation of demographic statistics – though both failed.

A good example of what could be achieved, and for what purpose, is provided by the national census in Denmark in 1787. The Danish government was no stranger to large-scale administrative enterprises of this kind. Already back in the 1680s it had completed a full land survey, measuring and evaluating the productivity and fiscal potential of every piece of land in the entire kingdom – a process which took years of work and generated an archive which now fills more than 2,000 large bundles of documents and notebooks. In 1769 it had also attempted a comprehensive national census, but the result had not been fully satisfactory. To try to remedy the defects, the plans for the 1787 census were much more detailed: there was to be a single census day (Sunday 1 July), to be used as the point of reference even if not all counting could be completed that day; every head of household regardless of rank would be obliged to report at a pre-arranged census centre, or personally complete a return by other specific arrangement; each head would be responsible for the accuracy for that household; and a standardised printed return form was to be used to ensure a uniform set of details on every household and on each of its members (name, age, occupation, marital condition and relation to head of household).

The result has, not surprisingly, been an invaluable resource for historians. But we also have some indication of what contemporary officials expected to use it for. A little can be gleaned from the official proclamations that were read from the pulpits prior to census day. The sample text distributed for that purpose emphasised that there was nothing to fear from the whole operation: the king personally assured that the census would not be used for fiscal purposes, but

> solely for the good of the whole country, to provide an accurate and reliable reckoning of how many people live in each place. By obtaining such information, his Majesty and the royal officials in the central government departments will have the best guide to the means whereby each locality might be helped, and such defects removed as here and there oppress the people, especially the great mass of ordinary people.

These assurances, of course, speak volumes: but the administrative context in which the census took place suggests that its real purpose was fact-finding. The census is merely the most complex of a great variety of information-gathering processes, without which government was no longer deemed capable of functioning effectively. The potential value of the census in terms of school reform, health, economic planning and poor relief was obvious; and whilst its contents could equally well be used for purposes of taxation or military recruitment, a reliable information base might well be mutually beneficial there as well. Most significant of all, perhaps, is the fact that the census came at a time when the government was itself (as we shall shortly see) becoming more open to public debate. It even sanctioned the first compendium of national statistical information to be printed for general reference.[6]

Rural reform

An obvious use for such detailed information might be to help improve agrarian productivity and rural economic stability. Tax officials, physiocrats and social reformers would all agree about the desirability of such an outcome, even if they might disagree about the means to achieving it. If we also accept the argument (above, p. 26) that the peasantry itself was far from

6 The details of the census are found in the background papers to the decree of 11 May 1787 (Danish Public Record Office, Danske Kancelli, Sjællandske Tegnelser, nos. 347–8). On censuses in general see also D.V. Glass, *Numbering the People: The Eighteenth-Century Population Controversy and the Development of Census and Vital Statistics in Britain* (Farnborough, 1973); P. Buck, 'People who counted: political arithmetic in the eighteenth century', *Isis* 73 (1982), 28–45.

impermeable to new ideas, we might expect the late eighteenth century to have been a period of agrarian experimentation, innovation and change. The reality was somewhat different – and the reasons are not hard to find.

Reading the growing eighteenth-century literature on agriculture and land management, broadly speaking two main approaches can be discerned. On the one hand, there was a wealth of advice on what we might call 'technical change' – improvements in land usage through new crops, more complex rotations, more systematic fertilisation, drainage, better tillage, as well as selective breeding of livestock. On the other was a growing recognition of the importance of the underlying rural relationships – the desirability of fostering longer-term tenancies, encouraging responsible contractual relationships between landowners and actual cultivators, and removing abuses or institutional obstacles to change. Both kinds of approach, it was argued, might result from the enlightened self-interest of landowners and tillers alike. A physiocratic deregulation of the market, or even total economic *laissez-faire*, might well provide an incentive for technical improvement. So indeed might the growing demands for taxation, provided such burdens were fairly distributed and predictable. Some commentators, however, argued that an improvement in peasant–seigneur relations would not be achieved by total de-regulation: on the contrary, rural social inequality was so great that external intervention was essential. The only possible provider of such controversial mediation, it was noted, would be central government.

Technical agrarian change in various forms became widespread by the later eighteenth century, its potential benefits clearly visible on those estates where it was tried. Across much of England, Lowland Scotland, northern and eastern France, northern Germany and southern Scandinavia 'improving' landlords furthered a host of changes based mostly on the techniques pioneered much earlier in the 'agrarian revolution' in the Netherlands. The diffusion of such ideas as far afield as Spain and newly reconquered Hungary was assured, thanks in part to the eighteenth-century mania for sending young sons from wealthy families on grand tours of Europe. Especially from the 1760s onwards, governments everywhere encouraged the spread of innovative techniques by means of promotional pamphlets, reform societies, prize essay competitions, show-case experimental work on crown estates, and other techniques. Although the lead was often taken on large estates, the prosperity of dairy farming in the United Provinces, East Friesland and Schleswig demonstrated that prosperity could equally well be attained within a traditional system of peasant landholding.

Agricultural 'improvement', however, was not without difficulties. Hostility was likely to be encountered in areas of partible inheritance, of land shortage resulting from strong population growth, or of tradition-bound adherence to monoculture (especially grain). Even mild proposals for technical change might become controversial if, for example, they affected the common grazing and forestry rights of a significant segment of a rural community, involved ending patterns of common strip-field cultivation, or were contingent on a temporary increase in labour services for fencing, clearance or other purposes. Analysis of rural unrest is outside the scope of this volume, but long-standing traditions of peasant revolt clearly did not die out. As Turgot discovered during his brief period as Controller General of French finances (1774–76), even relatively uncomplicated measures such as the removal of restrictions on the grain trade could be fatally undermined by changes in popular perceptions triggered by an accidental harvest failure. Nonetheless, the benefits of agrarian improvement were widely acknowledged in many parts of Europe by the last decades of the century, and actual implementation proceeded steadily in many areas.

For some forms of technical improvement, withdrawal from common cultivation was probably unavoidable. A re-location of peasant holdings outside the traditional village community was complex but feasible, as demonstrated for example in Denmark from the 1760s onwards. In some parts of England, however, improvement was implemented on a quite different scale, through the creation of large commercially oriented leaseholds. This often required enclosure and the destruction of customary peasant tenures and freeholds – essentially the removal of middling and smaller tillers from the land. Such shifts in landholding patterns had in fact already started before the main phase of enclosures, and could sometimes be achieved through private agreement or by other means. But during the period 1750–1830 the process of enclosure was greatly accelerated by means of parliamentary private bills – around 4,000 of which were passed during those 80 years, enclosing 21% of the total area of England. The overall consequences in the worst affected areas were truly dramatic: 'agrarian capitalism', commercial tenant-farming and large-scale production displaced older forms of agriculture. By 1800 the gains in agrarian productivity were sufficient to free a major part of the overall population for other work (notably in manufacturing). At one end of the social scale landownership became even more concentrated in relatively few hands. At the other end those who stayed in the countryside were increasingly likely to slide into the flexible but marginalised population of dispossessed rural wage-labourers, whilst those who left faced severe social dislocation and urban overcrowding. As many visitors to England noted, technical agrarian change on this scale was liable to have dramatic implications for society as a whole, and in no other part of Europe were the preconditions right to attempt anything like it.[7]

7 There is a very large literature, and considerable controversy, surrounding both the long-term gestation of the English agrarian revolution and the impact of enclosures. A striking comparative overview is provided by E.A. Wrigley, 'Urban growth and agricultural change: England and the continent in the early modern period', *Journal of Interdisciplinary History* 15 (1985), 683–728. See also the informed discussion in K.D.M. Snell, *Annals of the Labouring Poor: Social Change and Agrarian England, 1660–1900* (Cambridge, 1985), 138–227; T.C. Smout, 'Landowners in Scotland, Ireland and Denmark in the age of improvement', *Scandinavian Journal of History* 12 (1987), 79–97; the short overview by J.V. Beckett, *The Agrarian Revolution* (Oxford, 1990); and a significantly innovative argument in J.M. Neeson, *Commoners: Common Right, Enclosure and Social Change in England, 1700–1820* (Cambridge, 1993), reminding us that a recognisable peasant community survived in some areas.

The alternative approach, seeking to change the relationship between those who owned and those who tilled the land without dislocating either, could also be fraught with problems. Encouraging mutual enlightened self-interest amongst both landowners and tillers assumed at least some common understanding, and might require some re-education to overcome deeply engrained social inequality. Rural stability hinged on improvements in peasant security of tenure, moderation of labour services, regulation of land rents, standardisation of seigneurial rights, external scrutiny of seigneurial law courts, restraints on degrading corporal punishment, and minimalisation of the disruptive potential of tithes. Ultimately, reform was likely to affect the sacred right of landowners to make uninhibited use of their property: it thus had the potential of undermining one of the foundations of the whole social order. Some landowners argued logically that complete de-regulation would allow benevolent self-interest to prevail – and that the task of reform should in any case be entrusted solely to those who had practical experience of what they were doing. Others, however, pointed to England as an example to avoid. In their eyes, it was the duty of government to help the weaker side in those conflicts of interests that were bound to surface.

As a wealth of publications from all over Europe testify, these lines of argument were clearly identified at the time. It is therefore hardly surprising that eighteenth-century governments, largely staffed as they were by members of the elite closely linked to the landowning interest, hesitated to take action. The failure of Frederick II to pursue his *Bauernschutz* (peasant protection) policies in the face of landlord resistance is most readily explained in this way. Further east, if for rather more complicated reasons, Catherine II of Russia had to postpone reforms when her reform commission of 1767 proved abortive.

In France, the underlying social balance may well have been less clear cut. Titles to a third of the total land area of the kingdom were still in peasant hands, and another third in the hands of non-noble landowners. Revenue from the land thus did not depend primarily on those with a dominant political role. The return of agrarian instability around 1770 (and the growing fiscal difficulties of the crown which followed soon afterwards) brought increased rural tension. The government responded partly by pro-moting agrarian improvement (such as enclosure of commons and improvements in land management). With Turgot as Controller General more ambitious physiocratic intervention was to be expected, especially in matters such as the grain trade, commutation of compulsory labour for the state (*corvée*), and encouragement of innovative land usage. Despite the lack of ministerial continuity in central government, the need for improvement became widely recognised. Some historians have argued that this led to a 'seigneurial reaction', with landowners driving through changes which might maximise their own profits at the expence of smallholders. However, the evidence for this is conflicting and inconclusive, and recent work has instead pointed towards signs of disintegration in the seigneurial system, with the rights of lordship more and more vociferously challenged across many parts of France well before the Revolution. By this reckoning, the violent upheavals in many parts of rural France during the summer of 1789, in particular the widespread challenge to the 'feudal' rights of landowners, were the result more of accumulated tensions than of sudden resentments.[8] Even here, however, we see the resilience of vested interests, in that the reforms adopted by successive revolutionary governments fell very far short of expectations, and ultimately alienated the peasantry from the Revolution altogether.

Given the entrenched political power of the elite in most of Europe, it is quite surprising that any government managed to implement controlled reforms at all. In fact the two that achieved most, the Austrian and the Danish governments, both experienced severe difficulties, adopting significantly different tactics in order to avoid deadlock. The scale of the problem in Bohemia was described in a commission report in 1769 (some years before the worst revolts):

> The *robot* [labour service] gives rise to continual vexations. Even those nobles who have the best intentions are unable to protect their peasants, because their agents are rough, evil, violent and grasping ... In consequence of the arbitrary allocation of the *robot*, the peasants live in a condition of real slavery; they become savage and brutalised, and cultivate the lands in their charge badly. They are rachitic, thin and ragged; they are forced to do *robot* from their infancy. In their ruinous huts, the parents sleep on straw, the children naked on the wide shelves of earthenware stoves; they never wash, which promotes the spread of epidemics ... Even their personal effects are not safe from the greed of the great lords ... Even when the harvest has been good they are obliged to ask for seed from their lord, and he sells it to them at an extortionate price. The big landlords drive away the Jews, who make loans on better terms.[9]

8 P. Jones, ed., *The European Peasantry on the Eve of the French Revolution*, special issue of the journal *History of European Ideas*, 12 (1990), 328–418; and T. Scott, ed., *The Peasantries of Europe* (London, 1998), both provide a good range of articles which rightly emphasise the huge regional variations not just across western and central Europe but even within single countries. On France, see also O. Hufton, 'The seigneur and the rural community in eighteenth-century France', *Transactions of the Royal Historical Society* 29 (1979), 21–39; H.L. Root, 'Challenging the seigneurie: community and contention on the eve of the French Revolution', *Journal of Modern History* 57 (1985), 652–81; H.L. Root, *Peasants and King in Burgundy* (Berkeley, 1987); M.P. Fitzsimmons, 'New light on the aristocratic reaction in France, *French History* 10 (1996), 418–31; and P.M. Jones, *The Peasantry in the French Revolution* (Cambridge, 1988), 15–59. Although there was little detailed analysis of rural conditions by the most prominent intellectuals of the French enlightenment, there was no shortage of contemporary practical debate: see notably J.Q.C. Mackrell, *The Attack on 'Feudalism' in Eighteenth-Century France* (London, 1973). On the German lands, see also J. Gagliardo, *From Pariah to Patriot: The Changing Image of the German Peasant 1770–1840* (Lexington, 1969).
9 Commission report on Bohemia, submitted to the Austrian Council of State in June 1769; quoted in C.A. Macartney, *The Habsburg and Hohenzollern Dynasties in the Seventeenth and Eighteenth Centuries* (London, 1970), 173f.

By this stage, significant improvements were being piloted in the Austrian homelands on behalf of tenants on crown estates, notably to guarantee security of tenure and improve housekeeping. As elsewhere in Europe, it was hoped that private landowners would thereby be able to see the economic viability of change. But both Maria Theresa and Joseph II also recognised the need for active state mediation in peasant–seigneur relations in each of their different dominions. From the early 1770s, as economic instability brought widespread revolts, crown officials were instructed not to 'fraternise' with the landowning elite in implementing new restrictions on labour services (the so-called *robotpatenten* – open letters setting ceilings on the amount of labour that could be demanded). Enforcement, however, remained a problem, and from 1781 Joseph adopted a further series of measures designed to enhance peasant autonomy and curtail the rights of all landowners (ecclesiastical as well as private). The policies to some extent took into account divergent legal and economic patterns in the different provinces, and consequently appear rather uneven. But broadly speaking they included measures to improve crown monitoring of abuses in seigneurial courts, to clarify possible complaint procedures, and to curtail various aspects of serfdom (in Bohemia and Moravia notably marriage restrictions and compulsory service by peasant children over the age of 14). Efforts were made to limit the extent to which landowners there and in Hungary could exercise total economic dominion over their tenants through dues and labour services. The government even hoped to create a framework for tenants to buy freehold rights, in the hope that this would give them greater security against seigneurial rapacity. Yet Joseph, typically, remained ambivalent in his attitude towards the hereditary subservience which in one form or another was at the heart of rural instability: he recognised how oppressive it could be, sometimes appeared to want to break free from its traditions, yet on occasion seemed to adopt overbearingly autocratic expectations in his own dealings with his inferiors.

The Habsburg rural reforms were long overdue, and not without effect in some areas. But we need to remember that they were attempted not just out of humanitarian concern – real though that may have been on the part of Maria Theresa and perhaps also Joseph – but also to safeguard the fiscal interests of the state. This is more obvious in Joseph's plans from 1784 for a new universal land tax (on physiocratic principles), which involved a hugely ambitious general land survey as well as elusive calculation of the total maximum rents and dues which each peasant holding could support. The share of the gross yield payable to landowner and government alike was meticulously prescribed in the final scheme, which was ready for implementation in 1789. The primary purpose was to safeguard the revenue which Joseph required for his misjudged foreign and military policies; and to maximise, on possibly misguided physiocratic principles, agrarian production. But in so doing, he was on a collision course with local landowning interests. The risks had been apparent already at the end of 1784, with a large-scale and very violent anti-seigneurial insurrection in Transylvania, probably fuelled by the expectations of the reforms themselves, and requiring military repression. In 1789 the imminent new tax scheme helped release an even more dangerous revolt, this time by the Hungarian Magyar nobility. As he lay on his deathbed early in 1790, Joseph had no alternative but to retract the scheme and make various other concessions. His brother and successor Leopold was able to rescue some of the rural reforms when the Hungarian and international crisis abated, but the danger of head-on confrontation with the landowning elite had been clear for all to see.[10]

Government-initiated rural reform in Denmark came to a head at nearly exactly the same time. The political context, however, was very different. Denmark, too, was part of a composite monarchy which embraced different regions and cultures, but the crown wisely refrained from trying to universalise its reforms beyond the Danish lands proper. More fundamentally, the Danish-Norwegian monarchy, although on paper more absolute than most European states, was from 1766 headed by a monarch whose mental condition ensured that power had to be exercised rather tentatively through various regency arrangements. Although agrarian 'improvement' progressed significantly in many parts of the country from mid-century onwards, government initiatives were at first minimal. Even the flurry of activity during the short-lived administration of Struensee (1770–72) merely produced some hurried measures to limit seigneurial demands for labour services and other dues. Not until 1784, with the creation of a stable regency headed by crown prince Frederik, could more substantial legislation be contemplated.

It has been argued that the predominance of the Danish landowning interest – and in particular the rapidly mounting demands for rural labour services, combined with severe restrictions after 1733 on the mobility of males born in the countryside – was *de facto* pushing Denmark towards a variant of serfdom characteristic of east central Europe.[11] If so, this trend was

---

10 Much important work has been done in recent years on the tensions between tradition and innovation in the Austrian lands in the later years of Maria Theresa and during Joseph II's sole rule. A lively survey is provided by T.C.W. Blanning, *Joseph II* (London, 1994), including discussion of rural reform, 103–112. See also P.P. Bernard, *Jesuits and Jacobins: Enlightenment and Enlightened Despotism in Austria* (Urbana, 1971); G. Klingenstein, *Staatsverwaltung und kirchliche Autorität im 18. Jhr.: das Problem der Zensur in der Theresianischen Reform* (Munich, 1970); G. Klingenstein and F.A.J. Szabo, *Staatskanzler Wenzel Anton von Kaunitz-Rietberg, 1711–1794: neue Perspektiven zu Politik und Kultur der europäischen Aufklärung* (Graz, 1996); F.A.J. Szabo, *Kaunitz and Enlightened Absolutism 1753–1780* (Cambridge, 1987); D. Beales, Joseph II, vol. 1 (Cambridge, 1987); whilst the detailed work of P.G.M. Dickson, *Finance and Government under Maria Theresa, 1740–1780* (Oxford, 1987) has relevant information.

11 P. Jones, *The European Peasantry on the Eve of the French Revolution*, special issue of the journal *History of European Ideas*, 12 (1990), 330. The system of rural mobility restriction in Denmark from 1733, like its counterpart in Brandenburg-Prussia, was designed to facilitate military conscription and secure stability in the rural labour market. It affected all males between the ages of 18 and 36 (later extended to the range 4 to 40), but did not affect women, nor, in theory, limit the legal and other personal rights of the peasant population.

effectively reversed by the reforms of the new administration after 1784. The inner circle of advisors surrounding the crown prince, although consisting mostly of aristocratic landowners, quickly came round to the view that significant legislative reform of peasant–seigneur relations was essential to secure prosperity and stability. A routine enquiry into a particular instance of misuse of economic powers by a landowner was in 1786 transformed into a comprehensive review entrusted to a full Reform Commission. Headed by an enlightened cameralist landowner Christian Ditlev Reventlow, and at times driven forward by the acerbic Norwegian-born lawyer Christian Colbiørn-sen, this Commission of 16 members of the elite (including several conservative-minded landowners) ended up adopting some highly contro-versial measures. A range of preliminary matters were covered by legislation in 1787, notably restricting seigneurial rights of discipline, reinforcing secu-rity of tenure and imposing proper valuation procedures for peasant holdings at the start and end of each period of tenure. This was followed by detailed legislation in 1788 phasing out the mobility restrictions of 1733. Further legislation in 1789 and 1790 clarified tenure and enclosure proce-dures, and from 1791 onwards tackled the most controversial issue of all, contractual limitation of labour services.

The measures themselves were based firmly in contemporary cameralist thought, and had the detail typical of contemporary administrative practice. In public, Reventlow expressed optimism about the changes that would come, when, at a carefully managed ceremony in 1788 at which new hereditary leases were issued to some crown peasants, he appealed to God

> to make these peasants an example . . . to be followed by their brethren, and to make the formerly unappreciated estate of peasants a hard-working, happy and upright people, on whose welfare all other estates will blossom, and on whose loyalty and courage the king can depend as on the most secure defence.

The previous year, however, one of the Copenhagen journals had adopted a less optimistic tone when talking of the peasantry as

> that great mass of people, who without cultivating their intelligence, grow up in the dark night of ignorance, and, like speechless creatures, follow their habits and instincts, scarcely knowing any other writings than their almanac and their book of Christian instruction.

Understandably, therefore, most of the actual legislation emphasised the continuing obligation of the peasantry to submit to the authority of their landowner. The intention was to retain the division of rural society between secure tenants on the one hand, and poorer smallholders, cottagers or labourers on the other. Actual changes were to be phased in, or implemented as a result of local agreement; where outside arbitration proved necessary, as over labour services, the norms set by the government leaned strongly in favour of the landowning interest.

Even so, acceptance and implementation were far from easy. When the Commission started its work the government tacitly encouraged a significant level of public debate in the hope of fostering some degree of consensus – allowing an unprecedented range of books, pamphlets and government papers to be printed. Legislative initiatives were spaced out, to avoid too much controversy, and the work of the Commission itself was suspended for a while. Massive fiscal re-organisation, such as that attempted by Joseph, was firmly ruled out: the war against Sweden in the autumn of 1788 was conducted with as little enthusiasm as international treaty obligations allowed, and terminated quickly enough to ensure that a one-off tax levy would suffice. When a major landowning protest did nonetheless materialise in 1790, from Jutland, the government's tactics paid off handsomely: the common front of the ministerial team held its ground, with the nearly unanimous backing of Copenhagen public opinion. In a spectacular departure from normal practice, Colbiørnsen outmanoeuvred the protesters by publishing their complaints in a double-column text along with his detailed rebuttal. Government victory was finally secured in 1791 before the Supreme Court, when Colbiørnsen won a libel suit against the few landowners who, as ring-leaders, had not already capitulated.[12]

The Danish case is significant in the European context for a variety of reasons. Danish landowners were as keen as their counterparts elsewhere to experiment with innovative techniques in agriculture, but men like Reventlow explicitly rejected the English model of large-scale enclosures and the attendant social dislocation. By contrast, actual regulation of peasant–seigneur relations, not so much in the physiocratic mould as in the tradition of German cameralism, required more forceful state intervention than could be contemplated, it seems, in western European states like Britain and France. But even the Danish crown, despite its nominally absolute powers since 1660, was in no position to adopt a Josephist collision course. The actual outcome in Denmark may have seemed timid in Joseph's eyes, and costly for those amongst the peasantry who might have hoped for more positive protection; but it had the merit of being enough of a pragmatic compromise to survive quite significant challenges from both those peasants and those landowners who felt themselves cheated. Within these limitations, the Danish reforms at least demonstrated that the state could take on new areas of domestic responsibility in areas critical to the interests of the landowning elite.

---

12 For a fuller account in English of the run-up to this confrontation see T. Munck, 'The Danish reformers', in *Enlightened Absolutism: Reform and Reformers in Later Eighteenth-Century Europe*, ed. H. Scott (London, 1990), 245–63; T. Munck, 'Absolute monarchy in later eighteenth-century Denmark: centralized reform, public expectations and the Copenhagen press', *Historical Journal* 41 (1998), 201–24; and H. Arnold Barton, *Scandinavia in the Revolutionary Era, 1760–1815* (Minneapolis, 1986), especially 184–8, all of which include references to research work in Danish.

Poverty

Compared with the risks of interventionist agrarian reform, tackling poverty was fairly uncontentious. Unlike the peasantry, the poor had no economic leverage, rarely any collective identity, and never enough cohesion to initiate significant collective action. Contemporary complaints about the poor focused on their individual disorderliness, immorality or supposedly wilful idleness. At worst, beggars might be accused of using threats of violence or arson against reluctant donors, but there is little evidence of them doing so in gangs of any size. Parisian police records, though giving quite distinct profiles of detained beggars – their geographic mobility, age, gender, and state of ill health – provide no evidence of any conspiratorial infrastucture, even when the arresting officers specifically looked for it. The records also show that the vast majority of those arrested for begging, vagrancy or related offences were both illiterate and totally lacking any network that might either have facilitated self-help or have enabled them to exercise even modest socio-political leverage.[13] Like today's homeless, they were outcasts whom governments and private charities might try to help, but who had virtually no influence over what was done on their behalf. There was no lack of contemporary concern about the problems – every government in the later eighteenth century conducted increasingly detailed surveys of poverty, and sought to combat vagrancy and indigence by all means at their disposal – but the task invariably became overwhelming whenever serious economic downturns occurred, such as in the years 1768–75, 1789 and, worst of all, 1794–96.

Traditionally, poverty was regarded as a natural phenomenon, and even – to devout Christians – as a desirable state in itself. Those who were poor might be helped in various ways, according to circumstances. Minor charitable assistance continued to be routinely offered to tide over the so-called 'worthy' poor who had temporarily fallen on hard times through no fault of their own. In addition, institutional help was supposed to be on offer, at least in bigger towns, for orphans and children of indigent families, and for the elderly and sick. But for those who according to age-old norms (or prejudices) were deemed idle and 'unworthy', the customary response was much harsher, often involving punishment and the workhouse. Many of these we might now regard as conjunctural poor – that is, individuals suffering from misfortune brought on by economic instability, as opposed to the structural poor like children and the old who existed in every society at all times. Contemporaries were slow in recognising unemployment (or more frequently underemployment) as anything other than the responsibility of the individual concerned, and so had little difficulty justifying a harsh response. In a famous article in the *Encyclopédie*, under the keyword '*Fondation*' (charitable foundation), Turgot stated that:

13 See for example C. Romon, 'Le monde des pauvres à Paris au xviiie siècle', *Annales ESC* 37 (1982), 729–63.

It is precisely in those countries where such free [charitable] resources are most abundant, such as Spain and parts of Italy, that misery is more common and more general than elsewhere. The reason is quite simple, and many travellers have remarked on it. If you enable a large number of men to live gratis, you sustain idleness and all the disorders that stem therefrom; you make the condition of the do-nothing preferable to that of the man who works; in effect you diminish that resource of labour available to the state, and diminish the produce of the land – part of which necessarily becomes uncultivated. Hence the frequent dearths, the increase in misery and the resulting depopulation; the race of industrious citizens is replaced by a vile population consisting of begging vagabonds disposed to all kinds of crime.

What the state owes to each of its members is the destruction of obstacles which might hinder them in their industriousness, or which might trouble them in their enjoyment of the fruits which are the reward.[14]

The period of relative economic stability up to the later 1760s gave no obvious cause for re-evaluating the traditional distinction between worthy and unworthy poor, but there were nonetheless problems. In England, the only country with a compulsory poor rate, criticisms of both the principle of the levy and its practical administration recurred regularly. Especially in towns with scope for collective private initiatives, there was a growing emphasis on more focused initiatives, including charity schools, moral reform organisations, and, not least, voluntary hospitals (above, p. 34). Similar targeting was visible elsewhere in urban Europe. In Hamburg, for example, a new Patriotic Society was founded in 1765 to promote 'inwardly directed patriotism' – practical economic (cameralist) and social reforms for the benefit of all members of the community. It analysed poverty in terms of economic and demographic factors, and discussed measures ranging from poor rates to insurance and pension schemes, from workhouses to vocational training. The 1778 medical relief programme for out-patients grew by the 1790s into a substantial public health system. To this was in 1788 added the general poor relief (*Allgemeine Armenanstalt*) based on a central agency overseeing all forms of relief. Its 180 officials were split into teams covering individual areas of the city, under the direction of a panel of city fathers. They administered schooling for pauper children, relief against begging, and such types of work for able-bodied poor as would not destabilise the existing labour market. Despite the significant funding arrangements required, the system worked surprisingly well through the difficult years of the 1790s, demonstrating that it was possible to secure a system of practical relief which was more than merely a cosmetic exercise.[15]

14 Turgot, article headed '*Foundation*' (Foundation), in the *Encyclopédie*, vol. 7 (1757), 73f.
15 M. Lindemann, *Patriots and Paupers: Hamburg, 1712–1830* (Oxford, 1990), esp. 89–176.

Such substantial administrative efforts tended to brush aside traditional individual Christian charity in favour of the increasingly secular collective pragmatism characteristic of the later eighteenth century. Perhaps the distinction between religious altruism and enlightened self-interest mattered less for those who had grown up in an age familiar with Mandeville's *Fable of the Bees: Private Vices, Public Benefits* – the second edition of which (1723) had earned notoriety in puncturing contemporary self-satisfaction, notably by questioning the ulterior motives of all those who thought they were acting out of charity. Certainly there is evidence from different parts of Europe to suggest that traditional pious charity was becoming less universal than it had been. In France churchmen criticising the trend towards using the *hôpitaux généraux* as prisons for delinquents and undesirables were ignored. Most institutions were also affected by enlightenment criticisms of the church generally. In Aix-en-Provence, probably typical of a general trend, there were clear signs after mid-century of a fall in testamentary bequests and other donations to established charitable foundations, at the very time when costs of maintenance per inmate were increasing.[16] The French central government, like its counterparts elsewhere, did not rush to make up the shortfall. Rather, secular authorities began to turn to public works schemes as a means of both reducing begging and minimising the financial drain of relief.

Everyone in Europe eventually came to recognise the need for organised labour schemes to reduce idleness; but not everyone agreed on the level of compulsion that could or should be built into the system, let alone the financial basis on which it should be operated. Workhouses had existed since the late sixteenth century, and had not been conspicuously successful either in the quest for moral reform or in the search for a self-financing system of public relief for the able-bodied. Many government officials as well as entrepreneurs nevertheless continued, despite persistent contra-indications, to cling to the old hope that some kind of disciplinarian workhouse might become, if not financially self-supporting, then at least as minimal a public burden as possible. Others tried to solve the problem by means of selective intake, giving the scheme a more voluntary or even traditionally charitable appearance. Some institutions, like the Town Hospital set up in Glasgow in 1733, or the workhouse in Odense in 1752, combined voluntary and compulsory admissions in the same building.

As economic instability returned to much of Europe from the late 1760s onwards, the burden of the conjunctural poor again became more acute. With no obvious alternatives, refinement and further experimentation seemed the only answer. Accordingly, by the later eighteenth century a great spectrum of different types of institutions was evolving. At one extreme were

16 C.C. Fairchilds, *Poverty and Charity in Aix-en-Provence, 1640–1789* (Baltimore, 1976), 131–46; see also C. Jones, *Charity and Bienfaisance: The Treatment of the Poor in the Montpellier Region 1740–1815* (Cambridge, 1982), 76–94.

the rather grim houses of correction (German *Zuchthäuser*) designed to force able-bodied idlers to work and, increasingly, to discipline troublemakers. In France, at least some of the *hôpitaux généraux* clearly belonged in the latter category, even if they also continued to admit the old, the sick and the handicapped. To them were added from 1764 onwards the dreaded *dépôts de mendicité*, designed to take in the varying numbers of beggars and vagabonds picked up by the police, especially those who were not local. More hopeful, however, were some new developments. Amongst these we should probably count the nearly 2,000 open workhouses in England – helping perhaps as many as 90,000 individuals find work on an increasingly voluntary basis, and (especially after Gilbert's Act of 1782) facilitating flexible administration by the local authorities. Very similar in intent were the *ateliers de charité* in France from the 1760s onwards, developed nation-wide but directed especially at deprived rural areas. Relying on a mixture of state and private funding, the *ateliers* were intended to provide honest if low-paid work for the unemployed, on a daily basis and without social stigma – in other words, basic work opportunity precisely for those who had tradi-tionally been deemed 'unworthy', and who without help might slide from poverty into destitution and begging. The *ateliers* seem to have been carefully supervised, and on the whole well directed to meet local needs. Being intended as a temporary remedy, the *ateliers* fluctuated with varying eco-nomic conditions, accounting in 1789 for 31,000 men and women.

Grim though much poor relief was, we might note some signs of change in the late eighteenth century. For a start, the public policies do not seem to have displaced private philanthropic initiatives, which continued to evolve. Secondly, the trend towards a secularisation of poor relief paved the way for nationwide reform, such as the ambitious proposals put forward by the Committee for the Extinction of Begging set up by the National Constituent Assembly in 1790. And thirdly, while judgmental criteria for relief remained very pronounced, there were signs of a gradual recognition that some able-bodied poor would benefit more from work than from incarceration. Turgot was one of the many who argued that the *ateliers* were much more likely to produce long-term benefits than the servile forced labour of the *dépôts de mendicité*. In 1790 the Committee for the Extinction of Begging reflected a similar point of view when it emphasised not only that around one-fifths of all those admitted to the *dépôts* since their creation had died there, but also that collectively the *dépôts* had been a huge and uneconomic drain on resources.[17] The revolutionary government seemed to take these points of

17 The literature on workhouses and work schemes is very large, but see notably J.S. Taylor, 'The unreformed workhouse 1776–1834', in *Comparative Development in Social Welfare*, ed. E.W. Martin (London, 1972), 57–84; J. Innes, 'Prisons for the poor: English bridewells, 1555–1800', in *Labour, Law and Crime*, ed. F. Snyder and D. Hay (London, 1987), 42–122, who notes that there were probably at most 170 houses of correction in England in the later eighteenth century, and at most 19 in the United Provinces; G.R. Boyer, *An Economic History of the English Poor Law* (Cambridge, 1990), ch. 1; R. Ashcraft, 'Lockean ideas, poverty, and the development of liberal political theory', in *Early Modern Conceptions of*

view to heart, even including in the preamble to the 1793 Constitution a categorical statement of the state's responsibility to provide work as well as relief. But as always, good intentions did not by themselves produce results. The French government (like others in Europe during the difficult years of the 1790s) became ever more hampered by financial shortfalls aggravated by war. Even in Britain, the problems became so acute by 1794–95 that a substantive rethinking of the whole poor law system became necessary – as indicated in Frederic Morton Eden's monumental three-volume analysis of *The State of the Poor* published in 1797.

There is an additional dimension to this story. In most parts of Europe, and especially in rural society, forced labour of some kind was a burden borne intermittently by almost everyone. It could take many forms. Military conscription, naval impressment and the hiring out of conscripted troops as mercenaries to another state were common practice. It was but a short step from militia service to compulsory labour on fortifications and military transport duty, to the *corvée* (conscript labour) used to build royal roads all over Europe, or even (though mostly in areas of serfdom) to bonded labour in industries and mines.[18] In many parts of rural Europe, peasants also routinely provided compulsory transport and hospitality services for the crown, its administrators and its military – demands which were variable, unpredictable and sometimes arbitrarily iniquitous. Only urban communities had any scope for buying their way out of such mandatory service (and even they might not avoid military garrisoning).

The imposition of intermittent involuntary labour was bad enough, but continuous labour was also used, notably as a form of punishment for serious offenders who had avoided the death penalty. Following the abolition of the death penalty by the Habsburg government in 1776, for example, the labour of convicted criminals was increasingly used in Vienna for street cleaning and other deliberately demeaning tasks. In 1783, Joseph II decided

Property, ed. J. Brewer and S. Staves (London, 1995), 43–61; O. Hufton, *The Poor of Eighteenth-Century France* (Oxford, 1974), 227–42; R.M. Schwarz, *Policing the Poor in Eighteenth-Century France* (Chapel Hill, 1988), who suggests, 166–77, that there were on average 3–4,000 inmates in houses of correction in England and Wales in the early 1770s, roughly proportional to the 10–12,000 in the 80 or more French *dépôts* at the same time; T.M. Adams, *Bureaucrats and Beggars: French Social Policy in the Age of Enlightenment* (New York, 1990), 30–134 and *passim*; W. Olejniczak, 'Working the body of the poor: the ateliers de charité in late 18th-century France', *Journal of Social History* 24 (1990–91), 87–108; and on government attitudes during the French Revolution itself, see notably A. Forrest, 'Bienfaisance ou répression: l'état révolutionnaire et la question de la pauvreté', *StVEC* 311 (1993), 327–38.

18 Much unskilled labour in pre-industrial Europe was 'unfree' in one way or another, and both in eastern and western Europe the legal relationship between labourer and employer was normally based on assumptions of compulsion and inequality. Useful re-assessments include C.A. Whatley, 'The dark side of the Enlightenment?: sorting out serfdom', in *Eighteenth-Century Scotland: New Perspectives*, ed. T.M. Devine and J.R. Young (East Linton, 1999), 259–74, regarding bonded labour in the Scottish mines. See also M. Sonenscher, *Work and Wages: Natural Law, Politics and Eighteenth-Century French Trade* (Cambridge, 1989); and M. Vigié, 'La bagne des philosophes', *Revue d'Histoire Moderne et Contemporaine* 35 (1988), 409–33.

to use chain gangs of prisoners to pull barges on the Danube, where the land was too marshy for horses. Around 100 were sent to Hungary the following year, of whom 37 died within two months, and another 38 within a year. Despite similarly high death rates over the following years, the scheme was not abandoned until Joseph himself died in 1790.[19]

As we noted above (p. 155), most other states in Europe had equally brutal policies towards convicts. A particular example, however, will illustrate the kind of social categorisation which such policies fostered. The records of the forced labour camp in Copenhagen, the Stokhus, are not as full as one might wish,[20] but certain aspects are immediately striking. For a start, the admission protocol describes the inmates as 'slaves'. Slavery as such of course did not exist in Denmark, and was nowhere recognised in law. The use of the term as a short-hand for the inmates of the labour camp is therefore all the more revealing. When John Howard visited the institution in 1781, he found a total of 143 inmates committed to hard labour. The official archives indicate that many of these were male offenders from all over the country, typically in the age-band 20–40: soldiers and sailors who had deserted or had been found guilty of extreme violence, civilians who had committed capital offences but had had the penalty reduced, peasants who had fallen so foul of their seigneur that the local house of correction was not deemed sufficient, serious offenders against sexual morality, and some lesser categories. The terms they were expected to serve varied surprisingly. A few were allocated short sentences of some weeks, perhaps because they were in fact minor offenders of the kind that could just as well have ended up in the normal house of correction. The majority, however, were clearly regarded as serious criminals who (even after the penal reform of 1789) carried very long sentences of heavy penal servitude, sometimes for decades or for life. They appear also to have been the target for severe, sometimes recurrent, corporal punishment, and branding was common. The majority had no prospect whatever of rehabilitation or improvement, so their labour could not be deemed to have any 'corrective' function. As with Joseph's 'pardoned' convicts, these individuals had lost all rights of any kind and were effectively slaves of the state, forced to work until they dropped.

Slavery and enlightenment

In terms of highlighting the harshness of social relations, as well as emphasising the interdependency of economic systems, slavery and poverty had some points in common. But slavery also served to highlight two fundamental controversies within the enlightenment. One of these concerned the absolute

---

19 P.P. Bernard, *The Limits of Enlightenment: Joseph II and the Law* (Urbana, 1979), 34f.
20 The surviving records for the Stokhus are now in Landsarkivet for Sjælland, registered in *Københavns politi- or domstolsarkiver*, i–ii (Copenhagen, 1975–76). See also the provisional archival register for *Fængselsarkiver* (Copenhagen, 1965).

nature of property rights – the extent to which ownership gave the holder unlimited rights over his property and, by extension, over the ways in which he might exploit it for personal gain. As in the ownership of land, both tradition and the law seemed to guarantee unrestricted usage. On the other hand, unlike the relationship between seigneurs and peasants, most forms of slavery were not tempered by the nominal restraints of a shared Christian humanity. Slavery (at least outside Muscovy and the Mediterranean) could be justified through racial stereotypes – uneasy consciences salved by the argument that charity did not extend to heathens. Those who wished to protect the enormous profits generated especially in the growing African slave trade even argued that the suffering inflicted on blacks was morally outweighed by the access to Christian salvation afforded by the conversion of blacks in captivity – an argument officially sanctioned in the French law code of 1685 determining slavery and the slave trade, the so-called *code noir*.[21]

Before the eighteenth century only a few had voiced doubts about the compatibility of the slave trade with basic Christian beliefs – exceptions, such as Pope Urban VIII's condemnation of Indian slavery in Brazil in 1639, or initial hesitations in the Protestant North American colonies, being readily ignored. But as the trade grew, and channels of information improved, the horrors of the African slave ships also became more difficult to ignore. By the 1750s, meetings of the Quaker Society of Friends both in Philadelphia and in London warned that ownership of slaves was liable to be an obstacle to spiritual salvation, and by the end of the Seven Years War (1763) Quaker yearly meetings on both sides of the Atlantic had condemned the trade outright – a lead followed, after some delay, by other non-established churches.

Historians have disagreed substantially over the extent to which major enlightened writers condoned slavery and the racial stereotypes that it encouraged. Clear lines of argument were slow to emerge: most writers were restrained in their comments, partly (at least in France) because of fears of censorship, but perhaps also because the dazzling wealth of slaving ports like Liverpool, Bristol, Nantes and Bordeaux – and the novelty value of the few coloured persons who reached Europe – concealed the underlying reality. Montesquieu discussed slavery cautiously but in some detail in Book XV of his *Spirit of the Laws* of 1748, whilst Rousseau's *Social Contract* of 1762, though brief and generalised, was obviously critical. The *Encyclopédie* (1751–65) presented characteristically oblique arguments susceptible to multiple interpretations. A variety of articles compared exotic civilisations and beliefs to those current in Europe, the veiled irony of the text often concealing deep scepticism. The main articles dealing directly with slavery

---

21 On confessional and racial arguments for slavery, see C. Kidd, *British Identities before Nationalism: Ethnicity and Nationhood in the Atlantic World, 1600–1800* (Cambridge, 1999), 23–5, including note 51. See also C. Hunting, 'The philosophes and black slavery, 1748–1765', *Journal of the History of Ideas* 39 (1978), 405–18.

('*Esclavage*', volume 5) and negroes ('*Nègres*', volume 11) relied largely on Montesquieu. But in an article on the slave trade ('*Traite des nègres*', volume 16) Jaucourt was more openly critical, pointing out that 'if a trade of this kind can be justified by means of moral principle, then surely there is no crime, however atrocious it might be, that cannot similarly be justified'. He went on to say that:

> men and their liberty are not objects of trade; they can neither be sold, nor bought, nor paid for at any price. From that we must conclude that a man whose slave runs away has only himself to blame, for he acquired through money an illicit commodity, from possession of which he was barred by all the laws of humanity and justice.

Jaucourt added that if the colonies were not capable of making a profit without slavery it would be better that they were abandoned altogether; yet he also realised that those involved in the slave trade, and in the exploitation of slavery in the colonies, would not surrender their position lightly.

In fact the slave interest gained support from several directions, for in this as in other respects there was little unity of purpose amongst enlightened writers. Georges-Louis Leclerc de Buffon's multi-volume *Histoire naturelle* (1749–88), which became the standard *Natural History* of the enlightenment, lent explicit scientific support to the idea that human races had evolved hereditary differences attributable to the environment in which they lived. In contrast to the image of the noble savage that was still sometimes promoted in literature, Buffon regarded European whites as the most advanced race, and (though a critic of slavery) seemed to offer rational justification for racial discrimination against especially African blacks. Voltaire, noted for a great many prejudices, was even more outspoken in his view that racial hereditary differences were sufficient grounds for institutionalised segregation and discrimination, a view also supported by Helvétius. Even such independent minds as Hume and Kant seem to have accepted racial stereotypes.

Thus, as the slave trade reached its peak in the second half of the eighteenth century, with probably 60–100,000 Africans transported annually in the 1780s, there was no shortage of creditable enlightened opinion to draw on to justify continuation of the system. From around 1770 onwards, however, more detailed commentaries on slavery and the slave trade ensured an increasingly confrontational debate. Amongst the most influential contributions was abbé Raynal's *Histoire philosophique et politique ... des deux Indes* (*Philosophical and Political History of the Two Indies*), the first edition of which appeared in 1770 and caused an immediate stir. Its detailed and sometimes critical analysis of European relations with their colonies, its evaluation of the basis of commercial growth, and its insights into the impact of the West Indies on European civilisation, touched what had clearly become a sensitive area. Raynal described how the slave trade had affected African tribal life, and was bluntly critical of the slaving powers (not just Britain and France, but also the Dutch, the Portuguese and the Danes) who 'tolerate this cruelty, and who do not even blush in making it the basis of their strength'. He suggested that simple reforms would not only introduce a glimmer of humanity, but also improve survival rates and hence profits for the trade. When the slaves had reached their destination, a little understanding and foresight on the part of the owners could ensure much better long-term productivity and stability in the slave population. Nevertheless, in a passionate summing up, Raynal went much further:

> My blood boils at these horrible images: I hate, I flee from the human species composed of victims and tormentors; if it cannot improve itself, let it destroy itself ... If there existed a religion which authorised, which tolerated – albeit only by remaining silent – such horrors; if it regarded a slave's attempt to break his chains as a crime; if it tolerated within its community the iniquitous judge who condemns the fugitive to death; if such a religion existed, its ministers should be smothered under the debris of their altars.[22]

In Britain the Quaker campaign ensured that much of the debate centred on religious morality, but other aspects were also raised. The legal commentaries of George Wallace in Scotland (1761) or William Blackstone in England (1765–69) had questioned the validity of property claims by one man over another, and some extraordinary lawsuits in the later 1760s and 1770s tested the notion (current both in England and at least until 1716 in France) that ownership rights lost their validity if the slave was brought to Europe. Admittedly individual cases in law had little immediate significance in a society used to impressment, workhouses and other extra-legal infringements on personal liberty. The fact that no official sale of slaves appears to have taken place in Britain itself after 1779 does not mean that basic attitudes had changed much. But elsewhere in Europe, prohibitions on the entry of blacks into Portugal (1761) and France (1777), in particular, suggest not just a desire to end the legal squabbles, but probably also a growing concern to prevent racial mixing and ultimately to reduce the number of non-whites in Europe itself.[23]

To the legal arguments about slavery were added practical matters with no

22 Abbé Guillaume Thomas François Raynal (1713–96), *Histoire philosophique et politique des établissements et du commerce des Européens dans les deux Indes* (new edition, Amsterdam, 1774), 238–40. The work was rather loosely organised and not always consistent in its judgements, but between its first appearance in 1770 and the outbreak of Revolution there were 30 French editions, incorporating many changes (including some suggested by Diderot) to improve the text; there were also 18 English-language editions between 1776 and 1798, half of them in London and the rest in Edinburgh, Dublin, Glasgow and Aberdeen.
23 Pierre H. Boulle, 'In defense of slavery: eighteenth-century opposition to abolition and the origins of a racist ideology in France', in *History from Below*, ed. F. Krantz (Oxford, 1988), 219–46, argues that many recognisable elements of racism became apparent in France after 1750, but that it was prevalent mostly amongst those who were the main beneficiaries of colonial trade, and who tended towards the right once the Revolution erupted in 1789. See

doubt greater immediate impact on European and colonial opinion. Instances of unrest in the 1730s had already caused fears that the growing black slave populations in the Caribbean or in the southern colonies of North America might revolt: subsequent calls for restrictions on import numbers were in part a result of such fears. In the struggle that eventually led to independence, the North American colonists were on rather thin ice in their use of emotive terms like 'slavery' to sum up their reasons for revolt against the British government; but some states, starting with Pennsylvania in 1780, did in fact proceed with qualified and gradual emancipation of their own slaves. By then, Adam Smith's *Wealth of Nations* of 1776 had questioned whether slavery actually made economic sense – starting a debate, equally applicable to serfdom, regarding the value of labour delivered under duress compared to that of free contract workers.

Calls for legislative change were therefore often based on composite arguments. Philanthropic and religious considerations certainly mattered – and may have been the main drive behind the Quaker campaign for British abolition which, in gaining a full-scale parliamentary enquiry in 1775, put slavery on to the national political agenda. But all kinds of other factors came into play as soon as the political campaign gathered momentum both there and in France during the 1780s. By the time the Society for Effecting the Abolition of the Slave Trade was set up in London in 1787, headed by Thomas Clarkson and the evangelical reformist Member of Parliament William Wilberforce, there was widespread public interest. The collection of mass petitions against slavery in 1788 turned into the largest petitioning movement ever seen in Britain.[24] At the same time, Clarkson's work gathering information both on the economic and the humanitarian aspect of the slave trade encouraged a group of French reformist intellectuals to follow suit in 1788 and set up the Société des Amis des Noirs under the leadership of Jacques-Pierre Brissot (later leader of the Girondins). It counted amongst its members some of the most influential liberals of the day, including Condorcet, Grégoire and Lavoisier, but never seems to have won widespread public following. Despite a promising start in the National Constituent Assembly in 1789, the abolitionists rapidly lost ground, weakened by powerful lobbying from the slave ports and by the belated arrival of deputies to represent the whites of the Caribbean and other overseas possessions. In March 1790 the colonies were given self-government of a kind effectively protecting the interest of plantation owners, and a formal condemnation of slavery in principle in 1791 was tempered with ambiguity. Clarification of

also J. de Viguerie, 'Les "lumières" et les peuples', *Revue Historique* 290 (1994), 161–89; and S. Peabody, *'There Are No Slaves in France': The Political Culture of Race and Slavery in the Ancien Régime* (Oxford, 1996). It is not possible to quantify the actual presence of coloured and black people in Britain or France in this period, but the main ports may well have had enough for them not to be especially remarkable.

24 J.R. Oldfield, *Popular Politics and British Anti-Slavery: The Mobilisation of Public Opinion against the Slave Trade 1787–1807* (Manchester, 1995).

the rights of free non-whites in the colonies was deliberately avoided until 1792, when Brissot's influence in the Legislative Assembly was at its height. But by then the situation in the Caribbean had changed drastically: on 22 August 1791, following Vincent Ogé's unsuccessful mulatto rising the previous summer, a huge slave revolt broke out in Saint-Domingue (later Haiti), bringing the death of an estimated 10,000 blacks and 2,000 whites within a few months. In the end this became the only successful slave revolt in history, and created the second new republic in the Americas; but the cost in terms of human losses and economic destruction during the first 12 years of struggle (until the defeat of the French in 1803) was terrible.[25]

The British Parliament, on the other hand, debated slavery and the slave trade repeatedly from 1788, with very strong speakers pitched on both sides. After several attempts, and perhaps following news in 1792 that Denmark had decided to phase out the import of slaves to its small Caribbean possessions by 1803,[26] both Houses of Parliament passed an amended motion to abolish the slave trade at some future unspecified date – in the event, despite further efforts, not until 1807. In February 1794, the French legislature belatedly emancipated all French slaves (without specifically banning the slave trade), but it did not have the power to stabilise the situation in its Caribbean possessions; when Napoleon restored colonial slavery in 1802 he ensured the continuation of violence.

The eighteenth century created the anti-slavery movement – concentrating heavily on African slavery (rather than variants nearer home, notably in North Africa). In the process, however, an unintended impetus and focus also seems to have been given to particular forms of racial prejudice already inherent in the European outlook. As contemporary critics noted, some abolitionists worked more passionately in this campaign than anyone did over domestic social iniquities. Perhaps the image of the noble savage, and of exotic cultures hitherto unspoilt by European corruption, lingered on to give credibility to a moral crusade that seemed to suit liberal enlightened temperaments particularly well. Perhaps geographic remoteness made it easier to maintain a simple clarity in the main arguments and their implications. But at the end of the day effective reform (as Raynal recognised) needed much more than individual initiative – it required coordination between the major powers of the day. That was inherently unlikely, especially once the French revolutionary wars broke out in 1792 (involving Britain from early 1793).

25 D. Geggus, 'Racial equality, slavery and colonial secession during the Constituent Assembly', *American Historical Review* 94 (1989), 1290–1308; and S.M. Singham, 'Betwixt cattle and men: Jews, blacks, and women, and the Declaration of the Rights of Man', in *The French Idea of Freedom: The Old Régime and the Declaration of Rights of 1789* (Stanford, 1994), 114–53.

26 On the Danish decision, see S.E. Green-Pedersen, 'The economic considerations behind the Danish abolition of the negro slave trade', in *The Uncommon Market: Essays in the Economic History of the Atlantic Slave Trade*, ed. H.A. Gemery et al. (New York, 1979), 399–418. For the overall context, see H. Thomas, *The Slave Trade: The Story of the Atlantic Slave Trade 1440–1870* (London, 1997).

But in any case there was an even greater obstacle to reform, in the shape of the truly huge economic interests at stake in the trade. Procrastination and prevarication are therefore hardly surprising.

* * *

As in the previous chapter, we might see government responses to the issues discussed here as fundamentally weak or muddled. But as public debate increased, both social stability and the protection of property rights required difficult balancing skills, which the early modern state had struggled for generations to master. Ideas about fiscal redistribution, rural reform, poor relief and social engineering brought under the spotlight some of the most important assumptions underlying eighteenth-century society. The question of the abolition of slavery – threatening, in the eyes of some, the very life-blood of overseas commerce and hence of European prosperity – was just another of a whole set of problems with explosive potential. What is truly astonishing is not that eighteenth-century public debate in many respects failed to bring real change, but that it took as clear a shape as it did. The risks were plain for all to see, in terms of domestic instability, loss of economic prosperity and, ultimately, threats to the traditional social order. What we might note is not just the failures and inadequacies of government response, but the fact that a response – of any kind – was now not only contemplated but actually expected. The role of government had changed.

8

State, nation and individual in the late eighteenth century

Until around 1770, the relationship between state and subject in most of Europe was liable to appear almost unchanging, usually conveying an impression of stability that governments naturally tried to emphasise. As we noted in the last two chapters, specific government reform initiatives in the later eighteenth century turn out on closer examination to be highly context-sensitive and cautious – and much less intrusive (or indeed effective) than we might have assumed at first sight. Social and political relationships continued during this period to be shaped by long-standing traditions of religious belief, deference, dependency and power; yet they could also be affected by a variety of more immediate and sometimes disruptive influences nurtured by economic diversification and (especially in the last decades of the century) by mounting contradictions in social expectations. In the past, such discrepancies had been most obvious during periods of actual social unrest, when the fault lines in early modern society became clearly (if only temporarily) visible. In the last decades of the eighteenth century, however, many key aspects became the object of increasingly open debate in print.

In order fully to appreciate what was happening both before and after 1789, historians have in recent years paid more explicit attention to one of the most elusive aspects of their source material: the actual language in which it is couched. Language is subjective and transient, its elements and inflections constantly re-shaped, manipulated or distorted by individual users as well as through social assimilation. The study of the use of language – 'discourse analysis' in the current jargon – has always been important to the historian. But the norms of expression current in the eighteenth century can easily deceive, since they seem so deceptively familiar and unproblematic today. Because of the mobility and fluidity of much of eighteenth-century society, the subtle shades of social differentiation reflected in its language, and the remarkable diversity of dialects and idiom (not to mention spelling) at different levels in society, the historian may often feel as if on quicksand.

Methodologies derived from other disciplines are not readily re-deployed for our purposes.[1] And given the nearly inexhaustible supply of textual material from the period, only one thing is incontestable: namely, that historians have only begun to scrape the surface. This chapter will attempt to illustrate some of the directions we might pursue.

Social structure, 'the people' and public consensus

When Emmanuel Sieyes early in 1789 published his pamphlet entitled *What is the Third Estate?*, he felt it necessary to include an overview of the functional structure of society as a whole, as he saw it. The passage is worth citing at some length:

> What is required for a nation to survive and prosper? *Individual* employment and *public* services.
>
> All individual employment can be grouped within four classes. (1) Because land and water provide the raw material for man's needs, the first class, in logical order, will be that of all the families connected with working the land. (2) From the initial sale of goods through to their consumption or use, variable levels of further labour add secondary value of a more or less composite kind to these raw materials. Human industry thus succeeds in perfecting the gifts of nature, and the raw material doubles in value, increases tenfold or hundredfold. This is work of the second class. (3) Between production and consumption, as between different stages of production, a host of intermediate agents intervene to help both producers and consumers. These are the merchants and the dealers ... (4) Apart from these three classes of working and useful citizens, concerned with the normal *objects* of consumption and use, society also needs a range of individual work and of services which are *directly* useful or agreeable to the *person*. This fourth class includes everyone from the most distinguished scientific and liberal professions to the least valued domestic services ...
>
> Public services can also all, at present, be grouped under four known categories: the armed forces, the judiciary, the church and the administration.[2]

To suit his argument, Sieyes was in effect providing a social classification

---

1 General overviews are provided by P. Schöttler, 'Historians and discourse analysis', in *History Workshop Journal* 27 (1989), 37–65; and by J.M. Smith, 'No more language games: words, beliefs and the political culture of early modern France', *American Historical Review* 102 (1997), 1413–40, the latter including particularly helpful references to recent work on the eighteenth century. See also footnote 32 below.
2 Sieyes, *Qu'est-ce que le tiers-état?*, ch. 1 (this translation based on the third edition of 1789, reprinted by Flammarion, Paris, 1988, 33f). For informative comment on this text, see notably W.H. Sewell, *A Rhetoric of Bourgeois Revolution: The abbé Sieyes and 'What is the Third Estate?'* (Durham, N.C., 1994).

scheme based on practical function. In accordance with physiocratic norms, he placed cultivators of the land first; but he also recognised the value added by manufacture and commerce, and, reflecting recent economic trends, built in the service sector in its own right. His specific purpose, as was made very clear in the next part of his text, was to launch a full-scale attack on the privileged order of nobility, without whom, he argued, the nation would be much better off. Such a pragmatic and rational summary of society, significantly, corresponded neither to the traditional hierarchy of orders, nor to nineteenth-century views on social class. Sieyes' perspective was typical of the later French enlightenment,[3] and in turn paved the way for the more radical agendas of reform and social engineering of the Revolution.

In the rest of Europe – a few revolutionary enthusiasts of the 1790s excepted – such politically charged analysis was not common. Most people thought in terms of a fundamentally static hierarchical social structure in which the rich hereditary elite was always at the top, and (to use terminology customary in England at the time) the 'mean' or 'industrious' labouring sort somewhere towards the bottom. Variable degrees of descriptive refinement might be used to accommodate the middling layers, ranging from the gentry living off unearned income, through the 'upper middling sort' of merchants and wealthy professionals, to 'mechanics' reliant on their labour in ordinary trades. Below them were those who lived more precariously: ordinary country people from smallholders to rural labourers, unskilled urban labour, the poor, and those like vagrants and beggars who were totally destitute or 'indigent'. Of course no single layer was clearly definable or hermetically sealed – any individual could gain advancement through money and luck, and arguably only the clergy constituted a true order with clear boundaries (if little corporate identity) – but the hierarchy nonetheless had recognisable and meticulously observed steps.

Despite variations in substance and in nomenclature, a classificatory scheme along these lines would have been recognisable to most people in later eighteenth-century Europe. Its main layers were usually referred to by means of terms such as 'order', 'rank', 'degree', 'estate' or 'sort'. The term 'class' was not in common use in its modern sociological sense – though it did appear in specific contexts, for example to denote each of the 20 layers in Louis XIV's capitation tax of 1695. By mid-century, however, phrases such

---

3 In the *Encyclopédie*, the baron d'Holbach's article on representation ('*Representants*', vol. 14, 1765) had outlined a structure of orders which was more conventional in its ranking, starting with the clergy and the nobility, then proceeding to magistrates, trade and *cultivateurs* (farmers owning land), but which, like Sieyes, adopted the physiocratic emphasis on land as the prime producer. D'Holbach also argued that each of these orders was entitled to representation since none of them could on their own represent the nation as a whole.

as 'the lowest class of people' were beginning to gain currency at least amongst English-language writers, often in sharp contrast to the self-congratulatory 'middling sorts' who saw themselves as the backbone of British prosperity.[4] Subdivisions within the social hierarchy continued to matter a great deal, and, as Zedler's dictionary of 1744 made clear, an estate or order was definable precisely by 'the quality of a person that distinguishes him from others, and which in view of this distinction assigns him rights that are different from others'.[5] Such rights and privileges were not necessarily formalised in law, but were widely understood, jealously guarded and generally deemed essential for social stability. In short, eighteenth-century society was built on the inescapable premiss of engrained inequality.

Whilst especially the higher ranks of society were defined by a myriad of subtle distinctions and outward signs, there was little agreement regarding the meaning of such generic phrases as 'the people'. Most rational and enlightened observers in the eighteenth century had a deeply ambivalent attitude to the lower sorts: criticisms of excessive aristocratic luxury or ostentatiously insolent wealth notwithstanding, very few contemporary writers ever promoted arguments that were genuinely egalitarian. Many emphasised how utopian social equality could easily turn into violent individualism or even anarchy – as illustrated by the story of the Troglodytes in Montesquieu's *Persian Letters* (Letters 11–14), where the ideals of a community proved insufficient to prevent decadence and ultimately the election of a reluctant king. Voltaire, in his brutally dismissive remarks about the 'rabble' as irredeemably prone to superstition and unfit for greater things,[6] was probably closer to voicing a contemporary consensus than was Rousseau in his idealised *Discourse on Inequality* (1755) or *The Social Contract* (1762). Nevertheless, Rousseau was not alone in questioning the inherited and patronising dismissiveness of the elite. It is now clear that Coyer's 1755 *Dissertation sur la nature du peuple* (*Dissertation on the Nature of the People*), to which Jaucourt was deeply indebted for his article under the

---

4 P.J. Corfield, 'Class by name and number in eighteenth-century Britain', *History* 72 (1987), 38–61. See also the review of recent debate offered by S. Maza, 'Luxury, morality and social change: why there was no middle-class consciousness in pre-revolutionary France', *Journal of Modern History* 69 (1997), 199–229, which warns against terminological anachronism.

5 J.H. Zedler, *Grosses vollständiges universal-Lexicon*, vol. 39 (Leipzig/Halle, 1744), 1093, cited by J. van Horn Melton, 'The emergence of "society" in eighteenth- and nineteenth-century Germany', in *Language, History and Class*, ed. P.J. Corfield (Oxford, 1991), 134.

6 Voltaire made a number of forthright remarks in his private correspondence, noting for example that 'truth is not fit for everyone: the mass of the human race is not worthy of it' (*Voltaire's Correspondence*, ed. T. Bestermann (Geneva, 1968–71), 12 October 1764, Best.D.12138; cf. Best.D.10402 of 2 April 1762; Best.D.13212 of 19 March 1766; or Best.D.15461 of 3 February 1769). 'Equality' is in his *Philosophical Dictionary* (1764) seen as a chimera. However, it should be noted that at other times Voltaire seems more human-itarian – see for example his well-known draft letter to Linguet, 15 March 1767 (Best.D.14039) – and that in practice he was not a reactionary landlord on his own estate. For fuller discussion see R. Mortier, 'Voltaire et le peuple', in *The Age of the Enlightenment*, ed. W.H. Barber *et al.* (Edinburgh, 1967), 137–51; and for the wider context, H.C. Payne, *The Philosophes and the People* (New Haven, 1976).

keyword '*Peuple*' (people) in the *Encyclopédie* (published 1765), may have been influential not only in humanising the lower sorts, but in alerting contemporary consciences about the scale and exploitative degradation suffered by peasants, urban labourers and domestic servants.[7]

Throughout the later eighteenth century, therefore, a scale of meanings could be applied to the term 'the people'. At the benign and humanitarian end, the term could be used as a near synonym for 'the nation', often with vague implications of strength, unity and even patriotic loyalty. This was what was emphasised by Rousseau, and also hinted at in some German writings, notably those of Herder and the early Romantics. Other writers, however, used the term to denote 'the meaner sorts', what the French called the 'menu peuple', which might mutate into a mob during social unrest, and which Burke bluntly labelled 'the swinish multitude'. As we noted earlier in connection with property and taxation (above, p. 163), fears of the 'mob' might provide justification for the maintenance of social inequality itself – not just through continuing policing and censorship, but also, more insidiously, by the non-provision of adequate education for the 'lower sorts'. Such ambivalence towards the people persisted into, and arguably through, the revolutionary period. Significantly, the first revolutionary government in France simply ignored the difficulty by equating (as in the Constitution of 1791) 'the nation' with respectable citizens only. The nation, represented in the National Assembly, replaced the king as sovereign, and was rhetorically endowed with the kind of cohesive unity which it manifestly lacked in reality. Just how this 'nation' might incorporate the interests of the mass of the population was not explained. From 1792, the republican régime in France took the ideal of popular unity even further, reinforcing cohesion through elaborate imagery and ritual, and in accordance with Rousseau forcibly excluding or removing those deemed guilty of fostering faction. Ultimately – as in the Constitution of 1793 – 'the nation' was translated into 'the people', and the latter became the fulcrum and point of reference for all politics. Precision on the meaning of either term, however, remained as elusive as ever: it may have been one of Robespierre's great strengths that he could adhere to a vague if democratic vision of 'the people' without ever openly admitting that national interest and the will of the majority might not be identical.

Closely related to these changing ideals of collective identity was a growing awareness of the role of public opinion. As we noted at the end of Chapter 3, the existence of popular opinion outside government circles (and sometimes in opposition to it) had been recognised in various ways for a long time. The massive tax revolts of the seventeenth century, for example, relied for their success on sometimes quite sophisticated collective recognition of what the state or its tax collectors could or could not reasonably do. During the eighteenth century, 'opinion' was often used as a fairly vague term for

7 H. Chisick, *The Limits of Reform in the Enlightenment* (Princeton, 1981), 52–75.

something which could be verified in the streets and cafés – that is, something which governments needed to keep under observation by means of police agents and spies. It was fickle, volatile and potentially subversive, prone to being manipulated by irresponsible individuals, and susceptible to rumour, prejudice or superstition.[8]

The French *philosophes* themselves, however, had a clear impact on contemporary notions of public opinion. Since most of them were outside government, or in the case of the physiocrats on its periphery, it was in their interest to create a more abstract, cohesive and benevolent opinion than that traditionally associated with the crowd. As Keith Baker and Mona Ozouf, amongst others, have argued, the late enlightenment upgraded such a unitary opinion into a universal tribunal governed by the wisdom of the whole people – the very antithesis of Burke's 'swinish multitude' – now allegedly infallible and unchanging, sometimes above and always independent of the government of the day. Such a public-spirited universal opinion was buttressed above all by Rousseau, in whose eyes anything that was private was potentially suspect, divisive, factional and often selfish – in short prone to tempt the individual away from that 'public good' which civilised social existence required him to recognise.[9] Already a significant ideal by the 1780s, this new visionary public spirit was adopted enthusiastically by successive revolutionary governments as an abstract. However, what they meant was hardly 'public opinion' as that phrase might be understood today. A genuinely free (and potentially anarchic) public opinion was not what the revolutionary leaders had in mind: formal revolutionary consensus could never be created by genuine free exchange, but only by means of a carefully controlled (some would say manipulated) notion of what was in the 'public interest'. Such a public interest was initially embodied in the authority of national elected assemblies. Later, however, notably Robespierre and Saint-Just became habitual interpreters, in the name of 'the people', of a Utopian public interest which allowed no dissent and no deviation. If ever words were the tools of power, it was during the Revolution.

In reality, the dividing line between public and private was quite fluid

---

8 The French dimension is covered in detail in A. Goldgar, *Impolite Learning: Conduct and Community in the Republic of Letters* (New Haven, 1995); D. Goodman, *The Republic of Letters: A Cultural History of the French Enlightenment* (Ithaca, 1994); and J.A.W. Gunn, *Queen of the World: Opinion in the Public Life of France from the Renaissance to the Revolution*, StVEC 328 (1995), notably ch. 5, on 'Rousseau and a new language'. A. Farge, *Subversive Words: Public Opinion in Eighteenth-Century France* (Cambridge, 1994) provides a rich account from street level. For a different British perspective, see K. Wilson, *The Sense of the People: Politics, Culture and Imperialism in England, 1715–1785* (Cambridge, 1995), 17–22 and *passim*.

9 K. Baker, 'Politics and public opinion under the Old Regime', first published in *Press and Politics in Pre-Revolutionary France*, ed. J.R. Censer and J.D. Popkin (Berkeley, 1987), 204–46, and revised as 'Public opinion as political invention' in his *Inventing the French Revolution* (New York, 1990), 167–99; M. Ozouf, ' "Public opinion" at the end of the Old Regime', *Journal of Modern History* 60 (1988), supplement, S1–S21; D. Goodman, 'Public sphere and private life', *History and Theory* 31 (1992), 1–20.

during the eighteenth century. Domestic privacy, such as we would recognise it nowadays, barely existed at all at most levels of society: neither the king's dressing chamber nor the typical sleeping quarters of a workman was in any meaningful sense 'private'. In most European languages, neither 'private' nor 'public' were commonly used to describe personal property or ownership (which was itself sacrosanct and virtually beyond question). Rather, 'private' was synonymous with particular, with the life of an individual, sometimes also carrying connotations of secretive or even factional; whilst 'public' might apply to institutions of the state, but was more often used in vaguer contexts such as 'public spirit' or 'the public good'. A distinction between public and private would be particularly misleading in connection with opinion. For example, the republic of letters was essentially an unofficial network of private individuals with no formal membership and no written rules – yet at the same time ostentatiously egalitarian in its public sharing of knowledge and contact, and to all intents and purposes 'public' by comparison, say, with the exclusive Parisian salon.

Equally, it takes only a quick glance at eighteenth-century newspapers to realise that the ideal of a cohesive opinion or 'public spirit' as envisaged by the late enlightenment bears little or no relationship to reality. The lively, irreverent and increasingly politicised public opinion that was voiced in early eighteenth-century English papers was anything but united, constant or universal – and was certainly much more widely diffused and popular than some intellectuals welcomed. Public opinion in France may have emerged a little later and, as in the rest of monarchical Europe, rather more cautiously – furthered by corporate bodies such as the Jansenist *parlements*, by the cafés, salons and *musées*, by journals and journalists, and by a whole array of individuals who, as Rousseau himself so bitterly asserted, were divided by hatred and conspiracy. In some instances in the 1780s, as we have seen, government ministers themselves openly encouraged public debate – in ways that as often as not made factional interest more evident than 'public spirit'. Just as with 'the people', the reality of 'public opinion' was much more ebullient, irrepressible and complex than eighteenth-century writers and politicians wanted them to be.

Nation, homeland and patriotic identity

As we have already noted, the term 'nation' served various purposes during the later eighteenth century. Volume 11 of Diderot's *Encyclopédie* (published in 1765) followed earlier reference works in providing a simple lexical definition of nation as a 'collective word used to denote a considerable number of people, who inhabit a certain region of land, enclosed within clear limits, and who obey a single government'. Amongst German speakers, nationality was often seen more in terms of cultural identity and language rather than state boundaries – and there the abstract noun 'nationalism' even made a few rare appearances.[10] In the British Isles, stronger and more sophisticated political–ideological characterisations of collective identity had already evolved during the turbulent years of the mid-seventeenth century, including the National Covenanting movement in Scotland, and the English godly 'commonwealth' of the interregnum. Both embodied religious-based ideals which had not entirely lost their resonance by the eighteenth century – even though, as we shall see, many new dimensions were added.

The debate about national identity gathered momentum partly as a result of the innovative analysis in Montesquieu's *The Spirit of the Laws* (1748). He made much of the effects of climate and environment on national spirit, but other writers adopted quite different analytical frameworks. Adam Smith was more interested in economic and structural characteristics, whilst the cameralists took a pragmatic view dependent on social and political evolution. By contrast, factors such as past history, legal traditions and sociological evolution had been given prominence early on by Vico (in his little-read *New Science*, first published in 1725). Similar ideas were taken up by a number of German writers after mid-century in an effort to clarify linguistic, cultural and ethnic identities (as reflected in everything from folklore to the creation of symbolic folk costumes). German society as a whole remained socially conservative, and few writers were at first prepared to follow Herder either in his condemnation of the artificiality of aristocratic French culture (in his travel diaries of 1769) or in his quest for a non-elitist German cultural identity. Many did, however, share his interest in the German historical past, and especially in the great cultural heritage of the medieval period. The European-wide fascination with supposedly ancient texts, such as James Macpherson's fraudulent Ossian poems,[11] was part of this search for a cultural heritage. Rousseau took such nostalgia for the past more literally, making the classical republics of the ancient world a model for regeneration. As he emphasised in his *Considerations on the Government of Poland* of 1772, the values of the past could help, through public education, to create a new sense of national identity. Such quests for national identity (whether imaginary or real) could easily be exploited to reinforce prejudices already deeply engrained in European society: anti-Semitism (as systemic, it seems, in Voltaire's writings as in the popular culture of central Europe), hostility to minority religions (for example in the recurrent 'No Popery' riots in England), xenophobia (as in the defensive anti-German reaction in Denmark from the 1770s onwards), and a variety of more or less explicit racialist assumptions towards non-Europeans and especially to black slaves (above, p. 186). Equally, growing national awareness could have positive benefits, as

10 J. Godechot, 'The new concept of the Nation and its diffusion in Europe', in *Nationalism in the Age of the French Revolution*, ed. O. Dann and J. Dinwiddy (London, 1988), 13–26; see also other papers in that volume.
11 F.J. Stafford, *The Sublime Savage: A Study of James Macpherson and the Poems of Ossian* (Edinburgh, 1988), 163–83; see also R.B. Sher, *Church and University in the Scottish Enlightenment: The Moderate Literati of Edinburgh* (Edinburgh, 1985), 242–61.

in the growth of creative vernacular literature all over central, northern and eastern Europe from the 1770s onwards, designed to wean the elite from a perceived cultural dependence on the French, and encourage national self-awareness amongst a broader public. In Sweden, for example, this led to state patronage for Swedish-language theatre productions, and the foundation of the Swedish Academy in 1786 by one of the most francophile monarchs of the time, Gustavus III.

In the varied vocabulary that accompanied discussion of collective identity in many parts of Europe in the later eighteenth century, pride of place should be given to the highly emotive term 'patrie' (fatherland, homeland), commonly used from at least the fifteenth century to denote a subjectively defined region for which the user felt a sense of loyalty, commitment and love. The personal label 'patriot' had an equally long and ambiguous track record, but by the eighteenth century usually referred to a person who was perceived to have the best interests of his homeland at heart, protecting it from external threats or from the internal dangers created by mismanagement or instability. A patriot could therefore be either a reformer or a conservative – and sometimes both, as illustrated in the debates and publications of the Hamburg Patriotic Society of 1724, and those of its later namesake from 1765. In France, Jansenism became an increasingly powerful ideology of tradition-based loyal-patriotic resistance to an overbearing crown and episcopal establishment.[12] The Dutch Patriot movement of the 1780s similarly sought to restrict the deadening conservative power of the House of Orange, but when they took direct action in 1787 they faced crushing Prussian military intervention (against which the sympathetic French government was powerless to assist, because of its domestic financial difficulties).

Nowhere, however, were the complexities of patriotism more in evidence than in Britain. The seventeenth-century inheritance of protecting the 'birthright of Englishmen' against alleged government corruption and tyranny was in the 1720s and 1730s appropriated by leading Tory and Jacobite thinkers, notably Bolingbroke, as a form of patriotism which could make political opposition legitimate. But a variation on that same inheritance was also used to nourish the kind of aggressively xenophobic Protestantism which remained one of the most prominent and least attractive features of English self-identification throughout the eighteenth century. The definitive failure of the Jacobite rebellion in 1745 allayed suspicions of enemies within, but during the 1760s and 1770s little Englanders like Wilkes flamed resentment against Scots in British government service by playing on this same English national consciousness. As if these strands were not complex enough, the revolt of the American colonies added further twists. Reformist liberals in Britain, sympathetic to many of the grievances of the colonists whose intellectual ancestry they shared, also adopted the American usage of the

---

12 D. van Kley, *The Religious Origins of the French Revolution: From Calvin to the Civil Constitution, 1560–1791* (New Haven, 1996), 210–18.

term 'patriot' – only to find themselves directly challenged by the opposite kind of 'patriot', namely nationalists who wanted to defend imperial interests through war (especially once France became involved), and who by extension opposed most kinds of reform.[13] In the 1790s the French Revolution generated bitter and complex confrontations in Britain between loyalty and reform, resulting by 1794 in the near-destruction of the English and Scottish radical movements (see above, p. 74). In Ireland even deeper contradictions of loyalty emerged. Significant civil concessions to Catholics during the period 1778–93 had created a Protestant sectarian backlash of increasing violence, but the Irish parliament itself remained resolutely Anglican, unrepresentative and unreformed. The United Irishmen established in 1791 under the leadership of the lawyer Theobald Wolfe Tone, though building in the first instance on 'patriot' dissenting grievances, attempted to create a movement for radical parliamentary reform that would bridge existing religious divides and ultimately foster a national republic. Active assistance from France arrived in 1796, but when full-scale rebellion erupted in the spring of 1798 new French support came too late to make a difference. The British government responded by imposing a Treaty of Union (1800–1) which not only permanently changed British–Irish relations, but arguably also allowed a consolidation of loyalist sectarianism which effectively delayed reform in Ireland.

All over Europe, groups campaigning for modest political reform became sandwiched between a few vociferous radicals on the one hand, and conservative (often well-heeled) loyalists condemning French extremism on the other. Yet the stakes were now significantly higher because, as the French journalist and politician Brissot himself made clear in a letter he wrote in January 1791, being a patriot was no longer just the preserve of a narrow intellectual elite:

> A democrat or patriot (I shall use the two interchangeably) does not say: 'I love the people, I am the friend of the people', and so on. Such pedantry is as far removed from his thinking [*esprit*] as from his customary usage. He is too closely identified with the people to be able to place himself outside it in such a way.[14]

13 L. Colley, 'Whose nation?: class and national consciousness in Britain 1750–1830', *Past and Present* 113 (1986), 97–117, and her magisterial *Britons: Forging the Nation 1707–1837* (New Haven, 1992), 22–47, 105–32 and *passim*; C. Kidd, 'North Britishness and the nature of eighteenth-century British patriotisms', *Historical Journal* 39 (1996), 361–82, and his books *Subverting Scotland's Past: Scottish Whig Historians and the Creation of an Anglo-British Identity, 1689–c.1830* (Cambridge, 1993) and *British Identities before Nationalism: Ethnicity and Nationhood in the Atlantic World, 1600–1800* (Cambridge, 1999). See also E.H. Gould, 'American independence and Britain's counter-revolution', *Past and Present* 154 (1997), 107–41.
14 Jacques Pierre Brissot to Antoine Barnave, 31 January 1791; cited in A. Gestrich, *Absolutismus und Öffentlichkeit: politische Kommunikation in Deutschland zu Beginn des 18.*

The term 'patriot', then, was from the 1780s a badge of respect claimed with growing insistence by individuals of quite incompatible political inclinations. The revolt of the American colonies had set a clear precedent for the rejection of a distant government perceived to be unresponsive to the interests of its subjects; but the American constitutional debates of the 1780s, reported as they were over most of Europe, also highlighted the scope for moderate rational political innovation. The French Revolution greatly widened the agenda everywhere, providing new arguments that might clarify existing problems of identity or aspirations for change. In France itself, however, the burden of political inertia from the past was so great that it soon became necessary to abandon tradition in favour of a rationally reconstructed future – embraced during the summer of 1789 by leading patriot figures both from amongst the nobility and from the Third Estate. Their Declaration of the Rights of Man and the Citizen, approved by the Constituent Assembly on 26 August 1789, created the framework for an innovative national identity, the stakeholders of which were to be the 'citizens' of the new constitutional state. Until the American War of Independence, citizenship had been little more than a rather abstract ideal from classical Greece and Rome.[15] Now the French patriots made citizenship a central part of their reforms: those hitherto known as 'subjects' of the French crown were endowed with refinements of political and individual rights which implied a genuine contract between state and citizen.

Political rights and representation in revolutionary France

Like so much else during the French Revolution, the new concept of citizen went through several transformations in a short period of time. In the words of the preamble, the Declaration of the Rights of Man, 'constantly before all the members of the body politic, will incessantly remind them of their rights and duties' – the first principle of which was that 'men are born free and remain free and equal in their rights'. The Constitution of 1791, however, though prefaced by this same Declaration, did not give equal political rights

Jahrhunderts (Göttingen, 1994), 114. For the changing social impact of patriotism, see also H. Chisick, *The Limits of Reform in the Enlightenment: Attitudes toward the Education of the Lower Classes in Eighteenth-Century France* (Princeton, 1981), 215–25 and *passim*; and J. de Viguerie, 'Étude sur l'origine et sur la substance du patriotisme révolutionnaire', *Revue Historique* 295/597 (1996), 83–104.

15 That there was nevertheless a change in usage in some quarters well before 1789 is suggested by J. Merrick, 'Subjects and citizens in the remonstrances of the Parlement of Paris in the eighteenth century', *Journal of the History of Ideas* 51 (1990), 453–60.

to all Frenchmen. Citizenship itself was conferred either by birth (of a French father, or in France but of a foreign father); or by established residence (five years of domicile, possession of real estate or marriage) combined with taking the civic oath. Citizenship was lost by naturalisation in a foreign country, by conviction of certain criminal offences, or by membership of a foreign order carrying hereditary privileges or requiring religious vows. More crucially, a distinction was now made between active (voting) and passive (non-voting) citizenship: only French males over the age of 25 who paid a certain amount in annual taxation and who registered for the National Guard would qualify to vote in the primary round – which in practice probably amounted to around 15% of the total population (or around 60% of all males over 25). This relatively generous franchise was approved only because there was a higher property qualification which restricted eligibility to local and municipal offices, effectively eliminating perhaps another one-third of the active citizens. Those wishing to stand for election to the national parliament had to meet yet another requirement, the payment in annual taxation of one *marc d'argent* (just over 50 livres). This was high enough to ensure that some of the deputies elected to the Estates General in 1789 would no longer qualify (had they been allowed to stand again), and in practice ensured that at best only one active citizen in 10 qualified for national election.[16] Understandably, it was particularly this *marc d'argent* restriction which caused controversy during the elections to the Legislative Assembly in 1791. On 11 August 1792, the day after the fall of the monarchy, a decree was passed abolishing the distinction between active and passive citizens and lowering the minimum voting age to 21. Only domestic servants and those without work were henceforth barred from voting, so the third assembly, the Convention (1792–95) was elected on something approaching universal male suffrage.

The second Constitution, that of 1793, embodied another more generous Declaration of Rights, the formulation of which had been at least as tortuous as that of its predecessor in 1789. The first draft, compiled by a commission headed by the moderate *philosophe* Condorcet, was rejected by the Convention in February 1793 along with the rest of the draft Constitution, partly because of its Girondin associations. Robespierre then drew up an alternative, far more democratic, Declaration of Rights which was published in April. Its stated purpose was to ensure

> that all citizens, being able constantly to compare the acts of the government with the aim of every social institution, may never allow themselves to be oppressed and demeaned by tyranny; and that the people may always have before their eyes the foundation of their liberty and welfare.

16 P. Gueniffey, *Le nombre et la raison: la révolution française et les élections* (Paris, 1993), 78–101; M. Crook, *Elections in the French Revolution* (Cambridge, 1996), 38–46.

Whilst maintaining full protection for property rights, this draft also embodied a number of other principles: the need for redistributive progressive taxation, the obligation of the state either to provide work or to provide relief for those unable to work, and absolute equality in civic and political rights for all adult males. No doubt to help legitimise earlier popular insurrections, it included a formal statement that 'when the government violates the rights of the people, insurrection of the entire people, and of every section of it, is the most sacred of duties', adding for good measure that 'every institution which does not assume that the people are good, and the magistrate corruptible, is depraved'. It stated pointedly that elected deputies were merely mandatories of the people, subject to their continuous scrutiny. Finally, Robespierre's draft asserted the universal brotherhood of man, and proclaimed that 'kings, aristocrats, tyrants whoever they be, are slaves rebelling against the sovereign of the earth, which is the human race, and against the legislator of the universe, which is nature'.[17]

Not surprisingly, this text was not adopted either. Another attempt was made by a small *ad hoc* commission, working in some haste to produce a text which might help re-unify a republic torn both by foreign war and by serious civil conflict. This version, adopted by the Convention on 24 June 1793, incorporated some of the political rights of Robespierre's draft, but not its radical social provisions. It formed the preamble to the new Constitution, and as such was approved by national referendum shortly afterwards. However, it was never actually implemented – officially because of the war, but in reality because internal conditions had become too embittered. Ideological as well as personal feuds were not new to revolutionary France, but the outbreak of war, and the resulting crisis of government during the summer of 1792, had raised the stakes. Almost as soon as the Convention assembled in September it had become torn by deep animosities, which in turn were aggravated by the difficult trial of the king during the last two months of the year. Attempts were made to challenge the immunity of individual deputies through impeachment procedures (culminating in the case against Marat in April 1793); even worse, the inviolability of parliamentary government itself was broken by means of a direct assault on the Convention (31 May–2 June 1793), organised by a Parisian insurrectionary committee acting in the spirit of Robespierre's draft declaration. During June 1793, as exiled Girondins added fuel to the already serious revolts in provincial France, the unity of the French people was so palpably chimeric, the threat of anarchy so overwhelming, that visionary liberal or democratic

17 The Jacobin club on 21 April 1793 ordered this text printed, according to P.-J.-B. Buchez and P.-C. Roux, *Histoire parlementaire de la Révolution française*, vol. 26 (Paris, 1836), 93–7, and it was read to the Convention three days later. On the 1789 text, see S. Rials, *La déclaration des droits de l'homme et du citoyen* (Paris, 1988); J. Jennings, 'The 'Déclaration des droits de l'homme et du citoyen' and its critics in France', *Historical Journal* 35 (1992), 839–59; and on how the text actually emerged, K.M. Baker, 'The idea of a Declaration of Rights', in *The French Idea of Freedom*, ed. D. van Kley (Stanford, 1994), 154–96.

experiments understandably had to be postponed. The third Constitution, that of 1795, took no chances in this direction, reverting instead to a much more restrictive view both of citizenship and of political participation.

Such recurrent preoccupation with drawing up constitutions and declarations of rights to fit each stage of the Revolution may seem almost an obsession – or a pastime of the lawyers who dominated all three assemblies. Most contemporaries had learnt to regard democracy, much like citizenship, as an ideal of classical civilisation rather than as a practical system of guidelines for the present. Rousseau himself had recognised that, even if sovereignty might genuinely have resided in the people in ancient Greek city states, simple democracy was unworkable in practice in the much larger communities of his own time. As he had famously put it, 'if there were a people consisting of gods, they would govern themselves democratically: a government which is so perfect does not suit men'.[18] This offered little comfort to the French in 1789, once reform of existing structures had been abandoned in favour of wholesale reconstruction. The scale of change was such that political legitimacy had to be defined afresh, not just at the outset in 1789 (with the creation of a parliamentary monarchy), but even more so during the period 1792–93, when the failure of monarchy and its replacement by a republic threatened to bring anarchy. For each stage, but especially in the uncharted territory of the new republic, the legality of government could only be justified on the basis of 'the sovereignty of the people' – an ideal which alone seemed to offer a credible and rational alternative to discarded tradition. The members of the Convention knew perfectly well that the potential advantages of some degree of active public participation in (and consent for) the legislative process would have to be balanced against not only the risk of occasional collective lack of rational political judgement, but also the more insidious hazards of corruption, factional rivalry and demagoguery within a republic where the location of legitimacy might be open to question. Finding such a balance was the ultimate challenge facing the revolutionary government after 1792; and the emergence of the Terror a year later perhaps the clearest sign of its failure.

The only way popular sovereignty could work, it seemed, was through a system of representation. Rousseau had made clear that popular sovereignty, in the sense of a legislative general will determining a simple framework of universal laws, did not require a democratic organisation of the executive branch of government; indeed the application of democracy to the detail of government was likely to cause a disintegration of the general will into particular interests, and thus negate the true interest of the people. Rousseau, however, was also very critical of representative systems, where individuals

---

18 J.-J. Rousseau, *Du contrat social* (1762) (various editions), book III, chapter 4. It is worth noting that, until 1790, the word 'democrat' (or its derivative, 'democracy') was hardly ever used in any context other than that of the classical world of antiquity. The historical usage of this and many other terms is usefully summarised in R. Williams, *Keywords: A Vocabulary of Culture and Society* (London, 1983).

might be chosen to speak on behalf of the people. Already in 1789, therefore, in order for the National Constituent Assembly to function at all, the deputies had had to distance themselves from part of the Rousseauist orthodoxy. Not only had they laid formal claim to speak for the whole of the French nation/people (as announced by the Third Estate in their motion of 17 June 1789, and emphasised countless times thereafter), they had gone one step further, denying that they were in any sense bound or mandated to act on behalf of the particular constituency by whom they had been elected – or even to act in accordance with the *cahiers de doléances* so painstakingly compiled at each electoral meeting. For the deputies, personal liberty and individual rights (as defined in law) were supposed to be universal and unifying, rather than divisive, principles. As they asserted in July 1789, it was the responsibility of each deputy to interpret the general will of the whole nation, rather than to listen to the imperfect promptings of factions in a particular constituency.[19] Accordingly, elections were meant merely to determine who should be chosen as deputy, not to sound out the general will. The role of the primary voter ended the moment he had cast his vote – and the fact that some electoral assemblies, notably in Paris, continued to meet thereafter was fundamentally contrary to the general interest.

Some extremely important consequences followed from this initial interpretation of how political representation might work. First, the new Assembly, on the strength of its claim to represent the whole nation, took upon itself a much more comprehensive and detailed legislative remit than what the small group of 'democrats' amongst them wanted. One contemporary observer described the Constituent Assembly of 1789–91 as a 'decree factory',[20] its debates so badly managed that inconsistencies, self-contradictions and misjudgements littered its legislative record. Even more seriously, the Assembly gradually came to be seen as autocratic and out of touch. Its handling of the aftermath of the king's flight to Varennes (21 June 1791) and of the peaceful republican demonstration in the Champ de Mars a few weeks later (17 July) demonstrated its lack of political imagination and its brutal high-handedness in the face of popular politics. The Assembly seemed to claim to know the popular will better than the people itself, and seemed intent on enforcing its own agenda by means of repeated use of emergency powers against those who thought otherwise. However, the end of its mandate, and the holding of fresh elections in September 1791, saved the reputation of representative parliamentary government as such for a while. It took more than a year before the irreconcilable difference between being a 'representative of the nation' and a 'mandatory of the people' re-emerged to haunt and almost destroy revolutionary parliamentary politics.

19 For a discussion of this complex matter, see notably N. Hampson, *Prelude to Terror: The Constituent Assembly and the Failure of Consensus, 1789–1791* (Oxford, 1988), 62–65 and 101–10. See also K.M. Baker, 'Representation redefined', in his *Inventing the French Revolution* (Cambridge, 1990), 224–51.

20 Louis-Philippe [king of France, 1830–48], *Memoirs 1773–1793*, transl./ed. J. Hardman (New York, 1977), 97.

Followers of Rousseau would then interpret his recommendations on the legitimacy of a representative system in such a way as to subject deputies to a strict popular mandate, under the direct scrutiny of observers in the gallery of the assembly hall.

By 1793 it was increasingly clear how far the French representative system had taken a political course fundamentally different from that underpinning British parliamentary practice. This divergence was in part the result of another fundamental concept in Rousseau's political thought, the belief that the general will is always right. The individual could never be sure of his own interpretation of the general will, but guided by the majority he would come to see the truth. Compromise, or the reconciliation of differing views, was therefore not compatible with a Rousseauist reading of politics; nor was the existence of political parties, corporate bodies or any other associations that might cause institutionalised division within the general will. Already from 1789, serious effort had been made to attain substantive unanimity in French national politics: the seemingly inevitable failure to achieve such unanimity was regarded not simply as the result of imperfections of understanding, but rather as the result of deadly corruption within the body politic, or even the result of outright conspiracy, a crime against the people.

More frequent referrals to the popular will, for example through national referenda, might have been the obvious answer. But the Jacobins, for reasons of their own, became increasingly convinced that, until such a time when public education might succeed in creating a fully virtuous citizenry, the people should be given only simple and straightforward questions to which the answer was likely to be uncontentious. This line of argument secured the defeat in the Convention of a proposal for a referendum on the fate of the king (15 January 1793); equally, the groundwork for a national referendum in July endorsing the new Constitution was done with sufficient care to ensure both a good turn-out and an overwhelmingly favourable verdict. To the Jacobins, this was not political manipulation, but rather a process to facilitate the emergence of that 'true' general will untainted either by personal ambition or by the manipulations of parliamentary politics.

Perhaps the Jacobins were right in not entrusting difficult political questions to the electorate. It is one of the striking conclusions of recent research on French electoral politics in this period that, when the franchise was widened to include all adult males (from August 1792), the actual proportion of voters taking part fell. Electoral participation under the restricted franchise of 1789–91 was often upwards of 50%, and in some (especially rural) areas even higher. Signs of dwindling participation at national level are apparent already from 1791 in the primary assemblies (though less so for municipal elections). But the real failure came with the national elections in August–September 1792, which ushered in a period of very low turn-out (overall often in the range 15–20% of the now very large electorate). It may be that the lower ranks of the new electorate were not yet ready for electoral participation – many failed even to register – or that there was still a preference for traditional direct action. Alternatively, the atmosphere in which elections took place from now on may have been such as to discourage dissenting candidates from standing (and their supporters from turning up to vote). Violence and intimidation were noted in some areas during the elections of 1792. Equally, apathy or election-fatigue in the face of rather complicated but repeatedly modified voting systems may also have been a factor.[21] Barbaroux, who chaired the electoral assembly in Avignon in September 1792 and was himself duly elected to the Convention, described the mood of the election in the bitter memoirs he wrote before his execution as a Girondin in June 1794:

> Imagine an assemblage of 900 people, mostly ignorant, having difficulty in making themselves listen to those with any sense, but giving themselves over to the seething hot-heads, and, in this assembly, a crowd of men avid for money and preferment, eternal denouncers, who dream up trouble (or exaggerate it) in order to gain lucrative commissions; intriguers quick at disseminating calumnies, little distrustful minds, a few virtuous but unenlightened men; some who were enlightened but lacked courage; a great many patriots, but without balance and without philosophy: such was the electoral body of the *département* of Bouches-du-Rhône. One event describes it better than this very imperfect sketch: on hearing the news of the massacres of 2 September, the hall resounded with applause.[22]

If France demonstrated the enormous difficulties inherent in creating a new legitimate order which might balance popular will with practical stability, Britain, by contrast, demonstrated how difficult it was to update an inherited system. Since 1689, the existence of a workable (if unwritten) 'constitution' had made most political observers complacent. Yet the system was not without its flaws, and from the 1730s onwards the press contributed significantly (with its attacks on Walpole's government) to a rapid increase of public interest in politics. By the late 1760s, Wilkes could use his own repeatedly disqualified election to the Commons to demonstrate the real chasm between Parliament and its electorates. During the 1770s and 1780s, the American struggle for independence dramatically drew attention to more fundamental flaws in the representative system, on which critics within Britain could (and did) capitalise.[23] But serious analysis of the principles of political representation, let alone of a formal constitution or a declaration of rights, failed to get very far. Significantly, even Tom Paine in 1792 glossed over some major problems when he stated that 'by ingrafting representation

21 P. Gueniffey, entries under 'Elections' and 'Suffrage', in *A Critical Dictionary of the French Revolution*, ed. F. Furet and M. Ozouf (Cambridge, Mass., 1989), 33–44 and 571–81 respectively; P. Gueniffey, *Le nombre et la raison: la révolution française et les élections* (Paris, 1993); M. Crook, *Elections in the French Revolution* (Cambridge, 1996).
22 *Mémoires de [Charles] Barbaroux*, ed. A. Chabaud (Paris, 1936), 168.
23 For a survey of the debate on parliamentary, electoral and other political reform during this period, see notably H.T. Dickinson, *The Politics of the People in Eighteenth-Century Britain* (Basingstoke, 1994), esp. 174–89.

upon democracy, we arrive at a system of government capable of embracing and confederating all the various interests and every extent of territory and population'.[24] In the light of what happened in France, it is perhaps understandable why the British elite reacted so defensively against any demands for domestic electoral reform, wherever they may have originated.

It is very difficult to be precise about just who was really represented in any meaningful sense in the chaotically inconsistent British electoral system which prevailed before the Reform Act of 1832. Some counties, such as Yorkshire with its very large electorate of 15–20,000, were virtually impossible to control (or even predict accurately), and thus enjoyed quite interactive politics. In such relatively free county constituencies most male householders who met certain property qualifications could vote – in practice sometimes more than half the adult male population. At the other extreme were small boroughs with so few voters that meaningful political debate never occurred, where parliamentary election could be secured solely by means of patronage or by bribing the small self-perpetuating oligarchy who alone had the vote. In between were an impressive number of variants – including areas where electoral processes changed significantly during the period. Statistical averages are therefore liable to be misleading. Yet recent research indicates that the total electorate in 1689 in England and Wales was around 20% of the adult male population, declining (because population growth outstripped relaxation of the franchise) to around 17% by the end of the eighteenth century – in others words, the overall electorate was far more restricted than that in France during even the moderate early stage of the Revolution. On the other hand (and perhaps because of the restrictive electorate), turn-out in England of those entitled to vote seems to have been quite high.[25]

24 T. Paine, *Rights of Man*, Part II (1792), ch. 3 – 180 in the Penguin Classics edition (Harmondsworth, 1985); or 170 in Thomas Paine, *Political Writings* (Cambridge, 1989). Here he was referring primarily to America, but during the summer of 1791 (reported in the *Gazette nationale*, 16 July 1791) Paine had also challenged Sieyes in Paris to a public debate regarding the respective merits of hereditary monarchy compared with an elective 'republic' (in a loose sense of that word, meaning a publicly accountable open government). Much of his argument in *Rights of Man* was designed to undermine heredity in politics, rather than discuss electoral reform *per se*.
25 F. O'Gorman, *Voters, Patrons, and Parties: The Unreformed Electoral System of Hanoverian England, 1734–1832* (Oxford, 1989), 178–99. He estimates a total electorate at the end of the century of 338,000, in a population of around 8.5 million (4% of the total, 17.2% of adult males). These figures have generated some debate, and may need marginal adjustment; but even so, the proportion who had voting rights in France during the National Constituent Assembly is at least three times greater. As far as local elections are concerned, the contrast may seem less striking, in that some parts of Britain had quite lively and regular local contests. But in France, following the total re-organisation of both voting and local government in 1790, local elections became much more consistent throughout the country, for a wide range of offices. Comparisons with other European states with a representative system are much more difficult, but what little research has been done suggests that Scotland had a very limited franchise, and that even Sweden, despite its separate representation of the Fourth Estate, also had a long way to go. In any case, as D. Beales has pointed out in his review article of O'Gorman's book, 'The electorate before and after 1832: the right to vote, and the opportunity', *Parliamentary History* 11 (1992), 139–50, the right to vote is one thing, but problems of uncontested elections and actual turn-out are quite distinct.

Representing the other half: women and public life

In his *Encyclopédie* article on '*Citoyen*' (citizen), Diderot had taken for granted that, in effect, only the male head of household would have full citizenship: women, alongside children and servants, were granted no more than titular status 'as members of the family of a citizen properly so called', without themselves being true citizens.[26] This may well represent a common consensus of the enlightenment period, for the question of active political participation by women was not seriously discussed until well into the revolutionary period. Even Mary Wollstonecraft, in her *Vindications of the Rights of Woman* (1792), mentioned the subject only in passing, without risking any further elaboration:

> I may excite laughter, by dropping a hint, which I mean to pursue, some future time, for I really think that women ought to have representatives, instead of being arbitrarily governed without having any direct share allowed them in the deliberations of government.[27]

Remarkably, women had been given the franchise in a few of the North American colonies, in New Jersey and in Pennsylvania, but these instances were quite exceptional. In Europe, discussion of what we would now call 'gender issues' did gather some momentum in the 1780s – at the same time as discussion of slavery (see above, p. 186). By then the debating societies which had developed in London and other major British cities (above, p. 72) regularly included in their programmes a variety of issues relating to the position of women in society, sometimes touching also on matters of political rights. But much of the discussion was theoretical and generalised, and likely to conform strictly to contemporary claustrophobic norms of decency and morality. The radical reform movements of 1792–93 remained firmly male: thus the London Corresponding Society, whilst campaigning for electoral reform and at times even for universal male franchise, made no mention of the possibility that women might also be entitled to vote. Wollstonecraft too, despite her insistence that women be given a real education, seemed to accept that men and women should remain consigned to the separate spheres that Rousseau had so persuasively emphasised in the 1760s; whilst her slightly

---

26 Article on '*Citoyen*' in the *Encyclopédie*, vol. 3 (1753), 488. For the broader context, see L. Steinbrügge, *The Moral Sex: Woman's Nature in the French Enlightenment* (Oxford, 1995).
27 *Vindications of the Rights of Woman* (1792), 259f in the Penguin Classics edition (Harmondsworth, 1975).

older contemporary Hannah More condemned all notions of change as a threat to stability and morality.[28]

In revolutionary France, women's rights ultimately caused much more public controversy. The marquis de Condorcet (1743–94), one of the last *philosophes* and a very distinguished mathematician, had already in 1787 suggested that qualified (and propertied) women should have the right to be elected to public office. In 1790, in connection with his work on the reform of slavery and on Jewish emancipation, he published a short essay 'On the admission of women to the rights of citizenship' in which he stressed the illogicality of having a declaration of rights whilst debarring half of human-kind from its entitlements. Condorcet contributed to the debates of the Confédération des Amis de la Verité (Confederation of the Friends of the Truth), a political club founded in January 1790 by a group of reformers known as the Cercle Social, who also ran their own newspaper, the *Bouche de fer* (*Iron Mouth/Mailbox*). Alongside other current issues like educational and land reform, the journal tackled matters such as the inheritance and primogeniture system, domestic violence, divorce laws and women's voting rights. In March 1791, with around 5,000 members already enrolled, the Confédération established a women's branch led by Etta Palm d'Aelders and other mostly wealthy and well-educated women.[29] They debated additional topics like civic equality, the rights of single mothers, and women's work; but they also devoted much attention to the writings of Rousseau, seeming to turn a blind eye to his patronising and discriminatory attitude to women.

It is conceivable that the Confédération, or the articles in the *Bouche de fer*, may have inspired Olympe de Gouges to compile her idiosyncratic Declaration of the Rights of Women (probably dating from the late summer of 1791) – a text which not only rewrote the Declaration of the Rights of Man clause by clause, but also incorporated a passing reference to Caribbean slavery, an appeal to Marie Antoinette, and a proposal for an innovative

28 Both writers appear to have made a significant impression on contemporary opinion, though in opposite directions and on very different types of audience. As noted by R.M. Janes, 'On the reception of Mary Wollstonecraft's *A Vindication of the Rights of Woman*', *Journal of the History of Ideas* 39 (1978), 293–302, Wollstonecraft's book was generally well received by reviewers in 1792, especially its call for educational reform. It went through at least three editions in London, one in Dublin and three in the United States over the next few years, and was published in French by December 1792. Only after her death in childbirth in 1797, when the political mood had swung further to the right, did reviewers begin to use emerging details of her private life to discredit all her writings. Hannah More (1745–1833) was a prolific author, and her *Village Politics Addressed to all Mechanics, Journeymen and Day Labourers in Great Britain* (also 1792), a 24-page dialogue against Paine intended to appeal directly to a popular audience, quickly went through at least eight editions; but from 1795 she developed and marketed a more effective series of short tracts for the moral education of the poor, the so-called Cheap Repository Tracts. More was highly critical of the *Vindication*, whilst emphasising that she had no intention of ever reading it.

29 G. Kates, '"The powers of husband and wife must be equal and separate": the Cercle Social and the rights of women, 1790–91', in *Women and Politics in the Age of Democratic Revolution*, ed. H.B. Applewhite and D.G. Levy (Ann Arbor, 1990), 163–80; J. Landes, *Women and the Public Sphere in the Age of the French Revolution* (Ithaca, 1988), 112–29 and *passim*.

marriage contract which would allow easy divorce by mutual consent.[30] By the time this text appeared, however, the women's branch of the Confédération was already overshadowed by the political reaction which took place in Paris from July 1791 onwards. Nevertheless the Constitution of 1791 incorporated some of the liberal reforms which the Confédération and other political clubs had debated; and the Legislative Assembly, dominated by Brissot and other members of the Cercle Social, went further along this road, even legalising divorce at its very last full session on 20 September 1792. Condorcet himself sat in two successive assemblies: in the Legislative Assembly he presented a detailed report on national educational reform (20 April 1792), and in the Convention he sat on the committee drafting the new Constitution. That draft led to some discussion within the Convention (29 April 1793) as to whether women should now be given the vote. But Condorcet was a poor speaker, and the small minority of deputies who actively supported such reform failed to make any headway in the increasingly factionalised Assembly. Further appeals to the Convention from women's organisations were not acted on.

Even though successive national assemblies thus seem to have marginalised questions of women's rights, a number of political societies (including the Paris Jacobin club and many of its affiliated urban provincial branches) had admitted women as members already from 1790, or allowed women to form sister societies. With the outbreak of war in April 1792 some of these organisations called not just for more active female participation in education and community work, but also for admission into local politics and even into the armed forces. Such demands for female participation in public affairs, however, were not always well received; as the stakes of popular political participation increased, so did hostility amongst traditionalists (men as well as women). In May 1793 the constitution of the newly established Society for Revolutionary Republican Women indicated that it aimed to 'attend to public affairs, to succour suffering humanity, and to defend all human beings who become victims of any arbitrary acts whatever'. The society had close links with the radical populists (the *enragés*) around Jacques Roux; like them it was openly militant and strongly anti-elitist, its members adopting a uniform (including red liberty bonnet and trousers) and sometimes carrying firearms. The society participated prominently in section politics, and like other popular organisations campaigned both for stronger legislation against food speculators and for more effective enforcement of existing laws; but whether its members had long-term political aims such as securing voting rights for women is unclear, for internal divisions soon set in. Already by September elements within the society were openly critical of the Jacobin government, and on 30 October the Convention used recurrent and

30 The full text is cited in D.G. Levy, H.B. Applewhite and M.D. Johnson, *Women in Revolutionary Paris 1789–1795* (Urbana, 1980), 87–96. See also J.W. Scott, 'French feminists and the Rights of "Man": Olympe de Gouges's Declarations', *History Workshop Journal* 28 (1989), 1–21.

sometimes violent confrontations between its members and various groups of market-women in Paris as justification for a ban on all women's political organisations.[31] Although women continued to participate in sectional and other assemblies, the revolutionary leadership increasingly curtailed *sans-culotte* (popular) militancy, whether organised by men or by women. In short, the hopes and aspirations of the early 1790s, both for women's civil rights and for democratic reform more generally, foundered in 1793–94 – within France because of the bitter power struggles, outside France because of European-wide reaction against anything that might encourage the spread of French-style revolutionary radicalism in domestic politics.

The revolution of popular politics

A glance at the newspaper press all over Europe after 1789 suggests that events in France were followed with great interest; and it would be difficult to believe that contemporary political thinking was not affected in one way or another by such news. To those who had already been fascinated by the constitutional consolidation of the American republic in the 1780s, the relatively moderate early Revolution in France (1787–91) seemed a mostly unproblematic continuation of the ideas that had gained currency over the previous decades. From 1792 onwards, however, the war and the dramatic trial and execution of the king, combined with more innovative or intrusive forms of direct popular participation in politics in France, created dangerous and potentially alarming precedents for the rest of Europe which no-one with an interest in politics could ignore.

We have already observed how contemporary French thinking on representative government took a Rousseauist line which, in its insistence on the unanimity of the general will and its hostility to organised parties and parliamentary compromise, explicitly sought to avoid the kind of factionalism seemingly central to British parliamentary politics. With this French search for national consensus came a political vocabulary and a concept of public politics which in several respects broke new ground. As we noted, expressions of collective identity (people, nation, opinion), though far from new in themselves, gained greater prominence in French public consciousness – hammered home incessantly by such self-indulgent yet influential

31 D.G. Levy, H.B. Applewhite and M.D. Johnson, *Women in Revolutionary Paris 1789–1795* (Urbana, 1980), 143–220; on provincial women's societies, see notably S. Desan, ' "Constitutional Amazons": Jacobin women's clubs in the French Revolution', in *Recreating Authority in Revolutionary France*, ed. B.T. Ragan *et al.* (New Brunswick, N.J., 1992), 11–35. The ban of 30 October 1793 was imposed after a short and one-sided debate in the Convention, but in direct response to repeated appeals from the market women of Les Halles, who objected particularly to the regulatory economic demands of the Society for Revolutionary Republican Women. For a quite recent overview, see notably D.G. Levy and H.B. Applewhite, 'Women and militant citizenship in revolutionary Paris', in *Rebel Daughters: Women and the French Revolution* (New York, 1992), 79–101.

orators as Robespierre. Abstract ideals like liberty and equality also acquired universalist potential, whilst fraternity came to embody the internationalism so characteristic of the early days of the Revolution. Rather more ambivalent was the use of terms like 'federation' – at first a celebratory word for the new inclusive state (as in the Festival of the Federation marking the first anniversary of the fall of the Bastille on 14 July 1790), but soon an increasingly controversial term adopted by the Girondins in 1793, citing the American Constitution to justify their opposition to the Paris-dominated Revolution and the centralisation of government. Accordingly, a federalist came to be seen by the Jacobins as someone ultimately willing to question national unity and to foment factional armed rebellion in the provinces, as happened in the summer of 1793.

When we look at the speeches and writings of the militant leaders of the Paris Commune and of the radical Jacobin back-benchers (the Mountain) in the Convention, however, it is not difficult to see why many moderates even within France might find these developments frightening. The Convention deputy and maverick newspaper editor Jean-Paul Marat was from the start notorious for his inflammatory language: he not only helped turn words like aristocrat, *émigré*, *accapareur* (monopolist, hoarder) or *insouciant* (someone indifferent to revolutionary ideals) into terms of abuse, but also popularised rare words such as *agioteur* (speculator) and neologisms such as *moderantisme* (believing in moderation). Loaded terms like these could be used liberally but without specificity in denouncing perceived enemies of the people. Political correctness, by 1793, required awareness of the undercurrents of meaning in a growing and malleable vocabulary which included terms like *septembriseur* (supporter of the prison massacres in September 1792), *enragé* (left-wing agitator critical of contemporary *laissez-faire* economics and favouring *maximum* price controls), the increasingly ubiquitous *sans-culotte* (a person whose dress was evidence of a humble background), and naturally *mandataire* (a parliamentary deputy directly accountable to the people).[32] The great days of popular action (*journées*) in Paris, such as 10 August 1792 or 31 May 1793, provided a specific focus for the mythology of revolutionary celebration – the French people itself often symbolised by the

---

32 Changes in vocabulary can be documented by reference to the large database of texts held online by FRANTEXT/ARTFL. For more specific case studies, see notably H.J. Lüsebrink and R. Reichardt, 'La "Bastille" dans l'imaginaire social de la France à la fin du xviiie siècle (1774–1799)', *Revue d'Histoire Moderne et Contemporaine* 30 (1983), 196–234, and the book by the same authors, *Die Bastille: zur Symbolgeschichte von Herrschaft und Freiheit* (Frankfurt/Main, 1990); K.M. Baker, *Inventing the French Revolution* (Cambridge, 1990), 203–23, primarily regarding the word 'revolution' itself; M. Olsen, 'Enlightened nationalism and the early Revolution: the *nation* in the language of the *Société de 1789*', *Canadian Journal of History* 29 (1994), 24–50; J. Guilhaumou, *La langue politique et la Révolution française* (Paris, 1989); W.H. Sewell, 'The sans-culotte rhetoric of subsistence', in *The French Revolution and the Creation of Modern Political Culture*, vol. 4: *The Terror* (Oxford, 1994), 249–69; and the very substantial and innovative work of J. Markoff, *The Abolition of Feudalism: Peasants, Lords and Legislators in the French Revolution* (Philadelphia, 1996).

figure of Hercules, and its virtues by means of an array of visual icons. And, from 5 October 1793 onwards, the new revolutionary calendar sought not only to destroy all religious connotations like saints' days and Sunday worship, but also to promote a new litany of secular civic values eventually sanctified in the Worship of the Supreme Being instituted in May 1794.[33]

But it was not merely about abstract words. Popular politics, particularly in the radical districts of Paris, had already in 1789 acquired a distinctive momentum, encouraging frequent meetings of sectional assemblies and political clubs which concentrated on lengthy if often chaotic discussion of current affairs. It became common at these meetings to draw up formulaic petitions which were usually approved by acclamation and, in the omission of individual signatures, were intended to convey unanimity. When a sectional assembly or other group appointed a delegation to deliver such petitions directly to the sitting National Assembly, direct democracy appeared to be in the making. However, as such direct action became more common from 1792 onwards, so did the scope for denunciation and harassment of specific political opponents. Papers such as Marat's *L'ami du peuple* and Hébert's *Le père Duchesne*, designed to attract *sans-culotte* readers, turned denunciation into a hallmark of their style: thin on factual or analytic information, these papers deliberately encouraged a tendency for popular politics to focus on scapegoats. The way sectional meetings operated – even their habit of reading out newspaper reports *in extenso* as part of their discussion – made it easy to personalise all flaws in government, and to target individuals when something went wrong. Sectional politics became prone to defining the Revolution negatively, endlessly lambasting supposed conspiracy, faction, corruption, counter-revolution, and organised subversion.

Already in the 1770s and 1780s, economic and financial problems had routinely been ascribed to conspiratorial subversion, and the new National Assembly did not break with that tradition. In July 1789 a parliamentary committee had been established to identify subversive plots; ominously, the Paris Commune set up its own such committee in October, encouraging individual citizens to come forward with both evidence and denunciations. The public nature of such civic denunciation, before an open tribune of public 'opinion' and subject to legal checks, was meant to prevent a lapse into the secretive and divisive police procedures for which the *ancien régime* had been notorious. From the start, however, denunciations seemed to focus more on conspiratorial intent than on actual criminal action, and expectations of proof were accordingly low. For prominent individuals the effect

33 L. Hunt, *Politics, Culture and Class in the French Revolution* (Berkeley, 1984), ch. 3 and *passim*; J. Harris, 'The red cap of liberty: a study of dress worn by French revolutionary partisans, 1789–94', *Eighteenth-Century Studies* 14 (1981), 283–312. David's revolutionary iconography of Year II provided a stronger visual unity, but the fact that his designs for new national costumes (May 1794) were revived by the Directory after 1795 (with counterparts in other parts of Europe) suggests that his ideas do not represent merely the whims of one régime.

could be cumulative – as illustrated in the case of the king himself, who suffered a gradual erosion of credibility by press denunciation long before he was deposed. When war broke out in April 1792, fears of rapid military collapse significantly increased the scope for panic denunciations. During the months of uncertainty and prison massacres in late August and early September, officeholders and local magistrates in many parts of France were purged by more or less spontaneous popular action, and replaced by 'patriots'. Despite the often chaotic conditions under which this happened, the new Convention ratified such action on 22 September.

During the winter of 1792–93, as economic problems returned, the identification of conspiracies seems to have become a kind of safety valve, notionally justified in terms of civic education and purification, but in practice creating an endless supply of scapegoats. Local surveillance committees (*comités de surveillance*) were created in March 1793, to which secret denunciations could be made; the Revolutionary Tribunal was revived on 10 March 1793; municipal authorities began issuing so-called *certificats de civisme* (certificates of civic virtue) to individuals, with inevitable consequences for those who were refused such certificates; on 17 September 1793 the Law of Suspects improved surveillance under the Committee of General Security, not just in Paris but also in the troublesome parts of provincial France; and other measures were added up until the Law of 22 Prairial (10 June 1794), whereby a brutally efficient Terror machinery could minimise delays in identifying suspects, reduce the formality of verifying allegations, and make defence virtually impossible. Couthon, in presenting that law to the Convention on behalf of the Committee of Public Safety, had no hesitation in asserting that the law would provide a jury of patriots to defend those falsely accused, but none for conspirators.

What had happened to enlightened ideals of transparency and respect for the law? Clearly, if we measured the impact of the enlightenment by the politics of Year II, the tally would not be encouraging. Yet the very purpose of the process of denunciation had itself also changed: supposedly spontaneous and independent of government in 1789, intended to ensure the removal of *ancien régime* corruption and to strengthen popular support for good government, denunciation had by 1794 become a tool of government, a key part of the institutionalised fear and insecurity on which the Jacobin dictatorship had come to rely. It is difficult, on the basis of the formulaic language of accusations, to know whether the kinds of targets in fact changed significantly over those years.[34] But what we know about at least the high-profile victims of the Terror suggests that the Revolution had become hypnotised by its own rhetoric – by those endlessly repeated moral judgements which, like the general will, appeared to be transparent and

---

34 C. le Bart, 'L'imputation: un outil pour l'analyse des mentalités révolutionnaires', *Revue Historique* 282 (1989), 351–65; C. Lucas, 'The theory and practice of denunciation in the French Revolution', *Journal of Modern History* 68 (1996), 768–85.

egalitarian, but allowed no compromise or concession, and left no middle ground or escape.

It is worth remembering that surveillance tactics had been common long before 1789, the work of the Paris police and their spying agents likewise. The Revolution genuinely did seek to create civic unity and cohesion as a means of breaking with the long-engrained habits of factional *ancien régime* politics. The public ritual of taking an oath (something of an obsession at all levels of the Revolution) was an attempt to break the mould of the past, a symbolic re-affirmation of allegiance to the body politic – though, as demonstrated by the oath of allegiance required from priests after the adoption of the Civil Constitution of the Clergy in 1790, it, too, could serve as a means of identifying those who were ambivalent in their loyalties. Many contemporaries supported the idea of public scrutiny of government – assuring open accountability not so much through parliamentary procedures as through public scrutiny of the principles and aims of government. Barère re-affirmed that idea in 1794, and Condorcet continued to justify his educational reform programme as the only way of improving civic awareness – a view shared right across the political spectrum, even by Saint-Just. The programme of linguistic reform and standardisation energetically promoted by abbé Grégoire and others throughout the Revolution was intended to serve the same purpose.[35] Condorcet, a true disciple of the enlightenment, one-time collaborator of d'Alembert on the *Encyclopédie*, and a distinguished mathematician famous for his work on probability, remained optimistic about the perfectibility of man even after he was accused in 1793 of being an accomplice of the Girondins. His last work, written whilst he was in hiding immediately prior to his arrest and sudden death in March 1794, was entitled *Esquisse d'un tableau historique des progrès de l'esprit humain* (*Sketch for a Historical Overview of the Progress of the Human Spirit*): it re-affirmed his belief in a secular benevolent state, strengthened by legal and educational reform, and prospering under a system of tolerance and economic freedom.

* * *

This chapter has given some prominence to the way contemporary notions of citizenship, representation and national consensus changed during the French Revolution. It is not difficult, in the light of this discussion, to understand why many contemporaries in the rest of Europe were at first enthusiastic, then rapidly frightened by the consequences of what had happened. More traditional governments, whether parliamentary as in Britain or Sweden, or nominally absolute as in much of the rest of Europe, saw their sometimes quite carefully engineered programmes of gradual and

35 R. Balibar, 'La révolution et la politique de la langue', *Études sur le xviiie siècle*, 16 (1989), 9–21; P. Higonnet, 'The politics of linguistic terrorism and grammatical hegemony during the French Revolution', *Social History* 5 (1980), 41–69; M. de Certeau, *Une politique de la langue: la Révolution française et les patois – l'enquête de Grégoire* (Paris, 1975).

consensual reforms (which we noted in Chapters 6–7) suddenly endangered by what seemed an irresponsible revolutionary machine rapidly drifting out of control. They had no difficulty identifying the many problems that such overheated change could bring. More often than not they also had to deal with at least a few enthusiasts for such change within their own borders: Jacobins, Painites, organisers of Corresponding Societies, campaigners for democratic reform, dreamers and visionaries, whose experience of real government often seemed laughable. From hindsight we might be tempted to dismiss these groups as harmless enthusiasts. But in the light of developments in France one can have some sympathy for governments that were less certain, and that saw their different and more gradualist priorities foundering. Already well before 1789 the relationship between state and subject/citizen was undergoing finely balanced but quite substantial change. The French Revolution suddenly accelerated this process, and in effect opened up politics to mass participation in a way that few contemporaries either welcomed or had envisaged. It soon became clear that gradual transition was very difficult to control – by 1794, some would claim that France had proved it was impossible. Perhaps one had to be a visionary optimist, like Condorcet, to retain confidence in the enlightened perfectibility of man.

Conclusion

Rousseau, like many other *philosophes*, had several brushes with authority, and some hurried evasions of intended arrests. But when in 1776 he was knocked down by a large dog in Paris, he was treated with great civility by the police authorities: the outstanding order for his arrest was not implemented, and he was even offered some financial compensation. His former friend Diderot, whose four-month imprisonment in the Vincennes in 1749 had caused some stir amongst intellectuals in Paris, also gained enough sympathisers amongst those in authority to avoid further punishment. Nevertheless, few of the leading figures of the enlightenment had an easy time. As shown in the careers of writers as different in temperament and inclinations as Paine, Lessing or Mercier, tackling the complacent assumptions of your contemporaries could be both a thankless and a dangerous task. In his *Memoirs* for Catherine II (written around 1773 but characteristically left unpublished), Diderot showed that he was not unscarred by the environment in which he spent all his life:

> I have worked for more than 30 years on [the *Encyclopédie*]. Of all the persecutions that one can imagine, there is none that I have not endured. Leave aside all manner of defamatory lampoons. I have suffered loss of honour, of fortune and of freedom. My manuscripts were moved round from one repository to another, concealed now in one place, now in another. More than once attempts have been made to take them from me. I have spent several nights at the window in expectation of a violent order being carried out. I have been on the point of going into exile – and that was the advice of my friends, who saw no safety for me in Paris. The work has been proscribed and my person threatened by various royal edicts and several decrees of the Parlement. We have faced the declared enmity of the court, the magnates, the military (who never hold opinions other than those of the court), the priests, the police, the magistrates, those amongst men of

letters who did not work for the enterprise, high society, and those amongst the citizens who allowed themselves to be led by the major-ity.[1]

As we have noted, the eighteenth-century state only very gradually learnt not to over-react to expressions of opinion different from its own, and to allow a hesitant relaxation of censorship and press controls. Yet government policy was in reality rarely more than a working compromise between the opinions, prejudices and interests of those with the greatest influence: what historians have rather grandly called 'enlightened absolutism' can often be regarded merely as the political manifestation of a consensus or compromise between the most influential members of a government, who were in any case usually as familiar as anyone with contemporary ideas and writing. Perhaps, in some parts of Europe, the committed support of a particular ruler could be a real asset for would-be innovators: it is for example difficult to conceive of substantial reform in the conservative Habsburg lands without the active intervention of Joseph II and his younger brother Leopold. A similar case might be made for the Russia of Catherine II; whilst Frederick II of Brandenburg-Prussia, with his ability not only to absorb contemporary ways of thought but also to meet some of the *philosophes* fully on their own terms, was exceptional even amongst these remarkable crowned heads of Europe. Yet neither he nor any other ruler would have had any difficulty finding his intellectual match amongst the outstanding reformers and advisors who served some of the governments of post-1763 Europe. Enlightened reform in the later eighteenth century, then, is best regarded as a collective enterprise, the responsibility for which within any one state is as shared as the contem-porary political system would allow.

This goes a long way towards explaining why the hesitations, ambivalence and inconsistencies of government policies, which we noted especially in the last three chapters, need to be seen in historical context. Reform of rural conditions and agrarian practices was significant but slow – relying, as it invariably did, on the good will and economic self-interest of 'improving' landowners. New ways of tackling poverty, under-employment, economic planning and fiscal management achieved some modest results both amongst the cameralist administrations of central and northern Europe and amongst those influenced by the physiocrats. A glance at central government archives in many parts of Europe in this period soon reveals an innovative profession-alism and meticulousness which conforms with the spirit of the age. But most striking of all, from the 1780s onwards there are signs of a growing public expectation that government could and should make itself more accountable – ultimately, with the American and French revolutions, creating full-scale debate on political rights and representation.

1 D. Garrioch, 'The Police of Paris as enlightened social reformers', *Eighteenth-Century Life* 16 (1992), 43–59, at the start of which the Rousseau event is recounted. D. Diderot, *Oeuvres*, vol. 3, ed. L. Versini (Paris, 1995), 362.

That debate, however, also served to underline just how incompatible many aspects of enlightenment thinking were with the profoundly inegalitarian and convention-bound fabric of eighteenth-century society: much reform would have required fundamental structural change of the old order to make a real difference. Enlightened emphasis on justice was thus able to make some impression on the norms of criminal punishment, but made little headway in terms of reform of the law or of the judiciary. Similarly, demands for freedom of expression bore some fruit in the revised systems of censorship introduced in many parts of Europe, yet few governments adhered consistently to their own norms even before the events of the 1790s made them entirely lose their nerve. Not surprisingly, however, the extent to which the potential for change was limited by practical reality is above all apparent in the context of the religious controversies of the period. If the enlightenment was anything, it was about exposing all inherited beliefs to reason and open debate, and ultimately replacing passive acceptance with active participation; as we have noted, there was no shortage of religious enthusiasm during the eighteenth century, but tolerance was rarer. Most governments were so cautious about policies of religious toleration that they rarely implemented anything more than a grudging concession of limited civil rights to unproblematic minorities. Genuine and pervasive toleration of the kind envisaged by Lessing and others would have required real shifts in outlook across society as a whole. Lessing's very public conflict in the 1770s with the first pastor of Hamburg, Johann Melchior Goeze, shows just how fragile the enlightenment was, and how large a gulf still separated strict Lutheran traditionalism from genuine humanist tolerance even in a city which in this respect was better off than most.[2]

Nevertheless, we should be careful not to equate slowness of change – especially in areas as sensitive as religious belief – with simple failure. If we look at the eighteenth century as a whole, and at Europe as a whole, it is clear that there were many different routes to enlightenment. France contained by far the greatest contrasts, ranging from the insidious destructiveness of aristocratic boredom and intrigue reflected in Laclos' *Dangerous Liaisons*, to the contagious humour of Beaumarchais' *Marriage of Figaro*, or the brilliant iconoclasm and extraordinary versatility of Diderot and his friends. The intellectual life of the German lands, Scotland, and parts of Italy was undoubtedly less dazzling, yet the actual gains in terms of enlightening freedom of thought were at least as great. Precisely how we evaluate the repercussions of such enlightenment must of necessity depend in part on this

2 What was later dubbed the *Goezekrieg* may not have had the European-wide ramifications of, say, the conflict between Jansenists and Jesuits in the 1750s and 1760s, but nevertheless resounded throughout much of Lutheran and Calvinist Europe, where Goeze was portrayed as a rigorously orthodox legalist, incapable of seeing the need for religion to go beyond dogma, and in effect trying to destroy the hard-won peaceful religious co-existence between Protestant sects. See F. Kopitzsch, *Grundzüge einer Sozialgeschichte der Aufklärung in Hamburg und Altona* (Hamburg, 1982), 452–82; and J. Whaley, *Religious Toleration and Social Change in Hamburg 1529–1819* (Cambridge, 1985), 33 and 151–7.

context: someone looking back over a life spent in Edinburgh or Hamburg could, towards the end of the century, observe change which was at least as significant in scale, if sometimes different in nature, from that experienced by someone in Paris. But everyone (workers as well as the wealthy, women as well as men) could look in astonishment at the growth in book, pamphlet and newspaper reading across a broad band of urban society; they could point to novels as well as to popular scientific works, to prints and to irreverent political cartoons; they could go to the theatre or a debating society, or buy a pamphlet, for not much more than a few pints of beer; free of charge, they could listen to the soap-box orators in the Palais Royal, or rub shoulders with the elite in the annual exhibition of paintings in the Louvre; and, by the end of our period, in London they could sign a mass anti-slavery petition, in Paris they could add their voice to the political discussion of their sectional meeting, or perhaps cast their vote in a local election. By Kant's standard of an open-ended process of discovery and emancipation from authority, some real ground had been won.

Select bibliography

References to more specialised literature are provided in the footnotes to each chapter.

Studies on Voltaire and the Eighteenth Century, published in Oxford, is abbreviated as *StVEC*.

General studies (including parts of Europe not covered in separate sections)

The Blackwell Companion to the Enlightenment, ed. J.W. Yolton (Oxford, 1991)

Dictionnaire européen des lumières, ed. M. Delon (Paris, 1997)

R.P. Bartlett *et al.*, eds., *Russia and the World of the Eighteenth Century* (Columbus, Ohio, 1984)

I. Berlin, *The Age of Enlightenment* (New York, 1962)

P. Brockmeier, R. Desné and J. Voss, eds., *Voltaire und Deutschland* (Stuttgart, 1979)

E. Cassirer, *The Philosophy of the Enlightenment* (Princeton, 1951)

J.C.D. Clark, *The Language of Liberty 1660–1832: Political Discourse and Social Dynamics in the Anglo-American World* (Cambridge, 1994)

A. Cobban, *In Search of Humanity* (London, 1960)

M. Cranston, *Philosophers and Pamphleteers: Political Theorists of the Enlightenment* (Oxford, 1986)

L.G. Crocker, *The Age of Enlightenment* (London, 1969)

A. Cunningham and R. French, *The Medical Enlightenment of the 18th Century* (Cambridge, 1990)

H. Dippel, *Germany and the American Revolution 1770–1800* (Chapel Hill, 1977)

F. Engel-Janosi, G. Klingenstein and H. Lutz, eds., *Formen der europäischen Aufklärung* (Munich, 1976)

P. Francastel, ed., *Utopie et institutions au xviiie siècle* (Paris, 1963)

G. Gargett and G. Sheridan, eds., *Ireland and the French Enlightenment* (Basingstoke, 1999)

J.G. Garrard, ed., *The Eighteenth Century in Russia* (Oxford, 1973)

P. Gay, *The Party of Humanity: Essays in the French Enlightenment* (New York, 1964)

P. Gay, *The Enlightenment: An Interpretation, 2 vols.* (London, 1966–69)

J. Grieder, *Anglomania in France, 1740–89: Fact, Fiction and Political Discourse* (Geneva, 1985)

R. Grimsley, ed., *The Age of Enlightenment 1715–1789* (Harmondsworth, 1979)

N. Hampson, *The Enlightenment* (Harmondsworth, 1968)

P. Hazard, *European Thought in the Eighteenth Century* (Harmondsworth, 1965)

E. Hellmuth, ed., *The Transformation of Political Culture: England and Germany in the Late 18th Century* (Oxford, 1990)

P. Higonnet, *Sister Republics: The Origins of French and American Republicanism* (Cambridge, Mass., 1988)

S. Jüttner and J. Schlobach, eds., *Europäische Aufklärung(en)* (Hamburg, 1992)

F.E. Manuel, *The Eighteenth Century Confronts the Gods* (Cambridge, Mass., 1959)

F.E. Manuel, ed., *The Enlightenment* (Englewood Cliffs, N.J., 1965)

G. Marker, *Publishing, Printing and the Origins of Intellectual Life in Russia 1700–1800* (Princeton, 1985)

M. Maurer, *Aufklärung und Anglophilie in Deutschland* (Göttingen, 1987)

D. Outram, *The Enlightenment* (Cambridge, 1995)

F. Oz-Salzberger, *Translating the Enlightenment: Scottish Civic Discourse in Eighteenth-Century Germany* (Oxford, 1995)

H.C. Payne, *The Philosophes and the People* (New Haven, 1976)

R. Porter, *The Enlightenment* (London, 1990)

R. Porter and M. Teich, eds., *The Enlightenment in National Context* (Cambridge, 1981)

R. Shackleton, *Essays on Montesquieu and on the Enlightenment* (Oxford, 1988)

C.G. Stricklen, 'The philosophes' political mission: the creation of an idea, 1750–1789', *StVEC* 186 (1971), 137–228

M. Thom, *Republics, Nations and Tribes* (London, 1995)

F. Venturi, *Utopia and Reform in the Enlightenment* (Cambridge, 1971)

F. Venturi, *The End of the Old Régime in Europe, 1768–1776* (Princeton, 1989)

F. Venturi, *The End of the Old Régime in Europe, 1776–1789, 2 vols.* (Princeton, 1991)

I.O. Wade, *The Structure and Form of the French Enlightenment, 2 vols.* (Princeton, 1977)

L. Wolff, *Inventing Eastern Europe: The Map of Civilization on the Mind of the Enlightenment* (Stanford, 1994)

England

J. Brewer, *Pleasures of the Imagination* (London, 1997)

S. Burtt, *Virtue Transformed: Political Arguments in England, 1688–1740* (Cambridge, 1992)

L. Colley, *Britons: Forging the Nation 1707–1837* (New Haven, 1992)

P. Corfield, *Power and the Professions in Britain, 1700–1850* (London, 1995)

H.T. Dickinson, *Politics and Literature in the Eighteenth Century* (London, 1974)

H.T. Dickinson, *Liberty and Property: Political Ideology in Eighteenth-Century Britain* (London, 1977)

H.T. Dickinson, ed., *Britain and the French Revolution 1789–1815* (Basingstoke, 1989)

H.T. Dickinson, *The Politics of the People in Eighteenth-Century Britain* (Basingstoke, 1994)

D. Donald, *The Age of Caricature: Satirical Prints in the Reign of George III* (New Haven, 1996)

A. Goodwin, *The Friends of Liberty: The English Democratic Movement in the Age of the French Revolution* (London, 1979)

J.P. Hunter, *Before Novels: The Cultural Contexts of Eighteenth-Century Fiction* (New York, 1990)

C. Kidd: see section on Scotland, below.

P. Langford, 'British politeness and the progress of western manners: an 18th-century enigma', *Transactions of the Royal Historical Society* 7 (1997), 53–72

M. Philp, *The French Revolution and British Popular Politics* (Cambridge, 1991)

R. Porter and M.M. Roberts, eds., *Pleasure in the Eighteenth Century* (London, 1996)

J. Redwood, *Reason, Ridicule and Religion: The Age of Enlightenment in England 1660–1750* (London, 1976)

L.D. Schwarz, *London in the Age of Industrialisation: Entrepreneurs, Labour Force and Living Conditions 1700–1850* (Cambridge, 1992)

D. Spadafora, *The Idea of Progress in Eighteenth-Century Britain* (New Haven, 1990)

W. Speck, *Literature and Society in Eighteenth-Century England, 1680–1820* (London, 1998)

L. Stewart, 'A meaning for machines: modernity, utility and the 18th century British public', *Journal of Modern History* 70 (1998), 259–94

K. Wilson, *The Sense of the People: Politics, Culture and Imperialism in England, 1715–1785* (Cambridge, 1995)

D. Winch, *Riches and Poverty: An Intellectual History of Political Economy in Britain, 1750–1834* (Cambridge, 1996)

France

C. Blum, *Rousseau and the Republic of Virtue: The Language of Politics in the French Revolution* (Ithaca, 1986)

G. Bollème, *Les almanachs populaires aux xviie et xviiie siècles: essai d'histoire sociale* (Paris, 1969)

D.G. Charlton, *New Images of the Natural in France: A Study in European Cultural History 1750–1800* (Cambridge, 1984)

R. Chartier, *The Cultural Origins of the French Revolution* (Durham, N.C., 1991)

R. Darnton, *Mesmerism and the End of the Enlightenment in France* (Cambridge, Mass., 1968)

R. Darnton, *The Great Cat Massacre and Other Episodes in French Cultural History* (Harmondsworth, 1985)

D. Echeverria, *The Maupeou Revolution: A Study in the History of Libertarianism, France 1770–74* (Baton Rouge, 1985)

E. Fox-Genovese, *The Origins of Physiocracy: Economic Revolution and Social Order in 18th-Century France* (Ithaca, 1976)

D. Garrioch, *Neighbourhood and Community in Paris 1740–90* (Cambridge, 1986)

C.C. Gillespie, *Science and Polity in France at the End of the Old Régime* (Princeton, 1981)

D. Gordon, *Citizens without Sovereignty: Equality and Sociability in French Thought, 1670–1789* (Princeton, 1994)

J.P. Gross, *Fair Shares for All: Jacobin Egalitarianism in Practice* (Cambridge, 1997)

N. Hampson, *Will and Circumstance: Montesquieu, Rousseau and the French Revolution* (London, 1983)

H. Hömig, 'Absolutismus und Demokratie: das Reformprogramm des Marquis d'Argenson (1737)', *Historische Zeitschrift* 226 (1978), 349–80

M. Hulliung, *The Autocritique of Enlightenment: Rousseau and the Philosophes* (Cambridge, Mass., 1994)

L. Hunt, *Politics, Culture and Class in the French Revolution* (Berkeley, 1984)

F.A. Kafker, 'Les encyclopédistes et la terreur', *Revue d'Histoire Moderne et Contemporaine* 14 (1967), 284–95

D. van Kley, ed., *The French Idea of Freedom: The Old Regime and the Declaration of Rights of 1789* (Stanford, 1995)

A.C. Kors, *D'Holbach's Coterie* (Princeton, 1976)

S. Maza, *Private Lives and Public Affairs: The Causes Célèbres of Prerevolutionary France* (Berkeley, 1993)

R. Mauzi, *L'idée du bonheur dans la littérature et la pensée française au xviiie siècle* (Paris, 1960)

J.W. Merrick, *The Desacralization of the French Monarchy in the 18th Century* (Baton Rouge, 1990)

D. Mornet, *Les origines intellectuelles de la révolution française, 1715–1787* (Paris, 1933)

R. Mortier, 'Les héritiers des *philosophes* devant l'expérience révolutionnaire', *Dix-Huitième Siècle* 6 (1974), 45–57

D. Roche, *The People of Paris* (Leamington Spa, 1987)

D. Roche, *Les républicains des lettres: gens de culture et lumières au xviiie siècle* (Paris, 1988)

D. Roche, *France in the Age of Enlightenment* (Cambridge, Mass., 1998)

W.H. Sewell, *A Rhetoric of Bourgeois Revolution: The abbé Sieyes and 'What is the Third Estate?'* (Durham, N.C., 1994)

L. Steinbrügge, *The Moral Sex: Woman's Nature in the French Enlightenment* (Oxford, 1995)

A. Vincent-Buffault, *The History of Tears: Sensibility and Sentimentality in France* (London, 1991)

German areas, Netherlands and Scandinavia

H.A. Barton, 'Gustav III of Sweden and the enlightenment', *Eighteenth-Century Studies* 6 (1972), 1–34

H.A. Barton, *Scandinavia in the Revolutionary Era, 1760–1815* (Minneapolis, 1986)

H.E. Bödeker and U. Herrmann, eds., *Über den Prozess der Aufklärung in Deutschland im 18. Jhrh.* (Göttingen, 1987)

K.P. Fischer, 'John Locke in the German enlightenment: an interpretation', *Journal of the History of Ideas* 36 (1975), 431–46

G.C. Gibbs, 'The role of the Dutch republic as the intellectual entrepot of Europe in the 17th and 18th centuries', *Bijdragen en Medelingen ... der Nederlanden* 86 (1971), 323–49

M.C. Jacob and W.W. Mijnhardt, eds., *The Dutch Republic in the Eighteenth Century: Decline, Enlightenment and Revolution* (Ithaca, 1992)

F. Kopitzsch, ed., *Aufklärung, Absolutismus und Bürgertum in Deutschland* (Munich, 1976)

F. Kopitzsch, *Grundzüge einer Sozialgeschichte der Aufklärung in Hamburg und Altona* (Hamburg, 1982)

H.B. Nisbet, ' "Was ist Aufklärung?": the concept of enlightenment in eighteenth-century Germany', *Journal of European Studies* 12 (1982), 77–95

P. Pütz, *Die deutsche Aufklärung* (Darmstadt, 1978)

T.J. Reed, 'Talking to tyrants: dialogues with power in eighteenth-century Germany', *Historical Journal* 33 (1990), 63–79

R. Robertson and E. Timms, eds., *The Austrian Enlightenment and its Aftermath* (Edinburgh, 1991)

S. Schama, *Patriots and Liberators: Revolution in the Netherlands 1780–1813* (London, 1977)

I. Stephan and H.G. Winter, eds., *Hamburg im Zeitalter der Aufklärung* (Hamburg, 1989)

A.J. la Vopa, *Grace, Talent and Merit: Poor Students, Clerical Careers and Professional Ideology in Eighteenth-Century Germany* (Cambridge, 1988)

A.J. la Vopa, 'The politics of enlightenment: Friedrich Gedike and German professional ideology', *Journal of Modern History* 62 (1990), 34–56

M. Walker, *German Home Towns: Community, State and General Estate, 1648–1817* (Ithaca, 1971)

M. Walker, *Johann Jakob Moser and the Holy Roman Empire of the German Nation* (Chapel Hill, 1981)

K.H. Wegert, 'Patrimonial rule, popular self-interest and Jacobinism in Germany, 1763–1800', *Journal of Modern History* 53 (1981), 440–67

Scotland

D. Allan, *Virtue, Learning and the Scottish Enlightenment: Ideas of Scholarship in Early Modern History* (Edinburgh, 1993)

J.H. Brumfitt, 'Scotland and the French Enlightenment', in *The Age of the Enlightenment: Studies presented to Th. Besterman*, ed. W.H. Barbour *et al.* (Edinburgh, 1967), 318–29

C. Camic, *Experience and Enlightenment: Socialization for Cultural Change in Eighteenth-Century Scotland* (Edinburgh, 1983)

R.H. Campbell and A.S. Skinner, eds., *The Origins of the Scottish Enlightenment* (Edinburgh, 1982)

J.J. Carter and J.H. Pittock, eds., *Aberdeen and the Enlightenment* (Aberdeen, 1987)

A.C. Chitnis, *The Scottish Enlightenment: A Social History* (London, 1976)

D. Daiches *et al.*, eds., *A Hotbed of Genius: The Scottish Enlightenment 1730–1790* (Edinburgh, 1986)

T.M. Devine, ed., *Conflict and Stability in Scottish Society 1700–1850* (Edinburgh, 1990)

T.M. Devine and J.R. Young, eds., *Eighteenth-Century Scotland: New Perspectives* (East Linton, 1999)

J. Dwyer, *Virtuous Discourse* (Edinburgh, 1987)

J. Dwyer and R.B. Sher, eds., *Sociability and Society in 18th-Century Scotland* (Baltimore, 1991)

R.L. Emerson, 'Science and the origins and concerns of the Scottish enlightenment', *History of Science* 26 (1988), 333–66

I. Hont and M. Ignatieff, eds., *Wealth and Virtue: The Shaping of Political Economy in the Scottish Enlightenment* (Cambridge, 1983)

R.A. Houston, *Social Change in the Age of Enlightenment: Edinburgh 1660–1760* (Oxford, 1994)

P. Jones, *Philosophy and Science in the Scottish Enlightenment* (Edinburgh, 1988)

C. Kidd, *Subverting Scotland's Past: Scottish Whig Historians and the Creation of an Anglo-British Identity, 1689–c.1830* (Cambridge, 1993)

C. Kidd, 'North Britishness and the nature of eighteenth-century patriotisms', *Historical Journal* 39 (1996), 361–82

C. Kidd, *British Identities before Nationalism: Ethnicity and Nationhood in the Atlantic World, 1600–1800* (Cambridge, 1999)

E.W. McFarland, *Ireland and Scotland in the Age of Revolution* (Edinburgh, 1994)

N.T. Phillipson and R. Mitchison, eds., *Scotland in the Age of Improvement* (Edinburgh, 1970)

J. Rendall, ed., *The Origins of the Scottish Enlightenment* (London, 1978)

J. Robertson, 'The Scottish Enlightenment', *Rivista Storica Italiana* 108 (1996), 792–829

J. Robertson, 'The enlightenment above national context: political economy in 18th-century Scotland and Naples', *Historical Journal* 40 (1997), 667–97

R.B. Sher, *Church and University in the Scottish Enlightenment: The Moderate Literati of Edinburgh* (Princeton, 1985)

M.A. Stewart, ed., *Studies in the Philosophy of the Scottish Enlightenment* (Oxford, 1990)

H. Trevor-Roper, 'The Scottish enlightenment', *StVEC* 58 (1967), 1635–58

Education

J. Bloch, *Rousseauism and Education in Eighteenth-Century France, StVEC* 325 (1995)

L.W.B. Brockliss, *French Higher Education in the Seventeenth and Eighteenth Centuries: A Cultural History* (Oxford, 1987)

P. Burke and R. Porter, eds., *The Social History of Language* (Cambridge, 1987)

R. Chartier *et al.*, *L'éducation en France du xvie au xviiie siècle* (Paris, 1976)

H. Chisick, *The Limits of Reform in the Enlightenment: Attitudes toward the Education of the Lower Classes in Eighteenth-Century France* (Princeton, 1981)

R.L. Emerson, 'Scottish universities in the eighteenth century, 1690–1800', *StVEC* 167 (1977), 453–74

R. Engelsing, *Der Bürger als Leser: Lesergeschichte in Deutschland, 1500–1800* (Stuttgart, 1974)

R. Engelsing, *Analphabetentum* (Stuttgart, 1993)

F. Furet and J. Ozouf, *Reading and Writing: Literacy in France from Calvin to Jules Ferry* (Cambridge, 1982)

R. Gawthrop and G. Strauss, 'Protestantism and literacy in early modern Germany', *Past and Present* 104 (1984), 31–55

R. Grevet, 'La réforme des études en France au siècle des lumières', *Revue Historique* 297/601 (1997), 85–123

H.-C. Harten, *Elementarschule und Pädagogik in der Französischen Revolution* (Munich, 1990)

H.-C. Harten, 'Das niedere Schulwesen in Frankreich', in *Das niedere Schulwesen im Übergang vom 18. zum 19. Jahrhundert*, ed. P. Albrecht and E. Hinrichs (Tübingen, 1995), 25–47

R. Houston, *Scottish Literacy and the Scottish Identity: Illiteracy and Society in Scotland and Northern England 1600–1800* (Cambridge, 1985)

R. Houston, *Literacy in Early Modern Europe: Culture and Education 1500–1800* (London, 1988)

R.A. Houston, 'Literacy, education and the culture of print in enlightenment Edinburgh', *History* 78 (1993), 373–92

C.E. McClelland, *State, Society and University in Germany 1700–1914* (Cambridge, 1980)

I. Markussen, 'The development of writing ability in the Nordic countries in the 18th and 19th centuries', *Scandinavian Journal of History* 15 (1990), 37–63

J. van H. Melton, *Absolutism and the Eighteenth-Century Origins of Compulsory Schooling in Prussia and Austria* (Cambridge, 1988)

R.R. Palmer, *The Improvement of Humanity: Education and the French Revolution* (Princeton, 1985)

J. Quéniart, *Culture et société urbaines dans la France de l'ouest au xviiie siècle* (Paris, 1978)

H. de Ridder-Symoens, ed., *A History of the University in Europe*, vol. 2: *Universities in Early Modern Europe 1500–1800* (Cambridge, 1996)

T.C. Smout, 'Born again at Cambuslang: new evidence on popular religion and literacy in eighteenth-century Scotland', *Past and Present* 97 (1982), 114–27

Press and book trade

G. Barber, *Studies in the Booktrade of the European Enlightenment* (London, 1993)

J. Black, *The English Press in the Eighteenth Century* (London, 1987)

S. Boberg, *Gustav III och Tryckfriheten 1774–1787* (Stockholm, 1951)

G. Bollème *et al.*, *Livre et société dans la France du xviiie siècle* (Paris, 1965)

H. Bots, ed., *La diffusion et la lecture des journaux de langue française sous l'ancien régime* (Amsterdam, 1988)

A. Burius, *Ömhet om friheten: studier i frihetstidens censurpolitik* (Uppsala, 1984)

D. Castiglione and L. Sharpe, eds., *Shifting the Boundaries: Transformation of the Languages of Public and Private in the 18th Century* (Exeter, 1995)

J.R. Censer, *Prelude to Power: The Parisian Radical Press 1789–1791* (Baltimore, 1976)

J.R. Censer, *The French Press in the Age of Enlightenment* (London, 1994)

J.R. Censer and J.D. Popkin, *Press and Politics in Pre-revolutionary France* (Berkeley, 1987)

R. Chartier, *The Cultural Uses of Print in Early Modern France* (Princeton, 1987)

R. Chartier, *Lectures et lecteurs dans la France d'ancien régime* (Paris, 1987)

H. Chisick, ed., *The Press in the French Revolution*, StVEC 287 (1991)

M.E. Craig, *The Scottish Periodical Press 1750–1789* (Edinburgh, 1931)

P. Currie, 'Moral weeklies and the reading public in Germany, 1711–1750', *Oxford German Studies* 3 (1968), 69–86

R. Darnton, 'The high enlightenment and the low-life of literature in pre-revolutionary France', *Past and Present* 51 (1971), 81–115

R. Darnton, *The Business of the Enlightenment: A Publishing History of the Encyclopédie, 1775–1800* (Cambridge, Mass., 1979)

R. Darnton, *The Literary Underground of the Old Régime* (Cambridge, Mass., 1982)

R. Darnton, *Bohème littéraire et révolution: le monde des livres au xviiie siècle* (Paris, 1983)

R. Darnton, 'The facts of literary life in eighteenth-century France', in *The French Revolution and the Creation of Modern Political Culture*, vol. 1, ed. K. Baker (Oxford, 1987), 261–91

R. Darnton, 'The forgotten middlemen of literature', in his *The Kiss of Lamourette* (London, 1990), 136–53

R. Darnton, *Édition et sédition: l'univers de la littérature clandestine au xviiie siècle* (Paris, 1991)

R. Darnton, 'The forbidden books of pre-revolutionary France', in *Rewriting the French Revolution*, ed. C. Lucas (Oxford, 1991), 1–32

R. Darnton, *The Forbidden Best-Sellers of Pre-revolutionary France* (London, 1996)

R. Darnton and D. Roche, eds., *Revolution in Print: The Press in France 1775–1800* (Berkeley, 1989)

H. Duranton, ed., *Les gazettes européennes de langue française au 17e–18e siècles* (St Étienne, 1992)

E.L. Eisenstein, *Grub Street Abroad: Aspects of the French Cosmopolitan Press from the Age of Louis XIV to the French Revolution* (Oxford, 1992)

J. Feather, *The Provincial Book Trade in Eighteenth-Century England* (Cambridge, 1985)

L. Febvre, *The Coming of the Book: The Impact of Printing 1450–1800* (London, 1970)

L. Fontane, 'Les vendeurs de livres: réseaux de libraires et colporteurs dans l'Europe du sud (xviie–xixe siècle)', in *Produzione e commercio della carta e del libro sec. xiii–xviii*, ed. S. Cavaciocchi (Prato, 1992), 631–76

F. Furet, 'Book licensing and book production in the kingdom of France in the eighteenth century', in his *In the Workshop of History* (Chicago, 1982), 99–124

G.C. Gibbs, 'Government and the English press, 1695 to the middle of the 18th century', in *Too Mighty to be Free: Censorship and the Press in Britain and the Netherlands*, ed. A.C. Duke and C.A. Tamse (Zutphen, 1987), 87–106

A. Goldgar, 'The absolutism of taste: journalists as censors in 18th-century Paris', in *Censorship and Control of Print in England and France*, ed. R. Myers *et al.* (Winchester, 1992), 87–110

E.C. Goldsmith and D. Goodman, *Going Public: Women and Publishing in Early Modern France* (Ithaca, 1995)

V.R. Gruder, 'Political news as coded messages: the Parisian and provincial press in the pre-Revolution, 1787–88', *French History* 12 (1998), 1–24

B. Harris, *Politics and the Rise of the Press: Britain and France, 1620–1800* (London, 1996)

M. Harris, *London Newspapers in the Age of Walpole* (London, 1987)

R. Harris, *A Patriot Press: National Politics and the London Press in the 1740s* (Oxford, 1993)

E. Hellmuth, 'Enlightenment and freedom of the press: the debate in the Berlin Mittwochsgesellschaft, 1783–84', *History* 83 (1998), 420–44

C. Hesse, *Publishing and Cultural Politics in Revolutionary Paris, 1789–1810* (Berkeley, 1991)

G. Holzboog, 'Moses Mendelsohn und die Situation von Autor und Verleger im 18. Jhrh,' in *Moses Mendelsohn und die Kreise seiner Wirksamkeit*, ed. M. Albrecht *et al.* (Tübingen, 1994), 215–48

A.H. Huussen, 'Freedom of the press and censorship in the Netherlands 1780–1810', in *Too Mighty to be Free: Censorship and the Press in Britain and the Netherlands*, ed. A.C. Duke and C.A. Tamse (Zutphen, 1987), 107–26

C. Jolly, ed., *Histoire des bibliothèques françaises*, vol. 2: *Les bibliothèques sous l'ancien régime 1530–1789* (Paris, 1988)

C. Jones, 'The great chain of buying: medical advertisement, the bourgeois public sphere, and the origins of the French Revolution', *American Historical Review* 101 (1996), 13–40

P.J. Korshin, ed., *The Widening Circle: Essays on the Circulation of Literature in Eighteenth-Century Europe* (Philadelphia, 1976)

C. Labrosse and P. Rétat, *Naissance du journal révolutionnaire 1789* (Lyon, 1989)

J. Lough, *The Encyclopédie* (London, 1971)

J. Lough, *Writer and Public in France from the Middle Ages to the Present Day* (Oxford, 1978)

J. McLeod, 'Provincial book trade inspectors in 18th-century France', *French History* 12 (1998), 127–48

D.H. McMahon, 'The counter-enlightenment and the low-life of literature in pre-revolutionary France', *Past and Present* 159 (1998), 77–112

A. Machet, 'Librairie et commerce du livre en Italie dans la 2e moitié du xviiie siècle', *StVEC* 153 (1976), 1347–80

H.-J. Martin, *Le livre français sous l'ancien régime* (Paris, 1984)

H.-J. Martin, R. Chartier and J.-P. Vivet, eds., *Histoire de l'édition française*, vol. 2: *Le livre triomphant, 1660–1830* (Paris, 1984)

R. Munter, *The History of the Irish Newspaper 1685–1760* (Cambridge, 1967)

W.J. Murray, *The Right Wing Press in the French Revolution 1789–92* (Woodbridge, 1986)

R. Myers and M. Harris, eds., *Development of the English Book Trade, 1700–1899* (Oxford, 1981)

J.D. Popkin, *The Right-Wing Press in France, 1792–1800* (Chapel Hill, 1980)

J.D. Popkin, 'Pamphlet journalism at the end of the old régime', *Eighteenth-Century Studies* 22 (1988–89), 351–67

J.D. Popkin, *Revolutionary News: The Press in France 1789–1799* (Durham, N.C., 1990)

J.D. Popkin, 'The German press and the Dutch Patriot movement', *Lessing Yearbook* 22 (1990), 97–111

D.T. Pottinger, *The French Book-Trade in the Ancien Régime* (Cambridge, Mass., 1958)

P. Raabe, *Bücherlust und Lesefreuden* (Stuttgart, 1984)

J. Raven, *Judging New Wealth: Popular Publishing and Responses to Commerce in England, 1750–1800* (Oxford, 1992)

I. Rivers, ed., *Books and their Readers in Eighteenth-Century England* (Leicester, 1982)

M. Rose, *Authors and Owners: The Invention of Copyright* (Cambridge, Mass., 1993)

H. Rosenstrauch, *Buchhandelsmanufaktur und Aufklärung: die Reformen des Buchhändlers und Verlegers Ph. E. Reich (1717–1787)* (Frankfurt/Main, 1986)

J. Sgard, *Dictionnaire des journaux 1600–1789*, 2 vols. (Paris, 1991)

B. Tolkemitt, *Der Hamburgische Correspondent: zur öffentlichen Verbreitung der Aufklärung in Deutschland* (Tübingen, 1995)

A. Ward, *Book Production, Fiction and the German Reading Public 1740–1800* (Oxford, 1974)

M. Welke, 'Die Legende vom "unpolitischen Deutschen": Zeitungslesen im 18. Jahrhundert', *Jahrbuch der Wittheit zu Bremen* 25 (1981), 161–88

Public opinion

K. Baker, 'Public opinion as political invention', in his *Inventing the French Revolution* (New York, 1990)

J. Brewer, 'This, that and the other: public, social and private in the 17th and 18th centuries', in *Shifting the Boundaries*, ed. D. Castiglione (Exeter, 1995)

A. Farge, *Subversive Words: Public Opinion in 18th-century France* (Cambridge, 1994)

A. Gestrich, *Absolutismus und Öffentlichkeit: politische Kommunikation in Deutschland zu Beginn des 18. Jhrh.* (Göttingen, 1994)

A. Goldgar, *Impolite Learning: Conduct and Community in the Republic of Letters* (New Haven, 1995)

D. Goodman, *The Republic of Letters: A Cultural History of the French Enlightenment* (Ithaca, 1994)

J.A.W. Gunn, *Queen of the World: Opinion in the Public Life of France from the Renaissance to the Revolution*, StVEC 328 (1995)

M. Nyman, *Press mot friheten: opinionbildning i de svenska tidningarna och åsiktsbrytningar om minoriteter 1772–1786* (Uppsala, 1988)

M. Ozouf, 'Public opinion at the end of the old regime', *Journal of Modern History* 60 (1988), S1–21

M. Thale, 'London debating societies in the 1790s', *Historical Journal* 32 (1989), 57–86

A.J. de la Vopa, 'Conceiving a public: ideas and society in 18th-century Europe,' *Journal of Modern History* 64 (1992), 79–116

A. Würgler, *Unruhen und Öffentlichkeit: Städtische und ländliche Protestbewegungen im 18. Jahrhundert* (Tübingen, 1995)

Organisations

J.M. Burke, 'Freemasonry, friendship and noblewomen: the role of the secret society in bringing enlightenment thought to pre-revolutionary women elites', *History of European Ideas* 10 (1989), 283–94

R. van Dülmen, *The Society of the Enlightenment: The Rise of the Middle Class and Enlightenment Culture in Germany* (London, 1992)

R. le Forestier, *La franc-maçonnerie templière et occultiste aux xviiie et xixe siècles* (Louvain, 1970)

U. Im Hof, *Das gesellige Jahrhundert: Gesellschaft und Gesellschaften im Zeitalter der Aufklärung* (Munich, 1982)

M.C. Jacob, *The Radical Enlightenment: Pantheists, Freemasons and Republicans* (London, 1981)

M.C. Jacob, *Living the Enlightenment: Freemasonry and Politics in Eighteenth-Century Europe* (Oxford, 1992)

H. Reinalter, ed., *Aufklärung und Geheimgesellschaften: zur politischen Funktion und Sozialstruktur der Freimaurerlogen im 18. Jhr.* (Munich, 1989)

D. Roche, *Le siècle des lumières en province: académies et académiciens provinciaux, 1680–1789*, 2 vols. (Paris, 1978)

J. Voss, 'Die Akademien als Organisationsträger der Wissenschaften im 18. Jhr.', *Historische Zeitschrift* 231 (1980), 43–74

Church/religion

J.E. Bradley, *Religion, Revolution and English Radicalism: Non-Conformity in 18th-Century Politics and Society* (Cambridge, 1990)

C. Brown, *Religion and Society in Scotland since 1707* (Edinburgh, 1997)

W.J. Callahan and D. Higgs, eds., *Church and Society in Catholic Europe of the Eighteenth Century* (Cambridge, 1979)

O. Chadwick, *The Popes and the European Revolution* (Oxford, 1981)

L. Châtellier, *The Religion of the Poor: Rural Missions in Europe and the Formation of Modern Catholicism, ca.1500–1800* (Cambridge, 1997)

M. Fulbrook, *Piety and Politics: Religion and the Rise of Absolutism in England, Württemberg and Prussia* (Cambridge, 1983)

K. Gründer and K.H. Rengstorf, eds., *Religionskritik und Religiösität in der deutschen Aufklärung* (Tübingen, 1989)

K. Haakonssen, ed., *Enlightenment and Religion: Rational Dissent in 18th-Century Britain* (Cambridge, 1996)

C. Haydon, *Anti-Catholicism in 18th-Century England, ca.1714–80: A Political and Social Study* (Manchester, 1994)

M. Heyd, *'Be sober and reasonable': the critique of enthusiasm in the 17th and early 18th centuries* (Brill, 1995)

N.M. Hope, *German and Scandinavian Protestantism 1700–1918* (Oxford, 1995)

M. Hunter and D. Wooton, *Atheism from the Reformation to the Enlightenment* (Oxford, 1992)

D. van Kley, *The Religious Origins of the French Revolution: From Calvin to the Civil Constitution, 1560–1791* (New Haven, 1996)

R.A. Knox, *Enthusiasm* (Oxford, 1950)

B.R. Kreiser, *Miracles, Convulsions and Ecclesiastical Politics in Early Eighteenth-Century Paris* (Princeton, 1978)

J. McManners, *French Ecclesiastical Society under the Ancien Régime: A Study of Angers in the Eighteenth Century* (Manchester, 1960)

J. McManners, *Death and the Enlightenment: Changing Attitudes to Death among Christians and Unbelievers in Eighteenth-Century France* (Oxford, 1981)

J. McManners, *Church and Society in Eighteenth-Century France*, 2 vols. (Oxford, 1998)

R.R. Palmer, *Catholics and Unbelievers in Eighteenth-Century France* (Princeton, 1939)

J. Walsh, C. Haydon and S. Taylor, eds., *The Church of England c.1689–c.1833* (Cambridge, 1993)

W.R. Ward, *The Protestant Evangelical Awakening* (Cambridge, 1992)

J. Whaley, *Religious Toleration and Social Change in Hamburg 1529–1819* (Cambridge, 1985)

Culture (popular and elite)

L. Andries, *La bibliothèque bleue au dix-huitième siècle*, St VEC 270 (1989)

G. Bollème, *Les almanachs populaires aux xviie et xviiie siècles* (Paris, 1969)

P. Burke, *Popular Culture in Early Modern Europe* (London, 1978)

N.Ó. Ciosáin, *Print and Popular Culture in Ireland 1750–1850* (London, 1997)

M.C. Cook, 'Politics in the fiction of the French Revolution', *StVEC* 201 (1982), 233–335

B. Fort, 'Voice of the public: the carnivalisation of salon art in prerevolutionary pamphlets', *Eighteenth-Century Studies* 22 (1989), 368–94

T. Harris, ed., *Popular Culture in England, c.1500–1850* (London, 1995)

E. Kennedy, *A Cultural History of the French Revolution* (New Haven, 1989)

R.W. Malcolmson, *Popular Recreations in English Society, 1700–1850* (Cambridge, 1973)

M. Ozouf, *Festivals and the French Revolution* (Cambridge, Mass., 1988)

P. Rogers, *Literature and Popular Culture in Eighteenth-Century England* (Brighton, 1985)

R. Shenda, *Volk ohne Buch: Studien zur Sozialgeschichte der populären Lesestoffe, 1770–1910* (Munich, 1988)

D. Vincent, *Literacy and Popular Culture: England 1750–1914* (London, 1989)

M. Vovelle, *La mentalité révolutionnaire: société et mentalités sous la Révolution française* (Paris, 1985)

Music, art and theatre

D. Beales, *Mozart and the Habsburgs* (Reading, 1990)

A. Bermingham and J. Brewer, eds., *The Consumption of Culture 1600–1800: Image, Object, Text* (London, 1995)

A. Boime, *Art in an Age of Revolution* (Chicago, 1985)

M. Boyd, ed., *Music and the French Revolution* (Cambridge, 1992)

T. Crow, *Painters and Public Life in 18th-Century Paris* (New Haven, 1985)

T. Crow, *Emulation: Making Artists for Revolutionary France* (New Haven, 1995)

J.H. Johnson, *Listening in Paris: A Cultural History* (Berkeley, 1995)

E. Kennedy, M.-L. Netter *et al.*, *Theatre, Opera and Audiences in Revolutionary Paris: Analysis and Repertory* (Westport, Conn., 1996)

J.A. Leith, *Space and Revolution: Projects for Monuments, Squares and Public Buildings in France, 1789–1799* (Montreal, 1991)

D. Solkin, *Painting for Money: The Visual Arts and the Public Sphere in 18th-Century England* (New Haven, 1993)

B.M. Stafford, *Artful Science: Enlightenment, Entertainment and the Eclipse of Visual Education* (Cambridge, Mass., 1994)

D. Thomas and A. Hare, eds., *Theatre in Europe, a Documentary History: Restoration and Georgian England, 1600–1788* (Cambridge, 1989)

Individuals

K.M. Baker, *Condorcet* (Chicago, 1975)

F.M. Barnard, *Herder's Social and Political Thought: From Enlightenment to Nationalism* (Oxford, 1965)

I. Berlin, *Vico and Herder* (London, 1976)

G. Claeys, *Thomas Paine* (London, 1989)

J.C.D. Clark, *Samuel Johnson* (Cambridge, 1994)

M. Cranston, *Jean-Jacques: The Early Life and Works of J.-J. Rousseau* (Chicago, 1982)

M. Cranston, *The Noble Savage: Jean-Jacques Rousseau, 1754–62* (Chicago, 1991)

M. Cranston, *The Solitary Self: Jean-Jacques Rousseau in Exile and Adversity* (Chicago, 1992)

J.A. Downie, *Jonathan Swift: Political Writer* (London, 1984)

P.N. Furbank, *Diderot: A Critical Biography* (London, 1992)

P. Gay, *Voltaire's Politics: The Poet as Realist* (Princeton, 1959)

N. Hudson, *Samuel Johnson and Eighteenth-Century Thought* (Oxford, 1988)

E.J. Hundert, *The Enlightenment's Fable: Bernard Mandeville and the Discovery of Society* (Cambridge, 1994)

W.G. Jones, *Nikolay Novikov, Enlightener of Russia* (Cambridge, 1984)

D. Livingston and M. Martin, eds., *Hume as Philosopher of Society, Politics and History* (Rochester, N.Y., 1991)

J. Miller, *Rousseau: Dreamer of Democracy* (New Haven, 1984)

H. Möller, *Aufklärung in Preussen: der Verleger und Geschichtsschreiber Friedrich Nicolai* (Berlin, 1974)

E.C. Mossner, *Life of David Hume* (Oxford, 1980)

R. Pomeau, *Beaumarchais ou la bizarre destinée* (Paris, 1987)

J. Roger, *Buffon: A Life in Natural History* (Ithaca, 1997)

I.S. Ross, *The Life of Adam Smith* (Oxford, 1996)

R. Scruton, *Kant* (Oxford, 1982)

R. Shackleton, *Montesquieu* (Oxford, 1961)

J.N. Shklar, *Montesquieu* (Oxford, 1987)

K. Wellman, *La Mettrie: Medicine, Philosophy and Enlightenment* (Durham, N.C., 1992)

A.M. Wilson, *Diderot* (New York, 1972)

Index

NOTE ON MONEY-VALUES: In Britain the pound sterling was divided into 20 shillings, each shilling into 12 pence. In France the livre was similarly divided into 20 sols (sous), each of 12 deniers. In Britain, £20 a year constituted a subsistence wage, and more skilled workers could earn twice that. In France, the annual subsistence wage was in the range 250–400 livres (and was by 1790 officially reckoned at 435 livres); a compositor could earn 650 livres. See also entries below under EARNINGS AND INCOME, and PRICES.

academies of science, 68, 157

Addison, Joseph (1672–1719), English writer and journalist, 110

advertising in newspapers, 123–4

Aelders, Etta Palm d', Flemish feminist, 212

alehouses and social drinking, 38, 66

Alembert, Jean le Rond d' (1717–83), French mathematician and writer, 5, 100

American colonies and Republic, 2, 19, 97, 153, 187, 203

ancients and moderns, quarrel of, 5

Anglican church, 33–4, 135, 141–2

Anglomania, 6

anti-enlightenment, *see* counter-enlightenment

anti-Semitism, *see* Jews

Arbuthnot, John (1667–1735), Scottish physician, 161

art market, 63–5

Assembly of Notables (France 1787), 103, 167

atheism, 8, 32, 134

Austria-Hungary, *see* Joseph II

author's rights (book trade), *see* copyright

Avignon, 117

Bach, Johann Sebastian (1685–1750), German composer, 36

balloon flying, 13, 67

Bank of England, 164

Barbaroux, Charles-Jean-Marie (1767–94), French politician, 209

Basedow, J.H. (1723–90), educational reformer, 56

Baskerville, John (1706–75), English typographer and printer, 78–9, 83

Bastille prison, 87, 100, 153–4, 156, 215

Bayle, Pierre (1647–1706), French free-thinker, 1
his *Historical and Critical Dictionary* (1696), 100, 133

Beaumarchais, Pierre-Augustin Caron de (1732–99), French writer and entrepreneur, 2, 42–3, 83, 88
his *Marriage of Figaro* (1784), 43, 83

Beccaria, Cesare Bonesana di (1738–94), Italian reformer, 2, 151–2
his *Of Crimes and Punishments* (1764), 146, 151

begging, *see* poverty

Bentham, Jeremy (1748–1832), English philosopher and reformer, 149, 155

Berkeley, George (1685–1753), Anglo-Irish clergyman and writer, 12

Berlin, 10, 52, 69, 145 (*see also* Frederick II)

bibliothèque bleue, see chapbooks

Black, Joseph (1728–99), Scottish chemist, 12

Boerhaave, Hermann (1668–1738), Dutch physician, 158

Bohemia, rural conditions in, 176–7

Boisguilbert, Pierre le Pesant de (1646–1714), French economist, 166

Bolingbroke, Henry Saint John (1678–1751), English politician, 123

book-clubs, 98–9 (*see also* libraries)

books, demand for and production of, 80, 88, 89–101, 103

booksellers' networks, 11, 79–80, 97

Boucher, François (1703–70), French artist, 65

Bougainville, Louis Antoine de (1729–1811), French explorer, 25

Boullée, Etienne-Louis (1728–99), French architect, 39, 76

Brienne, Loménie de (1727–94), French clergyman and politician, 8n

Brissot (de Warville), Jacques Pierre (1754–93), French writer and politician, 190, 202, 213

British Museum and Library, 98

Buffon, Georges-Louis Leclerc, comte de (1707–88), French naturalist, 2, 13, 188

Burke, Edmund (1729–97), English writer and politician, 61n, 197

cahiers de doléances (France, 1789), 26, 28, 73, 207

Calas affair, *see* Voltaire

Calonne, Charles-Alexandre de (1734–1802), French finance minister, 127, 167–8

Calvinism, *see* Protestant churches

cameralism, 168–72, 180

capital punishment, 151–2

Capuchin religious order, 30, 54

Caribbean, 190–1

Catherine II, empress of Russia 1762–96, 83, 175

Catholic Church, Roman, 30–1, 37, 51, 139–40

hostility to, and relief for, in Britain and northern Germany, 34, 135–7

see also Jansenism

censorship of printed material, 84–9, 117–22, 128–9

reform of, by governments, 142–6

Cercle Social (in revolutionary Paris), 212–13

Chambers Cyclopædia (1728), 100

chapbooks, 24–5

charity, *see* poverty

Christian VII, king of Denmark 1766–1808, 144

churches, criticism and reform of, 133, 139–42, 218

citizenship, 203–5, 211

Clarkson, Thomas (1760–1846), anti-slavery campaigner, 190

class, *see* social structure

Cocceji, Samuel von (1679–1758), Prussian law reformer, 136, 149–50

coffee-houses, 38, 65–6, 112

Colbiørnsen, Christian (1749–1814), Norwegian lawyer, 179–80

Comédie française, *see* theatre

concerts, 70–1

Condillac, Etienne Bonot de (1714–80), French philosophe, 5, 12

Condorcet, Jean-Antoine-Nicolas Caritat, marquis de (1743–94), French mathematician and *philosophe*, 2, 68, 168, 190, 218

and educational reform, 55

and the French republican constitution, 204

and the rights of women, 212–13

Conger (association of London publishers), 81

Constituent Assembly (French parliament, 1789–91), 146, 168, 184, 190, 203, 207

Constitutional Convention (Edinburgh 1792–93), 74–5

Convention, National (French parlia-
    ment, 1792–95), 168, 204–6,
    213–14
Copenhagen, 39, 69, 94, 98, 116, 186
copper-plate engraving, 60–3
copyright, 80–4, 107n
Cordeliers club (in revolutionary Paris),
    73–4, 130
Correspondence Society (in London),
    73–5, 211
corvée (compulsory labour in France),
    175, 185
counter-enlightenment, 7–11
Couperin, François (1668–1733),
    French musician, 36
Coyer, Gabriel-François (1707–82),
    French writer, 196
criminal law, 150–1
criminal punishment, 151–6
Cullen, William (1710–90), Scottish
    physician, 160

Damiens, his attempted assassination of
    Louis XV (1757), 152
Darnton, Robert (20th-century histo-
    rian), 11, 96–7, 99
David, Jacques-Louis (1748–1825),
    French artist, 65
debating clubs and societies, 68, 72,
    211
de-christianisation (France 1793), 30–1,
    141
Defoe, Daniel (1660–1731), English
    writer, 24, 109, 153
    his *Robinson Crusoe* (1719), 90, 93
deism, 32, 142
democracy, 206–12, 216
Denmark, 19, 143, 167, 171–2, 191
    church and education, 52, 53–4, 137,
    rural reform, 27, 178–80
denunciation (during French Revolu-
    tion), 216–18
dépôts de mendicité, 184–5
Diderot, Denis (1713–84), French *phi-
    losophe*, 2, 25, 83, 102, 170
    as editor of the *Encyclopédie*, 100–1,
    211
    his precarious position, 20, 83, 87,
    220

his views on religion, 8, 134
dissent (in England), 8, 33, 135, 142
Dublin, 2, 81n, 91–2
Dupont de Nemours, Pierre Samuel
    (1739–1817), French economist,
    169
Dutch Republic, 10, 111, 115–16, 168
    and freedom of expression, 85, 117,
    126

earnings and income, 82–4, 100, 130,
    139, 141
Eden, Sir Frederick Morton
    (1766–1809), English reformer,
    185
Edinburgh, 9, 38, 68, 91–2, 98
    professional institutions, 57, 158–60
educational reform, 52–9
elections, *see* voting
Empfindsamkeit, *see* sensibility
empiricism, 5–6
enclosure (in England and elsewhere),
    174
Encyclopédie (1751–65/72), 8, 100–1
    and censorship, 86–7, 102,
    keyword entries, 134, 163–4, 166–7,
    169, 181–2, 187–8, 195n, 199,
    211
    see also Diderot
Encyclopédie méthodique (1782–1832),
    80, 101
England, 8, 60–62, 74, 148–9, 209
    role of press, 111–13, 123–5
    lapse of censorship controls, 42,
    80–1, 85, 112
    see also Anglican church; London
Engravers' Act (Britain, 1735), 61
enlightenment (*Aufklärung, lumières*),
    definition of, viii, 1–20
enlightened absolutism (despotism), ix,
    18–20, 144, 178n, 221–2
    and innovative administrative practi-
    ces, 170–2
    and the French Revolution, 218–19
    see also public opinion
enragés (in revolutionary Paris), 213
Estates General (France, 1789), 73,
    103–4, 146

ESTC (English-language Short-title Catalogue), 91–2

factions, political, 208, 214, 216
federalism (in revolutionary France), 215
Felbiger, Johann Ignaz von (1724–88), educational reformer in Austrian lands, 53
Fénelon, François de Salignac de la Mothe (1651–1715), French clergyman and writer, 165
Ferguson, Adam (1723–1816), Scottish philosopher, 2, 94
festivals, religious and secular, 37–8
feudalism, 163, 176
Fielding, Henry (1707–54), English writer, 60, 82, 93
flysheets, 23, 41
forced labour, 152, 155–6, 185–6
Formey, Jean-Henri-Samuel (1711–97), secretary of Berlin Academy of Science, 10
Fragonard, Jean Honoré (1732–1806), French artist, 65
France, 1–2, 9–10, 18, 28, 49, 147–8, 197
    arts and sciences, 64–5, 66–8
    books and the press, 94–7, 103–5, 117–22, 126–7, 131
    Catholic church, 30–2, 35–6, 140–2
    censorship, 86–9, 117, 120, 145–6
    constitution of 1791, 197, 203–4, 213
    constitution of 1793, 204–5
    educational reform, 55–7
    fiscal policies, 165–8, 169–70
    revolutionary change, 38, 43–4, 73–4, 128–30, 206–9, 212–18
    toleration, 134, 137–8
    see also Jansenism; Paris; *philosophes*; physiocrats
franchise, *see* voting
Francke, August Hermann (1663–1727), Lutheran educational reformer, 52
Frankfurt book fair, 79
Franklin, Benjamin (1706–90), American scientist and statesman, 13, 19, 70

Frederick II, king of Prussia 1740–86, 18, 19, 70, 149–51, 175
    and enlightenment, 136, 145, 221
Frederik V, king of Denmark 1746–66, 39
Frederik [VI], crownprince-regent of Denmark from 1784, 19, 178
freemasonry, 16, 38, 69–70
Fréron, Élie-Catherine (1718–76), French journalist, 9, 87, 108, 120

Gaelic, 49
Galiani, Ferdinand (1728–87), Italian political economist and writer, 2, 170
galley slaves and naval dockyards, 156
gazettes, French-language, 117–9
gender differences, eighteenth-century perceptions of, 17, 211–14
general will, 206–9
George III, king of Great Britain and Ireland 1760–1820, 152
German lands, 2, 4, 6, 27, 69, 197, 200
    books, 80, 92–4, 101–2
    education, 52–3
    free-lance writers and copyright, 81–2, 83–4
    political change, 18, 149–50, 169
    role of the press, 113–15
    religious beliefs, 33, 51–2, 136
    see also Hamburg
Gibbon, Edward (1737–94), English historian, 5
Gillray, James (1756–1815), English cartoonist, 26, 61
Girondins, French revolutionary group, 19, 205, 215
Girondin press, destruction of (1793), 129
Glasgow, 57, 91–2, 98, 135, 183
Goethe, Johann Wolfgang von (1749–1832), German poet, playwright and novelist, 2, 84, 101
    his *Sorrows of Young Werther* (1774), 101–2
Göttingen University, 53, 57, 98
Gordon riots (London, 1780), 135–6, 153
Gouges, Olympe de (1748–93), French

writer and women's activist,
212–13
Great Fear (peasant unrest in France in
1789), 28
Grégoire, Henri abbé (1750–1831),
190, 218
Grimm, Friedrich Melchior
(1723–1809), German *philosophe*,
108
Gustavus III, king of Sweden 1771–92,
19, 143

Habermas, J. (20th-century sociologist),
14–5
Halle University, 53, 57
Hamburg, 37, 94, 95, 113–5, 201
religious co-existence within, 136–7,
222
social welfare, 35, 182,
Hamburg Impartial Correspondent,
114
Handel, George Frederick
(1685–1759), composer, 72
Haydn, Joseph (1732–1809), composer,
72
Hébert, Jacques René (1757–94),
French revolutionary journalist,
128, 129–30, 216
Helvétius, Claude-Adrien (1715–71),
French *philosophe*, 86, 188
Herder, Johann Gottfried von
(1744–1803), 2, 8, 200
Herrnhut religious settlement, 33
Hogarth, William (1697–1764), English
engraver and artist, 60–3
Holbach, Paul Henri Thiry, baron d'
(1723–89), French *philosophe* of
German birth, 8, 66, 134, 195
his *System of Nature* (1770), 32, 96
Holland, *see* Dutch Republic
hospital charitable foundations, 34–5,
159–60
hôtels Dieu, 159
Howard, John (1726–90), English
prison reformer, 35, 154–5,
159–60, 186
Huguenots in France, 10, 51, 137–8
(*see also* Protestant churches)

Hume, David (1711–76), Scottish philosopher and historian, 2, 10, 82,
133–4, 170, 188
his scepticism, 12, 31–3,
Hungary, 178
Hutton, James (1726–97), Scottish
geologist, 13

improvement, agricultural, 173–4
Inns of Court (English law school),
148–9
inoculation, 161
insanity, 161
inventories after death, 94–5
Ireland, 4n, 81, 202
Italian enlightenment, ix, 2, 139, 151

Jacobin clubs (in revolutionary France),
73, 130, 213
Jacobins, 129, 208, 215
Jacobite crises (Britain 1715/45), 34,
201
Jansenists, 9, 35–6, 55, 100, 142
Jaucourt, Louis, chevalier de
(1704–80), 100, 167, 188, 196–7
(*see also Encyclopédie*)
Jefferson, Thomas (1743–1826), Amer-
ican statesman, 19
Jenner's smallpox vaccination (1796),
161–2
Jesuits, 30, 36, 55, 100
Jews, 126, 133, 136–7, 138, 200, 212
Johnson, Samuel (1709–84), English
writer and lexicographer, 8, 82
Joseph II, co-regent and emperor of
Habsburg lands 1765/80–90,
18–9, 133, 145, 177–8, 185
journals, 107–11

Kant, Immanuel (1724–1804), German
philosopher, 2, 7, 20, 69, 188
Kaunitz, Wenzel Anton, Fürst von
(1711–94), Austrian statesman, 18,
139–40

La Blancherie, Pahin de, 67
Laclos, Pierre-Antoine-François Cho-
derlos (1741–1803), French writer,
83

La Mettrie, Julien Offray de (1709–51), French physician and writer, 8, 10, 31, 88, 134

language, use of, 49–50, 122, 193, 195–7, 215

Lavoisier, Antoine-Laurent (1743–94), French scientist, 2, 13, 165, 190

law codification, 147

law reform, 146–50

Le Breton, Parisian publisher, *see Encyclopédie*

Leibniz, Gottfried Wilhelm (1646–1716), German scientist and philosopher, 4

Leipzig book fair, 79, 82, 92–3

Leopold, grand duke of Tuscany 1765–90 and successor to Joseph II, 133, 152, 178

Lessing, Gotthold Ephraim (1729–81), German writer, 2, 83–4, 222

his *Nathan the Wise* (1779), 136n

lettre de cachet, 153

libel, in British law, 85, 113

libraries, commercial and circulating, 98–9

Licensing Act (lapse of, in England 1695), 80, 85

Licensing Act (for the stage, 1737), *see* theatre

Linguet, Simon-Nicolas-Henri (1736–94), French lawyer, 10, 87, 121, 126, 130, 154

Linnaeus, Carl (1707–78), Swedish botanist, 12

literacy, 46–52

Locke, John (1632–1704), English philosopher, 1, 12, 133

London, 34, 66, 98
   book trade and the press, 81, 85, 91–2, 95, 98, 112
   debating clubs, 72
   music in, 71

Louis XV, king of France 1715–74, 19, 37, 39, 96, 120

Louis XVI, king of France 1774–92, 43, 126, 137–8, 148

Luzac family (French Huguenots in the Netherlands), 10, 117–18

Lutheranism, *see* Protestant churches

MacPherson, James (1736–96), author of *Ossian* poems (1765), 200

Malesherbes, Christian-Guilhaume de Lamoignon de (1721–94), French statesman and lawyer, 86–9, 95, 97, 100, 120, 137

Mandeville, Bernard (1670–1733), Dutch writer active in England, 85–6, 183

Marais, Marin (1656–1728), French composer and viol virtuoso, 37

Marat, Jean-Paul (1744–93), journalist in revolutionary France, 108, 128, 130, 205, 215–16

Maria Theresa, empress of the Habsburg lands 1740–80, 18, 177

Maupeou, René-Charles-Augustin de (1714–92), French statesman, 103, 120, 147–8

Maupertius, Pierre Louis Moreau de (1698–1759), French mathematician, 2

medical reform, 34–5, 156–62

Mendelsohn, Moses (1729–86), German Jewish philosopher, 2, 69

Mercier, Louis-Sébastien (1740–1814), French writer
   his *The Year 2440* (1771), 14, 89, 96
   his *Tableau de Paris* (1781–89), 26, 94, 138

Mercier de la Rivière, Pierre le (1720–93), 55, 169

mesmerism, 13, 157

Methodists, 33–4

metric system, 13

Millar, John (1735–1801), Scottish philosopher, 92

Mirabeau family, 108, 169

Mittwochsgesellschaft (Wednesday society, Berlin 1783–98), 10, 69

Moderates (in the Scottish enlightenment), 9, 135

monastic orders, 139–40

Montagu, Lady Mary Wortley (1689–1762), English writer, 161

Montesquieu, Charles-Louis Secondat baron de (1689–1755), 1, 161
   his *Persian Letters* (1721), vii–viii, 133, 196

his *Spirit of the Laws* (1748), 4, 146, 153, 187, 200
Moravian Brethren, 33
More, Hannah (1745–1833), English moralist, 212
Möser, Justus (1720–94), German writer and statesman, 69
Mozart, Wolfgang Amadeus (1756–91), Austrian composer, 14, 37, 70–1
Muir, Thomas (1765–98), Scottish reformer and political activist, 74
Muratori, Ludovico Antonio (1672–1750), Italian historian, 169
musée, see popular science
music, 36–7, 70–2

nationalism and national identity, 3, 197–8, 199–203
nature and 'natural', 11–14
Necker, Jacques (1732–1804), Swiss banker in French service, 127, 165
Netherlands, *see* Dutch Republic
Newgate prison, 153, 161
newspapers, *see* press
Newton, Sir Isaac (1642–1727), English scientist, 1, 6
Nicolai, Christoph Friedrich (1733–1811), German publisher and bookseller, 69, 80, 114, 145
novels, *see* books, demand for

oath-taking, public, 218
opera, 43–4
opinion, *see* public opinion
Orléans family, 41, 83
Ossian poems (1765), 200
Oxford, 8, 58, 91

Paine, Thomas (1737–1809), Anglo-American political theorist, 19n, 62, 74, 104–5, 209
Palais Royal (Paris), 38, 41–2
Palmer, Thomas Fyshe (1747–1802), English activist, 74
pamphlets, political, 103–5
Panckoucke, Charles-Joseph (1736–98), French publishing entrepreneur, 80, 88, 100–1, 119–20, 129
Paris, 6, 39–42, 65–7

arts, 42, 43–4, 63–5
book trade and the press, 62–3, 94, 128–9
festivals and celebrations, 37
Jansenism, 35–6
popular radicalism, 73–4, 215–18
see also France, revolutionary change
Parlement of Paris, 36, 100, 127n, 138, 147–8
regulating or influencing public debate, 88, 103, 118, 146
see also Jansenists
parliamentary reporting (in press), 125
parliaments, buildings for, 39–40
patriot, 201–3 (*see also* nationalism)
Patriot Movement (Dutch Republic), 10–11, 201
Patriotic Society (Hamburg), 114, 137
peasant protest movements, 26–9
peasant reform, *see* rural reform
penal reform, 150–6
penitentiary, *see* forced labour
'people', '*peuple*', 196–7
periodical publications, *see* press
Pestalozzi, Johann Heinrich (1746–1827), Swiss educational reformer, 56
philanthropy, 35, 159–60
philosophes, 1, 5–7, 14, 18, 20, 198
physiocrats, 169–70, 177
Pietists, 33–4, 52–3, 102
piracy (in book trade), *see* copyright
political economy, 168–71
Pope, Alexander (1688–1744), English poet, 5, 82, 92
popular culture, 22–9, 40–5
popular science, 67–8
population, growth and measurement of, 171–2
pornography, 96
poverty, 152, 159, 181–6
press, 106–31
    contents, 122–5
    control of, 111–22, 142–6
    output, 111–16
    political impact, 125–8
prices in consumer market for
    prints, 62
    tickets to entertainments, 42

books, 24, 79n, 83, 101
Priestley, Joseph (1733–1804), English scientist and non-conformist preacher, 13, 105
Priestley riots (Birmingham, 1791), 135
prints (engraved illustrations), 60–63
printing industry, 77–9, 106
prisons, 153–5 (*see also* Bastille)
private, concepts of, 199
privilège (French book trade), 81, 86–8
processions, *see* festivals
property rights, 15, 163–4, 205
Protestant churches, 8–9, 37, 135–7, 141–2
  and religious revival, 33–5,
  and literacy, 51–2
Provençal language, 49
public opinion, 14–17, 72–5, 144–5, 197–9
publishing, 77–84 (*see also* printing)
punishment, *see* criminal punishment

quackery, 157–8
Quaker campaign against slavery, 187, 189
quantification, 13
Quesnay, François (1694–1774), French physician and economic theorist (physiocrat), 2, 169

racialism, 12, 187–92, 200
radical reform, popular demands for, 72–5, 104–5, 202–3, 214–18
Rameau, Jean-Philippe (1683–1764), French composer and music theorist, 5
Raynal, abbé Guillaume-Thomas (1713–96), French writer, 88, 96, 188–9
reading habits, 77, 99
reason, 5–6
referendum, use of, 208–9
Reid, Thomas (1710–96), Scottish philosopher, 2
religious beliefs, 8, 29–37
  and toleration, 133–8
  see also Catholic Church; Protestant churches
representation, political, 206–12

republic of letters, 3–4, 67, 199
republicanism, 197, 200, 202, 205–6
Restif [Rétif] de la Bretonne, Nicolas-Edmé (1734–1806), French writer, 25
Reventlow, count Christian Ditlev (1748–1827), Danish reformer, 179
revolt, popular right of, 205
Richardson, Samuel (1689–1761), novelist, 82–3, 93, 102
Rights of Man, French declaration of (1789), 138, 146, 203–4, 212–3
  second version (1793), 204–5
Robertson, William (1721–93), Scottish clergyman and scholar, 9, 82, 135
Robespierre, Maximilien-Marie-Isidore (1758–94), French lawyer and revolutionary leader, 197, 204, 215
robot (labour services), 176–7
Roche, Daniel (20th-century historian), 94
Roland, Madame Jeanne-Marie (1754–93), French revolutionary activist, 156
Rousseau, Jean-Jacques (1712–78), Genevan philosopher, 1–2, 44, 77n, 166, 196–8, 200, 206, 220
  his *Discourse on Inequality* (1755), 196
  his *La nouvelle Héloïse* (1761), 99, 102
  his *Emile* (1762), 55, 87
  his *Social Contract* (1762), 96, 187
  his *Confessions* (1782), 8
  alienation from *philosophes*, 10, 102
  earnings from his writings, 81, 83
  views on role of women, 17, 211
Roux, Jacques (1752–94), Parisian priest and political radical, 74, 213
rural reform, 27–8, 172–80

Sade, Donatien-Alphonse-François, marquis de (1740–1814), French writer and sexual pervert, 156
Saint Domingue (later Haiti), 191
Saint-Just, Louis-Antoine (1767–94), French revolutionary leader, 55, 218

Saint-Médard, convulsions at (1731), 134
Salon (exhibition of Academy paintings in Louvre), 64
salons, 17, 66
sans-culotte, 215
satirical prints, 41
Schiller, Friedrich von (1759–1805), German poet and writer, 2, 84
his *The Robbers* (1781), 102
Schlözer, August Ludwig von (1735–1809), German writer and newspaper editor, 115
science of man, 13–14
Scotland, 6, 9, 18, 48, 91, 111, 170
churches in, 34, 135
education in, 12, 54, 57
political radicalism, 74
seigneurial power, 175–80
Select Society (Edinburgh), 68
sensationism, *see* empiricism
sensibility, 66, 102
serfdom, 178
Sieyes, abbé Emmanuel-Joseph (1748–1836), French political writer and politician, 70, 104, 194
slave revolts, 190–1
slavery and slave trade, 186–92
movement for abolition of, 189–92
smallpox, 161–2
Smith, Adam (1723–90), Scottish philosopher, 2, 11
his *Wealth of Nations* (1776), 167, 170, 190
social contract, *see* Rousseau
social structure, enlightenment concepts of, 15–17, 193–7
Societies for Constitutional Information/Reform (in Britain), 74–5
Sonnenfels, Josef von (1732–1817), Austrian academic and reformer, 169
Sorbonne (Paris University), 8
SPCK (Society for Promoting Christian Knowledge, in England and Scotland), 49–50, 54, 141
Spectator, 109–11
Stamp Act (Britain, 1712), 85, 111–12

statistics, national, 165–6
statues, impact of, 39
Steele, Richard (1672–1729), English journalist, 109–10
Steuart (-Denham), James (1712–80), Scottish political economist, 170
Stockholm, 69, 116, 143
Struensee, Johann Friedrich (1737–72), German physician and cameralist in Danish service, 41, 144, 152, 178
Sturm und Drang (Storm and Stress movement in literature and music), 2, 8
superstition, 22–3, 29, 32, 134–5, 158 (*see also* religion)
suicide, reactions to, 101–2, 151
Sweden, 19, 126, 137, 148, 201
education and literacy in, 48, 54
and publishing, 77, 116, 143
Swedenborg, religious leader, 34
Swift, Jonathan (1667–1745), Anglo-Irish writer, 14, 90, 93
symbolism of revolution in France, 215–6
systems of knowledge, 5

Tatler, 109–11
taxation, 163–8
proportional and progressive forms, 166
and public accountability, 164
Telemann, Georg Philip (1681–1767), German composer, 93
Terror (in revolutionary France), 43, 74, 217–18
theatre, 42–4
Thelwall, John (1764–1834), English radical, 72, 75
Toland, John (1670–1722), Irish writer, 133
toleration, 133–8, 222
Act of (England), 135
Tone, Theobald Wolfe (1763–98), Irish political activist, 202
torture, 151–2
translation (of texts), 4, 93–4, 101–2
transportation (of convicts), 74, 155
Turgot, baron Anne-Robert-Jacques

(1727–81), French statesman and economist, 18, 88, 137, 170, 174, 181–2

typography, 78–9

Tyburn (London place of execution), 153

Unigenitus (Papal Bull against Jansenism, 1713), 36

United Irishmen, 202

United Provinces, *see* Dutch Republic

university education, 12, 57

urban planning, 38–40

Vauxhall Gardens (London), 38, 65, 71

venal office-holding, 147–8

Venturi, Franco (20th-century historian), ix, 2

Vergennes, Charles Gravier, comte de (1717–87), French foreign minister, 88, 118

Vico, Giambattista (1668–1744), Italian philosopher and historian, 2, 200

Vienna, 158, 185

Vincennes prison, 87, 220

Voltaire, [real name François-Marie Arouet] (1694–1778), 1, 83, 94, 103, 145–6

his *Candide* (1759), 32

his *Philosophical Dictionary* (1764), 196n

his elitism, 94, 196n

role in Calas Affair, 32, 141

views on the church, 8, 134, 140–1

voting (in France and Britain), 204, 208–11

Watteau, Jean Antoine (1684–1721), painter, 63

Wesley, John (1703–91), Methodist preacher, 33

Wilberforce, William (1759–1833), English philanthropist and parliamentary reformer, 190

Wilkes, John (1727–97), English journalist and politician, 61, 126, 201, 209

Wolff, Christian (1679–1754), German philosopher and writer, 4, 10–11

Wollstonecraft, Mary (1759–97), English social campaigner and writer, 105

her *Vindication of the Rights of Woman* (1792), 211

women, role of, in enlightenment, 17, 48, 50–1, 58, 211–14

Society of Republican Revolutionary Women (in France), 74, 213–14

workhouses, 154, 183–5 (*see also* forced labour)

xenophobia, 136, 200–2

Zinzendorf, Nicholas Ludwig, Graf von (1700–1760), Pietist visionary, 33